Critical Thinking for Arts and Sciences

Custom Edition for Columbus State Community College

D1307088

Taken from:
Critical Thinking: Tools for Taking Charge of Your Learning and Your Life,
Third Edition by Richard Paul and Linda Elder

Learning to Think Things Through: A Guide to Critical Thinking Across the Curriculum, Fourth Edition by Gerald M. Nosich

Pearson Learning Solutions, 501 Boylston Street, Suite 900, Boston, MA 02116
A Pearson Education Company
www.pearsoned.com

Printed in the United States of America

2 3 4 5 6 7 8 9 10 V0ZN 17 16 15 14 13 12

000200010271653775

CW/TP

ISBN 10: 1-256-78290-4
ISBN 13: 978-1-256-78290-2

❖ Contents

❖ Copyright Acknowledgments

❖ Acknowledgments

This book has been a collaborative effort as all books are. Whether there is a single author or many, textbooks, especially, are created by the dedicated efforts of educators and their students. This is certainly the case with this book. The Freshman Seminar Committee has been unwavering in its commitment to an orientation program for Arts and Sciences students. Over the years, The Freshman Seminar program has been enhanced by the excellent suggestions from faculty teaching the course and from academic counselors in the Counseling and Advising Services who work individually with students as well as team-teach the transfer component of the course. Students enrolled in the Freshman Seminar have also contributed mightily to its success by offering feedback on the text and classroom activities.

❖ Welcome to the Columbus State Freshman Seminar

You may be wondering why you need to take this course. Don't most students just figure it out as they go? Not really. In fact, students who don't take a course are more likely to drop out of school than those who do. It's not that these students aren't smart or motivated; it's just that they are forced to spend too much valuable time and energy "figuring things out" when they should be studying and succeeding in college. Probably the most often heard comment from students who did not make it to their second year is, "I wish I'd known then what I know now"... about studying, signing up for classes, taking exams, transfer planning, etc. That's why you're taking this course: to find out how to succeed in college and avoid the "I wish I'd known" pitfalls. The Freshman Seminar is designed to introduce you to academic life and to your classmates for the next two years, students like you who are dedicated to helping you achieve your goals. This course will help you:

- ❖ determine personal academic goals;

- ❖ plan a course of study leading to a transfer degree;

- ❖ become familiar with academic reading and writing strategies, including critical thinking;

- ❖ learn to use various on-site support systems (ERC, Degree Audit program, *Blackboard*);

- ❖ become familiar with academic protocol.

The Freshman Seminar will also help you explore academic majors as well as career options. If you are undecided about a major, you will have the opportunity to discuss your interests with faculty from various academic disciplines. You will be introduced to career exploration options available on campus and through the Internet.

Your Freshman Seminar text was written exclusively for you as a Columbus State student. It is assigned to help you achieve success in college and to aid in the transfer process. In addition to the text, you will also need a Portfolio notebook or folder for keeping information and material relating to your educational experience at Columbus State (assessment scores, essays, exams and self-assessments). You should also have a copy of the Student Handbook and the most recent edition of the Columbus State Bulletin. Both contain important information about college policies and resources.

Now congratulate yourself. You have made a wise decision to enroll at Columbus State. Welcome to the first day of the rest of your life.

CHAPTER 1 Welcome to Columbus State

Chapter Goals

In this chapter you will:

❖ learn how to define
yourself as a student
❖ discover Columbus State
❖ learn how to set goals
❖ learn how to get expert
advice on how to succeed
in college

You have probably heard that each new beginning is the "first day of the rest of your life." This is certainly true for you today. Your decision to enroll in college signals your willingness to make changes in your life: to learn new things and meet new people. Just being here, you are already looking at a new future for yourself and, perhaps, for your family and friends as well. When you "choose" the academic life, you join the ranks of all those students who have gone before you (your instructor is one), and all those people who will follow you. As of this moment, you are a part of a **community** of learners: the Columbus State community.

At This Moment

Is College Just a Grown-Up Version of High School?

Although there are some similarities, being in college is not like being in high school.

In high school, your teachers were in control most of the time: they told you exactly what to do and when. They kept an eye on you. If you fell behind in your work, they let you know. If you missed classes, either your teachers or a school counselor would be on the telephone to your parents. That won't be the case in college. You're in charge of your education; you're the boss on the job.

Is College Just a Job, Then?

In some ways, the answer to that question is yes. Being in college is your job for the next two years. You need to prioritize your commitment to your college career just as you would to a job career. Success on the job depends on getting to work every day and on time, getting the work done, and being responsible to your employer and to your fellow employees. If you don't show up for work, or if you fall behind in your work, you risk losing your pay or even your job. Not getting along with your boss or your co-workers is also risky. On the job the choice is yours. Your boss may let you know that you're not working smart, but your boss isn't going to spend a lot of time and energy scolding you. On the job you make or break yourself. The same holds true for college. You need to be in class and on time every day; your homework must be done and turned in when it's due; you need to be responsible when dealing with the school and with your fellow students.

In college, when you don't show up for class or when you don't turn in work on time, you're risking a low or even failing grade. If you can't communicate with your instructor and don't participate responsibly in class, you also run the risk of losing points as well as the respect of your instructors and classmates. The choice is yours and so are the rewards. College is more than just a job, though. When you enter college, you enter into an academic partnership with your school and your instructors, a partnership based on mutual respect and effort.

Your college instructors make an assumption about you as soon as they see your name on a class roster. They assume you are an adult who is responsible for his or her behavior and performance in the classroom. They also assume you have made a conscious decision to be in college. No one has forced you to enroll; you are here for your own reasons. Let's look at some of the reasons why people go to college.

❖ *To Improve Employment or Career Opportunities*

Although a college degree is not a 100 percent guarantee that you will always be employed in the perfect job, as a college graduate your chances of a steady, satisfying career and promotion are much higher then they are for non-college graduates.

❖ *To Increase Income*

There is little doubt that a college degree increases your opportunity to earn as much as 50% more than a non-college graduate. Today's global marketplace demands a highly trained work force of well-educated people who can think critically and act resourcefully. Employers today want more than just problem-solvers. They want employees who can anticipate problems before they arise, and they will pay well for someone with these capabilities.

❖ *For Personal Growth and Satisfaction*

This is an area of potential that is sometimes overlooked, and it shouldn't be. A steady job and a good income are important, but without opportunities for self-improvement, life would be a pretty boring proposition. A college education is a lifetime investment in self-improvement (often referred to as lifelong learning) and self-esteem. In college, you come to know who you are and who you can become. You become more knowledgeable and interested in the world around you and, as a result, a more interesting person. You become a better consumer, a more informed voter, and a more critical evaluator of what you see and hear. In other words, college increases your aptitude for making the most out of life.

Who Are We?

Columbus State Community College is a teaching institution dedicated to the task of preparing students for academic success here, at four-year institutions and in their chosen careers. Columbus State's main campus is located near downtown Columbus. Columbus State also has branch campuses where students may take courses when it is inconvenient for them to come to the main campus. Columbus State is accredited by the North Central Association of Colleges and Schools, and has signed **articulation agreements** with a number of local colleges and universities.[1]

Students who enroll in the Arts and Sciences Division at Columbus State, and who successfully complete a prescribed course of study leading to an Associate of Arts degree (AA), or an Associate of Sciences degree (AS), satisfy the first two years of baccalaureate degree requirements with institutions with articulation agreements with Columbus State.

The Liberal Arts and Sciences

A liberal arts curriculum, or program of study, is designed to provide students with the opportunity to gain academic experience in several disciplines such as mathematics, the sciences, the humanities and English. At Columbus State the liberal arts are referred to as the Arts and Sciences. The ultimate goal of an arts and sciences program is to prepare you to take

---

1. You will find details about these agreements at the transfer workbook website: (http://global.cscc.edu/ASC/190/wkbkintro.htm)

your place in society as an informed, responsible, and successful citizen. The immediate goal of an arts and sciences curriculum is to invite you into a world of learning that allows you to connect with a rich past of academic achievements by scholars, scientists and artists from all over the world. At the same time you are entering the tradition of the liberal arts, you are also forging your own place in the tradition, your own identity. Eventually, you too will make your own unique contributions to this world of learning and continue the tradition.

Some Important Considerations

Full Time or Part Time?

When you signed up for classes you had to decide on the number of hours you would be responsible for in this quarter. At Columbus State a full time student is one who is registered for 12 or more credit hours per quarter; a part time student is registered for less than 12 hours per quarter. Some students go to school full time for their entire two years at Columbus State, while others complete their education here as part time students. Is one method better than the other? Not necessarily.

The decision to enroll as a full time or part time student depends on each student's individual situation. Going to school full time usually means it will take less time to complete your degree than it will if you go to school part time. On the other hand, if you work full time and try to take a full load of classes, you may find yourself falling behind at both jobs. In fact, many students who attempt this double load end up dropping classes because they just can't manage the schedule. The key to deciding whether to enroll full time or part time is to take a good look at your goals and your resources. You may want to refer to Chapter 4: Managing Your Time, as you respond to the following questions.

1. What are your short term and long term goals? What is a realistic time frame for achieving those goals?

2. If you work outside the classroom, how many hours per week are you on the job? Include travel time, too.

3. How many hours per week are you committed to personal activities (family responsibilities, exercising, recreation, etc.)?

4. Add up the hours, and then add in the number of academic hours you plan to take during the quarter.

5. Add in a study quotient. It has been determined by the Ohio Board of Regents that students at schools receiving funds from the State of Ohio should expect to spend about two hours of study outside of class for every hour spent in class.

When you have answered these questions, you will probably wonder if you have created an impossible life for yourself. Not so. It is only that your goals have exceeded your resources. Does this mean you can't go to school, work, and have a life? Of course not! It's only that your goals have exceeded your resources. It just means that you have to make some intelligent adjustments. Look at the list of questions again. Which items are negotiable and which are not? For example, your financial obligations require you to work 40 hours per week. That's not negotiable, then. You also know that you must allow yourself ample study time to do well in school. That's not negotiable, either. However, if you don't enroll as a full time student, you will need fewer study hours. True, dropping back your hours may require an adjustment in short and long term goals, but there are even options there!

You may decide to work full time and go to school part time for three quarters, and then take a quarter off work to go to school full time. You may also decide to look for a job where your employer pays your tuition, thus reducing some of your financial obligations. You may consider taking out a student loan and dropping back to a part time job/full time school scenario. The point is that there are many options available to you for meeting your financial obligations and completing your education. If you are armed with the right information for making wise decisions, there will be no stopping you from achieving your goals, whether you decide to enroll as a full time or part time student.

Advice for Commuters

Unlike many colleges and universities whose students may either live on campus or commute, Columbus State is an all commuter school. Every student at Columbus State lives off campus and commutes to classes on campus. Some students see this as a disadvantage, but if you think about it, being a commuter student has advantages.

First you live in your own apartment or home, surrounded by your own belongings (furniture, pictures, music). Second, you're able to maintain your family life. Resident students often share crowded space with several roommates, are limited to only a few personal items and are often miles away from family and friends. Commuter students also usually have access to their own cars, and are not completely reliant on public transportation systems to get to and from class or around the city. In other words, commuter students are generally self-reliant individuals who are fully responsible for their own lives and the choices they make. That kind of independence or self-reliance is a definite plus in college. Of course, commuter students also face challenges.

Commuter students spend quite a bit of time traveling to and from campus. They are usually employed outside the classroom or have family responsibilities, which makes time a precious item. The following tips should help you make the most of the opportunities/challenges on campus:

❖ Finding Parking

Accept the fact that parking is a challenge and plan ahead. Which parking lots seem to have the most available space when you come to campus? Don't forget to check the parking garage. Have a back-up plan. If you can't find a space in one lot, what's your next option? Remember that parking is always more difficult to find at the beginning of the quarter while new students are finding their way around. Finally, leave work or home in time to find a parking place on campus. "I couldn't find a place to park" is not an acceptable excuse for being late to class.

❖ Taping lectures

Consider recording lectures (be sure to get your instructor's permission first). Play the recording while you drive, or when you review your notes. Don't rely on the recording entirely for class preparation. You must still pay attention in class, take notes and ask questions on material that you don't understand. Listening to the answers again later will help you retain the information.

❖ Finding time to study

Be creative about when you study. Take advantage of breaks between class to review notes or read. You don't have to cover the entire chapter every time you sit down with a book. Set mini-goals for yourself each day—sections of material you can cover in the time you have between classes or work.

❖ Finding a study location

Be creative about where you study. Just because you don't have a dorm room nearby doesn't mean you can't study effectively on campus. There are designated study areas in the ERC (Educational Resource Center, otherwise known as the library, in Columbus Hall). Many students also make use of empty classrooms to study, or even study in their cars between classes. Of course, during good weather you can study outside at one of the picnic tables or in any green space.

❖ Studying together

Study with other students who are on campus when you are. Arrange to meet for lunch or coffee break. Perhaps you can even set up a car pool with another student and quiz each other as you drive.

Distance Learning at Columbus State

Columbus State students have the option of taking courses over the web or through televised offerings. Students who attend classes at one of Columbus State's off-campus sites may also participate in video-conferencing instruction that originates at the main campus.

Before signing up for a distance learning course, however, you need to be aware of the specific responsibilities of being a distance learner. The following guidelines are taken from The Ohio Learning Network's web site (http://www.oln.org).

❖ *Time management*

Distance learning requires more self-discipline than traditional learning. You need to have good time management skills. This is particularly true because so many people are drawn to distance learning because they are trying to balance a variety of roles within their lives: worker, wife, husband, mother, father, citizen, son, daughter, etc. For many people, taking courses, or pursuing a certificate or degree could not be possible if it were not for distance learning. However, the rest of your life does not stop because of your desire to pursue learning at a distance. Managing your commitments is critical to being a successful distance learner. *How good are your time management skills? Do you know how to avoid procrastination?*

❖ *Comfort level using technology*

You need to be familiar with using a computer and the Internet. *How would you rate your computer skills?* Most distance education instructors have listed specific technology requirements as the minimum for a student to complete the course successfully. Generally, you need to be comfortable with a sophisticated word-processing program (e.g., *MS Word*) and understand functions such as "copy" and "paste." You should also know how to use Columbus State's Student e-mail service and how to send attachments. This subject is discussed in more detail below.

❖ *General study skills*

Having good study skills is important to getting the most out of your distance learning experience. Having good basic reading comprehension, writing, computational, and exam taking skills are critical to success in the distance learning environment.

You should talk to the course instructor before enrolling to get a sense of what is expected from you.

You also should go to Columbus State's website http://global.cscc.edu/GettingStarted/index.asp for a distance learning orientation before you begin your distance learning course.

You will learn more about the instructor/student relationships in distance classes in chapter 4.

Computer Skills Needed for College

Even though you may not be enrolled in a distance learning class, your professors still expect you to use a computer and the Internet effectively. Not owning a home computer or not knowing how to use a computer are no longer excuses for work missed, work not submitted on time, or work submitted in the wrong format. Some of the activities you will participate in while taking classes at Columbus State are:

❖ accessing a computer regularly.

❖ using a computer program such as MicroSoft Word for word processing.

❖ saving a file to a disk or memory stick.

❖ saving a file in different formats (e.g., rich text format).

❖ printing a file from a writable CD or flash drive.

❖ E-mailing a clear, concise message and using e-mail responsibly.

❖ Attaching a file to an e-mail.

❖ Navigating the Internet efficiently to find appropriate material for course work.

❖ Using an online learning system such as Blackboard, to access course materials, participate in electronic discussions, submit assignments, and take quizzes.

In order to meet these expectations, you will need access to the following equipment necessary for college:

❖ Computer, monitor, keyboard, and mouse

❖ Operating system with software for connecting to the Internet

❖ Current and appropriate software for word processing.

❖ Speakers

❖ Printer, ink cartridges, paper

❖ Storage devices such as writable CDs or flash drive.

If you are serious about succeeding in college, you should make plans to invest in a computer, printer, and storage device. Columbus State also has computer labs available for student use (you will still need a storage device such as a flash drive to save your information). Familiarize yourself each quarter with lab locations and hours.

Student Resources

Columbus State Community College offers students numerous resources to help them achieve academic success. A majority of these services are free to students and offered at a variety of times. To learn more about the various student resources Columbus State offers, go to http://global.cscc.edu/Tools/StudentResources.asp.

❖ *The Writing Center*

Columbus State offers a free, one-on-one tutoring service for students in need of help at any stage of the writing process on various assignments, such as critical essays, research, documentation, and professional writing. A tutoring session with a skilled tutor from the

Communication Skills Department lasts for thirty minutes, and students are limited to no more than one thirty minute session a day and a maximum of three sessions per week. Franklin Hall 245/(614)287-5717.

❖ ESL Tutors

ESL tutors are available for ESL students currently enrolled in ESL courses. Modern Languages Deparment/(614)287-5400.

❖ Online Writing and Resource Center

Online tutoring is provided for students enrolled in distance learning courses. The Online Writing and Resource Center (OWRC) provides tutoring and writing help at any stage of the writing process. The OWRC can be accessed via Blackboard.

❖ Speech Lab

Instructors from the Communication Skills Department are available to help students prepare and rehearse speeches. Tutors will videotape students practicing their speeches and offer helpful advice. Nestor Hall 017/(614)287-5391.

❖ Learning Skills Center

The Learning Skills Center offers students enrolled in developmental courses additional help and tutoring. The Center also provides students with instructors and tutors to answer questions, computer help, and recorded math lectures. Aquinas Hall 213/(614)287-2478.

❖ Math Tutors

Students requiring additional help in math courses, from Math 102 to Math 104, may meet with a faculty tutor. Davidson Hall 313/(614)287-5313.

❖ Peer Tutors

Students may seek help from a peer tutor in the peer tutoring program run through the Student Success Center. Students may also apply to become a peer tutor. Aquinas Hall 241/(614)287-2474.

❖ IT Support Center

The Help Desk provides students with technical support dealing with computer, printing, and Blackboard issues. Columbus Hall 002/(614)287-5050.

❖ Personal Counseling

Counseling Services offers enrolled students one-on-one counseling to help them cope with such issues as stress, anxiety, academic concerns, family issues, grief, relationships, abuse, addiction, and eating disorders. Students may visit a trained and professional counselor six times for free and then referred to a counselor from the community. Advising and Counseling Services/Aquinas 116/(614)287-2668.

Extracurricular Activities

❖ *Recreation*

Students may enjoy the Fitness Center, which contains cardiovascular machines. The Fitness Center provides personal trainers and physical fitness assessment. Open recreation in the gym includes basketball, volleyball, and ping-pong. Free classes are offered in aerobics, yoga, pilates, self defense, and belly dancing.

❖ *Massage Therapy Student Clinic*

Students may receive a $10 Swedish massage from a student training in the Massage Therapy Program. Union Hall 319/(614)287-5943.

❖ *Student Publications*

Students may submit original work, such as poetry, fiction, creative non-fiction, artwork, and photography to *Spring Street*, Columbus State's literary magazine, published annually. Students interested in journalism and gaining experience may work on *Cougar News*, Columbus State's weekly newspaper.

❖ *Varsity Athletics*

Columbus State currently offers varsity sports.
    Basketball—Men's and Women's teams
    Golf—Men's teams
    Volleyball—Women's teams
    Cheerleading—Co-ed teams

❖ *Intramural Sports*

Columbus State also offers a variety of **intramural** sports for students, faculty and staff. Intramural sports include basketball, billiards, checkers, euchre, chess, and volleyball. The Delaware Hall gymnasium can be used for general exercise, weight training, and aerobic exercise.

❖ *Student Organizations and Clubs*

Organizations and clubs at Columbus State include honor societies, support and special interest groups, spiritual, cultural, and service organizations. For a current listing, visit the Office of Student Activities, Nestor Hall 116.

Opportunity Knocks: A Word About Diversity

One of the big advantages of a community college like Columbus State is the opportunity it gives students to meet people from different races, ethnic and cultural and socio-economic backgrounds. However, diversity doesn't stop there. Diversity also includes gender differences,

differences in sexual preferences, age, physical abilities, and differences in learning styles and abilities. Meeting and talking with people whose experiences and opinions differ from yours is a very important part of your college education. For example, the ability to think critically, a skill required of college students, depends on your ability to consider more than one side of (or perspective on) a situation, and arrive at a right or reasonable conclusion. Collaborative learning, working with others to solve a problem, is also a requirement in many classes across the curriculum. Finally, getting to know people whose background and life experiences are different from yours enriches your life. In fact, your future success in whatever career you have chosen for yourself depends upon your ability to communicate and work well and productively with others. While you are at Columbus State, do your part to build cooperation and consensus among all people.

❖ ***Keep an open mind***
❖ ***Respect difference; don't ridicule it***
❖ ***Speak out against injustice; help others to be heard***

Diversity means different, not separate. Remember who we are—the Columbus State Community College.

Academic Honesty

College students rarely set out to produce dishonest work on an exam or a paper. What usually happens is that the student is unprepared for an exam or hasn't started the six-page essay that's due the next day. The student feels trapped, pushed into a corner, and decides to take the easy way out by cheating on the exam or by turning in a paper that is not his or her own work. This is a big mistake. First, if you don't do the work, you don't learn. Sooner or later your lack of preparation is going to catch up with you. Second, not doing the work yourself is unethical and unfair. When you aren't honest with your instructors and your classmates, you're not just "cheating" the exam, you're taking advantage of their belief in you. Finally, in cases of academic dishonesty, the one who suffers the most, ultimately, is you. Your self-respect and self-esteem diminish, and as all the experts agree, these two, self-respect and self-esteem, are crucial to success in college.

Living with Integrity

According to the Kenan Institute for Ethics at Duke University, academic integrity can be defined as a commitment to honesty, trust, fairness, respect, and responsibility. These values form the basis of acceptable behaviors for students and instructors.

Consider the following statistics taken from the Kenan Institute's web site (www.academicintegrity.org):

❖ In a recent survey, three out of four college students admitted to cheating at least once during their undergraduate careers

❖ Nearly 80 percent of college-bound high school graduates believe that cheating is commonplace

❖ A web site providing free term papers for students averages more than 80,000 hits a day.

Having integrity puts your *ethics* (your sense of what is right and wrong) into daily action. You are responsible for your own integrity. You can choose actions that build your own confidence, ability, knowledge, and reputation. Make choices that serve you well. With a strong sense of integrity, you will learn throughout your life and use what you learn to adapt to change. Remember: if people can trust you to be honest, to be sincere in what you say and do, they will be more likely to encourage you and reward your work.

To ensure academic integrity:

❖ *Know the academic conduct rules*

Ignorance is not bliss, nor is it an excuse.

❖ *Be prepared*

Study for your exams and start essay assignments early.

❖ *Ask for help*

If you're falling behind in class, or don't understand the material, ask for help from the instructor. Take advantage of on-campus tutoring facilities.

❖ *Course withdrawal*

If, in spite of your efforts to do well in the class, you are still doing poorly, consider dropping the course and taking it later when you're better prepared. Drop deadlines are listed in the quarterly bulletin (schedule of classes), or are available in Madison Hall.

What if you decide to cheat on an exam or plagiarize a paper? What are the chances of getting caught? High, very high. College instructors are experienced professionals with an uncanny ability to spot dishonesty. Instructors are experts at reading student texts; they know when a student is not using his or her own voice or writing style. These same instructors are well aware of websites that encourage plagiarism, and the *will* take the time to check out cited sources, or surf the Net for undocumented material. Instructors are required to act on all cases of suspected cheating or plagiarism, so you can be certain that the consequences for taking a dishonest shortcut will be far more devastating than the poor grade you might earn because you are not prepared. Ask any student who has appeared before an academic misconduct board. The least you can expect is a failing grade on the exam or paper. You may also fail the entire course, and depending on the seriousness of the charge and the board's findings, you can be dismissed from school. That's not what you came here for, is it? You came for success, and once again, the key to success is within you.

The Modern Language Association uses the following criteria in evaluating whether or not a student has plagiarized.

You have plagiarized if

❖ you took notes that did not distinguish summary and paraphrase from quotation and then you presented wording from the notes as if it were all your own.

❖ while browsing the Web, you copied text and pasted it into your paper without quotation marks or without citing the source.

❖ you presented facts without saying where you found them.

❖ you repeated or paraphrased someone's wording without acknowledgment.

❖ you took someone's unique or particularly apt phrase without acknowledgement.

❖ you paraphrased someone else's argument or presented someone's line of thought without acknowledgement.

❖ you bought or otherwise acquired a research paper and handed in part or all of it as your own.

You can avoid plagiarism by

❖ making a list of the writers and viewpoints you discovered in your research and using this list to double-check the presentation of material in your paper.

❖ keeping the following three categories distinct in your notes: your ideas, your summaries of others' material, and exact wording you copy.

❖ identifying the sources of all material you borrow—exact wording, paraphrases, ideas, arguments and facts.

❖ checking with your instructor when you are uncertain about your use of sources.

Source:

Gibaldi, Joseph. *MLA Handbook for Writers of Research Papers*. Sixth Edition. New York: Modern Language Association, 2003. 75.

Learning Disabilities

If you have been diagnosed with a learning disability, you are not alone. Learning disabilities are not uncommon among students, and it is college policy to provide reasonable accommodations to all students. If you would like to request such accommodations because of a physical, mental, or learning disability, please contact the Department of Disability Services, Room 223, Franklin Hall or call 287-2570 (or 287-2624 TTY).

What if you only suspect that you have a learning disability? Get smart and get tested. The sooner you identify the problem, the better. Should you tell your instructor? The experts say yes. If you suspect a problem or if you have been diagnosed with a learning disability, your instructor should be made aware of this. It's up to you, though. Most colleges expect students to take the initiative in informing instructors and in arranging for the testing and assistance. Remember, you're the boss. You're in charge.

Service Learning

In some of your courses at Columbus State and beyond, you may be asked to participate in service-learning activities. Service learning is a teaching and learning method that integrates service to the community with academic coursework.

*Many educational theories have come to the same conclusion: students need to be invested in the process of learning. It has been proven that students learn best when they can either personally relate to what they are learning or can participate in some experiential way. Because of this, many academic institutions across the country are leaning toward requiring service learning.

Service learning offers you the opportunity to go outside of the classroom; learn about others; find out about their lives, thoughts, and struggles; reflect on what your work means; and finally discover how you fit into your own community.

Goals of Service Learning

❖ Develop opportunities to integrate theory and practice

❖ Increase your understanding of social issues

❖ Teach you to work collaboratively in teams

❖ Enhance your critical-thinking skills

* Taken from *Student Orientation Series: Service Learning* by Margit Misangyi Watts.

- ❖ Sharpen your problem-solving skills
- ❖ Strengthen your sense of social responsibility
- ❖ Provide you with a heightened understanding of human differences and commonalities
- ❖ Build your self confidence
- ❖ Illuminate your personal values and beliefs
- ❖ Help you discover a sense of empathy
- ❖ Allow you to reflect on what you learned and how it impacts the community

If your ASC 190 class includes a service-learning component, the following worksheets may be useful to you in planning and reflecting on your project:

*Service Learning: Preparation**

Name _____

Agency _____

Date _____

Awareness of the purpose of the service

- ❖ Who will this project help?

Application to your education

- ❖ Will this project help you understand things in your schoolwork?
- ❖ Will the things you learn in school help you do this project? How?

Responsibility to the community

- ❖ What would you like to do to help the organization?

Impact on your life

- ❖ Do you feel good about partnering with this agency? Why?
- ❖ Do you think you will do anything differently after you do this project? If yes, what?

---

* Taken from *Student Orientation Series: Service Learning* by Margit Misangyi Watts.

Critical Thinking

- ❖ Will this project give you any ideas about how to help other organizations? What?

- ❖ Do other people have different perspectives on the agency you have chosen?

- ❖ How can you tell whose ideas are best?

Definitions

- ❖ Service learning means _____

- ❖ Your organization is _____

---

*Service Learning: Reflection

Name _____

Agency _____

Date _____

What?

- ❖ What did you do for your project?

- ❖ What new areas of your community did you explore?

- ❖ Whom did you talk with, help, or work for?

- ❖ Did you like the people who worked with you on the project? Why?

- ❖ Did you do anything that you have never done before? Describe?

So What?

- ❖ How did you feel about doing the project?

- ❖ Were there things about the project that you did not like? Describe?

- ❖ Did this project actually help anyone? Who?

- ❖ Do you think that anyone cared that you worked on this project?

- ❖ Did this project help you understand things in your courses? What?

- ❖ Did the things you learned in your classes help you in the project? How?

---

* Taken from *Student Orientation Series: Service Learning* by Margit Misangyi Watts.

Now What?

❖ Now that you have done the project, can you see yourself doing it again?

❖ Will this experience help you in some way?

❖ In response to your work on this project, do you think you will do anything differently in your life?

❖ Is there anything you would like to do to help your agency?

❖ Do you want to keep working on these kinds of community projects?

❖ Could you now teach others about service learning?

Definitions

❖ Service learning means _____

❖ Your organization is _____

Some Final Words of Advice from the Experts

You might be thinking that the word experts refers to instructors or counselors. While it is true that these people are well trained and informed about the academic experience, the real college success experts are students who have been there, done that. Graduates of Columbus State, or those who are about to graduate, are often asked what advice they would give to new students. Following are the experts' Top Ten Tips for College Success:

1. Go to class.

2. Keep up with your assignments.

3. Use campus resources like the Writing Center or the Math Tutoring Lab.

4. Plan ahead. Set up a schedule and then stick to it.

5. Ask questions in class. See your instructors during office hours.

6. Take care of yourself. Don't push yourself to the point of exhaustion or skip meals.

7. Make friends. Study with others.

8. Identify with your school. Get involved in at least one campus activity or, if you don't have time for that, buy a Columbus State T-shirt and wear it proudly.

9. Don't whine. When you make a mistake, accept it, learn from it, and move on.

10. Look for the positive. Reward yourself for the great job you're doing.

Now that you have gotten to know yourself, your classmates, and your school better, you're ready to move on to the next step. Before you go, congratulate yourself again because:

❖ You chose Columbus State, a teaching institution.

❖ You chose to pursue a liberal arts education, one that prepares you to take your place in a tradition of lifelong learning and success.

❖ You enrolled in this class because you want to succeed in college.

Remember

❖ You are your number one resource

❖ Set reasonable, flexible goals

❖ Be open to new experiences

❖ Take advantage of on-campus resources

❖ You're the boss; you're in charge

Critical Readings

At the end of each chapter, you will find an article or essay that will give you practice in critical reading and thinking skills. The readings cover a wide range of topics in fields within the Arts and Sciences, and they often focus on contemporary social issues. Your instructor may ask you to focus on specific questions related to the readings.

This first reading explores the nature of the student/teacher relationship and the kind of challenges that some instructors face in getting to know their students.

Critical Reading: The Ins and Outs of the Closet

By IAN HOULIHAN

"That's so gay," the student said. "I mean, weird." He corrected himself quickly, with obvious discomfort. Clearly, he suspected something.

"Why did you say it that way?" I asked, in what I hoped was a lighthearted manner. I figured it was as good a time as any to have a serious discussion about my personal life.

"I'm trying not to do that anymore—to say 'gay' when I mean 'odd' or 'weird.' People do that all the time. Someone might be offended."

"You're right that some gay people take offense to that," I said. "But I know what you meant."

Jason's reaction was a mixture of shock and confusion. I could only guess what was running through his mind: Did my professor just come out to me? Or did I misunderstand him. Oh, man, this is gay. I mean, weird. Or both.

It wasn't clear to me that he knew what I was saying, and forcing the issue might make the situation worse, particularly if he were bothered by it. The fact that he quickly changed the subject made me wish I hadn't brought it up at all.

That was not the first time my sexuality came to the fore in my role as a professor in the social sciences at a Roman Catholic university. Last winter at a social engagement, a student told a staff member that she thought I was bisexual. And there were two encounters with gay students. The first occurred during my first semester at the university. It was an accidental, and at the time harrowing, encounter at a gay bar. The second, in an online chat room, was equally awkward but a bit less disconcerting.

It's not that I wished to hide my sexuality from my students or that I would ever lie about it, but I just didn't see the need to be open about it, especially since there was no one special in my life.

Even so, I am rather surprised that more people at the university do not know since it's not a large campus, and people love to talk. I've always felt that knowledge about my sexuality was like a snowball rolling down a hill. Every semester, each class, students would become more curious and, most likely, acquire more information about me. In addition to being "thin and neat" (for you *Seinfeld* fans), I am single and in my mid-30s. How many witty retorts can I give to the question, "Why aren't you married?"

The incident with Jason occurred during a recent conference in New York. Our group was able to save on the cost of a room (for four nights) by having one of the students stay with me. Since I envisioned my room would be our default headquarters, I didn't think it would be much of an inconvenience to have one of them sleep there. I also felt a tad guilty for the fact that students had to pay their own way, when so many other groups were financing the trip on their university's dime. I was willing to do whatever possible to cut costs. I select a student roommate (Jason) with whom I had a decent amount of familiarity.

He and I went out to lunch on the first day, and we talked about how his classes were going, his plans after graduation, and family life. It turns out that we had similar experiences with our fathers. Mine was an alcoholic who regularly hit my mother—before she gathered the will to leave him. His was a drug user who is now incarcerated. Things had gotten so bad that he thought it necessary to change his last name.

"Don't tell anyone," he pleaded. "No one knows."

"Of course," I said. "I'm glad you felt comfortable telling me. I'm sure your friends would be supportive if you were to tell them."

"Yeah, you're right," he said. "It's just a lot to deal with."

We also talked about the troubles he had with his former girlfriend. They had dated all through college but had grown apart. It was the first time since his early teenage years that he was not involved in a serious relationship, and he was looking forward to meeting new people and starting his career.

"What about you?" he asked tentatively.

"Well, I've had a couple serious relationships. But I moved twice for school and for work to come out here, so it's been tough."

"Nothing in four years, eh?"

"Not really," I responded somewhat dismissively.

I could tell he was dissatisfied with what I shared with him. And the conversation soon turned to issues related to the conference.

It was not until his "That's so gay" comment that I could revisit the issue and explain myself more openly, however unsuccessful I was. Thankfully, it was not the last that was said on the issue. Later that night, a few of us met at a nearby bar for food and drinks. After dessert, Jason found me at the jukebox. "Hey, I have a question."

I could tell by the tone of his voice that it was something serious. "Shoot," I said, glancing over his shoulder to gauge the distance between us and the rest of the group.

"Were you trying to tell me something earlier? I mean, I think I understood what you meant."

"Yes, I was." I took it as a good sign that he brought it up, but I wasn't sure how much he wanted to talk about it. "Are you OK with it?"

"Yeah, sure," he said quickly. "A couple of years ago, I don't know. But I'm different now."

It turns out that Jason was from a small town with small-town prejudices. It was not until he started college that he knew diversity of any kind. The dialogue I started with him became a teaching moment, as we discussed his background and how he has changed—or grown, he could have said—as a person.

Jason would later tell me that he was not surprised about my revelation. Others, too, he informed me, had suspected as much. A couple of my "favorites" have had lingering questions. I have since had discussions with a couple of them, and I'm supposing it's only a matter of time before the fact that I'm gay is common knowledge on the campus.

The truth is that the vast majority of young people could not care less about the sexual orientation of their professors. Those students who are put off by gay faculty members will have to learn tolerance, if not acceptance, if they are to succeed in their professional lives.

Others might find the idea of a professor being open with students about his sexuality objectionable for its political implications. "Our students need to be rescued from the liberals who have taken over the academy" is a common refrain from such circles.

But there is a difference between being comfortable with your sexuality and being an activist. More to the point, those who think students' minds are so easily shaped have obviously not spent too much time with today's young people. And those who think personal lives should be kept out of the classroom ought to try for one week to refrain from telling stories about their spouses, children, and friends. Only then would you realize how absurd such avoidance can become.

Given how difficult coming out can be, I would never judge someone who decides to dissemble or even deny their sexual orientation. Nevertheless, my admission to certain students, however minimal, has made me realize how misguided, and even silly, I had been about wanting to keep my sexuality from my students. Although the stories vary greatly, if there is one constant about coming out it is that the manner in which we let it be known determines to a large extent the reaction that others will have.

In his remarkable book *The Courage to Teach*, Parker J. Palmer contends that "we teach who we are." His approach is unique for its ability to consider technique as incidental, if not altogether irrelevant, to success in the classroom. Teaching is more about creating and sustaining an open and mutually supportive dialogue than it is about grading rubrics, research competency, or integrative technology.

I never wanted to be the "gay professor," but I especially don't want to be the shameful one. That is not the kind of person I am, and that is certainly not the kind of teacher I want to be. The closet is a dark, lonely, and, for the most part, unnecessary place, and it's not a particularly good place to teach.

Ian Houlihan is the pseudonym of a professor in the social sciences at a Catholic university in the Northeast. He considered using his real name, but he's not ready for that sort of large-scale public admission. Yet.

Exercises – Chapter 1

As your instructor directs, work on the following exercises:

Exercise 1.1 – Case Studies in Diversity

Scenario #1

One day on campus, you recognize Jack, a guy from your high school, who also is attending Columbus State. Jack is blind and uses a white cane to guide himself around campus. In high school, you never talked to Jack, even though you and he were in some of the same classes.

Since you have been in class with him at Columbus State, you notice that people tend to treat him differently from others. Sometimes people talk loudly to him, as if he couldn't hear. Although Jack seems to be friendly and personable, he is usually left out of the many pre-class social activities in which other classmates participate. You also see him eating alone in the cafeteria regularly.

1. How should you treat Jack?

2. Should you say anything to other classmates about what they can do for Jack?

Scenario #2

Douglas and Andy met in English 101 the first day of class. They struck up a conversation because Douglas saw him reading a copy of *Sports Illustrated* before class. The two decided to get together to play a game of basketball, and they discovered they had a lot in common. They were taking the same courses, and soon became friends. They studied together over coffee in the cafeteria once in a while.

Andy knew, however, that things would change. One day, well into the quarter, he chose his words carefully and told Douglas that he was gay and had been involved with someone for almost a year.

1. If you were Douglas, what would have been your reaction?

2. Should Andy have told Doug or kept it "his own business"?

3. If Douglas were to walk away from the friendship, what should Andy do?

Scenario #3

Jerry, a freshman at Columbus State, was walking to the parking lot one afternoon and he saw a pickup truck parked with two young men (presumably students) in it. One of the two men leaned out the window and called him a "n----." As the men drove off in the truck, Jerry saw a Confederate flag displayed on the back license plate.

1. How would you feel if you were Jerry?

2. What action, if any, should Jerry take?

3. Do you think racial discrimination is a problem at Columbus State?

Exercise 1.2 – Plagiarism and Ethics

Assume you have an essay due in a history class that counts for 20% of your final grade. You've had a lot of family emergencies over the last couple of weeks and unavoidably procrastinated your work on the paper. As the deadline approaches, you know you won't be able to finish the paper. You talk to some students in the cafeteria and they tell you about a web site, where for a modest fee, you can download typical undergraduate history papers. You go to the web site and find one that meets the assignment specifications.

What are the ethical issues raised by this situation?

A friend is taking English 102, a course you took last quarter, and asks to borrow the paper you wrote for the research requirement. You worked hard on the paper, and you fear that your friend wants to copy part or all of the assignment.

What can you do to help your friend without compromising your integrity?

For Your Journal

Keeping a journal of your experiences during your first quarter at Columbus State is a good way to keep track of your progress.

You will find the specific journal prompts for each chapter on your class' portal within Columbus State's *Blackboard* software platform at http://blackboard.cscc.edu/. In addition, your instructor will require you to submit your journal assignment through the *Blackboard* system with your Columbus State e-mail address.

To use *Blackboard* and your Columbus State e-mail, you will need a login password and you will need to establish a (free) Columbus State e-mail address. You may do so at http://password.cscc. edu/.

Since most of the instructors in your other courses are increasingly using features of *Blackboard* (even in traditional classrooms), learning how to access and submit your journal assignments this way will prepare you for using the *Blackboard* system in your other courses.

To find the topic for your first entry, then, go to your Freshman Seminar (ASC 190) portal on the *Blackboard* system.

CHAPTER 2   Laying the Groundwork for Success

Chapter Goals

In this chapter you will:

- ❖ Learn what is distinct about a college's culture
- ❖ Learn how to identify the outer and inner resources you'll need to succeed in this culture
- ❖ Learn to develop success behaviors

The goal of the Freshman Seminar is to help you succeed in college. Some people think of the Seminar as an orientation course, or a survival course. In part, it's both. But we go beyond orientation and survival, to skills and knowledge that will help you prosper in your academic work.

Adjusting to College Culture

The keyword to adapting to college culture is "different."

College is not only very different from high school; it's different from probably any other place you've been. We do things differently here. We hold values and assumptions that are subtly but profoundly different from those of the nonacademic world. College is a strange place, and it takes some time to get used to it.

Think of this analogy: You've won a trip to Rome, Italy. Your direct flight leaves from the Columbus airport and lands 12 hours later in Rome. A cab picks you up and delivers you into the heart of the city during a normal business day. You get out of the cab and look around.

The Italians are amazing! Here in the middle of an average day, everyone is expensively dressed, men in silk suits and women in stylish dresses, with high-heeled shoes. Everyone's walking very fast, and most are chain-smoking as they walk. You approach a crosswalk and discover that Roma has no stoplights at intersections. People simply step into the path of oncoming traffic, without glancing to either side, and dare drivers to run over them. Most astonishing of all are the couples. Young women and men are kissing on park benches, sprawled across each other on lawns, groping in doorways. Their displays of affection are at least R-rated, and all on public display. In Ohio, they'd be arrested. In Rome, nobody seems to notice, or to care.

The culture shock you experience in getting adjusted to college life may not be as dramatic as the one you might have on your first day in Rome. Nevertheless, you need to recognize that college, like Rome, is a different culture, and one of your tasks as a student is to learn and adapt to our ways and our customs.

So the Seminar is, in another sense, not only about orientation, survival and success. It's about acculturation. How well you do in this class will be a good indication of your overall likelihood of success in college.

Drawing upon Outer and Inner Resources

As a college freshman, you've embarked on what will be one of the most memorable, exciting and challenging journeys in your life. Make no mistake; the next several years are going to be hard on you. To succeed, you're going to have to draw upon your resources, both "outer" ones and "inner" ones.

Outer Resources

You'll need three types of resources from the outer world. The first will be the support of your family and friends, the people who believe in you and will be ready to provide emotional support as you strive to overcome the challenges of college.

The second outer resource will be your instructors and your classmates. You are going to need these people. Set your intention to establish friendly, respectful relationships with your instructors, whether or not you enjoy their classes. Get to know your classmates, because they can be some of the most effective allies you can have in your academic success.

The third outer resource will be the student services that are offered at Columbus State and at every other college.

Inner Resources

Your inner resources are personal character traits that you will need to cultivate and strengthen, in order to succeed in college. A short list of those resources would include the following:

Commitment

Academic success requires total, steady commitment to your work, in every class. You're going to have to put your courses ahead of other things in your life that are probably more pleasurable or that may claim prior importance. For the next several years, college will have to come first.

Focus

As well as commitment to the task, your ability to shut everything else out and focus on the academic task at hand—whether reading a chapter in a textbook, writing a report, or studying for an exam—will be vital to your success.

Stamina

To someone on the outside, studying doesn't look like very hard work, but we know better. College work involves long hours, early mornings and late nights, and a good bit of stress. You need to build up your strength and stamina. That means taking care of your health, exercising when you can, eating a healthy diet, and getting as much sleep as possible.

Open-Mindedness

When you're getting used to an unfamiliar culture, the best thing to do is to keep an open mind about the people around you and their strange ways. Some of your degree requirements may not make sense to you at the moment. Why must you take that English class or this math class? Trust that the requirements have a purpose, and don't waste your energy railing against them. In addition, the campus is a diverse place, filled with people of differing ideas and opinions. Part of academic culture involves showing respect to points of view that may be different from or challenging to your own—keeping an open mind.

Social Skills

You're going to be dealing with a lot of people in the coming years, probably hundreds of them before you've earned your degree. College isn't just a place; it's a society. Good social skills will serve you well.

Decision-Making Skills

Likewise, you'll have hundreds of decisions to make in the future, everything from what you plan to major in to what term you're going to take Algebra II.

Problem-Solving Skills

In both your coursework and your personal life, college work will pose problems to which you'll need to apply ingenuity, creativity, and wisdom to solve. Your outer resources of family, instructors, classmates and services can assist you, but you'll need to draw upon your inner problem-solving skills as well.

Self-Awareness of Strengths and Weaknesses

In addition to academic knowledge, you're going to acquire a great deal of self-knowledge through being in college. You'll discover motivations, assumptions, and styles that make you a unique individual. The best students generally possess a good understanding of their weaknesses as well as their strengths. They learn how to minimize the weaknesses and maximize the strengths in order to do their best work.

Planning Skills

Students chart a course through college by establishing goals and objectives—knowing exactly where you want to go, and how to get there. Think of college as a road trip to some place you want to reach, like a beach in San Diego or an amusement park in Orlando. Your task is to create a road map for your journey, plotting out each highway, stop, and obstacle along the way.

Success Behaviors

Older students who enter college after many years of experience in the business world or the military tend to be pretty good at adapting to the demands of academic protocol, since they've already learned from experience that different cultures reward different behaviors. The way to succeed is to adapt to the culture you're in.

Students who are entering college directly from high school, though, often encounter a period of adjustment in trying to learn the ropes. That's because they're suddenly given both a great deal more freedom and more responsibility than they've had before. The freedom is liberating, giving them the options to make good decisions for themselves, but also offering the temptation to make bad ones. The responsibilities can seem overwhelming, creating stress and tension.

Just as with any other culture, college tends to reward or "privilege" certain character traits and behaviors.

The successful college student usually displays character traits of promptness, respect, politeness, open-mindedness, acceptance of responsibility, flexibility, patience, and tolerance.

It's not hard to see how these behaviors would come in handy. The academic culture requires students to attend classes regularly, to arrive on time, and to submit all work according to deadlines. Students are expected to speak and deal respectfully with their instructors, acknowledging their authority both inside and outside the classroom. Keeping an open mind about new perspectives or controversial topics, and treating people with different points of view tolerantly are traditional values of the Arts & Sciences culture.

Even if these are behaviors you yourself don't personally value or intend to follow for the rest of your life, you'll find college a much more congenial place if you cultivate them at least while you're here. When in Rome, do as the Romans do.

Cultivating Effective Habits

Recently, a group of instructors and administrators met for a day-long conference to identify what they believe to be the most important habits students need to cultivate for their college work. Their final list boiled down to a handful of habits of conduct, mind, and success.

Habits of Conduct

CSCC students respect themselves and others.

CSCC students contribute to a positive teaching-learning environment by being courteous and honest, and by displaying personal integrity.

Habits of Mind

CSCC students are intellectually curious and open-minded.

CSCC students strive for success, and desire to learn much and perform well.

CSCC students work hard and are committed to meeting every obligation to the best of their ability.

Habits of Success

CSCC students set realistic goals and continually assess their progress.

CSCC students seek help from teachers, counselors, advisors and tutors in order to meet their goals.

CSCC students commit the time and personal resources necessary to succeed.

Stated and Unstated Rules

Much of what will be expected of you as a student is written down, public matters of college policy. For example, the Columbus State student handbook contains a section called the Student Code of Conduct. The instructor's syllabus in each course you take will establish other policies, specific to that course. Instructors usually review the syllabus thoroughly during the first session. If you've missed the first session, or your instructor doesn't review the syllabus, be sure you review it yourself, to know what rules you're bound by in that class.

Not every rule will be written down, however. Others will fall under the category of common sense and common courtesy. These might include prohibitions about eating during class, answering cell phones, texting, arriving late, talking during a lecture, reading a newspaper in class, or otherwise being disruptive or dismissive of what's happening in the course.

College instructors are professionals who have earned a right to be treated with respect, and who have the right to set reasonable rules about conduct, to assure that one or a few students don't disrupt the business of teaching and learning for the class as a whole.

It should go without saying—but ought to be said, anyway—that instructors are expected to treat students with the same respect and courtesy. The college campus is, ideally, a peaceful environment where conflict is kept at a minimum through the observed values of tolerance and open-mindedness.

"Working Together, Students and Instructors" will present more materials on how to develop a productive working relationship with your instructors and classmates.

Handling Stress

Stress is a natural part of life. In fact, moderate levels of stress can even be good for you. Stress is a sign of vitality, commitment to life. Stress can give you that "competitive edge." Stress out of control, though, is not good for you. If you are too uptight before an exam, you're not flexible; you might even become panicky and confused or suffer a memory block. In the chapters that follow, you'll find advice on how to deal with specific kinds of stress, like stage fright. For now it's important that you develop stress awareness. If you can answer the following two questions, you're already on your way to stress control.

1. What happens to you when you're stressed?
2. What situations produce stress in you?

Some students find it helpful to keep a stress diary or journal for a few weeks just to let them know when, where and why stress appears. You might wonder if such a journal will actually stress you more by focusing on stress producers. Not really. First, you will probably discover that you are not really as "stressed out" as you think you are. Second, identifying stresses is the first step toward eliminating them, or at least controlling them. The solution to stress management is simple. Take charge. You control the stress, not the other way around.

Here are some tips for taking charge of stressful situations:

❖ Anticipate stressful situations and be prepared to deal with them.

❖ Eat right and get enough sleep. Go easy on the tobacco and alcohol.

❖ Exercise regularly.

❖ "Take ten" when you start to feel overwhelmed (ten breaths, ten steps back, and a ten-minute break).

❖ Enjoy life. Do things that give you pleasure. Laugh.

❖ Choose serenity. Avoid stressful encounters whenever you can. Spend as much time as you can with people who are easy to be with, content and calm.

❖ Do something nice for yourself every day. Maybe it's candles and a bubble bath at the end of the day, a run in the park, or a double chocolate ice cream cone on the way home from class. Reward yourself on a regular basis—you deserve it.

If you feel stress getting the upper hand, ask for help. The Columbus State Counseling Center holds regular workshops on dealing with test anxiety, learning to balance work, family and school, dealing with substance abuse issues, and dealing with many other issues. These workshops are free and usually offered several times a week to accommodate commuters.

Other activities offered by the Counseling Center include the new student orientation program, placement testing, and academic advising assistance for students enrolled in the transfer programs.

Remember

❖ It is easier to succeed in college once you understand its cultural expectations and rules.

❖ You have access to both inner resources and outer resources that can help you succeed.

❖ You have the power to develop positive habits that will increase your chances of not only succeeding in college, but of enjoying the experience as well.

CHAPTER 3 Planning for the Future

Chapter Goals

In this chapter you will:

- ❖ Learn to understand the difference between setting goals and setting objectives
- ❖ Learn to use the college's academic calendar
- ❖ Learn to create a "vision" to support and guide you
- ❖ Learn to plan your academic hours
- ❖ Learn to plan for transferring hours to another institution

This chapter will cover the essential skills and tools you will need to chart your course from where you are now to the glorious day when you finally earn your college degree.

Setting Goals and Objectives

At a Columbus State curriculum committee meeting not too long ago, a faculty member volunteered a thought: she was glad that she'd gone to college back in days when planning out four years' worth of coursework wasn't as complicated as it is today.

Everyone in the meeting agreed. College requirements have become more complicated with every decade that has passed. Figuring out which courses to take, when to take them, at which school, whether or not they'll apply to hours required to graduate, whether or not they'll transfer to your next college—those can be daunting tasks.

Fortunately, lots of help is available to guide you through the academic maze.

Goals and Objectives: A Distinction

Let's start with goals and objectives. The difference between them is easy to grasp.

A goal is the final outcome, the thing or situation you hope to have at the end. An objective is a step you take toward accomplishing it. We used the example of planning a road trip.

If you're driving to Panama City Beach for spring break, you'll likely set a course down I-71, then I-65, and finally SR 79. Along the way you'll pass through Cincinnati, Louisville, Nashville, Birmingham and Montgomery. But you're not concluding your trip at any of those places. They're your objectives, points along the way you have to reach before you can achieve your goal, the warm sand and good times of Panama City.

Or consider a different example. If you've invited friends over for dinner on Saturday night, your goal is probably to provide a good meal and entertainment. Your objectives would include deciding on a menu, buying food from the store, cleaning the apartment, cooking the meal, selecting music or movies for your guests to enjoy, and so on. You'd probably create a schedule (at least a rough one) of when to take care of all these duties.

Academic planning is lengthier and more complex than preparing for a trip or a party, but the principle of objectives leading to a goal is the same. Your goal is to earn an Associates or Bachelors degree. Your objectives to reach it will include scheduling classes, maintaining a good GPA, choosing a major and a four-year school to transfer to, completing prerequisites, taking requirements and electives, earning sufficient hours to graduate, and so on.

Your goal is specific and measurable; you either arrive in Panama City or you don't. You either earn your degree, or you don't.

Your objectives are likewise specific and measurable. You either make your way through Birmingham, or you don't. If you don't, however, you won't make the beach. You either complete your Calculus requirement, or you don't. If you don't you can't earn the degree.

Planning Before Acting

In previous chapters, we talked about college as a unique culture, in the sense that its members tend to hold certain values and follow specific behaviors that may not be part of another culture. In the academic world, the ability to plan ahead is valued and "privileged." Students who display that skill adapt to our culture more easily and are rewarded for their conduct.

Students who, as a matter of their personality, prefer to act spontaneously, without planning ahead, tend not to be rewarded. This may seem unfair, but it's the way this culture works. Even if you're not a compulsive party planner by nature, you will need to develop some of the planner's attitudes, abilities and habits.

Success in the academic culture requires both long-term planning and short-term planning.

In a short-term plan, consider three, four or five specific objectives you hope to accomplish each term, things that help you take a few more steps toward your ultimate goal of earning the degree. These objectives should be concrete, and you should be able to report at the end of the term on whether or not you accomplished them.

"Being a better student" is a flawed objective, because it's too vague and can't be definitively measured. "Not cutting any classes this term" or "Making an A in Chemistry" would be better objectives; they're specific, and you'll definitely know whether or not you accomplished them by the end of the term.

For long-term planning, you need to think larger and peer into a more distant future.

Consulting the Academic Calendar

One of your most valuable resources for short-term planning is the official Academic Calendar that Columbus State posts online, with the schedule of class offerings, every term.

This calendar is important to you because it provides dates of when the term begins and ends, what days classes don't meet because of holidays, when fees must be paid, when you'll need an instructor's signature to enroll in a class, and when you can still drop classes with a full or partial refund of your tuition.

2010 Summer Quarter Calendar
June 28 – September 11
Please Note Deadline Dates

Fee Payment Deadline: Wednesday, June 23, 2010
The Web and CATS system will be unavailable beginning 11:00 PM on Wednesday, June 23, 1010

NOTE: Tuition refunds are based upon the percentage of time elapsed in each course. If the course is dropped within 10% of the time elapsed in the course, a 100% refund will be issued. If the course is dropped within 20% of the time elapsed in the course, a 50% refund will be issued. If the course is dropped within 30% of the time elapsed in the course, a 25% refund will be issued.

A course must be dropped before 20% of the course (50% refund date) has elapsed in order to avoid a "W" appearing on the academic transcript.

The last day to register for a flexibly scheduled course is the day before the course begins. The last day to drop and receive a 100% refund for a flexibly scheduled course is the last day before the course begins.

Please check with the Financial Aid Department regarding other term freeze dates.

A day marked with an "*" is either a weekend day, a holiday and/or the campus is closed.

	Full Term	First Term	Second Term	First 4-week Term	Second 4-week Term	8-week Term
Classes Begin	Monday June 28	Monday June 28	Thursday August 5	Monday June 28	Monday July 26	Monday June 28
Classes End	Saturday* September 11	Wednesday August 4	Saturday* September 11	Sunday* July 25	Sunday* August 22	Sunday* August 22
Instructor's signature required to add a class	Monday June 28	Monday June 28	Thursday August 5	Monday June 28	Monday July 26	Monday June 28
Late Registration Begins: Instructor's Signature Required	Monday* July 5	Thursday July 1	Sunday* August 8	Wednesday June 30	Wednesday July 28	Saturday* July 3
Last Day to Drop Classes	Thursday August 12	Tuesday July 20	Friday August 27	Wednesday July 14	Wednesday August 11	Saturday* July 31
Last Day to Drop with a "W"	Monday July 12	Sunday* July 4	Wednesday August 11	Friday July 2	Friday July 30	Thursday July 8
Financial Aid Freeze Date	Sunday* July 4	Wednesday June 30	Saturday* August 7	Tuesday June 29	Tuesday July 27	Friday July 2
Last Day for 100% Refund	Sunday* July 4	Wednesday June 30	Saturday* August 7	Tuesday June 29	Tuesday July 27	Friday July 2
Last Day for 50% Refund	Monday July 12	Sunday* July 4	Wednesday August 11	Friday July 2	Friday July 30	Thursday July 8
Last Day for 25% Refund	Monday July 19	Thursday July 8	Sunday* August 15	Monday* July 5	Monday August 2	Tuesday July 13

April 16	Deadline for FAFSA online application. www.fafsa.ed.gov
April 26	Open Registration for all Students
April 26	Readmission Deadline for Academic Dismissal and Academic Review Summer Quarter 2010
June 24	Drop for Non-Payment at 12:01 AM (Web and CATS system will be unavailable beginning 11:00 PM on Wednesday, June 23)
July 4 & 5	Independence Day observed – Campus Closed
July 9	**Petition to Graduate Summer Quarter 2010 due in Records and Registration, Madison Hall, Room 201 before 4:30 p.m.**
July 13	Drop for Non-Payment at 12:01 AM (Web and CATS system will be unavailable beginning 11:00 PM on Monday, July 12)
July 26	Readmission Deadline for Academic Dismissal and Academic Review Autumn Quarter 2010
August 7	Last day to remove Incompletes (I) incurred Spring Quarter 2010
September 6	Labor Day observed – Campus Closed
September 10	Graduation Ceremony
September 11	Summer Quarter 2010 Ends

In addition, the Academic Calendar lists important deadlines for forms and paperwork that you may need to file, such as the deadline for applying for Federal Student Aid or for filing your Petition to Graduate.

The school goes to a great deal of effort to make these dates and deadlines public. Ultimately, though, the student is responsible for knowing what the dates are and meeting the deadlines. One valuable success habit is to study the calendar for each new term.

Creating a "Vision" to Support You

A vision is something that will sustain you through the long ordeal of reaching your goal. Some people call it a "dream," but "vision" is a better term. Dreams are things that come to you unbidden, shaped by your subconscious. This vision, on the other hand, is something you yourself shape in your mind, deliberately and consciously.

Experiencing Success, Before it Happens

When the term "vision" is mentioned in conversation, people sometimes assume that we're talking about a mystical experience or some kind of New Age fad. That's not the case.

What's being referred to instead is your ability to imagine, in detail, what your final success will be like when you reach your goal. What will you see? Hear? Feel? What, in specific detail, will you experience?

For you as a college student, the vision of success may be the moment when you hear your name called at the commencement ceremony. You envision yourself walking across the stage in the long graduation gown, feeling the tassel on your cap tickling your cheek, approaching the President of the college, shaking hands, hearing congratulatory words. Then you feel the diploma in your hand as it's passed to you. You hear the roar of applause from the auditorium, and you make out the voices of your friends and family cheering for you. A beautiful, proud moment—not a fantasy, but something that could actually come to pass if you stick to your objectives and keep your goal in sight.

Others may have other visions: Opening the door to your office on the first day of your professional career. Buying a house with the salary you're earning because of your degree, signing papers with the realtor. Attending a conference or convention, maybe as a featured speaker at the event, and being greeted with respect by your colleagues.

Whatever the vision is, you need to imagine it as concretely and in as much detail as possible, and you need to return to it often, especially during hard times.

The Power of Imagination

What good is imagining something, though? Isn't it a waste of time to indulge in daydreams?

Not at all, because this is no ordinary daydream. Daydreams substitute wish-fulfilling fantasies for practical realities, and lead to inaction. A detailed vision of your success will promote and support constructive action toward your goal.

Educators and reformers talk a great deal about willpower, but psychologists and motivation experts have long known that the power of imagination is just as strong as willpower in creating desired outcomes. Sometimes, imagination is even a more powerful method. If you have high blood pressure, you can try to command it to decrease, using willpower; but it isn't likely to. Simply closing your eyes and imagining yourself at rest in the shade of a palm tree beside a peaceful sea at sunset would be much more effective.

Your vision is something that can happen, and is even likely to happen, if you continue to pursue your goals. If you treat your vision with conviction, it can even make it more likely that you will succeed.

Both professional and amateur athletes frequently report experiences of "seeing" themselves score a field goal or break a record in sprinting, before they do it. Surgeons "see" themselves performing successful procedures on patients before entering the operating room in life-threatening cases. Members of every profession know the secret of imagination. The genius Nikola Tesla, for example, frequently "saw" himself making a discovery in physics or inventing a new device before he actually did so.

Positive, constructive imagination leads to the development of positive, constructive habits, because the mind surrenders the subconscious resistance that frequently leads students to self-sabotaging behaviors like procrastination.

And, finally, your vision is something you can turn to on those late nights or early dawns when you're exhausted from being a student, tired of all the coursework, tired of struggling for money to support yourself in school, tired of not having fun with your friends. Those moments when you want to throw your goals away come to every student. And that's when your vision can help you the most. If you've shaped it carefully and imagined it fully, it can see you through those moments of despair.

Planning by Academic Hours

As you well know, you will need to complete a number of "hours" in college. Sadly, this doesn't mean you can sign up for any courses that interest you until you've completed the required number. Many of the hours belong to general education requirements, while others may apply to major requirements.

General Education Requirements

The general education requirements are part of what used to be called the Liberal Arts curriculum. They include courses in verbal and mathematical skills, the sciences, history and the humanities. If you're pursuing an AA or AS, with plans to transfer into a BA or BS program at another school, these are courses that you must take (and pass!).

Traditionally, students have come to Columbus State to spend two years completing most of their general education requirements—finishing all their English courses, for example, to get them out of the way. By doing so, students can begin to concentrate on courses related to their major program of study when they transfer to a four-year school.

Columbus State has started offering pre-major programs as well. The pre-major programs allow students to begin taking courses for their major without waiting two years. More information about the pre-majors will be presented by the college as the development process continues.

Major Requirements

In addition to a slate of courses that everyone is required to take, the academic departments of the four-year school you select will have other courses that they require their majors to complete. Many of these requirements will be in upper-level courses in the field.

An English major, for example, may take several 200-level literary survey courses, 300-level courses in Shakespeare and other authors, and 400-level courses in subjects like criticism and research.

Other requirements might include coursework in related fields, taught by other departments. A student majoring in Political Science, for example, might be required to take upper-level courses in Statistics, taught in the Math department.

In Ohio, the general education requirements are largely uniform among all the state-supported colleges. But major requirements may vary significantly from school to school. For that reason, students at Columbus State are encouraged to begin selecting a major and a set of schools that they might transfer to.

If you know, at least tentatively, your major and your school, you can begin investigating that school's major requirements and begin planning for completing them. That process is called Transfer Planning.

Transfer Planning

Transfer Planning 101

The professional counselors in Advising Services have created an introduction to this process that they call "Transfer Planning 101." This series of eight modules covers a comprehensive range of topics, from core requirements in AS and AA degrees to discovering both print and online transfer guides.

Transfer Planning 101 is available to all students on the Columbus State website (http://www. cscc.edu/Counseling/acdadv/TP101.html), but it's been specifically designed for students in this course.

Your instructor will probably devote at least one class session to reviewing the modules with you, and you have access to a link to the entire set on your Blackboard section. The following brief overview will explain what different modules offer:

Module 1—Introduction
Module 2—Associate of Arts & Associate of Science Degree Overview
Module 3—Transfer Resources: Transfer Guides
Module 4—Transfer Resources: Degree Audit Reports (DARS)
Module 5—Transfer Resources: u.select
Module 6—Term by Term Plan
Module 7—Resources for Undecided Students
Module 8—Advising Services Information/Conclusion

Planning Your Coursework, by Terms

Module 2 of the Transfer Planning presentation contains a great deal of vital information. Be sure to watch it carefully … and then to make an appointment with Advising Services to help you decide what courses you need to take, and when it would be best for you to schedule them.

Before watching Module 2, have a copy of either the AA degree requirements or the AS degree requirements. Both are available in .pdf format on the Columbus State website, or in the Advising Services offices.

As you'll see from Module 2, planning your coursework is one of the most complex tasks you'll face as a student. It isn't something you should attempt to do alone! You need an advisor to guide you through the process, and as a freshman you should begin with Advising Services.

If you haven't already done so, contact them today to make an appointment. There's not a moment to lose.

General Education Requirements

The general education requirements, the ones you should focus on during your first two years, differ slightly between the AA and AS degrees.

The AS degree, specifically, requires more Math coursework. Whether you pursue the AA or the AS will depend on the major(s) and the schools you're considering. If you think you want to major in communications at Ohio State, for example, you should follow the AA program, since that major at OSU is a BA degree.

Both degrees require a certain number of hours in the following fields:

❖ English/Communication

❖ Mathematics

❖ Humanities

❖ Social/behavioral sciences

❖ Biological/physical science

Many students will complete the hours for an AA or AS simply by fulfilling these requirements, but may still want to consider completing elective courses that will transfer to their four-year college as requirements there. Again, consult an advisor in making the best choices from the list of available electives.

Term-By-Term Plan

As Module 6 explains, the term-by-term plan is sort of a master schedule for planning a year or more in advance. With it, you decide which required courses you are going to take during each term.

The plan is tentative, of course, and can be changed if you need to or wish to. But it's an extremely useful tool for setting a course through this complex task.

Using Your Degree Audit Report (DARS)

Module 4 of the Transfer Planning presentation consists of two parts. Be sure to watch both of them, and take notes on the instructions provided for getting your report.

What it is

The report is referred to by the abbreviation **DARS** (Degree Audit Report). It's an individualized report generated for every student at Columbus State that lists what courses that student has completed, what courses the student is currently taking, and what courses remain to be taken in each of the general education categories (Writing, Math, Humanities, and so on).

DARS also assists students in planning ahead by enabling them to see what courses would be required in different programs and majors. Module 4 will demonstrate this function of DARS for you.

How to Read Your DARS

Since you are a freshman, perhaps in your first term at Columbus State, your current DARS will likely be simple. But it will become fuller and more helpful to you as you continue to acquire hours in future terms. Module 4 explains how the report uses color codes and other devices to alert you to what requirements you have already completed, and what others you still have to undertake.

Planning to Transfer to Another School

The information presented on this page provides an overview to what you will find in Module 5 of the Transfer Planning presentation.

Ohio Transfer Module

The State of Ohio requires all state-supported colleges to offer a similar "core" curriculum of courses that will transfer from one school to the next, in fulfillment of a student's general education requirements. Many private colleges have recognized the value of the system, and have voluntarily agreed to recognize the Transfer Module as well.

The system is a great advantage to Ohio students, since it makes their core coursework highly transferable between state colleges. Ohio was a pioneer in transferability; other states have since followed our lead.

Transfer Agreements

In addition to following the Ohio Transfer Module, individual colleges have formed agreements among themselves to transfer other courses outside of the core curriculum. These will be of interest to you if you are thinking of one of these institutions as your four-year school.

Transfer Assurance Guides

Columbus State has agreed to create Transfer Assurance Guides (TAGs) to help students seamlessly transfer to a number of area colleges including Capital University, the University of Cincinnati, Ohio Dominican, Otterbein and, of course, OSU.

Again, if you're considering one of those schools, check with Advising Services for assistance in reading its TAGs, or ask your instructor for assistance.

U.Select (Formerly Course Applicability System)

U.Select (https://www.transfer.org/uselect/login.htm) is a free website that enables you to determine the transferability of courses online.

Module 5 of the Transfer Planning presentation demonstrates the site's layout and functions. Again, please watch that module carefully and take notes.

U.Select was formerly known as the Course Applicability System (CAS). Many people still use the old name, and some printed and online guides still refer to CAS. When you see or hear "CAS" or "Course Applicability System," think U.Select instead.

Remember

❖ The only way to achieve a goal is to identify concrete objectives that will lead you toward it.

❖ Having a clear vision of your ultimate goal will help you reach it.

❖ Academic success requires both short-term and long-term plans.

❖ Columbus State provides many resources to help you plan your academic success.

CHAPTER 4   Working Together: Students and Instructors

Chapter Goals

In this chapter you will:

❖ find out what instructors expect of you
❖ find out what you can expect from instructors
❖ learn about classroom protocol
❖ get tips on how to talk to instructors
❖ learn how to deal with grade disputes
❖ learn to see your instructor as a partner in learning

When it comes to success in college, the only person you really can depend on is yourself. However, one of your greatest collaborators in your pursuit of success will be the instructors you meet as you move toward your goal of a college degree. Yes, you are in charge of your education, but learn to use your instructor as a resource to help you achieve your goals.

Find Out About Instructors Before Classes

The person teaching your class can make a tremendous difference both in how much you learn and in the grade you receive, and the time to research instructors is *before* signing up for courses. Seek out students who have already taken courses from the instructors you're considering for the following quarter. For each class, ask what you can expect in tests, grades, and the instructor's ability to teach the material. Success in later years in college and graduate school is dependent on hard knowledge, so getting the "easy" instructor in a key course or subject is not always the smart way to go. On the other hand, intentionally taking a course from a professor who is notorious for handing out low grades may not be good for your grade-point average. Keep in mind, though, who is giving you the information—with the study habits you'll learn in this book, you may well get an A from that "impossible" instructor.

Going through the grapevine is not the only way to find out about instructors. Here are others:

❖ Most colleges give awards to instructors for exceptional teaching, and a list of such award winners should be available.

❖ Student evaluations of courses and instructors are sought and made public by some schools, giving you access to a summary of student opinions instead of just the advice of a few.

❖ Instructors whose advice you trust may be able to recommend others whose classes you would enjoy or do well in.

Introduce Yourself Early in the Quarter

Most instructors care about students and are there to help them learn. They'll be even more interested in doing that if you make it clear you're there to do the learning. In a small class, it's possible that your class attendance, performance, and participation will speak for itself. In the many large classes you'll encounter, however, you'll be nothing but a student ID number on a computer printout unless you make a special effort to get to know your instructor. Introduce yourself to the instructors in all your classes, large or small, during the first week of the quarter. The instructor's concern for you is going to be considerably less if the first time you show up in the office is the day before an exam instead of early in the quarter.

How should you introduce yourself? Go to the instructors' offices during office hours. Let them know who you are and what your intentions are regarding their courses. Talk to them about how the courses fit into your long-range plans. If you're a science major taking an English composition course, let the teacher know that and explain why you want to do well. If you're a philosophy major taking introductory chemistry, tell the instructor what you're doing in the class. Don't waste the instructor's time: just introduce yourself briefly. Note also that while you want to let the instructor know that you want and plan to do well—that is, to get a good grade—you *don't* want to say, "I need to get an A." Instructors will be more receptive to someone who seems interested in learning than someone who seems only to want to get a good grade.

Instructors Do More Than Lecture

When you have trouble understanding class material, get help from the instructor. Instructors have weekly office hours set aside for students who require additional help. Seeking this help doesn't mean you're not a good student: on the contrary, asking questions shows instructors that you've been paying attention in class and thinking about what's been presented. Don't hesitate to take advantage of the additional help instructors can provide. Because few people take advantage of office hours, they can often turn into one-on-one tutorial sessions for you, enabling you to master the course material like no one else in your class.

It's important to be well-prepared with your questions when you approach an instructor. Instructors want to help you, but then don't want to waste time. Don't expect them to help if you haven't done your share. If readings or homework problems have been assigned, tackle them *before* you seek extra assistance. Then follow these steps:

1. Have questions written out so that you won't forget why you came.

2. Bring along your class notes if your question relates to them, or your textbook or handouts if they are relevant.

3. Be ready to show the instructor how you've already attempted to solve the problem.

4. Ask your question, and then listen carefully to the instructor's explanation; take notes to help you remember.

5. If you're not sure you understand what you're being told, thank the instructor, tell him or her that you'll go over the material (or try the problem) again, and ask if you may return for further help if you're still confused.

6. If you *know* you don't understand and feel the instructor has already done everything possible to explain, ask for recommendations for other sources for help.

Learning is a two-way street. To get the most out of an office conference, meet your instructor halfway. Be prepared to do your part by having questions ready.

The time spent in the office with your instructor is important for many reasons. First, it helps you understand the material better. Second, it shows your instructor that you are making an effort to learn the material and are concerned about doing well in class. Third, problems you may have in understanding lecture material are often the same problems other students are having, and pursuing these helps the instructor recognize questions the whole class may be having.

Many instructors offer occasional extra study sessions. *Don't miss these!* If instructors are willing to spend extra time helping you, you'd better show up for help. As in discussions during office hours, these review sessions can give you a good idea what questions will be on the exam and how to answer them. Also, other students' questions may provide clues you'd never think of on your own.

Instructors expect you to take *responsibility* for your own learning.

❖ You must make the effort to learn; instructors will be there to lead the class.

❖ You must take it upon yourself to do whatever it takes (required or not) to learn the material.

❖ You must realize that the work you do will result in the grade you get.

Classroom Protocol: It Goes Both Ways

In the past, the word *protocol* referred to ceremonial etiquette observed by diplomats and heads of state. Today, however, the observance of certain appropriate behaviors on the part of students and instructors applies to the classroom, as well. This is called *classroom protocol*. Of course, most instructors know what's expected of them in the classroom; students, on the other hand, often do not. Following is a list of commonly held myths about college classroom behavior.

Myth 1: It doesn't matter if I come to class late or if I come at all.

Wrong. It matters very much. When you come late to class, you miss important information given at the beginning of the lecture or lab. You also disrupt the class and interfere with the learning process of other students. Many instructors have late policies: you may be docked points for habitual tardiness or may receive a grade of zero for an activity conducted that day. As for missing class, isn't it obvious? When you miss class, you miss a day of your education, and if the day you miss is a quiz or exam day, you will probably earn a zero. Don't be fooled by the fact that your instructor does not call the roll every day. He or she knows who is in class ready to work and who is not. Be reasonable about your schedule and be honest with yourself. Excuses like "I'm just not a morning person," or "my car broke down," "My brother's getting married and I have to miss all next week," won't cut it. Make sure you are ready to devote the required time and effort to a class before you enroll.

Myth 2: If I don't have my book or if I haven't read the assignment, it really won't matter. All I have to do is listen to the lecture or get the information from other students.

Wrong again. Instructors don't read from the book when they lecture. They base their lectures on the assumption that *you* have read the material and understand it. Many instructors give pop or open-book quizzes on assigned material or call on students individually in class for answers. If you haven't read the material or don't have your book, you're in trouble. If you think you can rely on your lab partner to carry you through an experiment, think again. Students who have done the work are seldom willing to carry someone who hasn't. Finally, the surest way to show your lack of interest in learning is to ignore assignments or announce to the instructor, "I forgot my book. Can I borrow yours?"

Myth 3: All that matters is showing up for class. If I read the paper or do homework for another class, that's my business.

Just being a body in the classroom isn't enough. Your mind must be there, too. Your instructors expect you to answer questions, give opinions, and actively participate in class discussions. Don't imagine you can appear to be taking notes in art history class when you're really doing your math assignment. Although they may say nothing to you at the time, instructors are experts at spotting such behavior. Your body language says a lot about you, too. Don't slouch or look bored, and don't fall asleep in class! If you're too tired to stay awake, stay in bed.

Myth 4: I don't have to raise my hand to talk in class. I can also chat with my neighbor if I feel like it as long as I don't talk too loud.

Respect for others applies to the college classroom just as it does anywhere else where a discussion is in progress. Don't blurt answers; wait to be called on. Give others a chance to respond, too. If your instructor announces at the beginning of the lecture that he or she will answer questions at the end, don't raise your hand and wave it frantically while the instructor is speaking. Jot down your question and voice it at the appropriate time. Don't hold a conversation with another student while someone else is speaking. It's not polite, and it's not smart. Your "whisper" is a lot louder than you think and your instructor will probably view this as a classroom disruption. Don't interrupt when others have the floor; this applies to your classmates as well as the instructor. Listen. You'll get your chance to be heard.

Myth 5: It's okay if I bring a snack or a can of pop to class, when I don't have time to eat before class.

It's not okay. In fact, it is against school policy at Columbus State to allow any food or drink in the classroom. You should plan your schedule from the beginning to allow for time to eat a balanced diet. If you find yourself in a bind, pack some energy bars and snack on the way to class or at breaks. If you're thirsty, stop at a drinking fountain.

Myth 6: I can bring my cell phone to class, since my work needs to get in touch with me at any time.

A recent survey of teachers and students confirmed that beeping pagers and ringing cell phones are at the top of the list of irritating distractions in a college classroom. If you must bring either to class, ***turn off the sound alert!*** Never answer a phone during class and carry on a conversation. If you must receive an emergency call during class, excuse yourself and leave the room quietly. If you are involved in an emergency situation, perhaps it would be better to leave it outside of class so that you can give your full attention to your coursework.

Myth 7: If I work really hard and do everything my instructor tells me to, I will get a good grade.

Not necessarily. Hard work certainly pays off, but it is no guarantee of a good grade. It may be true that if you are a math whiz, your strong effort may, indeed, result in an A. However, if math is not your strong suit, you may have to put in extra effort just to get a respectable C. Of course, the more experience you have with any subject, the better you become. Eventually your hard work will pay off, but you may have to be patient for results you want.

Myth 8: My instructor is really nice and seems to like his students. I guess that means he's an easy grader.

This is, perhaps, one of the most common mistakes new students make about college, where instructors and students generally interact on a friendly and open basis. This makes sense. Your instructors are there because they want to be. They enjoy teaching and working with students. This does not mean they do not uphold grading standards. In fact, they are required to do so by the college. Your college degree and transfer credits would have very little value otherwise. Your instructors honor your trust in them by making sure you are well prepared for further study. No instructor worth of the title would allow a student to leave his or her class with a "good grade" knowing that the student is unprepared for the future. Instructors do like students; that's why they grade them fairly.

Your instructors are human so they are always forming opinions. You need to be aware that the impression you make can have an effect on your grade. Even the way you sit and where you sit communicates to your instructor. Three good rules to follolw:

1. Get to know your instructor personally.

2. Be prepared for class.

3. Be an active part of the class.

Freedom of Speech in the Classroom?

Freedom of speech—your right to hold an opinion and express it, whether or not others agree with you—is one of the great hallmarks of a democracy.

The college classroom is a forum for open discussion and the exchange of information, a place where everyone is given the opportunity to be heard. The college classroom is a place where ideas are explored, where convictions may be affirmed and minds changed. However, just because we have the right to speak our opinions does not mean that we don't have a responsibility to others in the sharing of those opinions. In the course of your education, your instructor may find it necessary to raise controversial issues that people disagree about and feel strongly about. That is part of the responsibility of being a college instructor. However, in the discussion of these issues, there is no place in the classroom for bigotry or disrespect for others. Deliberate racist or sexist remarks are not acceptable. This applies to your instructor, as well. On the other hand, your instructor may say things that shock you or even make you angry. Be aware that no instructor ever sets out to shock or anger a student just for the sake of doing it; the real purpose of controversial statements is to get you to examine your belief and opinions, to think critically about them, and to explain or defend them rationally. If you really feel uncomfortable about a topic for discussion, or feel that you can't control your reactions, talk to your instructor privately. Don't avoid class or leave in the middle of a discussion. To become educated means to become aware of the whole picture and not just one corner of the canvas.

What Can You Expect From Your Instructor?

So far the discussion has centered mainly on student responsibilities. What about student rights in the classroom? What should you expect from your instructor? In order to answer these questions, you need to know something about college instructors.

Your instructor is a professional educator. He or she has completed an intense program of study leading to a master's degree or a doctorate in a specific academic discipline such as psychology, literature, physics, or music history. In addition to academic credentials, your instructor is also an experienced teacher who has taught many different students and many different courses. Each quarter, full time instructors at Columbus State teach 20 hours of classes a week and maintain 10 office hours a week. They develop lesson plans, make up exams, and grade papers; many serve on college committees and volunteer in the community. Also, instructors are expected to keep up with the latest developments in their fields; they read extensively in their disciplines, attend workshops, give conference presentations, write articles and books, and even take courses. You are in good hands. College instructors expect a lot of themselves, and they take their responsibilities to their students very seriously. Following are ten characteristics of college instructors:

1. Instructors meet classes. If they must be absent due to conference attendance, they provide a qualified substitute. If they must miss class due to illness or an emergency, they

make every effort to provide a substitute, if possible, or to notify students that class is canceled.

2. Instructors are available for office hours. If an instructor must cancel or rearrange an office hour due to a conference or professional meeting, he or she will leave a note on the door explaining the situation.

3. Instructors treat students with respect.

4. Instructors create and maintain an atmosphere conducive to learning. College instructors do not choose to spend valuable class time disciplining students. However, if a student demonstrates rude or disruptive behavior that interferes with the educational process of other students, the instructor will correct the situation. If the disruptive behavior continues or if the instructor feels that a student's behavior is a threat to himself or to any member of the class, the instructor may notify Public Safety and ask the student to be removed from the classroom.

5. Instructors involve students in the learning experience.

6. Instructors use a variety of teaching methods which might include lectures, student presentations, response journals, or videotapes.

7. Instructors answer questions in a clear and timely manner.

8. Instructors return corrected work on time.

9. Instructors give positive reinforcement as well as constructive criticism.

10. Instructors provide students with a written syllabus which describes the course and course objectives, lists requirements and grading standards, and daily assignments.

Things to Never Say to Your Instructors

❖ Why do we have to learn this stuff anyway?

❖ This isn't an English class: we shouldn't have to worry about grammar.

❖ I couldn't come to class because I had to study for a test in an important class.

❖ You know, this isn't the only class I have.

❖ You must have made a mistake. I worked too hard to get this grade. You need to look again.

❖ I missed class last week; did we do anything important?

❖ Is this going to be on the exam?

❖ Do we have to take notes?

❖ Are we getting out early?

❖ I learned all of this in high school.

Maximize Your Team Work

Whether you aim to complete a project or study for an exam, what can you gain from working with other?

Increased knowledge. When group members share knowledge, each member spends less time and energy learning the material. Another benefit: Talking about concepts or teaching them to others helps solidify what you know.

More motivation. Knowing that you are accountable to others and that they will see how prepared you are—or aren't—may encourage you to work hard.

Better teamwork skills. Nothing teaches you how to work effectively in groups better than experience. What you learn will be invaluable throughout college and in the workplace.

Working with students from a variety of backgrounds creates team strength. The more diverse the team, the more varied the approach to problem solving.

Strategies for Group Success

The way a group operates may depend on members' personalities, motivation, and knowledge; what your are studying; group size; and where you are meeting. These general strategies will help all groups succeed:

❖ **Set long-term and short-term goals.** At your first meeting, decide what the group wants to accomplish. You may want to have an agenda (a meeting plan) for each meeting.

❖ **Set a regular schedule.** Determine how many meetings are needed and what members' schedules can handle. If you are studying for a final, you might start a month before the test with a weekly meeting. As test day nears, you may decide to meet more frequently.

❖ **Choose a leader for each meeting.** Rotating the leadership among members willing to lead helps everyone take ownership of the group.

❖ **Share the workload.** Your willingness to pitch in and work is more important than how much you know.

For groups with a study focus, here are further tips:

❖ **Create materials for one another.** Give each group member one topic to compile, photocopy, and review for the others.

❖ **Help each other learn.** Have group members teach each other information, work on problems, give feedback on responses to essay questions, or go through flash cards together.

❖ **Pool your note-taking resources.** Compare notes and fill in any information you don't have.

Key 4.1 The group process needs leaders and participants

For Participant

- ❖ Do your share of the work.
- ❖ Stay organized and focused.
- ❖ Be open and willing to discuss.
- ❖ Perform your responsibilities on schedule.

For Leader

- ❖ Define projects, and focus everyone's efforts.
- ❖ Assign work tasks, and set a schedule and deadlines.
- ❖ Set meeting and project goals.
- ❖ Keep everyone on target and moving ahead.
- ❖ Set a fair, respectful, and encouraging tone.
- ❖ Evaluate progress, and make changes if needed.

Study groups and other teams need both leaders *and* participants to accomplish their goals. Lidia, who rarely has time or energy to take a leadership role, needs to understand that she is a crucial part of a group no matter which role she plays (see Key 4.1).

Defuse Potential Problems

As beneficial as it is to work in a team, issues can arise. Be prepared to address them if they happen to you:

- ❖ **People not pulling their weight.** At some point in almost every group, one or more people will not fulfill their responsibilities. If it's a one-time incident due to an illness or a personal problem, it's best to let it go. However, if it happens regularly, take action. Try reassigning tasks or having a group problem-solving session.

- ❖ **Trouble scheduling.** Finding a time and location that works for a group of people can be challenging. Coordinate everything on a group e-mail first. Once you find a time and day that works, schedule meetings consistently. You may want to rotate locations if there isn't one that is convenient for all group members.

- ❖ **Too much talking.** Although it may not be realistic to keep friends out of your study group, you can set boundaries. Set up some talking time at the end as a "reward" for accomplishing a goal.

Identifying your core values, setting goals that reflect them, learning techniques to manage the stress that can keep you from reaching your goals, and tapping the wisdom of the group will help you stay on target toward what you want most to achieve in college and beyond.

Course Protocol: Distance Learning

As you've seen, students have many misconceptions about appropriate behaviors and attitudes in traditional classrooms. Now, with the increasing popularity of web-based learning environments like online, hybrid, and blended classes, new myths have spring up regarding what students can—and can't—do in a distance learning class:

Myth 1: I can fit an "extra" class into my schedule by adding a distance learning class.

Wrong! In fact, this is the most common myth about taking a distance learning class. True, you will not spend time driving to class, finding a parking space, walking to class, and sitting for the same hour or so, two or three days a week, in the classroom. However, you can expect to spend *at least* as many hours—and possibly more—in a distance learning class as would in a traditional class. You'll be reading online lectures, interacting with other students and the instructor, and of course, completing your assignments, many of which are more extensive than those in the traditional versions of the same class. So, if you think you'll be able to squeeze in an "extra" class by adding a web course to your schedule, you might want to think about the "extra" hours of sleep you might lose as a result!

Myth 2: I won't interact with my instructor or with other students in a distance learning class.

Here's another myth we can debunk. The kinds of interactions you have with instructors and students in a traditional class will be duplicated in the distance learning format. For example, you can have a conversation with your instructor via email exchanges or in a chat room during specific online "office hours" or "class discussions." (Many distance learning instructors are available during on-campus office hours to meet with you in person or talk on the phone as well.) Also, most distance learning classes require that students interact with each other (with partners, in groups, or as an entire class) in chat rooms or on the discussion board. Finally, some distance learning classes (especially hybrid or blended versions) do have an "in-person" component, with students and their instructor meeting at specified times throughout the quarter. No matter what the course format, "attendance" is mandatory in distance learning classes!

Myth 3: I need to be a computer genius, have up-to-the-minute computer equipment, and be very organized and self-motivated to succeed in an online class.

As you learned in Chapter 1, part of this myth is true: the organized and self-motivated part, that is! You do need to have the ability to work independently and use your time efficiently when you take a distance learning class. But aren't the same skills valuable for success in a traditional class?

Review the "Computer Skills Needed for College" section in Chapter 1 to see what skills you *will* need before you begin any class at Columbus State.

For more specific information about skills and technical requirements for distance classes, go to http://global.cscc.edu/index.asp. Once you're on this link, you can take a quick self-test called Readiness for Education at a Distance Indicator (READI) to see if you're ready to take an online course.

The Syllabus Is a Contract With the Instructor

Most instructors will provide a **syllabus** and a brief outline of the course, including specific details about exam dates, quizzes, and what components of the course will be used to determine your grade. This is, in effect, a contract for performance. In exchange for certain work in the class, you receive a final grade.

Make sure at the beginning of the quarter that there are no hidden agendas, no blind corners, and no misunderstandings regarding this contract between you and the instructor. Go over the syllabus carefully, and be sure you understand what's expected of you. Quizzes, homework, term papers, lab reports, and tests should all carry specific weights in the final grade. Class participation or attendance may be considered in your final grade: be sure you have that defined. What constitutes "good" class participation? What should you do if you must miss a class? If there are any uncertainties about any part of the syllabus, discuss them with the instructor at the beginning of each quarter.

Students Do Have Rights

Students have the right to be treated with respect, but it's possible that at some time during the four years (or more) it takes to get an undergraduate degree you'll find yourself feeling ill-used. If you ever feel that you're being discriminated against, unduly harassed, or otherwise unfairly treated, be very serious and careful in your approach to the problem. Take some time to cool off and think things over. Are you overreacting? Misinterpreting something? Or is there really a problem?

If you're sure there is a problem, there are steps you can take to solve it. Refer to the Student Handbook for Guidance Procedures and Policy.

Grade Disputes Can Be Resolved

If you feel you have been dealt with unfairly with regard to classroom assignments, exams or your final grade, take at least a day to cool off and consider the circumstances and your preparedness as objectively as possible. Sometimes the problem is a simple one. Instructors are human, and it may be that they copied a final grade incorrectly or made a mistake in adding up the grades for the quarter. In other cases, however, it may be a matter of a difference of opinion: you feel your work on an assignment, or your answer on an exam, was worth a higher grade than your instructor does. Again, think things through carefully before acting.

If, after this period of reflection, you feel the same way and are confident in your argument, approach your instructor after class to set up an appointment to discuss the matter. Most teachers welcome students' input on grading and will admit openly that mistakes are occasionally made.

Before you talk to the instructor, however, carefully check the grades you received from every homework or paper assignment. If you feel it's relevant, take past tests with you. Plan your presentation. Make a scratch outline and rehearse what you plan to say. If you've been keeping a personal score card of your progress in the class, you will be in a much better position to present your case.

When you arrive for your appointment with the instructor, set the tone for an open discussion. Don't be confrontational and don't be defensive. This is a conference, not a debate. It hardly needs to be said that your class attendance and participation may be a factor in the resolution of the dispute. The changes for a satisfactory outcome are better if you have shown yourself to be a conscientious student.

If, in spite of your best efforts, your claim is rejected by the instructor and you still feel the grade is unfair, you have the right to make an appointment with the department chairperson. Bring all materials with you to the meeting. Again, do not act in a confrontational or defensive manner. Simply present the evidence in a calm, clear, logical way. If your grade dispute is not satisfactorily resolved at this level, you may make an appointment to discuss the situation with the dean of the Arts and Sciences division. If you are not satisfied with the results of this meeting you have the option of submitting a written request for arbitration. Your request will be forwarded to a Grade Dispute Committee for consideration. Every student has the right to due process when it comes to grade disputes. However, it should also be obvious that pursuing your claim can be a long, drawn-out process. The best way to avoid grade disputes is to be sure you understand the course requirements and grading standards from the first day of the quarter. Ask for clarification if you do not. Go to class; do the assignments; see the instructor during office hours for additional help. Keep the lines of communication open and remember that there are always two sides to every misunderstanding.

How Your Instructors See You Matters

The rapport you establish with your instructors can be critical to your grade. The teacher's view of you as a student is crucial. If you are *perceived* as a great student, many minor mistakes may be overlooked because the instructor will be looking for your successes. This is just human nature at work. If you are seen as a marginal student, then every mistake, major or minor, sticks in your instructor's mind and helps to lower any grade he or she may be considering for your work. This may not be fair, but it is the nature of the game. The impression you make will help elevate you to the top of the class or depress your grade to the point that you may never break away from the pack.

Your instructor's perception of you as a student will unavoidably influence your grade. If you project the image of a great student, he or she will treat you like a winner, and often this will reflect itself in higher marks. You can get this process off to a good start by introducing yourself at the beginning of every quarter and letting the instructor know you'll be taking the class very seriously. Then follow it up by *being* a great student.

Quality matters. The quality of your work is important. Your assignments and the way you turn them in tells the instructor a lot about you and how much you care about the course. It doesn't matter what the assignment is; you should make an effort to complete it on time and fully. The more information you can give, the better. Getting by is not good enough in college. Not understanding is never an excuse, nor is not having enough time.

See the Instructor as a Person

Your relationship with your instructor is a key factor in getting good grades. It helps you make the most of your education if you think of yourself as the boss, but you also need to have a genuine respect for your instructor's knowledge and for their profession. Don't make the mistake of thinking the person before you is "just a teacher." Often students fail to realize that their instructors may have given up more lucrative careers because they recognized and wanted the personal rewards that teaching offers. Indeed, the majority of instructors care about their students and are there to help them learn. Also, most instructors care, some passionately, about their subjects. They may be engaged in research in some specialty in their fields, and if you show an interest in what they've dedicated their lies to, they're much more likely to want to talk to you—and to remember you favorably.

A good relationship with your instructors is valuable for letters of recommendation or references when you're applying for jobs. For this purpose, it is a good idea to contact instructors while your class performance is still fresh in their minds. Ask them if they would be willing, when needed, to write a letter of recommendation or serve as a reference for you. Some instructors like to write the letter while they still remember you clearly and then keep it in a file until it's needed, which is another good reason to ask right after you've taken their classes. Most instructors are more than willing to write letters for good students, so don't hesitate to ask.

E-Mail between Students and Instructors

Certain tones in online communication can affect the relationship between instructors and students. To promote a good relationship, consider the following guidelines:

1. Proofread for mechanical errors. Sloppy editing can create a bad impression of you (as it does in a printed message).

2. Can the sarcasm. Humor or sarcasm might fall flat or offend someone when you put it in writing.

3. Put out flames. *Flaming* takes place when an online message is tinged with sarcasm or even hostility. Avoid sending such a message, even if you are responding to one that engages in it.

4. Remember common courtesy. Whenever you're at the keyboard typing something, ask yourself one question: "Would I say this to the person's face?"

Remember

❖ Research instructors before each class

❖ Introduce yourself early in the quarter

❖ Make use of office hours and extra study sessions

❖ Observe classroom protocol

❖ Be a responsible partner in learning. Deal with misunderstandings and grade disputes rationally

❖ See your instructor as a valuable resource in helping you reach your academic goals

Critical Reading 1: "Hey Dude!"

by J. R. EGAN

Introduction:

In this reflection, the author wonders whether the frustrations of the student/teacher relationship are just "part of the territory."

My reverie about retiring to work at Wal-Mart or Home Depot or anywhere other than where I was at the moment (grading papers while waiting for students to appear during my designated office hours) was broken by someone knocking timorously at my open door.

What's this? A student actually showing up to ask for help? "Come in," I said, moving my briefcase and jacket off the rarely used chair set aside for student visitors.

I listened as she rattled off the usual excuses—I was out of town, I was too busy, I didn't know your number, I needed to wash my hair—for her two-week absence from my class with nary a phone call or e-mail. I handed her a tissue as she cried about her hard life.

Later that very day, as I drove off campus, I saw her whisk by in a shiny new BMW while chatting away on her cell phone. She had felt it was unfair to count the absences and missed assignments against her grade—as was stated clearly in the syllabus that she had obviously not read—because her parents *insisted* she go along on the family vacation trip to Cancún.

My field is communications. While many in academia, myself included, long to escape the increasingly disrespectful classroom and the tedium of grading stacks of final papers that read like half-thought-out rough drafts, many of my former colleagues working in private industry are clamoring to get in. The fantasy of returning to academia in the twilight of one's career to share one's knowledge and experiences with legions of attentive and bright students is a powerful stimulant.

As a reality check, I herewith share some of my recent experiences in higher education to help focus the expectations my professional colleagues should have when considering a move to college teaching. I hope others have had different experiences.

Let me set aside the standard wailings and lamentations that students are dumber than they used to be (although they indeed may be). When I say I believe that students have, on the whole, changed for the worse, I'm not talking about standardized test scores or grade-point averages. I am talking about behavior, and I am basing my stance on 30 years in the college classroom.

In the past, students seemed to see going to class as their main activity during their years enrolled at a university; work was something they did to earn enough money to survive.

Today, nearly all my students work—many of them full-time—and class attendance and homework are things they squeeze in as long as it doesn't interfere with the rest of their lives. I have received complaints that a mere 10 pages of reading for the next class were too many because the students were *so busy*. They expect you to provide make-up lectures, exercises, and tests at their convenience. Most drive nice cars, wear the latest fashions, and have both a cell phone and an iPod yet tell me they can't afford a $25 textbook.

Disrespect in the classroom is rampant. Many students don't even know their professor's name or how to pronounce it by mid-term, much less recall the names of faculty members from the previous semester. During a timed lab exercise recently, I had a student call out to me across the room, "Hey, dude!"

Once, while discussing the nature of classroom manners and decorum, I had a woman pipe up from the back row: "Listen, man, I paid $300 for this class, and if I want to sit here and trim my toenails, that's what I am going to do."

That detachment from the classroom environment works the other way as well. Students from the immediate past semester routinely are amazed when I recognize them in the new semester's class or when I see them in the hall and actually say hello using their name. They probably find me only vaguely familiar.

The faculty have become a nameless wait staff, paid to deliver what the customer wants, when it is wanted, in an entertaining fashion, with a B grade or better. The students seem to think their role is to sit passively or check e-mail while you are trying to run a class. The tuition check is merely the tip for good service.

Students also look at us, standing at the front of the class, as entertainment. The professor is the television set droning off in the corner. It (you) can be attended to or not, conversations can be carried on while the "show" slips to background noise, and personal interaction is only necessary when making up excuses for absences or wheedling for a higher grade.

Despite repeated invitations to students to come to my office hours when they are struggling or if they want to discuss careers, or whatever, my office hours are spent alone 95 percent of the time. And then the rare student visitor usually asks a question that is clearly answered in the syllabus.

In one recent instance, a student tried to explain why he hadn't shown up for the past three classes because he was out of town for a "family emergency" (based on my experience, that is the new excuse of choice, surpassing both homework-eating dogs and flat tires). Turned out that he was having a fight with his out-of-town girlfriend, as another student let slip.

Just this semester, I had a student walk up to me at the lectern two minutes past the beginning of our third class session. I was finishing getting the computer and projector fired up to start the discussion, but no, her need to talk to me on her schedule trumped the start of class. She wanted me to sign paperwork to allow her into the class late, saying she didn't realize not attending the first day of class would bump her for someone on the waiting list—another tidbit clearly stated in the college catalog and online class schedule.

I asked her what caused her to miss class. She said she went snowboarding with friends. They "made" her come, she lamented. I declined to sign and started the class. She stomped off, probably to complain to the dean, the provost, or even the president, which is done more frequently than you would imagine.

It is as if someone with a Microsoft software glitch went straight to Bill Gates to complain. Students, however, are where the money comes from, so they always get an audience upstream.

Students in a particularly surly class last semester continued to ignore my requests that they stop their computer play during the class discussion. I exaggerated my irritation by telling them that their behavior had driven me to retire and that I was going to take that job as a Wal-Mart greeter. One student was so offended by my hyperbole that she complained to my chair, the dean, and even the provost.

Who knows exactly what she said, but did anyone ask me my take on the incident? No. The dean just said that I should apologize.

That's why it's tough to ignore student misbehavior: They are cash cows that make the place run. Once the admissions office lets them in, you are expected to let them out so that the desks can be filled with the next year's fresh student harvest.

Then, just as you feel the bitterness becoming more than you can stand, you get a reminder of what keeps you in the business.

Just today, I got not one, but two such reminders—e-mail messages from former students thanking me for my rigorous approach to education. Looking back, they said, it not only has helped them in their careers, but in their lives.

I suppose teaching is, like golf, a maddening endeavor. In golf, even after 50 bad shots, if you accidentally hit a beauty, life is good and you love the game and you don't throw the clubs in the lake after all. In teaching, even if you get 50 students who don't care, it's those one or two each term who keep you coming back.

Wal-Mart is going to have to wait.

J. R. Egan is the pseudonym of a professor of communications at a state university in the South.

Critical Reading 2: Letter From Birmingham Jail

Introduction

Our reading is King's "Letter from Birmingham Jail" (published in *Why We Can't Wait*), an essay King wrote in 1963 when in jail for protesting segregation at lunch counters and discrimination in hiring practices. King's essay is a response to eight members of the clergy who had published a statement criticizing his civil rights activities as "unwise and untimely." King explains that blacks in America have waited for over three centuries to gain their basic human rights—and that they should wait no longer. In answer to the objection that his nonviolent activities sometimes violate laws, King distinguishes just and unjust laws. Just laws should be obeyed, but unjust laws are not binding because they contradict moral laws and degrade human beings. There are some situations in which even just laws are not binding, however. For example, a law requiring a permit for a parade is just, but it need not be obeyed when it is used for the unjust purpose of denying citizens the right of peaceful assembly and protest. King explains that a person who breaks a just law as a form of protest must do so openly and with a willingness to accept the penalty. Responding to the charge that he is an extremist, King points out that nonviolent protest is certainly less extreme than violence. He admits, however, that in a certain way he is an extremist—an extremist for love and justice.

Dr. Martin Luther King, Jr. (1929–1968) was born in 1929 in Atlanta, Georgia. He attended Morehouse College and during his senior year decided to follow in his father's footsteps and become a Baptist minister. Upon graduating in 1948, he entered Crozer Theological Seminary in Chester, Pennsylvania. There he was deeply influenced by Mahatma Ghandi's philosophy of nonviolence and became convinced that black Americans should use this strategy to attain their civil rights. King received his bachelor of divinity degree in 1951. He then began doctoral studies in theology at Boston University, completing his degree in 1955. While still working on his doctorate, King became pastor at Dexter Avenue Baptist Church in Montgomery, Alabama. In 1954 he led a boycott of the city transit company to protest segregated seating on buses. Within a year the buses were desegregated. Encouraged by this success, King began to work for civil rights on a national basis by forming the Southern Christian Leadership Conference.

In 1960 he moved to Atlanta, where he directed the Conference and served as co-pastor (with his father) at Ebenezer Baptist Church. In 1963 he and many others were arrested and jailed for participating in a demonstration in Birmingham. Later that year King helped organize a massive demonstration in Washington, D.C., for civil rights legislation. King addressed the crowd, proclaiming, "I have a dream"—a dream of interracial equity and harmony. The following year King received the Nobel Prize for Peace. In 1968, while in Memphis to support a strike by sanitation workers, he was shot and killed by a sniper's bullet.

King's works include *Stride Toward Freedom: The Montgomery Story* (1958), *Why We Can't Wait* (1964), and *Where Do We Go From Here: Chaos or Community?* (1967).

Letter from Birmingham Jail

Dr. Martin Luther King, Jr.
April 16, 1963

My Dear Fellow Clergymen:

While confined here in Birmingham city jail, I came across your recent statement calling my present activities "unwise and untimely." Seldom do I pause to answer criticism of my work and ideas. If I sought to answer all the criticisms that cross my desk, my secretaries would have little time for anything other than such correspondence in the course of the day, and I would have no time for constructive work. But since I feel that you are men of genuine good will and that your criticisms are sincerely set forth, I want to try to answer your statement in what I hope will be patient and reasonable terms.

I think I should indicate why I am here in Birmingham, since you have been influenced by the view which argues against "outsiders coming in." I have the honor of serving as president of the Southern Christian Leadership Conference, an organization operating in every southern state with headquarters in Atlanta, Georgia. We have some eighty-five affiliated organizations across the South, and one of them is the Alabama Christian Movement for Human Rights. Frequently we share staff, educational and financial resources with our affiliates. Several months ago the affiliate here in Birmingham asked us to be on call to engage in a nonviolent direct-action program if such were deemed necessary. We readily consented, and when the hour came we lived up to our promise. So I, along with several members of my staff, am here because I was invited here. I am here because I have organizational ties here.

But, more basically, I am in Birmingham because injustice is here. Just as the prophets of the eighth century B.C. left their villages and carried their "thus saith the Lord" far beyond the boundaries of their home towns, and just as the Apostle Paul left his village of Tarsus and carried the gospel of Jesus Christ to the far corners of the Greco-Roman world, so am I compelled to carry the gospel of freedom beyond my own home town. Like Paul, I must constantly respond to the Macedonian call for aid.

Moreover, I am cognizant of the interrelatedness of all communities and states. I cannot sit idly by in Atlanta and not be concerned about what happens in Birmingham. Injustice anywhere is a threat to justice everywhere. We are caught in an inescapable network of mutuality, tied to a single garment of destiny. Never again can we afford to live with the narrow, provincial "outside agitator" idea. Anyone who lives inside the United States can never be considered an outsider anywhere within its bounds.

You deplore the demonstrations taking place in Birmingham. But your statement, I am sorry to say, fails to express a similar concern for the conditions that brought about the demonstrations. I am sure that none of you would want to rest content with the superficial kind of social analysis that deals merely with effects and does not grapple with underlying causes. It is unfortunate that demonstrations are taking place in Birmingham, but it is even more unfortunate that the city's white power structure left the Negro community with no alternative.

In any nonviolent campaign there are four steps; collection of the facts to determine whether injustices exist; negotiation; self-purification; and direct action. We have gone through all these steps in Birmingham. There can be no gainsaying the fact that racial injustice engulfs this community. Birmingham is probably the most thoroughly segregated city in the United States. Its ugly record of brutality is widely known. Negroes have experienced grossly unjust treatment in the courts. There have been more unsolved bombings of Negro homes and churches in Birmingham than in any other city in the nation. These are the hard brutal facts of the case. On the basis of these conditions, Negro leaders sought to negotiate with the city fathers. But the latter consistently refused to engage in good-faith negotiation.

Then, last September, came the opportunity to talk with leaders of Birmingham's economic community. In the course of negotiations, certain promises were made by the merchants—for example, to remove the stores' humiliating racial signs. On the basis of these promises, the Reverend Fred Shuttlesworth and the leaders of the Alabama Christian Movement for Human Rights agreed to a moratorium on all demonstrations. As the weeks and months went by, we realized that we were the victims of a broken promise. A few signs, briefly removed, returned; others remained.

As in so many past experiences, our hopes had been blasted and the shadow of deep disappointment settled upon us. We had no alternative except to prepare for direct action, whereby we would present our very bodies as a means of laying our case before the conscience of the local and national community. Mindful of the difficulties involved we decided to undertake a process of self-purification. We began a series of workshops on nonviolence, and we repeatedly asked ourselves, "Are you able to accept blows without retaliating?" "Are you able to endure the ordeals of jail?" We decided to schedule our direct-action program for the Easter season, realizing that except for Christmas, this is the main shopping period of the year. Knowing that a strong economic-withdrawal program would be the by-product of direct action, we felt that this would be the best time to bring pressure to bear on the merchants for the needed change.

Then it occurred to us that Birmingham's mayoralty election was coming up in March, and we speedily decided to postpone action until after election day. When we discovered that the Commissioner of Public Safety, Eugene "Bull" Connor, had piled up enough votes to be in the run-off, we decided again to postpone action until the day after the run-off so that the demonstrations could not be used to cloud the issues. Like many others we waited to see Mr. Connor defeated and to this end we endured postponement after postponement. Having aided in this community need, we felt that our direct-action program could be delayed no longer.

You may well ask: "Why direct action? Why sit-ins, marches, and so forth? Isn't negotiation a better path?" You are quite right in calling for negotiation. Indeed, this is the very purpose of direct action. Nonviolent direct action seeks to create such a crisis and foster such a tension that a community which has constantly refused to negotiate is forced to confront the issue. It seeks so to dramatize the issue that it can no longer be ignored. My citing the creation of tension as part of the work of the nonviolent-resister may sound rather shocking. But I must confess that I am not afraid of the word "tension." I have earnestly opposed violent tension, but there is a type of constructive nonviolent tension that is necessary for growth. Just as Socrates felt that it was necessary to create a tension in the mind so that individuals could rise from the bondage of myths and half-truths to the unfettered realm for creative analysis and objective appraisal, so must we see the need for nonviolent gadflies to create the kind of tension in society that will help men rise from the dark depths of prejudice and racism to the majestic heights of understanding and brotherhood.

The purpose of our direct-action program is to create a situation so crisis-packed that it will inevitably open the door to negotiation. I therefore concur with you in your call for negotiation. Too long has our beloved Southland been bogged down in a tragic effort to live in monologue rather than dialogue.

One of the basic points in your statement is that the action that I and my associates have taken in Birmingham is untimely. Some have asked, "Why didn't you give the new city administration time to act?" The only answer that I can give to this query is that the new Birmingham administration must be prodded about as much as the outgoing one, before it will act. We are sadly mistaken if we feel that the election of Albert Boutwell as mayor will bring the millennium to Birmingham. While Mr. Boutwell is a much more gentle person than Mr. Connor, they are both segregationists, dedicated to the maintenance of the status quo. I have hope that Mr. Boutwell will be reasonable enough to see the futility of massive resistance to desegregation. But he will not see this without pressure from devotees of civil rights. My friends, I must say to you that we have not made a single gain in civil rights without determined legal and nonviolent pressure. Lamentably, it is an historical fact that privileged groups seldom give up their privileges voluntarily. Individuals may see the moral light and voluntarily give up their unjust posture; but, as Reinhold Niebuhr has reminded us, groups tend to be more immoral than individuals.

We know through painful experience that freedom is never voluntarily given by the oppressor; it must be demanded by the oppressed. Frankly, I have yet to engage in a direct-action campaign that was "well timed" in the view of those who have not suffered unduly from the disease of segregation. For years now I have heard the word "Wait!" It rings in the ear of every Negro with piercing familiarity. This "Wait" has almost always meant "Never." We must come to see, with one our distinguished jurists, that "justice too long delayed is justice denied."

We have waited for more than 340 years for our constitutional and God-given rights. The nations of Asia and Africa are moving with jetlike speed toward gaining political independence, but we still creep at horse-and-buggy pace toward gaining a cup of coffee at a lunch counter. Perhaps it is easy for those who have never felt the stinging darts of segregation to say, "Wait." But when you have seen vicious mobs lynch your mothers and fathers at will and drown your sisters and brothers at whim; when you have seen hate-filled policemen curse, kick, and even kill your black brothers and sisters; when you see the vast majority of your 20 million Negro brothers smothering in an airtight cage of poverty in the midst of an affluent society; when you suddenly find your tongue twisted and your speech stammering as you seek to explain to your six-year-old daughter why she can't go to the public amusement park that has just been advertised on television, and see tears welling up in her little eyes when she is told that Funtown is closed to colored children, and see the ominous clouds of inferiority beginning to form in her little mental sky, and see her beginning to distort her personality by developing an unconscious bitterness toward white people; when you have to concoct an answer for your five-year-old son who is asking: "Daddy, why do white people treat colored people so mean?"; when you take a cross-country drive and find it necessary to sleep night after night in the uncomfortable corners of your automobile because no motel will accept you; when you are humiliated day in and day out by nagging signs reading "white" and "colored"; when your first name becomes "nigger," your middle name becomes "boy" (however old you are) and your last name becomes "John," and your wife and mother are never given the respected title "Mrs."; when you are harried by day and haunted by night by the fact that you are a Negro, living constantly at tiptoe stance, never quite knowing what to expect next, and plagued with inner fears and outer resentments; when you are forever fighting a degenerating sense of "nobodiness"—then you will understand why we find it difficult to wait. There comes a time when the cup of endurance runs over, and men are no longer willing to be plunged into the abyss of despair. I hope, sirs, you can understand our legitimate and unavoidable impatience.

You express a great deal of anxiety over our willingness to break laws. This is certainly a legitimate concern. Since we so diligently urge people to obey the Supreme Court's decision of 1954 outlawing segregation in the public schools, at first glance it may seem rather paradoxical for us consciously to break the laws. One might well ask: "How can you advocate breaking some laws and obeying others?" The answer lies in the fact that there are two types of laws: just and unjust. I would be the first to advocate obeying just laws. One has not only a legal but a moral responsibility to obey just laws. Conversely, one has a moral responsibility to disobey unjust laws. I would agree with Saint Augustine that "an unjust law is no law at all."

Now, what is the difference between the two? How does one determine when a law is just or unjust? A just law is a man-made code that squares with the moral law or the law of God. An unjust law is a code that is out of harmony with the moral law. To put it in the terms of St. Thomas Aquinas: An unjust law is a human law that is not rooted in eternal law and natural law. Any law that uplifts human personality is just. Any law that degrades human personality is unjust. All segregation statutes are unjust because segregation distorts the soul and damages the personality. It gives the segregator a false sense of superiority and the segregated a false sense of inferiority. Segregation, to use the terminology of the Jewish philosopher Martin Buber substitutes an "I–it" relationship for an "I–thou" relationship and ends up relegating persons to a status of things. Hence, segregation is not only politically, economically and sociologically unsound, it is morally wrong and sinful. Paul Tillich has said that sin is separation. Is not segregation an existential expression of man's tragic separation, his awful estrangement, his terrible sinfulness? Thus it is that I can urge men to obey the 1954 decision to the Supreme Court, for it is morally right; and I can urge them to disobey segregation ordinances, for they are morally wrong.

Let us consider a more concrete example of just and unjust laws. An unjust law is a code that a numerical or power majority group compels a minority group to obey but does not make binding on itself. This is difference made legal. By the same token, a just law is a code that a majority compels a minority to follow and that it is willing to follow itself. This is sameness made legal.

Let me give another explanation. A law is unjust if it is inflicted on a minority that, as a result of being denied the right to vote, had no part in enacting or devising the law. Who can say that the legislature of Alabama which set up that state's segregation laws was democratically elected? Throughout Alabama all sorts of devious methods are used to prevent Negroes from becoming registered voters, and there are some counties in which, even though Negroes constitute a majority of the population, not a single Negro is registered. Can any law enacted under such circumstances be considered democratically structured?

Sometimes a law is just on its face and unjust in its application. For instance, I have been arrested on a charge of parading without a permit. Now, there is nothing wrong in having an ordinance which requires a permit for a parade. But such an ordinance becomes unjust when it is used to maintain segregation and to deny citizens the First Amendment privilege of peaceful assembly and protest.

I hope you are able to see the distinction I am trying to point out. In no sense do I advocate evading or defying the law, as would the rabid segregationist. That would lead to anarchy. One who breaks an unjust law must do so openly, lovingly, and with a willingness to accept the penalty. I submit that an individual who breaks a law that conscience tells him is unjust and who willingly accepts the penalty of imprisonment in order to arouse the conscience of the community over its injustice, is in reality expressing the very highest respect for law.

Of course, there is nothing new about this kind of civil disobedience. It was evidenced sublimely in the refusal of Shadrach, Meshach and Abednego to obey the laws of Nebuchadnezzar, on the grounds that a higher moral law was at stake. It was practiced superbly by the early Christians, who were willing to face hungry lions and the excruciating pain of chopping blocks rather than submit to certain unjust laws of the Roman Empire. To a degree, academic freedom is a reality today because Socrates practiced civil disobedience. In our own nation, the Boston Tea Party represented a massive act of civil disobedience.

We should never forget that everything Hitler did in Germany was "legal" and everything the Hungarian freedom fighters did in Hungary was "illegal." It was "illegal" to aid and comfort a Jew in Hitler's Germany. Even so, I am sure that, had I lived in Germany at that time, I would have aided and comforted my Jewish brothers. If today I lived in a Communist country where certain principles dear to the Christian faith are suppressed, I would openly advocate disobeying that country's anti-religious laws.

I must make two honest confessions to you, my Christian and Jewish brothers. First, I must confess that over the past few years I have been gravely disappointed with the white moderate. I have almost reached the regrettable conclusion that the Negro's great stumbling block in his stride toward freedom is not the White Citizen's Councilor or the Ku Klux Klanner, but the white moderate, who is more devoted to "order" than to justice; who prefers a negative peace which is the absence of tension to a positive peace which is the presence of justice; who constantly says: "I agree with you in the goal you seek, but I cannot agree with your methods of direct action"; who paternalistically believes he can set the timetable for another man's freedom; who lives by a mythical concept of time and who constantly advises the Negro to wait for a "more convenient season." Shallow understanding from people of good will is more frustrating than absolute misunderstanding from people of ill will. Lukewarm acceptance is much more bewildering than outright rejection.

I had hoped that the white moderate would understand that law and order exist for the purpose of establishing justice and that when they fail in this purpose they become the dangerously structured dams that block the flow of social progress. I had hoped that the white moderate would understand that the present tension in the South is a necessary phase of the transition from an obnoxious negative peace, in which the Negro passively accepted his unjust plight, to a substantive and positive peace, in which all men will respect the dignity and worth of human personality. Actually, we who engage in nonviolent direct action are not the creators of tension. We merely bring to the surface the hidden tension that is already alive. We bring it out in the open, where it can be seen and dealt with. Like a boil that can never be cured so long as it is covered up but must be opened with all its ugliness to the natural medicines of air and light, injustice must be exposed, with all the tension its exposure creates, to the light of human conscience and the air of national opinion before it can be cured.

In your statement you assert that our actions, even though peaceful, must be condemned because they precipitate violence. But is this a logical assertion? Isn't this like condemning a robbed man because his possession of money precipitated the evil act of robbery? Isn't this like condemning Socrates because his unswerving commitment to truth and his philosophical inquiries precipitated the act by the misguided populace in which they make him drink hemlock? Isn't this like condemning Jesus because his unique God-consciousness and never-ceasing devotion to God's will precipitated the evil act of crucifixion? We must come to see that, as the federal courts have consistently affirmed, it is wrong to urge an individual to cease his efforts to gain his basic constitutional rights because the quest may precipitate violence. Society must protect the robbed and punish the robber.

I had also hoped that the white moderate would reject the myth concerning time in relation to the struggle for freedom. I have just received a letter from a white brother in Texas. He writes: "All Christians know that the colored people will receive equal rights eventually, but it is possible that you are in too great a religious hurry. It has taken Christianity almost two thousand years to accomplish what it has. The teachings of Christ take time to come to earth." Such an attitude stems from a tragic misconception of time, from the strangely irrational notion that there is something in the very flow of time that will inevitably cure all ills. Actually, time itself is neutral; it can be used either destructively or constructively. More and more I feel that the people of ill will have used time much more effectively than have the people of good will. We will have to repent in this generation not merely for the hateful words and actions of the bad people but for the appalling silence of the good people. Human progress never rolls in on wheels of inevitability; it comes through the tireless efforts of men willing to be co-workers with God, and without this hard work, time itself becomes an ally of the forces of social stagnation. We must use time creatively, in the knowledge that the time is always ripe to do right. Now is the time to make real the promise of democracy and transform our pending national elegy into a creative psalm of brotherhood. Now is the time to lift our national policy from the quicksand of racial injustice to the solid rock of human dignity.

You speak of our activity in Birmingham as extreme. At first I was rather disappointed that fellow clergymen would see my nonviolent efforts as those of the extremist. I began thinking about the fact that I stand in the middle of two opposing forces in the Negro community. One is a force of complacency, made up in part of Negroes who, as a result of long years of oppression, are so drained of self-respect and a sense of "somebodiness" that they have adjusted to segregation; and in part of a few middle class Negroes who, because of a degree of academic and economic security and because in some ways they profit by segregation, have become insensitive to the problems of the masses. The other force is one of bitterness and hatred, and it comes perilously close to advocating violence. It is expressed in the various black nationalist groups that are springing up across the nation, the largest and best-known being Elijah Muhammad's Muslim movement. Nourished by the Negro's frustration over the continued existence of racial discrimination, this movement is made up of people who have lost faith in America, who have absolutely repudiated Christianity, and who have concluded that the white man is an incorrigible "devil."

I have tried to stand between these two forces, saying that we need emulate neither the "do-nothingism" of the complacent nor the hatred and despair of the black nationalist. For there is the more excellent way of love and nonviolent protest. I am grateful to God that, through the influence of the Negro church, the way of nonviolence became an integral part of our struggle.

If this philosophy had not emerged, by now many streets of the South would, I am convinced, be flowing with blood. And I am further convinced that if our white brothers dismiss us as "rabble rousers" and "outside agitators" those of us who employ nonviolent direct action, and if they refuse to support our nonviolent efforts, millions of Negroes will, out of frustration and despair, seek solace and security in black-nationalist ideologies—a development that would inevitably lead to a frightening racial nightmare.

Oppressed people cannot remain oppressed forever. The yearning for freedom eventually manifests itself, and this is what has happened to the American Negro. Something within has reminded him of his birthright of freedom, and something without has reminded him that it can be gained. Consciously and unconsciously, he has been caught up by the Zeitgeist, and with his black brothers of Africa and his brown and yellow brothers of Asia, South America, and the Caribbean, the United States Negro is moving with a sense of great urgency toward the promised land of racial justice. If one recognizes this vital urge that has engulfed the Negro community, one should readily understand why public demonstrations are taking place. The Negro has many pent-up resentments and latent frustrations, and he must release them. So let him march; let him make prayer pilgrimages to the city hall; let him go on freedom rides—and try to understand why he must do so. If his repressed emotions are not released in nonviolent ways, they will seek expression through violence; this is not a threat but a fact of history. So I have not said to my people: "Get rid of your discontent." Rather, I have tried to say that this normal and healthy discontent can be channeled into the creative outlet of nonviolent direct action. And now this approach is being termed extremist.

But though I was initially disappointed at being categorized as an extremist, as I continued to think about the matter I gradually gained a measure of satisfaction from the label. Was not Jesus an extremist for love: "Love your enemies, bless them that curse you, do good to them that hate you, and pray for them which despitefully use you, and persecute you." Was not Amos an extremist for justice: "Let justice roll down like waters and righteousness, like an ever-flowing stream." Was not Paul an extremist for the Christian gospel: "I bear in my body the marks of the Lord Jesus." Was not Martin Luther an extremist: "Here I stand; I cannot do otherwise, so help me God." And John Bunyan: "I will stay in jail to the end of my days before I make a butchery of my conscience." And Abraham Lincoln: "This nation cannot survive half slave and half free." And Thomas Jefferson: "We hold these truths to be self-evident, that all men are created equal." So the question is not whether we will be extremists, but what kind of extremists will we be. Will we be extremists for hate or for love? Will we be extremists for the preservation of injustice or for the extension of justice? In that dramatic scene on Calvary's hill three men were crucified. We must never forget that all three were crucified for the same crime—the crime of extremism. Two were extremists for immorality, and thus fell below their environment. The other, Jesus Christ, was an extremist for love, truth and goodness, and thereby rose above his environment. Perhaps the South, the nation and the world are in dire need of creative extremists.

I had hoped that the white moderate would see this need. Perhaps I was too optimistic; perhaps I expected too much. I suppose I should have realized that few members of the oppressor race can understand the deep groans and passionate yearnings of the oppressed race, and still fewer have the vision to see that injustice must be rooted out by strong, persistent and determined action. I am thankful, however, that some of our white brothers in the South have grasped the meaning of this social revolution and committed themselves to it. They are still too few in quantity, but they are big in quality. Some—such as Ralph McGill, Lillian Smith, Harry Golden, James McBride Dabbs, Ann Braden and Sarah Patton Boyle—have written about our struggle in eloquent and prophetic terms. Others have marched with us down nameless streets of the South. They have languished in filthy, roach-infested jails, suffering the abuse and brutality of policemen who view them as "dirty nigger lovers." Unlike so many of their moderate brothers and sisters, they have recognized the urgency of the moment and sensed the need for powerful "action" antidotes to combat the disease of segregation.

Let me take note of my other major disappointment. I have been so greatly disappointed with the white church and its leadership. Of course, there are some notable exceptions. I am not unmindful of the fact that each of you has taken some significant stands on this issue. I commend you, Reverend Stallings, for your Christian stand on this past Sunday, in welcoming Negroes to your worship service on a nonsegregated basis. I commend the Catholic leaders of this state for integrating Spring Hill College several years ago.

But despite these notable exceptions, I must honestly reiterate that I have been disappointed with the church. I do not say that as one of those negative critics who can always find something wrong with the church. I say this as a minister of the gospel, who loves the church; who was nurtured in its bosom; who has been sustained by its spiritual blessings and who will remain true to it as long as the cord of life shall lengthen.

When I was suddenly catapulted into the leadership of the bus protest in Montgomery, Alabama, a few years ago, I felt we would be supported by the white church. I felt that the white ministers, priests and rabbis of the South would be among our strongest allies. Instead, some have been outright opponents, refusing to understand the freedom movement and misrepresenting its leaders; and too many others have been more cautious than courageous and have remained silent behind the anesthetizing security of stained-glass windows.

In spite of my shattered dreams, I came to Birmingham with the hope that the white religious leadership of this community would see the justice of our cause and, with deep moral concern, would serve as the channel through which our just grievances could reach the power structure. I had hoped that each of you would understand. But again I have been disappointed.

I have heard numerous southern religious leaders admonish their worshippers to comply with a desegregation decision because it is the law, but I have longed to hear white ministers declare: "Follow this decree because integration is morally right and because the Negro is your brother." In the midst of blatant injustices inflicted upon the Negro, I have watched white churchmen stand on the sideline and mouth pious irrelevancies and sanctimonious trivialities. In the midst of a mighty struggle to rid our nation of racial and economic injustice, I have heard many ministers say: "Those are social issues, with which the gospel has no real concern." And I have watched many churches commit themselves to a completely other-worldly religion which made a strange, un-Biblical distinction between body and soul, between the sacred and the secular.

I have traveled the length and breadth of Alabama, Mississippi and all the other southern states. On sweltering summer days and crisp autumn mornings I have looked at the South's beautiful churches with their lofty spires pointing heavenward. I have beheld the impressive outlines of her massive religious-education buildings. Over and over again I have found myself asking: "What kind of people worship here? Who is their God? Where were their voices when the lips of Governor Barnett dripped with words of interposition and nullification? Where were they when Governor Wallace gave a clarion call for defiance and hatred? Where were their voices of support when braised and weary Negro men and women decided to rise from the dark dungeons of complacency to the bright hills of creative protest?"

Yes, these questions are still in my mind. In deep disappointment I have wept over the laxity of the church. But be assured that my tears have been tears of love. There can be no deep disappointment where there is not deep love. Yes, I love the church. How could I do otherwise? I am in the rather unique position of being the son, the grandson and the great-grandson of preachers. Yes, I see the church as the body of Christ. But, oh! How we have blemished and scarred that body through social neglect and through fear of being nonconformists.

There was a time when the church was very powerful—in the time when the early Christians rejoiced at being deemed worthy to suffer for what they believed. In those days the church was not merely a thermometer that recorded the ideas and principles of popular opinion; it was a thermostat that transformed the mores of society. Whenever the early Christians entered a town, the people in power became disturbed and immediately sought to convict the Christians for being "disturbers of the peace" and "outside agitators." But the Christians pressed on, in the conviction that they were "a colony of heaven," called to obey God rather than man. Small in number, they were big in commitment. They were too God-intoxicated to be "astronomically intimidated." By their effort and example they brought an end to such ancient evils as infanticide and gladiatorial contests.

Things are different now. So often the contemporary church is a weak, ineffectual voice with an uncertain sound. So often it as an archdefender of the status quo. Far from being disturbed by the presence of the Church, the power structure of the average community is consoled by the church's silent—and often even vocal—sanction of things as they are.

But the judgment of God is upon the church as never before. If today's church does not recapture the sacrificial spirit of the early church, it will lose its authenticity, forfeit the loyalty of millions, and be dismissed as an irrelevant social club with no meaning for the twentieth century. Every day I meet young people whose disappointment with the church has turned into outright disgust.

Perhaps I have once again been too optimistic. Is organized religion too inextricably bound to the status quo to save our nation and the world? Perhaps I must turn my faith to the inner spiritual church, the church within the church, as the true *ekklesia* and the hope of the world. But again I am thankful to God that some noble souls from the ranks of organized religion have broken loose from the paralyzing chains of conformity and joined us as active partners in the struggle for freedom. They have left their secure congregations and walked the streets of Albany, Georgia, with us. They have gone down the highways of the South on torturous rides for freedom. Yes, they have gone to jail with us. Some have been dismissed from their churches, and lost the support of their bishops and fellow ministers. But they have gone with the faith that right defeated is stronger than evil triumphant. Their witness has been the spiritual salt that has preserved the true meaning of the gospel in these troubled times. They have carved a tunnel of hope through the dark mountain of disappointment.

I hope the church as a whole will meet the challenge of this decisive hour. But even if the church does not come to the aid of justice, I have no despair about the future. I have no fear about the outcome of our struggle in Birmingham, even if our motives are at present misunderstood. We will reach the goal of freedom in Birmingham, and all over the nation, because the goal of America is freedom. Abused and scorned though we may be, our destiny is tied up with America's destiny. Before the pilgrims landed at Plymouth, we were here. Before the pen of Jefferson etched the majestic words of the Declaration of Independence across the pages of history, we were here. For more than two centuries our forebears labored in this country without wages; they made cotton king; they built the homes of their masters while suffering gross injustice and shameful humiliation—and yet out of a bottomless vitality they continued to thrive and develop. If the inexpressible cruelties of slavery could not stop us, the opposition we now face will surely fail. We will win our freedom because the sacred heritage of our nation and the eternal will of God are embodied in our echoing demands.

Before closing I feel impelled to mention one other point in your statement that has troubled me profoundly. You warmly commended the Birmingham police force for keeping "order" and "preventing violence." I doubt you would have so warmly commended the police force if you had seen its dogs sinking their teeth into unarmed, nonviolent Negroes. I doubt you would so quickly commend the policemen if you were to observe their ugly and inhuman treatment of Negroes here in the city jail; if you were to watch them push and curse old Negro women and young Negro girls; if you were to see them slap and kick old Negro men and young boys; if you were to observe them, as they did on two occasions, refuse to give us food because we wanted to sing our grace together. I cannot join you in your praise of the Birmingham police department.

It is true that the police have exercised a degree of discipline in handling the demonstrators. In this sense they have conducted themselves rather "nonviolently" in public. But for what purpose? To preserve the evil system of segregation. Over the past few years I have consistently preached that nonviolence demands that the means we use must be as pure as the ends we seek. I have tried to make it clear that it is wrong to use immoral means to attain moral ends. But now I must affirm that it is just as wrong, or perhaps even more so, to use moral means to preserve immoral ends. Perhaps Mr. Connor and his policemen have been rather nonviolent in public, as was Chief Pritchett in Albany, Georgia but they have used the moral means of nonviolence to maintain the immoral end of racial injustice. As T. S. Eliot has said: "The last temptation is the greatest treason: To do the right deed for the wrong reason."

I wish you had commended the Negro sit-inners and demonstrators of Birmingham for their sublime courage, their willingness to suffer and their amazing discipline in the midst of great provocation. One day the South will recognize its real heroes. They will be the James Merediths, with the noble sense of purpose that enables them to face jeering, and hostile mobs, and with the agonizing loneliness that characterizes the life of the pioneer. They will be old, oppressed, battered Negro women, symbolized in a seventy-two year old woman of Montgomery, Alabama, who rose up with a sense of dignity and with her people decided not to ride the segregated buses, and who responded with ungrammatical profundity to one who inquired about her weariness: "My feet is tired, but my soul is at rest." They will be the young high school and college students, the young ministers of the gospel and a host of their elders, courageously and nonviolently sitting in at lunch counters and willingly going to jail for conscience sake. One day the South will know that when these disinherited children of God sat down at lunch counters, they were in reality standing up for what is best in the American dream and for the most sacred values in our Judaeo-Christian heritage, thereby bringing our nation back to great wells of democracy which were dug deep by the founding fathers in their formulation of the Constitution and the Declaration of Independence.

Never before have I written so long a letter. I'm afraid it is much too long to take your precious time. I can assure you that it would have been much shorter if I had been writing from a comfortable desk, but what else can one do when he is alone in a narrow jail cell, other than write long letters, think long thoughts and pray long prayers?

If I have said anything in this letter that overstates the truth and indicates an unreasonable impatience, I beg you to forgive me. If I have said anything that understates the truth and indicates my having a patience that allows me to settle for anything less than brotherhood, I beg God to forgive me.

I hope this letter finds you strong in the faith. I also hope that circumstances will soon make it possible for me to meet each of you, not as an integrationist or a civil rights leader but as a fellow clergyman and a Christian brother. Let us all hope that the dark clouds of racial prejudice will soon pass away and the deep fog of misunderstanding will be lifted from our fear-drenched communities, and in some not too distant tomorrow the radiant stars of love and brotherhood will shine over our great nation with all their scintillating beauty.

Yours for the cause of Peace and Brotherhood,

Martin Luther King, Jr.

Exercises – Chapter 4

As your instructor directs, work on the following exercise:

Exercise 4.1 – Classroom Protocol

Below is a list of "bad classroom experiences" that former students of ASC 190 have shared with their instructors. Read each one and then be prepared to discuss 1) what perception the student has of the teacher and vice versa; and 2) what you think would have been the best way for the student or the teacher to resolve the problem.

1. I was in an English class and had to leave the class without permission because I felt sick to my stomach. The next time I saw the teacher at the next classroom session a week later and asked him for the assignment handout, he told me I was rude.

2. I couldn't afford to buy the book for the class, and when the teacher found out he got mad.

3. Right after the class on the day I got my test back, I went to talk to the teacher; we got into an argument about my grade.

4. The teacher came across as being distant and gave me a negative impression from the very beginning of the term.

5. When I didn't come to class prepared for the assignment, the instructor called on me to respond.

6. When I fell over a chair coming in to Math, everyone laughed, even the teacher. I got really upset.

7. I told my teacher I had to be 10 minutes late for class every day, and she told me to drop the class.

8. The instructor got an attitude when I returned from being sick and asked, "Did we do anything in class last time?"

9. I was doodling during class, and my teacher told me to stop in front of the entire class.

10. When I had to rush a friend of mine to the hospital, I missed class the day of an exam. The instructor asked for documentation from a doctor, which I thought was insensitive.

11. During our chemistry class, many students were asking questions. Suddenly, the teacher vented by saying, "Are you all idiots?"

12. My Spanish teacher told me how bad I was doing in front of the class.

13. My teacher told me in front of the class to stop reading a newspaper.

14. My cell phone was on vibrate, and my teacher still got mad when I got up and left the room to answer it.

15. My instructor refused to tell me what was going to be on the exam when I missed class on the day he had done so with the class.

Exercise 4.2 – "Is there an E-Mail Etiquette for Student/Professor Interaction?

(a) Read the following e-mail from Jarrod to the Professor:

Dear Dr. Jones:

I apologize for missing class today, but I woke up with a fever of 102 and did not think it was a good idea to go. I do not plan to make a habit of this, but I didn't want to pass around what I have. I will keep up with the syllabus and will be on class Friday to turn my paper in on time.

Sincerely,
Jarrod

Is this e-mail appropriate? Why or why not? What sort of response should Jarrod expect?

(b) What about the following response by the teacher?:

> I received your e-mail. Don't bother me with trivial matters like this! I have 85 other students besides you. Everyone gets sick, but people shouldn't whine about it to their teachers. Show up or deal with the consequences

(c) Here's another example:

> My apologies for missing class today. Thursday night at work was kind of ugly, and not getting home until 8 am this morning pretty much wiped me out. The next thing I knew my wife was waking me up at 5 pm to head to the office again. Have a great weekend, and see you Monday

(d) Rewrite the following e-mail in a way you think is appropriate.

> I was too mad in class to talk to you about the grade you gave me. I have never gotten below an A and now you give me a B–! I am trying for a scholarship, and your class cannot stop me. I will be in class Wednesday to talk to you about changing my grade.

For Your Journal

Go to your course's *Blackboard* site for your journal assignment on Chapter 4

Chapter 5
What Is Critical Thinking?

Often, a good way to begin the process of thinking critically about a subject is to do some conscious thinking about it *before* you do any reading or hear any presentations in the subject. Thus, if you are going to study biology or sociology or writing, a good way to begin is by writing down some of the main ideas you already have about biology or sociology or writing itself *before* you do any reading or listen to lectures. This allows you to be an active listener rather than a passive recipient of information. It helps you to become aware of your assumptions about the subject so that you can assess them more accurately in light of what you will later read and hear.

Some Definitions of Critical Thinking

Here are three definitions of critical thinking by leading researchers. First, Robert Ennis's classic definition:[1]

> Critical thinking is reasonable, reflective thinking that is focused on deciding what to believe or do.

Even before you start reading this text, begin by examining your own concept of critical thinking. Respond to the following in a paragraph or two:

What is your concept of *critical thinking*? (You can respond by giving a description. An alternative way to address it, though, is to use examples: Describe a situation in which you thought through something critically; then describe a situation in which you did not think through something critically.)

Next, write a paragraph describing how, in your best judgment, critical thinking is necessary within the subject matter you are studying?

Next, Matthew Lipman's definition:[2]

Critical thinking is skillful, responsible thinking that is conducive to good judgment because it is sensitive to context, relies on criteria, and is self-correcting.

Finally, in informal presentations, Richard Paul uses this definition:

Critical thinking is thinking about your thinking, while you're thinking, in order to make your thinking better.

Each of these is an excellent definition of critical thinking. It pays to read them several times and to stop and reflect on every aspect of each definition. Why did the expert include this word rather than another? Just what are the experts trying to capture with the words they have chosen? What overlap is there in the definitions, and what main differences of emphasis are there?

It may seem hard to believe, but each of these definitions, brief as they are, is the product of a long period of intense pondering about how best to describe critical thinking. Each definition is an attempt to convey in words the essence of an activity, a "thing"—critical thinking. Before trying to define it, each expert had an intuitive grasp of what critical thinking is, based on years of working with it. This was what the experts tried to capture in the words they chose.

So in reading the experts' definitions and in the discussion ahead, one very important goal to keep in

Revise your concept of critical thinking over the semester. Reformulate it (maybe starting over entirely) so that it accords with your deepening grasp of what critical thinking is.

mind is for you to develop a solid intuitive grasp of just what critical thinking is and what it is not.

Some Prominent Features of Critical Thinking

Critical Thinking Is Reflective

Critical thinking is different from just thinking. It is metacognitive—it involves thinking about your thinking. If I enter a social studies course where one of the topics to be studied is conformity, it is likely that I already have views about conformity: what it is, how prevalent it is, what influences people to conform or not conform. I have these views even if I haven't formulated them explicitly for myself. Each view is an example of thinking, but not necessarily an example of critical thinking. Critical thinking starts once I reflect on my thinking: Why do I have these views about conformity? Since my views are really conclusions I have drawn, what evidence are they based on? How do other people look at conformity differently? What are their views based on? How can I tell which are more accurate, their views or mine?

Critical Thinking Involves Standards

Critical thinking involves having my thinking measure up to criteria. I can think about something accurately or inaccurately. I can use evidence that is relevant to an issue or irrelevant, or somewhere in between. When I reason out and try to understand the main ideas in a course I'm taking, I can do so on a superficial level or I can try to understand them deeply, trying to get at the heart of the matter.

Accuracy, relevance, and depth are examples of standards or criteria. The words "critical" and "criteria" come from the same root, meaning "judgment." For my thinking to be critical thinking, I have to make judgments that meet criteria of reasonableness.

Critical Thinking Is Authentic

Critical thinking, at its heart, is thinking about real problems. Although you can reason out puzzles and brainteasers, the essence of critical thinking comes into play only when you address real problems and questions rather than artificial ones. Critical thinking is far more about what you actually believe or do. It is about good judgment. Puzzles and narrow problems may help occasionally when you want to hone or practice special skills, but even those skills help only if you consciously transfer them to real-life settings. Honing your skills at guessing the endings of murder mysteries is not likely to be good preparation for becoming a criminal investigator. In murder mysteries, all the clues are provided, the murderer is one of the characters, and someone (the author) already knows the murderer's identity. None of that is so in a criminal investigation.

Real problems are often messy. They have loose ends. They are usually unclear: clarifying and refining them are part of thinking through them. They often have no single right answer. But there are wrong answers, even disastrous answers: there may not be any unique right person to take as your partner in life—but there are certainly people it would be disastrous to choose.

AUTHENTIC PROBLEMS

To get the feel of authentic problems (in contrast to "school problems"), think of good novels you have read, or plays or movies you have seen. (Exclude contrived movies where everything automatically works out according to a formula.) Now consider the problems that are facing some character. Those will likely be *authentic* problems. They are full of complications and other people's cross-purposes; actions don't work out exactly as planned; emotions and desires are heavily involved in the decisions people make.

Choose an example or two like that, and try to reason through decisions that the character could make.

Critical Thinking Involves Being Reasonable

There are no surefire rules of reasoning. There are no rules so foolproof that they guarantee your reasoning will be successful. There are guidelines; there are even "rules" sometimes, but these always need to be followed thoughtfully. You need to apply them with sensitivity to context, goals, and a whole host of realities. For thinking to be critical thinking, it must be reasonable thinking.

Compare critical thinking to driving a car. There are rules for good driving (e.g., merge when entering an interstate), but merely following the rules won't make you a good driver. To be a good driver you have to follow the rules *mindfully*. What does that mean? It means, for example, following the rules while being aware that the purpose of merging is to allow traffic to flow more smoothly and reduce collisions between fast- and slow-moving cars, that weather and traffic conditions affect how you should merge, and so on. Notice that this is an open-ended list of what a mindful driver is aware of while merging.

We often long for surefire, step-by-step procedures, and the more personally important or threatening a situation is, the more we want foolproof rules. But there are no rules that guarantee our thinking will be correct—and that is especially true in very important or threatening situations. We must use our reasoning to evaluate rules, rather than vice versa. The only way we can decide whether to follow certain rules is if we use our best reasoning to determine that those rules are reasonable, that they lead to reasonable results when followed. Critical thinking is "self-correcting" at least partly because it is the court of last resort. There is no level of greater certainty beneath it that we can use to evaluate our reasoning.

Three Parts of Critical Thinking

Full-fledged critical thinking involves three parts. First, **critical thinking involves asking questions**. It involves asking questions that need to be asked, asking good questions, questions that go to the heart of the matter. Critical thinking involves noticing that there are questions that need to be addressed.

Second, **critical thinking involves trying to answer those questions by reasoning them out**. Reasoning out answers to questions is different from other ways of answering questions. It is different from giving an answer that we have always taken for granted but never thought about. It is different from answering impressionistically ("That reminds me of . . ."), or answering simply according to the way we were raised, or answering in accordance with our personality. It is also different from answering by saying the first thing that comes into our mind, and then using all our power of reasoning to defend that answer.

Third, **critical thinking involves believing the results of our reasoning**. Critical thinking is different from just engaging in a

CRITICAL WRITING

Write down three questions you have about critical thinking. Then, write down three questions you have about how you will be using critical thinking *in this course*.

(If you can't think of any real questions, even after pushing, what conclusions do you draw from that?)

mental exercise. When we think through an issue critically, we internalize the results. We don't give merely verbal agreement: we actually believe the results because we have done our best to reason the issue out and we know that reasoning things out is the best way to get reliable answers. Furthermore, when we think critically through a decision about what to do in a situation, then what follows the reasoning is not just belief, but action: Unless something unforeseen occurs, we end up taking the action we concluded was most reasonable.

Asking the Questions

Critical thinking begins with asking questions. If a teacher assigns a homework problem to solve, a good question to ask is "How can I best solve this problem?" Often, though, students don't ask this question at all. Instead, they just jump in and try to solve the problem by any method that springs to mind. Thinking critically about solving a problem, on the other hand, begins with asking questions about the problem and about ways to address it:

- What is the purpose behind the problem?
- What is a good way to begin?
- Do I have all the information I need to start solving the problem?
- What are some alternative ways of solving the problem assigned?
- Can the problem be solved? Does it even make sense?

All of these questions are relevant when a problem is assigned. But when teachers assign problems, they have already done a fundamental part of the questioning. Posing a problem is asking a question. So, a major part of learning how to think critically is learning to ask the questions—to pose the problems—yourself. That means noticing that there are questions that need to be addressed; recognizing that there are problems. Often, this is the hardest part of critical thinking.

This is true not just in school, but in daily life as well. People often do not ask themselves, "How can I best get along with my parents (my partner, my co-workers, my friends) in this situation?" Instead, they continue relating to them in habitual and unexamined ways. If your goal is to improve some aspect of your daily life, begin by asking yourself some questions: What are some concrete things I can do to make better grades? To meet new people? To read more effectively? To make the subject matter of this course meaningful in my life?

To be effective, you need to really *ask* these questions. It's not enough just to say the words. In fact, when you look at the questions just posed, they can seem empty. But that's not because they are empty. Whether a question is empty or not depends a great deal on the spirit in which you ask it. If you ask it in an empty way, just going through the motions, then it's not a genuine question at all, not for you, and it will not be the beginning of thinking critically through that question.

Here are some questions that teachers list as ones that students do not ask, but should be asking, in their courses:

- How does what I learn in this course relate to my own experience?
- How can I use what I learn here in my own life?
- Can I think up my own examples?
- How does this subject matter relate to other courses I am taking?
- What is the evidence behind this?
- How do the topics in this course fit together?
- What is the purpose of the course?
- Why?

Identify some situations in your life that are problematic, ones that are not going as well as you think they should. Write them as questions. Be specific in how you describe them. Don't just say "How can I get along with my friends?" Focus it: "How can I best deal with Arthur when I feel him pressuring me to do X and I really don't think I should be doing X?"

Write a list of some further questions you should be asking about those situations?

Reflect on your educational experience a little. Which of the questions listed by teachers are ones you tend to ask yourself in courses you are taking? Which of them do you never (or almost never) ask?

Try keeping a journal of questions that arise during a course you are taking now. Questions maybe about the subject matter itself, about how it affects you (or *does not* affect you), about how you can use it, about implications of the course, about the way it is taught, about the assignments given, about assignments *not* given.

Reasoning It Out

Though asking questions is necessary to begin critical thinking, merely asking the questions is not enough; the questions need to be answered (or at least addressed). Often we raise questions only to worry about them, or to torment ourselves, or even to put off action, instead of trying to answer them by thinking them through.

For example, a significant number of students have difficulty in math-related fields. They sometimes ask the question, "Why am I so bad at math?" They then use this question to make negative judgments about themselves ("I'm just hopeless at math, and I always will be") or about the field ("I don't need to know math to be a nurse"), or they answer it with unhelpful generalities ("I'm no good at it because of the way I was taught"). Reasoning it out, however, requires approaching the question in a different way and with a different spirit. It is the spirit of *intellectual engagement*, of genuinely wanting to figure out a clear, accurate answer to a question that is important to you. It might begin with reformulating the question in a more neutral and helpful way: "What are the main causes of my problems with math, and what are some good ways to begin dealing with them?" You might then read a little about what causes problems in learning math and apply the information to your own case. You could talk to counselors about alternative approaches that have helped other students, take seriously what the counselors say, and note any resistance you feel to the new approaches. Reasoning it out may not "solve" the problem, but it does provide a significantly better way of addressing the problem than not reasoning it out at all.

On the other hand, there are many *uncritical* ways to try to answer questions, ones that do not involve much reasoning. You can:

- Ask someone (and simply accept the answers uncritically)
- Answer according to the way you have been raised (without examining whether it was a healthy way to be raised)
- Answer without looking for information, even if it's readily available
- Answer in accordance with your personality (without examining the extent to which your "personality" helps or hinders you in this kind of situation)
- Answer with what first comes into your head

It is easy to misunderstand questions about reasoning. Thus, you might interpret the second item listed as implying that critical thinking is opposed to the way you were raised, but that is not what it means. What critical thinking is opposed to is acting in the way you were raised, without examining it. For example, someone raised in a family where violence and abuse were taught, or where blind obedience to authority was taken for granted, should not simply follow those values.

The two greatest difficulties in reasoning are not what you might expect. It isn't that people aren't good at reasoning, or that they make mistakes. People are good at it in some areas and not so good in others; everyone makes mistakes; everyone can improve. But these are not the most crucial difficulties. They go deeper. The first is that, when presented with a problem, people often don't think to reason in the first place. It's just not the usual human reaction to a problem. This is partly because societies do not encourage reasoning as an approach to important questions. The second difficulty is that people often do not know the difference between reasoning through something and other ways of responding. As a result, people respond with what seems to be reasoning, but isn't.

For example, a discussion is not automatically an example of critical thinking. Often in discussions, each participant says what he or she believes, and that's the end of the matter. In a reasoned discussion, on the other hand, listening is as important as speaking. Participants try to understand the reasons behind other people's beliefs, and they try to identify both the strong and weak points of the views expressed. The whole spirit is different.

So, "reasoning things out" really means reasoning them out well. What does it mean, then, to reason through something well?

Reasoning itself is drawing conclusions on the basis of reasons. Good reasoning, therefore, is drawing conclusions on the basis of reasons and giving due weight to all relevant factors. Relevant factors include the *implications* of drawing those *conclusions*, the *assumptions* on which the reasoning is based, the *accuracy* of the reasons used, the *alternatives* available, and a number of other elements (Chapter 6) and standards.

Though it's not difficult to define good reasoning in an open-ended way, the challenge is to spell

> **REASONING VERSUS NON-REASONING**
>
> What are some important differences between a debate and a reasoned debate? Between writing a reaction paper and a reasoned reaction paper? Between evaluating an essay and giving a reasoned evaluation of an essay?

it out in a way that is usable by you, one that lays a foundation so that your ability to reason well can improve and deepen during the rest of your life. A good deal of the rest of this book is devoted to that.

Believing the Results

Critical thinking, in the fullest sense, results in belief. It even results in action. Here is an example. A teacher lowers my course grade because I missed too many classes, and I feel unfairly treated. So I raise the question: "Was my teacher being fair in giving me this grade?" Next, I reason my way to an answer: I collect information (maybe I ask the teacher about it; I check what the syllabus said about missed classes; maybe I check to see if other students were treated the same way); I consider the teacher's point of view on the issue and her purpose in lowering my grade because of absences. After reasoning it through—reasoning it through well, I believe—I come to the conclusion that my teacher was fair in what she did. The next step seems so obvious as not to need stating: I believe the results of my reasoning; I believe that my teacher's actions were in fact fair.

However, taking this last step isn't always easy. Even after reasoning it out, I may still have feelings of being unfairly treated, and I may still suspect that I was treated unfairly.

What is going on in this example is an indication that I have not thought through the issue critically, at least not in a complete enough way. Maybe there are other questions I should be raising ("Could my feelings of being treated unfairly arise from other circumstances in my life?" "What concept of fairness am I using in my thinking?"). Maybe there are alternative explanations to consider; maybe I am making some unstated assumptions that are influencing my feelings. Or else, maybe I should just believe the results: the teacher was being fair and my original estimate of unfairness was really off the mark (and I need to remember that feelings of being unfairly treated, even if they are unjustified, often take time to go away).

Believing the results is a rough test or measure of the completeness of your critical thinking. If you have reasoned something out and come to a conclusion but find you still don't really believe it, that indicates the reasoning is probably not complete. Important factors probably are missing—factors that lead you to resist internalizing the results.

It is more controversial to link critical thinking to action. Suppose, for example, I continue to smoke or to eat too many saturated fats despite the fact that I've done a lot of reasoning about the importance of giving them up. Is that a flaw in my critical thinking? If I can state all the compelling reasons but still do not act on my reasoning, how good is my critical thinking? Experts disagree on the answer.

The suggestion here is that there is some flaw in the critical thinking. The flaw can lie in how I think about my own body, about my life, or about the relation between abstract statistics and my chances of survival. I might have an overriding background belief that those statistics don't apply to me, or that even though it's important for me to give up smoking, it's not important that I do it now. Sometimes you can even get the impression that certain people don't believe that they will ever die. There is a subtle relation between denial and lack of critical thinking, one that has not yet been fully explored.

It is difficult to identify examples of not believing the results of our own reasoning. That's because, paradoxical as it may sound, it's hard to become aware of what we actually believe and don't believe. There are four indicators of when we are not believing the results of our reasoning (but only the last one is even moderately easy to spot in ourselves):

1. I reason something out, but strong emotions arise within me against the result.
2. I find myself believing contradictory things.
3. I believe something very strongly, but I find I am unable to come up with any good reasons for the belief. In fact, I don't think I even need reasons. Thinking the opposite seems ridiculous.
4. I reason something out, but my actions do not follow my reasoning.

The following are examples of the first three indicators (but they may not be convincing to you, especially if you share the beliefs in question):

1. ■ Michael reasons out the issue of capital punishment as a deterrent. He gathers information and concludes that it does not significantly deter murder or other violent crimes. But after his investigation, he feels angry. He says, "Maybe that's true, but I'm still in favor of capital punishment because you have to do something to stop criminals."

   ■ Maria, taking a course in gender studies, reasons her way through the argument that there is no non-sexist reason why a woman should adopt her husband's name at marriage. Like Michael, Maria discovers that the more she follows the argument, the angrier she gets.

2. ■ Pete believes that all cultures and all cultural practices are equally valid. He believes that people do not have a right to say that a particular culture's practices are wrong. But he also believes that it's part of our Western culture to impose our ideas on others, and that it's wrong for us to do that.

   ■ Most of us believe that everyone should be treated equally, but that does not prevent us from thinking that we deserve special breaks.

3. ■ Some people think that eating dogs, cats, or seagulls is revolting, but that eating cows or chickens is quite reasonable. They believe this despite the fact that all their reasoning shows the cases are identical. They find themselves trying to make up reasons that they know don't work (such as "Dogs and cats are pets! That's why it is wrong to eat them").

   ■ In critical-thinking presentations, Vincent Ruggiero asks, "Why not turn cemeteries into parks where children can play?" (Can you give a good reason against it?) "We're running out of room: why not bury people in the median strips of highways?"

When you've thought through something critically and come to the conclusion that seems most reasonable to you, it should follow (a) that you believe it, and (b) that you start acting in accordance with that belief.

An appropriate exercise would be to ask you to identify situations where you do not believe the results of your reasoning, where each of the four causes applies to you. But that is extremely difficult. Can you identify any examples where indicators (1), (2), and (3) apply to you? If you can find even one, that's a major insight into yourself. (It sometimes helps to begin with other people, and then apply the results to yourself.)

With indicator (4), on the other hand, it should be easy to identify some examples of actions you continue to engage in even though your best reasoned thinking tells you that you should not.

What Critical Thinking Is *Not*

There are a number of widespread misconceptions about critical thinking. These can throw off your understanding of critical thinking and influence the way you develop in your thinking skills.

Critical Thinking and Negativity

Critical Thinking Is Not Negative

The word *critical* often has negative overtones. A "critical person" is one who does a lot of faultfinding. To "criticize" someone usually means to say something negative. A "critic" is often thought of as someone who is against something.

But the word *critical* in "critical thinking" has no negative connotations at all. It is related to the word *criteria*: it means thinking that meets high criteria of reasonableness. To learn to think critically is to learn to think things through, and to think them through well: accurately, clearly, sufficiently, reasonably. Some people have proposed the term *effective thinking* as a synonym for "critical thinking," and using that term can help in removing negative overtones.

The Importance of Negative Feedback

Another aspect of negativity must be considered. Sometimes sensitivity to negative feedback gets in the way of critical thinking. Suppose someone makes a judgment about your work—that it is inaccurate or unclear, or not relevant to the question asked. Maybe the person even personalizes it, criticizing you when he or she is actually talking about your work. The person might say that you are unclear or inaccurate. Maybe the person even says it harshly.

You need to sort out the judgments, separating out the harshness or the over-generalization on the speaker's part. You are left with feedback about your work on this occasion. Many people view such feedback as negative, but you don't have to view it that way. Instead, you can choose to view it as a source of valuable information. If you can distance yourself from the negativity, you can free yourself to look for the kernel of truth it may contain.

Because the judgment is not binding on you, you can choose what to learn from it. You may learn something about the other person ("My teacher values grammar very highly. Just how important is grammar?"); but you may also learn something about your work and the way you think ("Oh, I didn't even realize I was being unclear! Maybe I should elaborate more").

Critical Thinking and Emotions

Critical Thinking Is Not Emotionless Thinking

One of the most widespread myths about critical thinking, and one of the most harmful too, is that critical thinking is somehow opposed

> Using the word *critical* in the sense of *critical thinking*, what would you say are the main earmarks of critical reading? What is the difference between reading your text and reading it *critically*?
>
> How about critical listening? What is the difference between listening to a lecture in a course and listening to it *critically*?
>
> Can a person listen critically and not disagree at all?

to emotions. According to this myth, the best way to think critically is to be devoid of emotions or, if emotions arise, to put them aside, don't let them influence your conclusions. The image in this myth is of someone coldly rational, someone who puts aside his or her feelings in order to be "logical."

This is one of the most misleading myths there is, and it is all the more damaging because there is a grain of truth in it. Some emotions do indeed get in the way of critical thinking: rage and panic, for example. It is extremely difficult for people to think clearly about a decision when they are enraged. But, by contrast, certain other emotion-laden states actually help with critical thinking: the love of truth is an example. So are the joy of discovery, anger at biased presentations of information, and fear of making an unreasonable decision in a crucial situation.

Consider as an example something that intrinsically involves a lot of emotion: love. Suppose you are the mother of a child. What will help you in being a good mother? A good mother is one who acts in accord with high standards of critical thinking: she has the best interests of her child at heart; she does not neglect her own well-being, but she nurtures and makes wise decisions in the best interests of her child, weighs relevant alternative courses of action, and understands the child's growing need for both autonomy and safety; she is creative about finding ways to help her child develop in a healthy way. Now, what is the role of love in this? It should be clear that love—far from being an impediment to clear thinking—is *essential* to being a good critically thinking mother. Love is a large part of what motivates the thinking, grounds it, helps her to assess choices that confront her as a parent. The emotions that go along with love are not in any way opposed to the thinking required to be a good parent.

The same can be said about romantic love. Sometimes it may seem that being in love is opposed to critical thinking, but often this stems from a superficial concept of love. For example, people who are in love often engage in wishful thinking. Suppose Ashley is in love with Lou and Lou is an alcoholic. A common scenario is that Ashley keeps thinking that Lou will be cured any day now, even though it may be clear to others that Lou is not on the road to recovery. But thinking, against all the evidence, that Lou's cure is just around the corner is not an example of love interfering with critical thinking. It's deeper than that.

To sort through this example requires thinking through the concept of love in a deeper way and distinguishing it from neediness and from a desire to mold the person according to an image. Part of loving someone, romantically or not, is seeing what that person is actually like, respecting his or her boundaries. To love someone, rather than just to love an image of that person, is to accept the person as he or she is. Loving the person is exactly what can help you see clearly who that person is and your relationship to him or her.

Emotions Give Us Data

There is another area in which emotions are essential to critical thinking. Emotions often give us data, and much of the time it's foolhardy to ignore that data. For example, if two people are in love, it is *unreasonable* for them to ignore that fact when they make important decisions about, say, whether to go to schools that are far apart. Being in love is directly relevant to that decision. Ignoring important data is *not* thinking critically. (For the same reason, it would also be unreasonable to base the decision *only* on the fact that they are in love. There are other facts that are relevant as well.)

In a more general way, though, we receive important data from our emotions all the time. Suppose that while walking through a neighborhood at dusk, you become afraid that you are in danger. Sometimes people have a narrow view of rationality. If they cannot pinpoint what is dangerous about the situation, they draw the conclusion that their fears are unfounded. But under most circumstances, that's not reasonable at all. There is a good chance that you are picking up clues you are not aware of, triggering your fear. There

Describe some situations where, in your best judgment, your emotions led you astray in your reasoning. Then, describe some situations where, in your best judgment, your emotions made a positive contribution to your reasoning.

Try to discover patterns in your emotional reactions, so that you can assess when your emotions tend to be accurate responses to reality and when they tend not to be.

For example, think about the people you have been in love with in the past. Have they generally been caring, respectful people who, on the whole, treated you well? If so, that's a pretty good reason to rely on your feelings of love as an indicator of who is good for you: you're pretty good at picking good people. On the other hand, if they were abusive or manipulative, that's a good reason not to let your feelings of being in love with someone guide you too strongly in your choices.

is nothing unreasonable about heeding that data. On the contrary, what is unreasonable is to pretend that you are not afraid when you are. The reasonable thing to do is neither to ignore the data of your emotions, nor to give them too much weight.

Being Logical Is Linked to Having Feelings

If we think of desires as intertwined with emotion, then the tie between critical thinking and emotions is even stronger. That is because, in the end, it is not possible to engage in critical thinking without desires and their attendant emotions. Unless I have goals—desires, things I want, things I'm emotionally attached to—I have no reason to think critically, no reason to take action X rather than action Y.

In the movie *Star Trek* (2009), the character Mr Spock is based on a character in an old TV series. In the series, Mr. Spock often said that he puts aside whatever feelings he has in order to be what he called "logical." But he also saves the ship and the crew again and again. The problem with this scenario is that if he is not emotionally attached to the crew members, he has no reason to save them. Unless he *wants* them to live, it is not "logical" for him to save them. Spock's answer is that saving the *Enterprise* is the "right thing to do." But, unless he's emotionally attached to doing the right thing, he has no reason to do the right thing either. The question is always: Why should he try to achieve *any* purpose? It is "logical" for him to do something only if achieving his purpose is something that matters to him, matters to him in terms of his emotions and desires. Being logical requires having goals that are emotionally important.

The relation between emotions and critical thinking is a complicated one, without easy solutions. (For example, not all philosophers would agree that emotions and desires underlie rationality.) There is no doubt that emotions can cloud judgment, but they can also illuminate it. Fear can make you run from a decision that is in your best interests. But fear can also alert you to dangers in decisions, dangers that you're not consciously aware of. Anger is often a very sophisticated emotion, alerting us to subtle evidence of people's willingness to cross our boundaries. Whether to rely on emotions in any particular case, and how much to rely on them, is itself a matter for critical thinking.

Impediments to Critical Thinking

The way we think is an adaptation to the surroundings we have lived in. The patterns in our thinking are ways that we have developed to make sense of what goes on around us. These patterns can be effective, but they can also be dysfunctional. Most likely, for each of us, the patterns are variable: effective in some areas, wildly ineffective in others, and mixed most of the time.

Many aspects of the world we live in can be impediments to learning to think more critically.

Forming a Picture of the World on the Basis of News Media

Most of us form a picture of what the world is like based, directly or indirectly, on news media: TV news, blogs, newspapers, and so forth. Even if you don't watch the news much, you indirectly form a good deal of your picture of the world from it. You get a picture of what the world is like by talking to friends, by connecting through Facebook or Twitter, by listening to comedy shows or reality TV, or just through hearsay. But when we trace it back, all those people form their picture of the world ultimately from the news media. So, indirectly, you and I do too.

Here is a question I ask students in Louisiana. (You may not know much about Louisiana, but answer the question anyhow):

> Consider people who are convicted of murder in Louisiana, and sentenced to life imprisonment. How much time do such people, on the average, actually spend in prison? (Remember: the question is not how many years they are sentenced to; it is how many years they end up actually spending in prison.)

a. 0–5 years
b. 5–10 years
c. 10–20 years
d. 20–50 years
e. until they die.

Choose an answer before you read on.

I have asked thousands of students this question over the last few years or so; almost no one ever gets it right. Even with myself, it was hard to become convinced of the right answer. The first few times I heard it, I simply didn't believe it. (The answer is in the footnotes.[3])

Now, this is a purely factual question, not a critical-thinking one. But there is a critical-thinking question behind the mistaken answers. Where do we get our false impression? We get it, directly or indirectly, from the news media. But how? We do not get the wrong answer because the news tells us the wrong answer. News media are very careful to check the accuracy of factual statements they report.

Rather, the news media tell us *stories*. They report on someone getting released from prison early. Maybe over the course of time they report several such stories, including some where a criminal then commits a violent crime while on parole. Maybe we hear politicians or relatives of a victim talking about how life means only twenty years, and we believe them. (These people too get their impression from the news.) These stories are vivid. They are simplified and made dramatic. Often there is stirring footage. They register in our minds. Whether we are aware of it or not, we form a general picture that violent criminals (including murderers sentenced to life in Louisiana) are getting out of prison early all the time.

Any picture like that one, formed on the basis of news presentations, is likely to be seriously distorted. This is because the news media report not on what is usual or typical, but on what is *unusual*. That's why it is called news: it reports on what is out of the ordinary. That's also why it works so well as entertainment. In contrast, what is usual is for people to wake up in the morning, eat breakfast, go to work, eat lunch, come home at the end of the day, watch TV for a while, go to bed. That is not a news event. Rather, what the news reports on is Afghanistan (hardly a typical country), a tornado hitting a trailer park (not a common event), a postal employee going berserk (extremely unusual), or a highly controversial bill in Congress (not the hundreds of bills that are passed on a regular basis).

If you want an accurate picture of what the world is usually like, you need to look to reputable books, studies, or web sites that deal with the subject in depth. Textbooks are usually an excellent source. And, of course, you have to do some intensive critical thinking about the topic as well.

This doesn't imply that it's wrong to consult the news media regularly. On the contrary, the news—especially if it has more in-depth coverage—is an excellent way to keep up with the unusual, even earthshaking, events of our time.

Discuss how likely you are to get a false picture of the following topics from the news media:

- The danger of small airplanes
- The amount of crime in your area
- New findings in science
- The chances of winning the lottery

(continued)

(Continued)

Write down a few important topics of your own where your picture of the world is likely to be seriously distorted if you base your impression mainly on what is reported by news media. Where, specifically, would you look to get a more accurate impression?

In the Discipline. Are there topics related to the discipline you are studying that appear from time to time in the news? Is the picture you receive from the media likely to be distorted? In what ways? Again, where specifically would you look to get a more accurate picture?

Forming a Picture of the World on the Basis of Movies, TV, Advertising, Magazines

If forming a picture of the world on the basis of the news results in distortion, forming a picture on the basis of fictionalized or sensationalized material results in vastly more distortion. Sometimes the distortion is obvious, at least to reflective adults: people do not get thrown through plate-glass windows and emerge intact; there is no reason to believe that there are aliens among us; the clothes in the glossy picture will not make most of us look like the model in the picture; products often have unmentioned defects. Other examples are more subtle and affect our attitudes in deep and disturbing ways: trying your hardest, though it may give you personal satisfaction, will not usually result in beating the competition (especially since they may be trying their hardest too); most people's grades (or height or intelligence or abilities) cannot be above average; everyone cannot be glamorous, young, physically attractive, or strong; being a lone-wolf rebel who can't get along with superiors does not usually bring success.

List some of the subtle messages acquired from movies, TV, magazines, or advertising that tend to give people a false sense of what the world is like. How about school in particular? How is high school or college usually depicted? How is the subject matter of your classes presented in these sources? Are there stereotypes?

All-or-Nothing Thinking (Black-and-White Thinking), Us-versus-Them Thinking, Stereotyping

Each of these ways of thinking is deeply ingrained in us. Each stands in the way of critical thinking, and for similar reasons—they give us a way of simplifying our in fact, though, each of them vastly over-simplifies the complexity of reality, and each serves as an excuse for not thinking things through.

Effective thinking requires us to pay attention to the complexity of things. It requires us to develop a tolerance for ambiguity and an acceptance of less-than-certain answers. It requires a commitment to seeing both sides of an issue and to trying to find out the truth, rather than merely trying to bolster our side: our country, our race, our gender, our political views.

Describe a situation—either from your own life or from disciplines you have studied—where you engaged in all-or-nothing thinking.

Then describe a contrasting situation, one where you were tempted to engage in all-or-nothing thinking, but instead addressed the subtleties of the situation and therefore came up with a more careful answer.

Describe a similar pair of contrasting examples for us-versus-them thinking, then for stereotyping.

Fears

Although, as we have seen, all fears are not automatically an impediment to critical thinking, some fears do tend to become obstacles. That's especially true of:

- Fear of making mistakes
- Fear of trying something new, of sticking your neck out
- Fear of looking foolish

The full exercise of critical thinking requires that you develop intellectual courage. For example, making mistakes is an essential part of critical thinking. What important skill have you ever learned that did not involve making many mistakes? Most critical-thinking experts believe that you learn a great deal more from mistakes than from successes. In fact, though you may make fewer critical-thinking mistakes as your higher-order thinking skills develop, there will always be mistakes to be made and learned from.

The same will be true when you try new ways of thinking, when you risk looking foolish by exposing how you think about issues, and when you take the risk of giving original solutions to old problems.

Some Educational Practices Discourage Critical Thinking

Some prevalent educational practices discourage critical thinking, and internalizing them as a model of what education should be can seriously affect your critical thinking. These practices are based on assumptions like:

- The student's role is to be a passive recipient of knowledge.
- The student's role is to memorize and regurgitate information.
- The teacher's role is to dispense knowledge.
- Questions on exams should be taken only from what has been covered in class.
- Problems assigned to students should always be clearly formulated.
- There is an adequate answer to every question.
- Everything is just a matter of opinion.

> How much of your past education has emphasized the teacher or student roles listed?
>
> Formulate your idea of what education should be about, your philosophy of education.
>
> Make some well-considered judgments about how the roles listed fit in with or oppose your idea of education.

Deeper, More Pervasive Impediments to Critical Thinking

In addition to the specific impediments listed previously, there are other, deeper and more pervasive obstacles to critical thinking. Four of them are briefly discussed below, but they are not separate from one another. All four are deeply interwoven. In addition, they are difficult impediments to come to terms with. Maybe it is fair to say that none of us ever completely overcomes them. We can, however, gain deeper insights into how they work, and that can help us overcome their influence.

Egocentrism

Each of us is at the center of our own experience. We live in the middle of our feelings, pains and pleasures, the things we want and the things we are afraid of, the experiences that have shaped our lives and our attitudes, whether we know it or not. Our experience is heavily influenced by how we think and, conversely, how we think is influenced by our experience.

In accord with this, people often have a way of thinking that always puts themselves first. When they are engaged in such egocentric thinking, they tend to make judgments about how things are, but they may base those judgments on wishful thinking or mere self-interest. This occurs in all of us, probably a good deal of the time. Sometimes it's so blatant that, when it is pointed out to us, we easily see it. Most of the time, though, it operates far beneath the surface. It is easy to delude myself into believing that I am working in the best interests of humanity as a whole when in fact I am working for my own interests and even against the interests of humanity. This is always easier to see in other people than it is in myself.

Egocentrism interferes with critical thinking on all levels, from the deepest to the most superficial. It stands in the way of the empathy that is such an important part of critical thinking. If I am in the health-care professions, for example, it's easy to stay bound up in my own desires and needs and not see things from the patient's point of view. Egocentrism stands in the way of fair-mindedness too, another essential critical-thinking trait. Part of thinking effectively is being able to understand points of view that are opposed to my own. Sometimes when I feel threatened, though, I can't even hear what the other

> Write a brief response to the following questions (your response can be just a few lines, but it is important that it be written):
>
> 1. Advertising. In your judgment, how heavily are people influenced by advertising?
>
> 2. Conformity. In your judgment, to what extent do people conform to roles dictated by the society they live in?
>
> 3. Driving. In your judgment, are people generally good drivers?
>
> Write your responses before you look at the answers (see Exercise 5.3 at the end of the chapter).

person is saying. For many people, when someone critiques their country or culture or religion or family, all they hear is the fact that they are being criticized. Anger rises, and often they can't even repeat the substance of the comments the person made. This interferes with their ability to give a fair evaluation of their country, culture, and so on. If I can't hear a critique, then I can't come to a balanced conclusion, and that deprives me of information I can use to assess the validity of my beliefs.

In course work, egocentrism can lead to my seeing education only in terms of grades, in effect causing me to miss out on all the other benefits to be derived from education. It can lead to plagiarism and cheating, or thinking that teachers are unfair even if they're not.

One of the most valuable things to be gained from critical thinking is an increased ability to see the egocentricity of our own thinking.

Developmental Patterns of Thinking

We acquire many of our patterns of thinking as we go through different stages of psychological and physical development. As children, we have a number of deeply felt needs: a need to feel safe, a need to be loved, a need for physical contact; we have a need to individuate ourselves from others as well as a contrary need to join completely with another person. Moreover, many of our standard ways of thinking were acquired during childhood, even during early childhood. After all, that's when we

Think about the need to feel safe. This is a need that develops in early childhood and never really goes away.

Begin by focusing on other people. Use obvious examples of persistent irrational behavior in people you know: maybe they are abrasive and drive friends away; maybe they identify with groups or with causes that don't seem to serve their interests; maybe they continue to hold beliefs when the vast preponderance of evidence goes against those beliefs. Now try out the hypothesis that this behavior is partly the result of looking for feelings of safety along paths established during childhood. (If I drive people away, for example, it can feel as though I don't have to take the risk of depending on them; identifying with groups can give me a feeling of belonging, of safety.)

A much harder exercise is to apply this not just to others, but also to yourself.

first learned how to conceptualize and deal with emotions, frustration, authority figures, strong desires, pain and hurt. Many of the strategies we devised back then still persist, beneath the surface, throughout our lives. Thus, when we feel threatened, we can easily revert back to a child's way of thinking. Problems that can be solved may seem overwhelming. (Think of how overwhelming problems can be to a child.) People can be going about their business with no reference to us at all, and we may feel victimized by it (e.g., waiters who don't see us at their table or drivers who go slow in the left lane). We might resort to manipulation or even physical bullying when we don't get our way.

So, another great benefit of learning to think critically is that you can start identifying the *assumptions* you used to make about life, and you can distinguish them from the more mature assumptions you can make now. You can separate your past from your present *purposes*. You can take seriously the much more extensive *information* you have now, the *context* in which you now live, the *alternatives* that are now available to you that were not available when you were younger. You can draw different *conclusions*. (The italicized terms are essential critical-thinking concepts, elements of reasoning; see Chapter 6.)

Previous Commitments, Previous Personal Experience

Suppose someone makes a point about a controversial issue, about politics maybe, or capital punishment, or the benefits of a trade agreement. The most usual way to evaluate the person's statement is first to see how much it agrees with my views, and then give reasons for or against it based on the amount of agreement.

This might be reasonable if my views were the product of extensive critical examination on my part. But often my views are ones I just happen to hold; they only seem to be the result of previous examination. There may be no reason to think that my previously held beliefs are more likely to be correct than the newer points I am evaluating for the first time.

We can also think in a biased way with respect to evidence. If I lean toward a certain belief, then just a small amount of evidence weighs heavily in its favor for me. If I believe in aliens visiting earth, or herbal remedies for cancer, or homeopathic cures, or predestination, then even the negative fact that such views have not been absolutely disproven counts heavily in their favor in my eyes.

On the other hand, if I oppose a belief, then a vague piece of evidence, or just the fact that it has not been absolutely proven, weighs heavily against it:

"I don't believe in global warming. Nobody has *proved* the earth is getting warmer. Last winter it was very cold."

"You can't prove that I won't win the lottery. There's always a chance. You can't win if you don't play."

That is, we slant the amount of evidence to fit in with our predispositions. We require a mountain of evidence to make us doubt something we already believe, but we require only the slightest of evidence to make us more sure of it. Even our own ingenuity can work against us. No matter how bizarre or farfetched a point of view is, if we become convinced that it is true, our ingenious minds can almost always construct at least *some* evidence in its favor.

How should we make judgments? If we are interested in accuracy, in knowing the truth or what is likely to come closest to the truth, we should go with the *preponderance of evidence*, regardless of whether we started out for or against a particular conclusion. That is often extremely difficult to do because decisions can be made below the level of our awareness and because our beliefs are so often bound up with our egos and developmental ways of thinking. We can increase our awareness and open-mindedness by using critical thinking.

This is also true when we are basing judgments on personal experience. Personal experience gives us a valuable supply of information, one that we can use to draw conclusions, make decisions. One of the main ways teachers get students to think critically about a discipline is by asking them to relate the discipline's concepts to their personal experiences. No one would deny the value of personal experience in critical thinking.

However, personal experience can also be an impediment to critical thinking. That's particularly true of vivid personal experiences, the kind that are unusual and imprint themselves on our minds. For each of us, our personal experience is limited. If we make generalizations from it that go beyond what we are acquainted with, we stand a good chance of drawing distorted conclusions. Your own experience has far more impact on you than the experiences of a hundred other people you hear about. But, if you want to draw accurate conclusions about what is likely to happen, then (other things being equal) you should put more faith in the experiences of a hundred people than in the experience of one—even if that one happens to be you.

What do you need to do to broaden your knowledge-base so as to take account of a wide variety of experiences and conclusions beyond your own? You should look at reputable books, studies, journal articles, sources that gather and assemble information from a great variety of human experience. If you own a Kia that repeatedly gives you trouble, that is an excellent reason not to trust that car in the future. But if you want to make a wise decision about whether the next car you buy should be a Kia, your personal experience is too limited. It would be wiser to consult *Consumer Reports* or some other neutral agency that evaluates cars.

How Deep Is Our Need for Critical Thinking?

One of the great things about critical thinking is its versatility. It is valuable at all levels of our thinking.

At the Level of Practical Decision Making

Critical thinking helps when we are simply trying to deal with ordinary tasks: how to study more efficiently, find a strategy when we are stuck in an airport, decide what kind of clothes to buy. This is thinking about the means to use to accomplish our goals. It is problem solving of the most authentic kind. This is an important level of critical thinking, one that addresses all those ordinary decisions we make.

Developing thinking skills helps you envision alternative paths you could take. It helps you identify and discard outdated assumptions you may be making. It helps you anticipate some of the consequences, both positive and negative, of decisions you or others may make. It helps you keep your goals in sight and think of more effective means of achieving those goals.

At the Level of Meaningfulness

Learning to think critically also helps people deal with the much larger issues of living their life. Critical thinking frees people, the way nothing else really can, from habits of thinking they are often ruled by. Not completely of course, but substantially. Critical thinking opens up other viable courses of action that leave people far more fulfilled, paths that otherwise might never occur to them. Finding a life partner or a new occupation; incorporating the profound knowledge that's available in your courses into your way of thinking about your life; developing reasonable attitudes toward self, toward others, toward your values, toward all the things that make life meaningful for you—all of these can be made richer and more attainable when you examine them thoughtfully.

At the Level of Concepts

We think in terms of concepts, and these inevitably shape our life to a considerable degree. Very often the concepts we think in terms of are ones we accept uncritically. We may understand what love is from movies and from the way we feel. We may understand what freedom is simply by having heard the word over and over and making vague associations with it. We may grow up thinking justice means getting even. We all have concepts of what it is to be a student, a teacher, a woman, a man, a religious person, an atheist, a scientist, an artist, a professional in the field we are studying. We have concepts of what it means to be brave, to be treated fairly, to be intelligent, to fit in, to be anything you can name or describe. We can reach a deep level of critical thinking by examining our concepts critically, becoming more aware of the way individual concepts help us or hurt us, limit us or free us.

Even aspects of ourselves that are distinct from thinking are heavily influenced by our concepts. Desires, for instance: If you like something, or hate it—a person, a movie, a subject in school, a kind of car—the liking or the hating is not itself an instance of thinking. Rather, the liking or hating is influenced by the concepts you use in your thinking. It is only recently that anyone thought suntans were beautiful, that beaches were a desirable place to spend a vacation, that thinness in men and women was attractive, that wilderness held value, that toleration was a virtue, that democracy was workable, that it was unhealthy to be a caretaker in a relationship. Our standard concepts for each of these key terms has changed, becoming strikingly more positive or negative. The concepts may well change again. It can be liberating to step out of the fads that come and go with respect to what is desirable. Re-examining the concepts you have of the things you desire will help you rise above the fads.

Similarly, your concepts have an immense influence on what you are afraid of and what brings you joy. If you are afraid of the dark, afraid of math, or even afraid of dying—these are not universal fears. There are many people, not very different from you, who don't share these fears. Some people feel safe in the dark, delight in math (even if they are not very good at it), and find peace and acceptance in contemplating death. We fear things in part because of the concepts we have of those things, because of how we classify them and think about them.

Emotions are not really under our direct control, though how we act on those emotions often is. Many of the ways people try to gain direct control over their emotions actually hurt. If you are afraid of speaking in public, for example, but feel you shouldn't be afraid of it, you can try to suppress the fear. Maybe you can even force yourself to speak in public, or pretend to yourself that you are not afraid of it. You can reason as follows: "It doesn't make sense to feel fearful of speaking in public. There's really nothing to be afraid of. Therefore, I am not afraid of speaking in public." This is called *denial*. Denial is when you keep yourself from seeing something you know is true. The classic case is alcoholics who refuse to see that they are alcoholics. Many people confuse denial of this sort with being rational. Neither suppression nor denial is very healthy. Neither is very effective either, at least not in the long run. Both have high psychological costs.

Though our emotions are not under our direct control, we can indirectly affect them by addressing our concepts. You can work on

Many people automatically assume that bravery is good. But here are some possible examples where bravery makes a situation worse, where being brave does damage:

- Someone who is brave but a Nazi

- A sports figure who bravely plays despite a serious injury

- Criminals who bravely risk their lives in committing their crimes

- Achilles, the hero of *The Iliad*. Did his bravery accomplish what you would call worthwhile purposes?

Plato would say that these examples are not part of the concept of bravery at all. How might someone believe that?

In your view, are these examples of bravery, or of something else? Why? If they are examples of bravery, would you admire the action in each case? Or would you say, "We would all be better off if these people were not brave?"

your concept of public speaking and try to understand why you see it as fearsome. You can admit and honor the fear that arises. You can investigate what its roots are, what associations you have with it that generate the fear, and build new associations. You can rethink the concept over time, and usually this will be effective in changing your reaction to it.

The Experience of Learning to Think Things Through

You may already be good at thinking critically. In some areas, you may be very good at it. In fact, in some areas you may be so good at critical thinking that it occurs naturally—you no longer even recognize it as good thinking. For example, suppose you are driving down a street and a ball bounces out in front of you from between parked cars. You instinctively put your foot on the brake; you instinctively look around, searching for the child who might dart out. Another example: There's a sudden accident in the cars ahead of you. To get out of the way, you instinctively pull to the right rather than to the left.

These *seem* instinctive, but they're not. You've *learned* to do these things by reflecting on likely consequences. You've internalized the critical thinking so well that it seems natural, instinctive. But these actions are still the product of critical thinking.

As you work your way through this book, you can be confident that your thinking skills will improve significantly. Of course, it's not enough *just* to read the book. You have to engage in the activities, try them out in this class, in other classes, and in your life outside school. If you *do* the critical thinking, your skills will improve.

The trouble is, you may not *feel* as if your skills are improving. The improvement is unlikely to be obvious. Many people have the opposite reaction. They feel they are getting worse at reasoning as they work through a course that emphasizes critical thinking.

That happens for a number of reasons. First, working through a disciplined process of critical thinking will slow your thinking down. A problem that you once effortlessly thought your way through will now take much longer. You will have to focus on all the parts of the thinking that you previously took for granted.

Second, questions will start to arise for you where none arose before. "Am I being clear?" "Is this really an implication?" "Maybe I'm jumping to a conclusion here." "How can I check on this?" Questions are a sign of growth, of opening to new ways of thinking. But we often believe that questions are a sign of *not* understanding, that it is better to have no questions at all. Critical thinking lives in questions.

Third, the reflectiveness of critical thinking can cause you to start second-guessing yourself, especially at the beginning, or when you are feeling down on yourself. Before, you might have confidently asserted an answer; now, however, you might reflect, "Wait a minute, maybe I'm jumping to a conclusion here," or, "Is this really an implication of this author's position? Maybe I'm being unduly influenced by the fact that I disagree with her."

Fourth, some of your certainty about things can be a bluff to cover up the threatening fact that you really don't know, or don't know for sure. The main person you are bluffing may be yourself. Studying how to think critically often calls your bluff. You start asking, "What assumptions does my automatic response rest on?"

Finally, as Michael Scriven explained in a classic text on reasoning, if you are a swimmer or a tennis player and you start studying with a professional coach, you'll find that you have to change many of the ways you do things, unlearning certain moves and learning others. This will feel awkward, and it will slow you down—at first. But that slowing down is really the only way to build up proficiency and reliable speed. "Speed builds slowly."[4]

Here is a list of reactions many people have to studying critical thinking. You should not be surprised, or troubled, by experiencing many of them. (In fact, as a teacher I would be troubled if you experienced none of them.)

- Difficulty applying critical-thinking terms in practice
- Not being able to tell if you have applied them correctly
- Becoming very concerned with how concepts overlap
- Becoming confused about things that seemed clear before
- Persistently doubting that you will ever improve
- Having initial confidence in an answer, followed by nagging doubt
- Feeling that your teachers are not teaching enough because they generate more questions than answers

Again, when trying to learn to think critically, what's important is to engage in the activities of critical thinking, including getting feedback, and to be open to how they can enrich your life.

Getting Started: Clarifying with SEE-I

As we have seen, critical thinking begins with asking the questions you need to ask. Asking questions is a way of starting to get clearer: by formulating questions you are focusing your mind on what you need to address. In general, a good way to begin any critical-thinking process is by *clarifying*, by making things clearer.

A very useful process for clarifying almost anything is called **SEE-I**. This book contains many critical-thinking processes that accomplish far more than you would ever expect at first glance, and SEE-I is one of them. The letters stand for four steps that help make whatever you are working on clearer:

S: State it

E. Elaborate [explain it more fully, in your own words]

E. Exemplify [give a good example]

I. Illustrate [give an illustration: maybe a metaphor, a simile, an analogy, a diagram, a concept map, and so forth]

Statement

To **state** something is, essentially, to say it briefly, clearly, and as precisely as possible. Sometimes it means constructing a good definition, but it can also mean stating the thesis of a chapter by trying to capture the heart of what the chapter is saying in a single, clear, well-formulated sentence.

Elaboration

To **elaborate** on something is to expand on it, to explain it in your own words, at greater length, so that the reader gets more of the fullness of what is meant. For instance, I can **state** the law of conservation of energy; I can then **elaborate** on it, explaining it in more depth, in greater detail, spelling out what it is saying. You can begin your elaboration by saying, "In other words, ..."

Exemplification

Here, the goal is to give a good **example**—not just any example, but a well-chosen one, one that will clarify for yourself or for a reader what you mean. Usually, it should be your own original example, not one from the book or the teacher, and it should fit well with your statement and elaboration. Thus, I might try to clarify the concept of *falling in love*: first I would try to **state** in a sentence what *falling in love* is; then I would **elaborate** on it; and then I would give a good **example** of falling in love, one that the reader can connect with. (Romeo and Juliet come to mind, but it could be a personal example as well.) You can begin your exemplification by saying, "For example, ..."

Illustration

An illustration is literally a picture (as in "an illustrated book"). To clarify something, it helps to give readers something they can picture in their minds. Sometimes, it can be an actual picture (Figure 5.2 on page 114 of this book is a visual illustration of the process of critical thinking). In some cases, it can also be a graph, a diagram, or a concept map. More often, your illustration will be a picture in words: an analogy, simile or metaphor that captures the meaning. For instance, Rush Cosgrove was clarifying the concept of *civil disobedience*. He stated his definition of it in a sentence; then he elaborated on it; and then he gave a good example of civil disobedience. (His example was Rosa Parks refusing to sit in the back of the bus.) Then he gave an **illustration**: He said that civil disobedience was like being a cliff at the edge of the ocean—the waves crash against it, but the cliff remains there. To me, that illustration captures vividly what Cosgrove means by *civil disobedience*. You can begin your illustration by saying, "It's like... ."

There are two aspects of clarifying something. The first is getting clear in your own mind; the second is communicating clearly to

When students are assigned a five-page paper to write, they often have difficulty "filling up" the five pages. (Teachers are often amazed by this because teachers usually have the opposite problem: they have difficulty "cutting down" what they want to say to five pages.) Using SEE-I gives you a way to "fill up" those pages—but without just adding filler. With every major point you are making in your paper, you can state it, elaborate on it, give examples, and top it off with an illustration that conveys the point. This will "fill up" your paper with writing that is clear and directly relevant to the development of your paper (see pages 111–112).

others, so that they understand you well. SEE-I works well for both of them. You can improve your writing in a major way by taking each main idea and developing it in your paper with an SEE-I. The result, with practice, can be a smooth flow of richly understood and well-communicated ideas. SEE-I can make both your thinking and your writing dramatically better. It is also a way of testing your understanding of what you learn (and is thus a valuable way to study for exams). If you can accurately S, E, E, then I a concept or a principle in a course, it means you almost certainly have a good grasp of it, that you understand it to a much greater degree than if you are merely able to state it. Similarly, SEE-I is a method your teacher may use to test your understanding, to assess how clear you are about concepts and issues in the course.

The Flexibility of SEE-I

All of the critical-thinking processes in this book are flexible and adaptable. They can be shaped to a great variety of circumstances that call for critical thinking. Critical thinking is seldom simply a linear activity. That is true for SEE-I also: it is not a rigid process. For instance:

- Though the idea is to go step by step—*first* state, *then* elaborate, *then* give an example, *then* illustrate—you don't simply finish one step and then you're done with it. You will find that as you *elaborate*, you will often need to revise the *statement* you formulated in step one. Similarly, both your example and your illustration may cause you to refine or even change your mind about the earlier steps.

- An ideal clarifying statement is a single, clear, well-formulated sentence. But in some cases it may take two. Similarly, you will usually elaborate in one or two paragraphs—but with complex ideas, more elaboration than that may be needed. The point is not really *how long*—the point is to capture the *essence* in a **statement**, and to explain it in its *fullness* in an **elaboration**.

- Sometimes you can skip the illustration-step with very little loss. Often, though, a striking illustration will make the subject suddenly come into focus. It allows your creativity to come forward.

- In exemplification, you give an example. But sometimes what really clarifies the issue is to give both an example and a **contrasting example**. Thus, with civil disobedience, I can say that Rosa Parks is an example of it, but that cheating on my income tax in order to protest tax laws is *not* an example—it is doing something self-serving under the guise of civil disobedience.

- Much of the time, the statement-part of your SEE-I will be your own formulation, a definition or thesis statement that you yourself construct. But sometimes it is beneficial to take the statement-step from some authoritative source, such as your teacher or the textbook. You then clarify your understanding of that statement in your elaboration, give a good example of your own, and an illustration that conveys it well. Thus an Anatomy and Physiology text gives a definition of "anatomy" as "the study of internal and external structures of the body and the physical relationships among body parts."[5] Writing out this statement does not, of course, show that I grasp what anatomy is, or how it is different from physiology. But I can clarify my understanding of it in my own mind, and convey that understanding accurately to a reader, by elaborating on that definition in a paragraph or two, by giving a good example of an anatomical structure (and maybe a contrasting example of a non-anatomical process), and by giving an apt illustration of anatomy.

SEE-I IN THIS BOOK

STATE

A **statement** of what *critical thinking* is can be found on pages 79–80. In fact, there are three statements of it there.

ELABORATE

Pages 81–82 are an **elaboration** of what *critical thinking* is. Pages 83–90 are another elaboration.

(*continued*)

SEE-I IN THIS BOOK (*Continued*)
EXEMPLIFY

There are many **examples** of *critical thinking* in this book. One is on a reasonable way to deal with math anxiety on page 86; another is reasoning out the fairness issue on page 88. More extended examples are Chris's analysis of marriage (pages 149–153) and the analysis of the logic of earth sciences (pages 236–237). Other examples will come from you: Any of the outcomes listed at the end of any chapter in this book are examples of critical thinking. Some **contrasting examples** (examples of *not* thinking critically) are also found throughout this book: for instance, the bulleted list on page 87.

ILLUSTRATE

There are several **illustrations** of critical thinking in this book. A picture of critical thinking is given on page 114; a visualization of thinking through the elements of reasoning is given on pages 141–142. But I could also say, as an illustration, that critical thinking is like a pair of binoculars: it allows you to get up close, explore detail, put what you see in context, and understand more of what you are seeing. That is an analogy. It is not an example of critical thinking; it is something that critical thinking is being compared to. Another illustration: when people give me a ride someplace in their car, or if I follow GPS instructions, even if I pay close attention I usually cannot find my way on my own next time. If on the other hand, I figure out my own way there, maybe using a map, I can almost effortlessly retrace my path every time. It stays with me indelibly. The illustration: critical thinking is like figuring out your own way there.

Critical-Thinking Template

Here is a simple critical-thinking template, which can be applied in any area where you and others are trying to think things through:

- ■ Find four or five other people who are also trying to think critically about this area. (This can be done in person or on-line.)

- Figure out the three most central organizing concepts or ideas that underlie the area. (For example, the three main concepts in a chapter you are studying for this course.)
- Begin with writing an SEE-I: State, elaborate, give an example of, and illustrate each of the three concepts.
- Next, write a paragraph or so explaining how the concepts fit together, how they operate in the world, in your life, in the subject matter. Duplicate both pieces of writing so that everyone has a copy. (It is important that your responses be written, even if they are just jotted down. Written responses are concrete and allow you to confront your thoughts in black and white.)
- Critique one another's thinking. (Remember that critiquing is not the same as criticizing or finding fault.) In the critique,
- Focus on the elements from Chapter 6. Does the writer specify the purpose behind the concepts? Identify key assumptions? Look for consequences, for alternatives? and so on.

An Overview of the Book That Lies Ahead

Here is the basic model of this text, in a nutshell.

When people engage in critical thinking, they start off with some question. They try to answer it by reasoning their way through it.

1. **There are elements of reasoning.** The elements are the basic building blocks of reasoning or thinking. *Assumption* is an element. When people reason things out, they make assumptions. So one way to examine their reasoning is to focus on that element of their reasoning: *assumption*. We can ask, "What assumptions are they making?" (The elements are explained in Chapter 6.)

    So if the question is Q, we can picture the reasoning process thus far as shown in Figure 5.1.

2. **There are also standards of reasoning.** They can also be called "standards of critical thinking." These standards determine whether people are reasoning through the question well or not. *Accuracy* is an example of a standard. So one way to examine how well they have reasoned it out is to focus on that standard of reasoning: *accuracy*. We can ask, "Are the assumptions they have made accurate?" You can picture the standards as a set of filters as shown in Figure 5.2. They are used to filter out reasoning that doesn't meet the standards.

FIGURE 5.1   *The process of reasoning.*

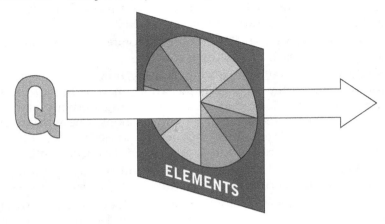

3. Suppose the question being addressed is one **related to the discipline or field you are studying**. Maybe it is a question your teacher has assigned; maybe it's from the textbook in the subject; maybe it's your own question.

There are ways of thinking that lie at the heart of the discipline you are studying. These include fundamental and powerful concepts, and central questions of the discipline. Disciplines are not bits and pieces; they are not assemblages of facts. Instead, there is a logic to thinking in each discipline. For example, in biology, the goal is to think biologically, to think the way a biologist thinks. In history, the goal is to think historically.

The concepts will differ from field to field. *Social patterns* is an example of a fundamental and powerful concept in sociology. So one way to examine how well people have reasoned out a question in the discipline of sociology is to focus on that fundamental and powerful concept: *social patterns*. We can ask, "Have they drawn conclusions,

FIGURE 5.2   *The process of critical thinking: reasoning through the elements and standards.*

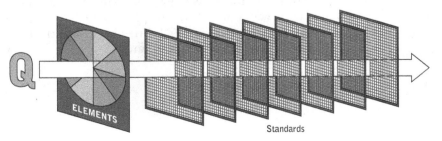

FIGURE 5.3   *The process of critical thinking in a discipline.*

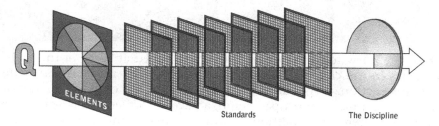

accurate conclusions, in terms of what we know about social patterns?" (Critical thinking in a discipline is explained in Chapter 10.)

You can picture the discipline as a lens or set of lenses through which people reason. Figure 5.3 gives us a full picture.

Some Outcomes

At the end of this chapter . . .

1. You should be able to run your finger slowly down the table of contents and identify the main concepts of Chapter 5:
   - reflective thinking; reasonable thinking
   - misconceptions about critical thinking
   - the role of emotions in critical thinking
   - impediments to thinking more critically
   - and so on

2. With the book closed, you should be able to state, elaborate, exemplify and illustrate each of these concepts, using examples from your own life, learning and experiences. You should be able to give contrasting examples as well (e.g., of unreflective thinking, or of a mistaken idea of the role of emotions in critical thinking).

3. You should be asking more questions—about your thinking, about the discipline you are studying, about everything. You should also be reflecting more on your reasoning.

4. You should be able to identify which aspects of critical thinking are getting clearer for you and which are still unclear.

You should not expect to achieve the outcomes listed above in a way that is perfect. But you can expect to be improving in them, to find them increasing in your behavior. Not all of these will be directly observable by your teacher. You yourself may often not notice them. Changes in critical-thinking abilities are usually gradual and subtle.

Ideas for Writing

Here are a few ideas for writing. They are aimed at some of the main themes in the chapter. There is a lot of flexibility in what you write in this section. Depending on what you decide or your instructor assigns, you may write a paragraph, a page, or something larger. (If it's a deeply interesting question to you, you may want to consider pursuing that question in your later research and education, possibly even becoming a professional who focuses in that area.) The writing may be for a take-home assignment, for a term paper, or something you write in your journal. Your teacher may assign some of these ideas (or similar ones) to write on, but you might also choose to write about some of them on your own. Also, after you've read the chapter, you may want to construct some ideas to write about that interest you personally. Since this is the work of critical thinking, explain your ideas in enough detail for a reader to understand you well.

1. In your best judgment, what role should questions play in the way people live their day-to-day lives? What role should they play in school? What role do they play in learning a discipline?

2. Pick one emotion to reflect on (anger, for instance). State what that emotion is, elaborate on it, and give a good example of it. Then explore in writing how that emotion interacts with critical thinking. When might it help, and when might it hurt?

3. What are some widespread misconceptions people have about critical thinking? How are they misconceptions?

4. Suppose there is a centrally important idea in one of your courses, and many people in the course do not understand the idea well enough to be able to SEE-I it. Is it possible for them still to get a good test grade on a question about that idea? If your answer to that is "Yes," the next question is: *Should* it be possible? Should education work that way? Or should good grades be achievable only to the extent that the person actually understands the idea?

5. Near the end of this book (pages 351–352), some critical-thinking character traits are described briefly. Even this early, though, you should feel your *intellectual perseverance* being challenged: there is a lot to revise in your thinking. In your judgment, to

what extent is intellectual perseverance essential for becoming better at critical thinking?

6. Create your own ideas for writing about an aspect of Chapter 5.

Tell Your Story

The "Tell Your Story" section of each chapter asks you to reflect on your personal history, especially with respect to aspects of critical thinking that have been involved in your life long before you took this course. The kind of thinking you do is strongly influenced by your life so far—the people you've associated with, your family, the values you've grown up with, the activities you've grown to like, and so forth. Your personal history, "your story," also influences the way you do critical thinking, the aspects of it you respond to or don't respond to. The idea behind this section, then, is to become more consciously aware of "your story" and how you've been shaped by it. That then lays a foundation for you to become more intellectually autonomous, to gain substantially more ability to shape your own present and future through critical thinking.

1. How do you feel about asking questions? (The answer may be different in different contexts.) What aspects of your personality or experiences have led you to feel that way? How comfortable are you with the idea of reasoning things out?

2. What has been your attitude toward the topic of critical thinking before you began this course? Where did you acquire that attitude? Do you think you are open to changing or modifying your attitude toward it?

3. Think of your life as a whole. How has your own native egocentrism changed in your life from childhood to the present?

4. What are some impediments to critical thinking that affect you? Reflect on how they have operated in your personal history.

5. When you have had an important decision to make in your life, how did you go about it? (Be sure not to describe here how you think you *should have* gone about it, but how you actually did.)

6. At this point, how open are you to critical thinking, to letting it become an important part of the way you live your life?

CHAPTER 5 Exercises

Some of the questions in this and later chapters call for the straightforward application of concepts from the text, but some are more than that. Some ask you to extend concepts in the text to new areas and then to think critically about these extensions. Some of the exercises are designed to teach new concepts. Answering them is part of learning to think critically.

Starred exercises (✱) are ones that have answers (or at least responses) at the back of the book. The responses there are not necessarily complete. Sometimes they are very sketchy. Often they simply point out one dimension it would be wise to consider when answering the question. Sometimes the starred response will contain additional questions as well.

5.1 What are some "good questions" you have about this course? Ask some good questions in each sense (ones that open up central areas and ones that you really want to know the answer to). What are some "bad questions" you could raise about the course (bad in the sense of superficial or bad in the sense that you don't really care about the answer)? Compare the questions you raise here with those you raised on page 86.

5.2 Envision a prospective employer who might hire you after graduation. What are the most important understandings he or she would want you to have learned from your college education? How does this relate to critical thinking?

✱5.3 Go back to the box on page 100 and look at the responses you gave about advertising, conformity, and driving. Now turn the question to yourself: To what extent are *you* influenced by advertising? To what extent do *you* conform to roles dictated by society? Are *you* a better-than-average driver?

5.4 Raising central questions. Here are some "facts" or alleged facts. Formulate good questions about each. Explain why each is a good question.

a. The U.S. is #1.

b. In 1996, "Dr. Ian Wilmut of the Roslin Institute in Edinburgh, Scotland, cloned the first adult mammal, the famous Dolly."[6]

c. "Art is not a luxury, as many people would have us believe, but an integral part of daily life.... We feel better about ourselves when we are in environments that are visually enriching and exciting."[7]

d. Smoking causes more deaths per year in the U.S. than alcohol, illegal drugs, murder, suicide, and AIDS all together.

e. Our stereotype of Neanderthals as "dim-witted, ugly people who are like apes" or "shambling cave people" comes from "mistaken studies of Neanderthal skeletons.... In fact, the Neanderthals were strong, robustly built humans.... There is every reason to believe that they were expert hunters and beings capable of considerable intellectual reasoning."[8]

5.5 Review the definition of denial and the examples given there. (Here's another standard example: Smokers who deny that smoking causes early death.) Identify three of your own examples of denial. (they can be from your own life or someone else's). Explain how denial can appear "rational" to the person engaged in it.

5.6 A woman goes for a haircut at a national hair-cutting chain. The hairdresser asks her what brand of shampoo she uses. He then puts some of her hairs under a microscope and shows her that there is a white film on the hairs. He recommends that she buy the store's brand of shampoo rather than the one she has been using.

What would be some good questions for her to ask herself about this situation?

5.7 **Group activity.** Individually write out some factors that you see as impediments to developing your own critical-thinking skills. Then, prioritize the list, choosing that factor that is the greatest impediment for you.

Sit in groups of four. Person A begins, explaining how that factor is an impediment for him or her and giving a good example. Proceed through person B, C, and D in the same way. Discuss the extent to which all four share the same impediments.

Then, the whole group should focus on Person A's impediment. Together, try to devise a practical strategy to counteract some of the influence that impediment has on critical thinking. Do the same for each group member.

5.8 Without looking back in the book, explain how SEE-I works to make your thinking clearer.

5.9 On page 80, you described a situation in which you thought through something critically, and another in which you did not think through something critically.

For each, what criteria did you use to decide? That is, what earmarks of the first situation told you that it was an example of good thinking? And what earmarks of the second situation told you that you did not think it through critically?

5.10 Look back at page 99, at the list of educational practices that the text says discourage critical thinking. Which of those practices seem "right" to you? That is, which of them seem to you to be a genuine way education should be? Why?

Then address this question: How could the practices listed actually get in the way of learning to think better within the discipline?

5.11 Name three things you have seen in movies that tend to give people a distorted view of the world. Discuss how they are misleading. Give an example of each.

Now, name three things you have seen in movies that have been seriously misleading for *you*. Explain briefly how they were misleading.

5.12 Watch a segment of a news program on TV or look at the news section of newspaper. Make a list of the news events reported there. Now make a list of events that could have been reported on, but weren't. In your best judgment, what criteria did the news compilers use to select the particular events they reported on?

5.13 It is one of those days when people seem to be driving erratically. Far more than usual, people are cutting you off, slamming on their brakes unexpectedly, or driving too slow. What are some good hypotheses to explain the way people are driving?

5.14 **In the discipline.** Look again at the impediments to critical thinking discussed in this chapter. (Eight major ones are listed.) Choose three and describe how they might be impediments for learning the discipline or subject matter of this course in a critical-thinking way.

5.15 In a book about how the sense of taste and smell work, the author explains that if you get sick and nauseated after eating a certain food, you will probably have an aversion to that food for a long time afterward. She notes that this is true even if the food you ate had nothing in fact to do with your getting sick. She says: "Intellectually knowing that it isn't a particular food that has made one sick does not override the instinct to avoid it .... The 'irrational' override of intellectual knowledge is based on our primeval past."[9] *Is* it "irrational?"

5.16 The topic of Chapter 6 is the elements of reasoning. Three of those elements are *conclusions*, *assumptions*, and *points of view*. Think of a difficult situation in your life, a problem in your relationship with someone, a decision you have to make, or something important about this course. Formulate three good questions about that situation, using each of the three elements listed. Then answer the questions, as well as you can.

5.17 Near the end of this book (pages 351–352), there is a brief discussion of some of the traits that are part of being a critical thinker. Read the descriptions of the traits there, and then focus on intellectual courage. Go deep: Look for a good example of how intellectual courage will be needed for you to think critically within the discipline you are studying, an example of when it will require courage for you to take ownership of some of the concepts or conclusions or points of view in the discipline. If you find a good example, describe it, including the role intellectual courage would play. If you can't find an example, write a paragraph considering the possibility that you are not taking the discipline seriously enough to believe the results.

5.18 **Work in pairs.** Each person chooses one written answer to an exercise in this chapter. (Alternatively, you could choose a written answer you gave to a critical-thinking problem about the discipline.)

Exchange papers with the person next to you. Each of you then writes comments on the reasoning in the other person's paper. Return the papers.

What can you learn about your paper from what the other person has said? What can you learn about what the other person values?

5.19 **Group work.** Use the template on pages 112–113 to address the topic of critical thinking as you understand it so far.

- Gather with four or five people to discuss the topic critically.
- In a discussion, figure out the three most central organizing concepts that underlie the conception of critical thinking being presented in this book. Try to come to consensus, but if you can't, use your own.
- Write out an SEE-I for each and a paragraph on how they work and fit together. Make duplicates for everyone.
- Each person critiques the responses of the others in the group. Focus on two standards: → (a) Are the responses clearly stated? → (b) Are they accurate?

DAILY PRACTICE
At incorporating critical thinking into your life
and your learning

Two of the difficulties in learning to think critically are dramatically different from one another. The first is how to do it: how to acquire the skills of asking good questions, reasoning your way through them, and believing the results of your reasoning. One way to look at this book is as a guide for developing those skills.

The second difficulty is deeper, harder to reckon with: as you learn *how* to do it, you actually have to *do* it. Even *after* you acquire skills, your tendency may well be to let them slide, to engage in them only when given a specific assignment.

A subsection of the exercises at the end of each chapter is designed to help you incorporate critical thinking into your life and learning in a more ongoing way. (Here, it's Exercises 5.20 through 5.24.) The key to these is to do them as often as possible, daily if you can, in small repeated intervals, rather than in a single big burst of effort. It's like daily exercise—only this is mental exercise. Thus, spending ten intense, focused minutes per day on practicing applying the critical-thinking concepts to your life and learning will be more effective than spending the same number of minutes all crowded into a single day.

5.20 **Engage with questions.** Spend some time just noticing questions, and then writing them down in your journal. You can notice (a) asked questions: ones you ask, other people ask, questions in print or on TV. Get a feel for the places and times where people ask questions and the kind of questions they ask. But notice also (b) the questions that are not asked: write down examples you come across where questions would have made a difference, where they should have been asked, but weren't. That includes places where you should have been asking questions.

5.21 **Engage with reasoning.** Again, this is an exercise in noticing, and then in critical writing about what you notice. In your journal, write down examples of good reasoning, bad reasoning, and non-reasoning that you come across. Again, these can be on TV, in ads, in what people say, in what you say, anywhere. The goal is to start using the concept of reasoning as you observe what's around you.

5.22 **Engage with believing the results.** Spend some time noticing and recording examples where people (including you) don't believe the results of their reasoning. These will usually be most apparent when people's actions are at odds with what they say they believe.

5.23 **Confront the impediments to critical thinking.** Over a period of a number of days (say, two per day for four days), practice noticing and overcoming the impediments. There are eight major ones mentioned in this chapter. Start with one of them (such as "Forming a picture of the world on the basis of the news media") and identify that kind of thinking when you come across it. But more than that, search out examples: watch the news, ponder how people internalize it and take it for normal; notice things that people say that reflect a view that's based on the news media. That means you will spend at least part of the day being on the alert for that impediment. That's a major part of the exercise. Keep a journal of the examples you find.

Then, do the same with another impediment.

5.24 **Engage with SEE-I.** As you work through this book, you will often be asked to write out an SEE-I. Extend this idea on your own. That is, when you are reading this book and you come across something that is important for critical thinking, state, elaborate, exemplify and illustrate that point *without* being asked to. Do this with other books also, in other courses as well as this one.

Then extend it farther. Use an SEE-I in some other class where there is written work. It can be a paper you are writing, an essay exam response, a presentation you are making. Try actually using the key words: after you state a point you are making, say "In other words ...," "For example ..." and "It's like ...." Notice how it makes your writing richer, more substantive, and clearer.

Chapter 6
The Elements of Reasoning

Critical thinking is not the same as thinking. Thinking is any activity in which you process things with your mind. So, forming a closely reasoned judgment after paying close attention to the evidence is an example of thinking. But so is jumping to a conclusion without considering any evidence. Similarly, weighing both sides of an issue and carefully checking for biases are both examples of thinking. But so is stubbornly holding on to prejudices and using stereotypes to judge people.

Although all four descriptions are examples of thinking and reasoning, only the first and third are examples of *critical* thinking. Two conditions are necessary for critical thinking. First, the thinking has to be reflective; it has to involve thinking-about-my-thinking. Second, this reflective thinking must meet high standards; it must be reflective reasoning that is done well. This chapter focuses on the elements of our thinking. When we reflect on our thinking, the elements are what we reflect *about*.

The Nuts and Bolts of Critical Thinking

There are at least two or three dozen basic concepts in critical thinking, maybe as many as 50. The most central concepts number around 20 and can be grouped into 8 categories. These are called the *elements of reasoning*.

Some of these concepts map out very different aspects of critical thinking; some overlap and are closely related to one another. Being able to think critically means being able to use these elements as tools in your thinking—being able to use them with sensitivity and the knowledge of how they interact. You can produce thinking that is reliable and trustworthy (though not infallible).

Let's look briefly at an example of an element: conclusions. This is a central concept of critical thinking. When we reason, we draw conclusions. We want to draw reasonable conclusions, not unreasonable ones. That is, we want to draw conclusions that are *accurate*, that have *sufficient* evidence to back them up, and that are *relevant* to the issue we are investigating. (Accuracy, sufficiency, and relevance are *standards* for using the element *conclusions*.)

Notice how thinking in terms of *conclusions* changes our thinking, makes it more reflective, more critical. It starts to lead us logically from step to step. Someone says something and you realize, "That's a conclusion." Then you are led to the next question, "Well, since it's a conclusion, what is it based on?" When you ask that, you don't necessarily mean to be skeptical. The conclusion might be based on excellent evidence. But calling it a conclusion brings home the idea that it's not an absolute, not a given. It is a result of human reasoning and based on some evidence, some information. Now, that leads you to two more questions: "Well, since it's a conclusion based on evidence, is that evidence accurate?" and "Is the evidence it's based on enough to support this conclusion?" Just thinking it out this far puts you deep in the process of critical thinking.

The Elements of Reasoning

Figure 6.1 is a chart of the elements of reasoning.[1] (Compare it to the overview in Figure 5.3 on page 115.) Each of the eight wedges shown in Figure 6.1 is an element of reasoning. Whenever we reason through anything, all eight are always present. Thus in any piece of reasoning, you can reflect on any or all of those eight and be assured of finding them there. In addition to the eight elements, the chart also contains *context* and *alternatives*. *Context* is the background to the reasoning rather than being literally an element in

FIGURE 6.1   *The circle of elements.*

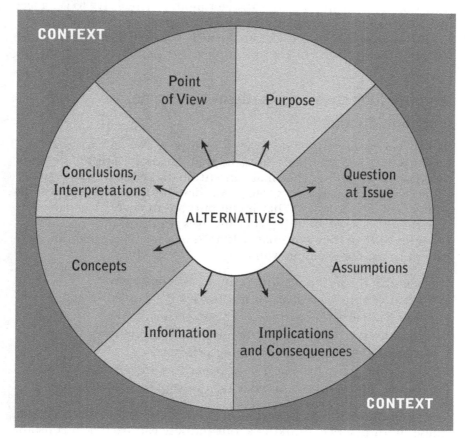

it, and *alternatives* encompass the different choices that could be made in the reasoning. Whenever we reason through anything, there is always a context in which the reasoning takes place, and there are alternatives that shape it.

The eight elements plus context and alternatives are called the 8+ elements. They are arranged in a circle, but they are not numbered because there is no required order. The order in which it is most beneficial to apply them depends on the question being addressed.

For each of the 8+ elements, this book will be saying roughly the same three things. It will first introduce the element and give you a sense of how that element is present in all our reasoning. Second, it will illustrate how identifying that element in many contexts is essential to thinking critically. Third, it will describe briefly a number of other critical-thinking activities that center on that element.

The initial description of each element is abstract, but the examples that follow will make the abstract more concrete. Try to get a feel for each element, for its flexibility and usefulness. Each of the elements is essential, and each can furnish you with insight into the heart of the subject you are reasoning about.

Purpose (objectives, goals, desired outcome, intention, function)

Whenever we reason, we do so with a purpose. People have goals and objectives in all their activities, in their reading, writing, decision making, in the things they make intentionally (books, theories, equations, cars, advertisements, etc.). All have purposes. Therefore, it's always relevant to ask, "What is the purpose in that?" You can identify the purpose of anything that involves reasoning.

Flexibility: Here is a small selection of areas where you can identify purpose. For example, you can:

- Identify the author's purpose in an assigned essay
- Identify your own goals in reading it
- Ask, "What is the purpose of this experiment?"
- Identify the purpose of all homework assignments
- Ask why this case study is being presented
- List your main goals in a term paper you are writing
- Figure out your goals in your relationship with a close friend

Notice how it is always relevant and central to ask questions like these. With practice, thinking about purpose can become a constant in your reasoning, and it will often bring insight.

Question: What is the *purpose* of the course or discipline you are studying?

All the examples just listed have to do with *identifying* a purpose in something. But the concept of purpose has other uses as well. You can not only identify your purpose:

→ You can keep it firmly in mind as you work through a whole host of details. That can be difficult to do—seeing the forest while looking at the trees.
→ You can question your purpose, or an author's purpose, asking whether it is worth achieving, and at what cost.
→ You can compare my goals to yours, or one textbook's goals to another's.

Thus, purpose serves as a center for asking a host of relevant, reflective questions, as well as for performing a large number of higher-order thinking activities.

Question at Issue (problem, topic, "the point," "Q at I")

Whenever we reason through something, we are trying to answer some question or address some problem. So in any act of reasoning, ask, "What is the question at issue? What is the problem being addressed?"

If *purpose* is what you are trying to accomplish, the question at issue (q at i) is the more specific question you are addressing to achieve that purpose. The purpose of this book, for example, is to guide people to think their way critically through a subject. By contrast, the question at issue is "What is the best way to help people accomplish that?" Since all reasoning is about some question, it's always relevant to ask what is the question being addressed.

Flexibility: Here are some areas where you can identify questions. For example, you can:

- Ask, "What is the question at issue this author is addressing?"
- Ask, "What, specifically, is the problem being addressed in this piece of art criticism?"
- Identify the major questions at issue in this math problem, in this marketing strategy, in this physical education exercise
- State the question at issue you are addressing in writing a term paper
- See the point of a cartoon

Questions are vital to all critical thinking. The central question of a course (see pages 246–249) is vital to critical thinking in a discipline.

Question: What are two important questions at issue in the course or discipline you are studying. What is a question about your life that the discipline may help you understand?

Notice that in any area that involves thinking, there is a question at issue, and you can identify it. In addition, after you *identify* a question at issue, you might have to go further:

→ You can ask, "What *other* questions at issue need to be addressed? What major questions have been left out?"
→ When you identify the question at issue in a term paper you are writing, also be mindful and stay focused on that question all the way through.

→ You can create a set of guideline questions on a topic or for reading a chapter.

→ A good pro-active question to ask is, "If I try to solve this problem this way, what further problems are likely to arise?"

All of these are rich ways to explore your thinking and the thinking of others, and all of them revolve around the element *question at issue*. As with each of the elements, to learn how to answer questions like these is to develop a range of higher-order thinking skills.

Assumptions (background theory, what is given or what is taken for granted, axioms)

Whenever you reason through something, you always have to begin somewhere. You can't "begin at the beginning" because there is no beginning. What you begin with are your assumptions, everything you take for granted when you think through something. Sometimes people can state their assumptions up front. More often, though, the most crucial assumptions we make are those that are unstated. In fact, it is often a major insight to identify assumptions an author may be unaware of even though they underlie his or her reasoning.

Any area where reasoning is taking place is an area where it is important to identify assumptions. If you are having an argument with your friends, maybe a heated argument, a good question to ask is, "What are their main assumptions?" But it is at least as important to ask, "What are my own assumptions?"—and to hold yourself to the same standards you apply to your friends.

If you're doing a writing assignment, it is crucial to ask, "What assumptions am I making about the person who will read this?" Whether you ask this question or not, you automatically do make assumptions about the reader. The critical-thinking question is not whether you *make* assumptions—we all do that all the time. The critical-thinking question is whether you are *aware* of the assumptions you're making. Only by becoming aware of your assumptions can you then evaluate them, so you can be more in charge of your thinking.

Flexibility: You can find (or identify) assumptions in anything that involves reasoning. For example, you can:

■ Identify the assumptions an author is making

■ Ask, "What is the background theory to keep in mind while formulating this political science questionnaire?"

■ Identify the assumptions behind the famous Milgram experiment

■ Describe your assumptions in designing a health plan

■ With your family, identify your mutual assumptions about how and when it is appropriate to express anger with one another

Question: What are two important assumptions in this course? If you take the discipline seriously, is there a personal assumption you make about your life that might be challenged?

So far we have been talking about *identifying* assumptions, but you can reflect critically on assumptions in any number of other ways:

→ You can evaluate people's assumptions in the light of evidence.

→ You can compare your assumptions to other people's.

→ You can put people's assumptions (including your own) in a larger context, asking how they are rooted in their upbringing or their cultural background.

→ You can seek out others with different assumptions as a way of becoming more aware of your own.

Assumptions, then, like all the elements, serve as a core idea around which to investigate a large number of critical-thinking questions.

Sometimes we are told, "Never make assumptions," "Don't assume anything," or "When you ASSUME, you make an ASS of U and ME. So don't assume."

But that advice makes no sense. We *have to* make assumptions. The speaker of the advice above is *assuming* that the hearers follow the play on words, that they care, that advice can help, and so on. It is *impossible* to avoid making assumptions.

We don't need to stop making assumptions: we need to check our assumptions to see if they are reasonable.

What are two areas of your life where you need to check your assumptions?

Implications and Consequences (what follows, costs and benefits)

Just as your reasoning has to begin somewhere, it also has to end somewhere. The area *beyond* where it ends constitutes the implications and consequences of your reasoning. To ask about the implications and consequences of a piece of reasoning is to ask, "What *follows* from it?" If you have a certain position on capital punishment, you need to ask, "What are the implications of that position?" That is, what further things must I adhere to if I hold that position? What further beliefs does this commit me to?

Flexibility: Consider a few of the many areas where you can identify implications and consequences. For example, you can:

- Identify the consequences, both positive and negative, of making this decision rather than that one
- Ask, "What are the costs and benefits of implementing this marketing strategy?"
- List the implications noted by the authors of a case study
- Identify the implications of creating a design, of not following a schedule, of consistently being late for classes

Question: What are two implications or consequences of the discipline you are studying? How might your learning in this course have implications and consequences in your life?

But to think critically, you need to become skillful at handling implications and consequences in ways that go beyond simply identifying them:

- In most real-world situations, consequences are seldom automatic, so you need to do something more subtle: not just *identify* consequences of an action, but *assess* the likelihood of various possible consequences, few of which are certain.
- Because many decisions have both a plus-side and a minus-side, you need to be able to weigh the costs and benefits of decisions.
- You sometimes have to accept the unwelcome implications of your positions.

Focusing on the element of *implications and consequences* allows you to see aspects of situations and thought processes that, previously, you saw only occasionally, in a hit-or-miss sort of way. This element allows you to focus on something that is one of the keys to reasoning well, to taking charge of your thinking.

Each of the elements in fact functions in this way. As you get better at internalizing them and using them, they will change how you

---

CRITICAL WRITING: SEE-I.

You have just read through sections on four of the elements of reasoning (purpose, question at issue, assumptions, implications and consequences). Close your book. For each element, write out an SEE-I: state, elaborate, give a good example, and illustrate it.

think about your life as well as about the subject matter you are studying in school.

Information (data, evidence, observations)

Whenever you reason, you use information. Therefore, it always makes sense to ask, "What information is relevant to this issue?" You might ask, "What information do I have, and what information do I not have, but *need*?"

Flexibility: Here is a sample of ways you can look for information. For example, you can:

- Identify the information the author of an article supplies and the information the author omits
- List the data an experiment yields
- Ask, "What evidence do I have to back up my claim?"
- Describe what you observe about these cells in the microscope
- Identify the main observations you've made about the children in this special education setting

Question: What are the main sources you will use to gather information in this course or discipline? What is another reliable source you *could* use (but won't)?

Notice that people use information even when they reason badly through an issue. People who draw prejudiced conclusions often base their reasoning on incomplete or incorrect information. So you often need to do more than simply identify the information in a piece of reasoning:

→ You need to be able to evaluate both information and sources of information.
→ You need to distinguish information from your interpretation of that information.
→ You need to decide when you need more information to draw a reasonable conclusion.
→ You can learn how to find other reliable pieces of information on a topic.
→ You can organize information in a coherent way, and present it clearly.

Information is an essential element of reasoning. But information by itself is seldom enough to decide important issues. We need the other elements of reasoning just as much. If you know some information, but you don't know its implications, you can be seriously misled even by the facts. If you know some information, but you don't know the questions at issue that the information is relevant to, then the information just floats in your memory, like pieces of trivia.

Concepts (organizing ideas, categories)

All reasoning exists in terms of concepts. If you are reasoning about democracy in America, you have a concept of *democracy* that is operative in your thinking. It is part of being reflective to ask, "What is my concept of *democracy*? What is my understanding of that term?" If you are trying to figure out whether an office is running efficiently, it helps to step back from that question and ask, "What is my concept of *efficiency* here? What earmarks do I use to decide whether an office is running efficiently?"

The same is true with less familiar concepts like real numbers, or cognitive dissonance, or iambic pentameter. A major goal of courses in a field is to help students grasp its most important concepts. Teachers and texts often try to accomplish this by using definitions. Thus an environmental science text defines *biotic potential* as "Reproductive capacity—The potential of a species for increasing its population and/or distribution."[2] But it's important to realize that the definition is a means to an end, not an end in itself. To grasp it, you must understand both how a species increases its population or distribution, and how that increase is limited by factors such as food, water, predation, and disease. Thus a good question to ask yourself about important but unfamiliar terms is, "What is my *understanding* of the concept that term represents?"

One helpful way to look at concepts is to describe them using a word or a term rather than a sentence. Thus *honesty* is a concept, whereas "Honesty is the best policy" is an assumption rather than a concept. The *Treaty of Versailles* is a concept (of course, it is also a document), whereas "The Treaty of Versailles formed the peace terms of World War I" is a piece of information rather than a concept. Why is that important? Because that difference is the feature that allows concepts to be so versatile, to be usable in a wide variety of contexts. You can use the concept of honesty or the Treaty of Versailles to think through hundreds of important problems. The sentences containing these concepts, however, are far more specific and therefore usable in a much more limited set of contexts.

It is a considerable skill to learn to identify the main concepts in our reasoning. It is very similar to identifying assumptions, and it is difficult in much the same way. Just as we tend to make unexamined assumptions, we use unexamined concepts also. If I have the inner conviction that I've been treated unfairly, it doesn't often lead me to ask, "What is my concept of fairness? What do I mean when I classify this action as unfair?" For example, I can feel an action to be unfair simply when I've been hurt by it. If I don't then go on to explore the concept of fairness that is at work in my reaction, I may continue to draw the conclusion that I've been unfairly treated even when it is just bad luck.

Flexibility: Consider some areas where you can identify *concepts*. For example, you can:

- Identify the concepts that an argument turns on
- List the main concepts in a scientific theory
- Spell out the key concepts that define historical or artistic epochs
- Identify the most fundamental and powerful concepts in the discipline you are studying (see pages 241–244)
- Identify your concept of being a loving father, mother, daughter, son, spouse

Question: What are three main concepts or organizing ideas in this course or discipline? How might one of these concepts give you insight into your life?

In addition to identifying concepts,

→ You can refine your concepts.
→ You can compare and contrast different concepts.
→ You can amend your concepts in response to new situations.
→ You can create concepts to cover new cases.

Notice again that concepts are always present in everyone's thinking. Every single thought you have is guided by concepts. The question for the critical thinker, then, is not whether you are using concepts, but whether you are aware of the concepts you're using.

Conclusions, Interpretations (inferences, solutions, decisions arrived at)

To think about the world you live in is to interpret it, to draw conclusions about it. So it's always relevant to ask, "How are you interpreting this?" "What conclusions are being drawn?"

Flexibility: There are conclusions to be found in all reasoning. For example, you can:

- Identify your interpretation of this situation, this poem, this philosophical issue, this equation, this anything
- Clearly state the conclusion of an argument you are making

■ Ask, "What is the inference this author is making?"
■ Figure out solutions (or partial solutions) to problems in your life

> **Question:** What are two major conclusions experts have come to in this discipline? If you took the subject matter in this course to heart, how might you interpret events in your life differently as a result?

It is often vitally important in critical thinking to distinguish information from someone's *interpretation* of that information. We see people's faces (information) and we interpret the look we see there as anger, maybe as anger at *us*. But we can easily be mistaken in that *conclusion*. The person may be feeling sad or tired rather than angry, or the person may indeed be angry but at something that has nothing to do with us. People who diagnose patients need to be constantly aware of the information they are receiving about the patient and also of their interpretation of that information. They then need to reflect on their interpretation and question whether alternative interpretations are more plausible.

In addition to *identifying* interpretations and conclusions, to be an effective critical thinker you need to develop other skills centering on this element:

→ You need to compare your interpretation of a situation to the interpretations given by others.

→ You need to decide which interpretations are most reasonable.

→ You need to be able to contextualize interpretations: the distinction between information and interpretation depends heavily on context. (For example, when a beginner looks through a microscope, the data might be the fuzzy orangish blob she sees, and the interpretation might be that it is a cell. For a more advanced practitioner, the data might be that she sees a cell, pure and simple, and the interpretation might be that the cell is beginning to undergo mitosis.)

→ You can group a set of interpretations to see how they all follow from an underlying background system. (For example, evolutionary biologists interpret the hibernation of bears, the day-long lifespan of a mayfly, or the shape and size of a palm frond— indeed, almost all plant and animal characteristics—in terms of how that characteristic increases the organism's chances at reproductive success.)

You are constantly drawing conclusions—so is everyone else— based on what you observe (information), on the beliefs you carry (assumptions), on what you think will happen (implications and consequences). Conceptualizing your own thoughts (and those of others) as conclusions gives you an insight into what those conclusions are based on.

Point of View (frame of reference, perspective)

Whenever we reason through something, we do so within some point of view. So it always makes sense to ask, "From what point of view am I addressing this issue?" Addressing the same question from a different point of view can produce a whole different set of purposes, assumptions, conclusions, and so on.

It is sometimes difficult to distinguish point of view from assumptions. Indeed, the two often overlap. For example, to have a conservative's point of view on a political issue is to make certain assumptions about the importance of promoting free enterprise and reducing the role of government. But point of view is often quite distinct from assumptions. For example, consider psychological point of view: if you write your name in the blanks below, you'll end up with an accurate (and sometimes profound) sentence:

_____ is at the *center* of my point of view. Everything I think about is from the point of view of _____'s mind.

But the uniqueness of your psychological point of view does not necessarily mean you making the assumption that your point of view is more valid than other people's.

At least one point of view is distinctly relevant to the course you are taking, and that is the point of view of the discipline itself. If it's a course in sociology, you will be expected to address most questions from a sociological point of view—not, usually, from a biological, religious, personal, business, or even an ethical point of view. These may be relevant, and they may well be extremely important. But they are different points of view from a purely sociological one. It is important to think about sociological findings from an ethical point of view, and in many cases, sociologists contend that an ethical perspective should in fact take priority over a sociological one. However, the two points of view are distinct, and you should be able to think in terms of either. Learning to think from the point of view of a discipline is one of the most valuable outcomes a course in the discipline can provide (see pages 252–254). The goal of a course is not simply to provide you with new facts to fit into your old point of view; it is to provide you with new perspectives, fresh and reputable points of view you can use to see things in a way you couldn't before.

That is not the end of the matter, however. Part of being a critical thinker is having the ability to bring to bear a variety of relevant points of view. This is addressed directly in multidisciplinary courses, which explicitly require thinking from the points of view of several disciplines. But identifying multidisciplinary points of view is valuable even within a course in a single discipline.

Flexibility: Consider places where it would be useful to identify points of view. For example, you can:

- Identify the points of view of different characters in a drama or story
- Identify the audience's point of view in a report you are writing
- Ask, "What is my teacher's point of view on absences, academic integrity, completing homework assignments?"
- Describe an argument from your spouse's (parent's, child's, friend's) perspective

Question: How would you briefly describe the point of view of the course or discipline you are studying? How could you use this course to enrich your personal point of view on the world?

In addition to identifying points of view, you need to develop other, related skills:

→ You can think within someone's point of view, applying it to new situations.

→ You can contrast the nursing point of view with the patient's point of view—also with the point of view of the doctor, the hospital, the patient's family, the insurance company. Some of these are always relevant. Others are relevant in one case but not in another.

→ A major critical-thinking skill to develop is the ability to evaluate points of view. Clearly it is not enough just to know what my point of view is. Bigots, for example, sometimes openly admit that they look at things from a bigoted point of view. (They sometimes even seem proud of it!) Obviously, that is not

CRITICAL WRITING: SEE-I.

Close your book. For each of the four elements you have just read about (information, concepts, conclusion, point of view), write out an SEE-I. This may reveal to you what you are clear and unclear about.

an example of critical thinking. Once I've identified a point of view on an issue, my own or anyone's, I need to evaluate how plausible it is, how well it fits the evidence, how biased it is.

Alternatives (other possibilities, options, choices)

Whenever you reason, there are alternatives. One of the great benefits of learning to think critically is that you gain the freedom of having alternatives to your normal ways of approaching things.

Flexibility: The search for alternatives applies to each of the elements we've discussed.

- If you have a purpose, ask, "What alternative purpose should I be trying to accomplish instead?" or "What other purpose can I accomplish *in addition*?"
- If you are reasoning through a question at issue, ask, "What other questions at issue should I be considering?"
- You can also ask, "What alternative assumptions could I make?" "What other sources of information could I consult?" and so forth, for each of the elements.

Each of the elements of reasoning is empowering, but thinking about the elements in terms of *alternatives* is empowering in a more direct way. *Thinking outside the box* means envisioning alternatives where before there seemed to be only the sides of the box. Getting in the habit of searching for alternatives allows us to see many potential paths ahead of us, where before there seemed to be only one. Both psychologically and practically, this is empowering:

- You can identify alternative ways of reasoning through experiments, health-care issues, information systems, math or business problems—through anything.

Question: What are two alternative paths or choices you could pursue within the course or discipline you are studying? What alternative choices in your life might this course open up for you?

For most people, simply *seeing* alternatives (where there seemed to be none before) opens paths for them, puts doors in the sides of the box. But, in addition to *identifying* alternatives:

- You need to be able to think your way down alternative possible paths, and then compare them before deciding which path is the best one to follow.
- You need to cultivate the ability to live with ambiguity, realizing there are multiple paths you could follow.

- You need to see that you can combine alternatives, that a third possibility might allow you to accomplish both of two seemingly irreconcilable courses of action.

For example, it often seems as though we have to choose: either fight for our own point of view or give in to the other person's. There are, however, usually alternatives that are different from either choice: discuss the issue; ask for what we need (rather than demanding it); compromise; find the good in the other person's point of view; take turns; seek arbitration; let the other person prevail, but do so out of generosity rather than giving in.

There is also something else to live with once you start taking alternatives seriously. In all major events in your life or in your thinking, there are likely to be alternative reasonable paths to follow, and each one will have its own consequences, both positive and negative. Therefore, it is unusual for any one path to accomplish all you wish for. If you choose to major in English, you give up other fields you may well be interested in. If you have a long-term relationship with X, even when you find a good deal of happiness, you automatically give up other possible futures. When doctors operate on patients unsuccessfully, the consciousness that other paths could have been followed can be a source of deep guilt (even if they chose the one that was most reasonable beforehand). It might be nice if we didn't feel guilt or regret or the loss of other directions our life might have taken, but that's not the way our minds work. We humans do have such feelings. And telling ourselves that we shouldn't feel what we in fact do feel is unreasonable—both because it's unproductive and because it involves denying reality. So:

→ We need to develop the ability—one that involves emotions in a strong way—to give up desired alternative paths, accepting that it's often important to grieve for paths we could not follow.

Context (setting, background)

We do not reason in a vacuum. Our reasoning always takes place in a context, and the question at issue always exists within that context. So it is always relevant to ask, "What is the context in which this reasoning is being done?"

Flexibility: It is beneficial to identify context in innumerable areas. For example, you can:

- Identify the personal histories that led writers to produce their work
- Identify the path that brought you to your present point of view
- Ask in what context a drama is being performed, an experiment is being carried out, a managerial decision is being made

■ Describe some of the different backgrounds of students in a diverse classroom

Question: What are two contexts that are relevant to understanding the course or discipline you are studying? How could you incorporate the findings of this discipline into the context of your life?

In addition to identifying the context, you may need to exercise other critical-thinking skills as well:

→ You can gather more information about the context.

→ You can compare the political backgrounds of John Adams and Thomas Jefferson.

→ You can spell out the context to someone who is unfamiliar with it.

→ You can ask, "How does the context of the writing make the writer *not* address certain questions?"

The following is a list of some of the main contexts that you may need to consider when reasoning through a particular question:

■ historical   ■ scientific

■ economic   ■ personal

■ cultural   ■ social

■ linguistic

This completes the quick survey of the 8+ elements from the circle shown in Figure 6.1. A major critical-thinking activity is to *go around the circle*: that is, to analyze a question, problem, or topic in terms of the 8+ elements and synthesize them to see the logic of how they fit together.

A Visualization

Here's a way to visualize the elements. It's only one of many you could construct yourself.

You are on a journey. Picture yourself walking down a path. It is the path of inquiry.

Ahead of you, where you can see it in the distance, is your *purpose*.

You think about why you are headed there, how far it will be, whether it will be worth it: your *questions at issue*.

Behind you, where you came from, are your *assumptions*.

Your mind-set, as you walk the path, is your *point of view*—it's the frame of reference you use to view the things around you.

The whole environment around you is the *context*.

As you walk, you gather *information* about the world—about the path ahead, about the forests and mountains you see, about the breeze you feel, about the friends you meet on the road, the beautiful places and the obstacles that lie ahead.

You gather that information by taking your impressions and classifying them according to the *concepts* you carry with you: "path," "mountain," "breeze," "friend." Some parts of the landscape you conceptualize as "places of beauty" or as "obstacles."

What will happen to you as you journey down the path can be pictured as *implications and consequences*: you will reach your goal, or you won't; you'll travel on afterward; you'll feel tired; you'll be excited; you'll encounter old friends.

You draw *conclusions* as you travel: you conclude you will reach your goal before nightfall, that the path will be longer than you assumed. You *interpret* your journey as an important one in your life.

You think of all the other paths you could be walking, the other goals you could be heading toward, the *alternatives* that still lie before you.

Three Additional Elements of Reasoning

Three other elements must be mentioned. They are not explicitly in the circle because they overlap categories. Still, they are important concepts in critical thinking.

Reasons

Reasoning can be defined as drawing conclusions on the basis of reasons. So, reasons are always present when someone is reasoning. It's crucially important to identify reasons: "What reasons do I have for my beliefs on this issue?" "What reasons does this author give for her conclusions?"

Reasons is a much broader category than the other elements of reasoning. Reasons can include pieces of *information, assumptions,* and *interpretations and conclusions* someone has come to on other grounds—almost any of the elements.

Claims (judgments)

People who teach courses specifically on critical thinking tend to emphasize the word *claim* a great deal, and it's a useful term to get in the habit of using. It is a very general word. It has roughly the same meaning as the term *judgment*. The terms *claim* and *judgment* overlap all the other elements. When I say, "This is my *purpose*," "This is the *question at issue*," "These are the *assumptions* I am making," and so on—all of these are *claims*. People can make claims about anything, and (except for questions and commands) most of what you read and hear consists of claims.

Aristotle says that humans are rational animals—that is, he makes the *claim* that humans are rational animals. Notice how explicitly calling it a claim—rather than just describing it as what Aristotle says—helps you think about it in a slightly different way. Calling it a claim holds it up before your mind as something to be wondered about: What reasons did Aristotle have for making that claim? Is it true that humans are rational animals?

To call something a claim does not necessarily call it into question, but it does leave the statement *open* to question. It reminds us that we can ask further questions about the evidence for believing the statement, how to interpret it, and what significance it has. That is why *claim* and *judgment* are such useful critical-thinking terms.

Run your finger down three or four pages in your textbook. Pick out some sentences that are important. (Don't pick incidental statements or mere examples the author is providing.) Describe those sentences to yourself as *facts*. Then describe those sentences to yourself as *claims*. When you describe them as claims, you should notice that you no longer take the statements as absolutes. What questions about those specific sentences arise in your mind when you call them claims?

Hypothesis

The term *hypothesis* is a central part of reasoning in the sciences. It does not play such a prominent role in other fields (though perhaps it should). A hypothesis is a type of assumption that I make or a conclusion that I draw, usually about the way a situation will turn out, but I hold it tentatively while waiting to see whether the situation will turn out the way I thought it would, waiting to see whether my hypothesis will be confirmed or disconfirmed, often by experimentation.

This is a fairly formal use of the term *hypothesis*, but actually we form hypotheses all the time in our thinking. We may not call them hypotheses, but we make predictions about how things will work out, and then we check to see if they do work out that way. If they do, then we usually conclude we were right; if they don't, we (at least sometimes) conclude we were wrong.

Being reflective means recognizing the hypotheses you are making. When you read a novel or watch a movie, you make predictions about what will happen and how characters will change. When you read a textbook attentively, you do the same kind of thing: you have a tentative awareness of where you think the book is heading. When you write, you make hypotheses about how the reader will understand what you are saying. So critical writers pay a lot of attention to feedback about their writing because that allows them to refine their writing in the light of whether their hypotheses were confirmed.

We are unaware of most of the hypotheses we make in our day-to-day living. A major part of becoming a critical thinker, however, is becoming aware of how you think. That is the process of reflection. Reflection helps you take control of your habitual patterns of thinking, rather than letting the habitual patterns control you. John Maynard Keynes said, "When somebody persuades me that I am wrong, I change my mind. What do *you* do?"

A Misleading Element: Facts

The term *fact* is not in the list of elements. Facts fall under information, but habitually using the word *fact* can do a disservice to critical thinking. Pieces of information we are very certain about we often call "facts." We believe they have been proved. These are usually pieces of information that seem to us to be completely unproblematic. For example, it's a fact that Neil Armstrong was the first person to walk on the moon, that smoking causes lung cancer, that Michelangelo sculpted the statue *David*, that Lee surrendered at Appomattox, that I like chocolate ice cream, that A got angry when B insulted him. There is nothing automatically uncritical about using the word *fact*, as long as we do it carefully.

Still, it's a term that tends to shut down inquiry rather than promoting it, and it tends to conceal problematic aspects of those claims that are labeled facts. In the previous list of facts, all are (as far as I know) true, but the second, fourth, and sixth facts have something problematic about them. Smoking does cause lung cancer, but calling it a "fact" may hide the *statistical* nature of the claim; it does not necessarily mean that everyone who smokes will get the disease, and therefore it cannot be refuted by giving examples of people who managed to smoke to a ripe old age. It means that a significant percentage of those who smoke will have a greater chance of developing lung cancer, and at an earlier age, than those who do not smoke. Similarly, it is true that Lee surrendered to Grant at Appomattox, but surrendered *what*? The statement, though true, is elliptical: It leaves out an important part and can easily be misleading. Many people draw the conclusion that Lee surrendered the *Confederacy*, but that is not true at all. Similarly, it may be a fact that A got angry when B insulted him. It may be true as far as it goes. However, it may be a *superficial* truth and therefore misleading. We often get angry at insults because the insult connects with some fear we have about ourselves, often a childhood fear. It may be more beneficial to A for him to realize that B's remark tapped into his own pre-existing fears in some way. But if A calls it a *fact*, he tends to close off further exploration of what is really going on inside him.

It is probably better to think of facts as pieces of information that we assume do not require questioning or clarification in the context of a particular discussion.

How to Analyze a Piece of Reasoning Using the Elements

The reasoning you are trying to understand may be written: an argument, a news story, a chapter from a textbook, a novel, a poem, a text message, almost anything. Or the person doing the reasoning may instead be speaking to you. It could be someone you know or someone giving a lecture. The person whose reasoning you are trying to understand may be you.

The point of analysis is to understand, in a fairly deep way, just what the person is saying, how he or she is reasoning through an issue.

The following questions are *guides* only. Sometimes you will have to be flexible and adapt a question to fit the piece of reasoning you are trying to understand. (For example, you may often have to change the singular to the plural, and vice versa. If the questions are phrased one way to understand an argument, you may have to ask them somewhat differently to apply them to a novel or a chapter in a text.) That flexibility is also part of learning to reason well. Sometimes you may need to do an analysis in greater depth and detail, or you may need to focus on different aspects of how the elements enter a piece of reasoning. So some further analysis questions are suggested in parentheses after the basic ones.

Going Around the Circle: The Basic Process of Analysis

1. What is the person's main *purpose* in this piece of reasoning? (Also, what other goals or objectives does the person hope to accomplish in this piece of reasoning?)

2. What is the key *question* or problem the person is addressing? (Also, what are two or three of the most important subsidiary questions at issue?)

3. What is the most important *information* the person is using to reason through this issue? (Also, what other information or data does the person need in this piece of reasoning?)

4. What are the person's major *conclusions*? How is the person *interpreting* this issue? (Also, how does the person answer the main question at issue? What solutions are being offered?)

5. What are the main *concepts* the reasoning depends on? (Also, how does the person understand those concepts? How do those concepts fit together in the person's reasoning?)

6. What are the main *assumptions* the person is making in this piece of reasoning? (Also, what are the crucial stated and unstated assumptions the author is making?)

7. What are the main *implications and consequences* of the person's reasoning? (Also, what are some of the unforeseen consequences of this line of reasoning?)

8. From what *point of view* is the person addressing this question? (Also, what other points of view are necessary to understand this piece of reasoning? What discipline's point of view is being used to address this issue? What other disciplines would help illuminate this reasoning?)

9. What is the *context* of the issue the person is addressing? (Also, what circumstances led up to the issue and to this person's reasoning? What is the background in the discipline [scientific, artistic, cultural, business, sociological, etc.] in which this issue is being addressed?)

10. What *alternatives* are there? (Also, what alternative answers could you reasonably give to the preceding questions? What alternatives are there to the person's reasoning?)

Working with the Elements: The Logic of Something

Becoming a critical thinker means becoming adept at using the elements explicitly and reflectively in your thinking. This involves being able to take a piece of reasoning, your own or someone else's, and analyze it using all 8+ elements from the circle in Figure 6.1. It may seem unrealistic to go through all 8+ elements with respect to every reasoning problem you encounter, but it's a good way to become more proficient in using the elements (and you will quickly get faster at it).

There is another benefit to analyzing a problem in terms of the 8+ elements. Going around the circle displays the *logic* of that problem. The elements, after all, are *parts* of a *whole*. You may notice that as you go around the circle, your responses to the different elements will gear together. Sometimes they will almost seem to repeat the same set of themes. Though the elements are valuable individually, they are even more valuable when you think through a question in terms of how they fit together. So going around the circle involves not just analysis but *synthesis* as well: not just breaking an issue down into its component parts, but also seeing it as an integrated whole.

Some things, however, do not have a logic to them. Their parts don't fit together to make a coherent whole. You can't figure such things out because there is no rhyme or reason to them. Maybe the best you can do in such cases is to memorize individual bits of information. People's first names are like that. You can't look at someone intently and then figure out that her first name is Janis. In cities and towns, street names may or may not have a logic. If Oak Street is followed by Main, that gives no clue as to what the next street is.

> Find two examples of topics that have no logic to them. Find two examples of topics that do have a logic to them.

There is no logic to it. Sometimes, however, there is a logic: if 24th Street is followed by 25th, it doesn't take much effort to figure out what the next street is likely to be. In that situation, street names have a logic.

Any reasoning topic has a logic to it, however. This will be especially important to grasp when it comes to analyzing the logic of a discipline (see pages 233–239). Going around the circle is versatile: it applies to any topic, question, or problem in the discipline. Indeed, a central part of understanding a field is developing the ability to think through topics like the following in a deep and thorough way:

- supply and demand
- how to prepare and give a speech
- plate tectonics
- what will happen as global warming continues
- the way the concept of "the frontier" has shaped Americans' view of their country.

Similarly, thinking critically about your personal life means that you think through topics like the following, grasping the logic of them:

- taking this course
- how fears get in the way of your personal growth
- the most effective way for you to study for exams
- why your boss repeatedly takes his anger out on you
- adolescence, gender, race.

In working through the elements, you may need to adapt the way a particular element fits in with the demands of the question being considered. In the previous lists, the items are described in different forms—questions, concepts, topics, incidents, fragments of a thought process—to emphasize how versatile the circle of elements is. There is no magic formula for how to apply the elements uniformly to any question that arises. Making that adaptation is also part of thinking critically.

Analyzing Positions You Disagree With

Sometimes you will be called on to analyze a position that you disagree with deeply. That's an important part of critical thinking because

Take some point of view you deeply disagree with:

- communism,   ■ capitalism
- al-Qaeda,   ■ patriotism
- atheism,   ■ religion
- conservatism,   ■ liberalism

Analyze it. Go around the circle. Be sure to analyze it in a fair-minded way.

Apply the three tests, especially the second one: An advocate of the point of view (a communist or whatever) should be able to say, "Yes, you have captured it well. That is exactly what I believe in."

before you can evaluate a position reasonably, you have to understand it accurately. Here are three quick tests of whether you have given an accurate, fair-minded analysis of a view you disagree with.

First, no words of evaluation should lurk beneath the surface of your analysis.

Second, a person who holds that position should be able to say, "Yes, you have captured it well. That is exactly what I believe in."

Third, a neutral critical-thinking observer, reading your analysis, should not be able to tell if you agree or disagree with the position. If anything, because you have been empathetic in your analysis, the observer's suspicion should be that you advocate the position (even though, in fact, you may disagree with it deeply).

Example: Thinking Through the Logic of Getting Married

Chris and Sean are considering getting married, and Chris tries to think through the question as deeply as possible. [The italicized remarks in brackets are a critical-thinking commentary on Chris's reasoning.]

Chris starts by asking questions based on each of the elements.

- What is the purpose of marriage?
- To live as full and as satisfying a life as possible, for both of us.

  [*Notice that this would not be everyone's purpose in getting married. Chris's response did not mention children, for example, and the purpose of marriage for many people includes children. Also, notice that Chris could have listed more purposes, not just that one.*]

- What is the main question at issue?
  - Should I marry Sean?
  - Should I marry Sean now?

  [*Chris could have asked other questions, and these might influence subsequent answers: Do I love Sean? How can I tell whether marrying Sean would help us live the happy and satisfying life I want? How can I tell this with good reason, not just an impression?*]

- What are the main assumptions I make about marriage?
  - That it's a commitment to monogamy.
  - That marriage is a lifelong commitment.

  [*This assumption leads Chris to identify a different kind of assumption:*]

  - That we will both grow older, and our looks will change.

  [*Chris is not going through the elements mechanically, without thinking, but as part of a process of genuinely thinking through the idea of marrying Sean. Therefore, Chris takes the time to notice an implication of the last assumption: That though how they look may*]

be important to both of them, it should not be the crucial factor
if marriage is a lifelong commitment and their looks will change
over time.]

- What are the main implications and consequences of marrying?
  - First, there is the implication already mentioned, that marriage should not be based too heavily on how we look.
  - There are many legal consequences of marrying someone.
  - Children may or may not be a consequence.

    [*This leads Chris to notice another question at issue: Should*
    Sean and I discuss our attitudes toward children (including, maybe,
    adopted children) before we address the question of marriage?]
  - There will probably be conflicts of interest in the future. In fact, there will probably be some serious conflicts of interest.
    → It would be especially good to have some psychological tools available to deal with these conflicts when they arise.

    [*Chris wonders if the statement about future conflicts of interest is*
    a consequence or an assumption, and decides that in a way it is both:
    The conflicts of interest themselves are a consequence; the claim there
    will be such conflicts of interest is an assumption.]
- What information do I have (or need to have) about marrying Sean?
  - I have a lot of information about myself: about my likes and dislikes, about my long-term goals, about how I see marriage, about my religious beliefs, about how I was raised.
  - I have a lot of information about Sean as well, but not nearly as much as I have about myself. fi Maybe we should talk about this.
  - I have heard that certain kinds of dysfunctionality run in families. My father was an alcoholic. I really don't know much about Sean's childhood. It would be a good idea to get more information about this so that we know how to deal with problems stemming from our backgrounds as they arise in our marriage.
  - I know I have a certain amount of fear about committing to marriage. → I assume Sean does too. → We should talk about this. We both need more information.
- What are the main concepts I use when I think about marriage?
  - Well, the main one is the concept of marriage itself. What is my idea of marriage? What is involved in being married for me? What is Sean's concept of marriage?

- What is my concept of *loving someone*? My concept of being *in love*? What do I understand by those terms and how they apply to us?

- Is *being a friend* part of being married to a person? What do I understand by being a friend?

- One thing I want with the person I marry is to share unconditional love. But what is unconditional love? Does that mean that I would love the person *no matter what*? That's an extremely broad commitment, and—once I start imagining possible scenarios—a scary prospect to me. Is it even possible to love people no matter what they do?

[*Concepts often influence our behavior below the level of awareness. That is why it's so important to identify the concepts that operate in us. Suppose Chris and Sean had radically different concepts of marriage and were unaware of this. One might have a concept of marriage as, for example, a union that links two whole families, while the other might think of it as being only between two individuals, with their families being completely irrelevant. Because of their different concepts, Sean's behavior with respect to their families might be completely inexplicable to Chris, and vice versa. Both may see their own behavior as entirely appropriate—and the other's behavior as entirely irresponsible.*]

- What conclusions should I draw? What interpretations am I using?

[*Chris has already come to a number of conclusions while reasoning out the elements so far: the importance of talking about their attitudes toward children, getting some information and tools for conflict resolution, and acknowledging the potential effects of having an alcoholic father. Chris may also be coming to a tentative conclusion (a hypothesis, maybe) that the concept of unconditional love is one that does not apply in marriage.*]

  - Whether to get married to Sean or not is the main conclusion I am trying to decide. But there are more specific conclusions and interpretations as well.

  - That Sean is a loving, caring, affectionate individual.

  [*Notice that Chris calls this an interpretation rather than information. Chris's information may be that Sean has acted in a loving, caring, affectionate way before marriage. This is often very different from being a loving, caring, affectionate individual.*]

  - That this is the right time for me to consider marriage seriously.

- ■ That our interests, personalities, and the way we view life are compatible.
- ■ What points of view should I consider?
  - ■ My own, of course: the point of view of someone who has had a certain kind of upbringing, in the society we live in, who has certain expectations and hopes about the future.
  - ■ Sean's.
  - ■ Are there male and female points of view on marriage? → I don't know. Maybe that's just a stereotype.
  - ■ Our families' points of view.
  - ■ Is it important for me to consider society's point of view, or a legal point of view, or a psychological point of view?

    [*It is important to consider other points of view if they are relevant, and if they are likely to give a person insight into the problem being reasoned out. This is often difficult to decide beforehand.*]
- ■ What alternatives are there?
  - ■ Continue as we are now.
  - ■ Decide that marriage is not in the cards for us.
  - ■ My Al-Anon book talks about not forcing solutions: "Instead of redoubling my effort, I can slow down and reassess the situation."[3] That seems reasonable under the circumstances. So we could defer the decision to the beginning of next year when some of the uncertainties in our lives will, I hope, be sorted out a little.
  - ■ Consciously decide to enter into some new relationship with one another. → Each of these brings up a host of new possibilities and new feelings as well. Those are all alternatives to the main question at issue I'm addressing. But there are also alternatives to the other elements I've just gone through:
  - ■ I've thought a lot about my concept of marriage, and the legal point of view just entered my mind. Does my concept of marriage automatically bring with it the idea of legality? → Could we have a relationship with one another that we would consider being married, even if it was not legally binding?
  - ■ An alternative source of information: I should buy a good book that deals with the decision to get married. I know I can't learn everything I need to know from a book, but I don't want to be afraid to consult books either, especially about such an important decision. I can probably learn some things I haven't considered at all. And all I stand to lose is a little time.

[Chris could also have considered alternative purposes, consequences, interpretations, and so on.]

- In what context is this question being addressed?
    - Well, it's a real context for me. It's not a problem in a textbook where filling in an answer merely results in a grade. This is my life I'm talking about. If I don't carefully consider the important parts of the decision to get married, it may have an impact on the rest of my life.
    - There is the context of where we are in our relationship, how long we've been together, our ages and backgrounds, the influence of friends, family, and society (and some influences I may not even be aware of).
    - I realize that the issue of same-sex marriage is one that is very serious to a great many people. I have put off considering it until now, maybe because I have such strong views about it. So does Chris. Still, it is part of the social, ethical and legal context in which we live, and it has consequences for how we feel about the institution of marriage.
- Should I have addressed context first, before I did any of the other elements?

    [Remember, there is no right order to apply the elements. The most useful order may vary from question to question. Many people have the experience that no matter which one they start with, it feels as if they should have done another one first. It often helps to describe the context at the beginning, so we can anchor the problem in its actual setting and not let it become an abstract puzzle.]

Context, purpose, and *question at issue* are often good places to start. So is *point of view,* for example when you are reasoning within the point of view of a particular discipline. But keep alternatives in mind as you go through each element. It is good to revisit alternatives at the end of your analysis to open up new insights you may have overlooked.

Trusting the Process

You may have a number of concerns as you finish Chapter 6, particularly if you have tried to work through the elements in the subject you are studying. You may be concerned with how the elements fit together. You may see that they sometimes overlap, that their application is not always completely clear, that what you thought was an *assumption* may be an *implication* or a *point of view* in another context. You may find yourself concluding from concerns like these that the elements are confusing. These are natural concerns. They are a part of many people's reactions.

A good thing to do is give the elements a chance to develop in you. Trust the process—maybe not completely, but give it a chance to take hold. The benefits start to come when you get familiar enough with the elements to use them in your day-to-day practice of thinking, both inside the course and out. That takes some time. Expect to feel some resistance inside you. Most of us have a strong tendency to continue down more familiar paths. It will probably feel unsafe to have your thinking process slowed and broken into parts. It will likely feel unsafe to face the multitude of questions and doubts that may arise as you go through this process.

Some Outcomes

At the end of this chapter . . .

1. You should be able to state, elaborate, exemplify, and illustrate what is meant by "the elements of reasoning" and "analysis."

2. You should be able to name most of the elements of reasoning without looking back at the list. (You should be able to do this not by having memorized them, but by seeing how they are involved in reasoning and then by using them in practice. A future outcome: By the end of the course they will start to become spontaneous parts of your thinking.)

3. Running your finger slowly around the Circle of Elements, you should be able to give a clear explanation of each of the elements.

4. You should be able to give your own examples of each element and to show how each can be used in different contexts.

5. You should be able to apply the elements to almost any question or problem. Your application will of course not be perfect. You should be able to apply some of the elements easily in some contexts; other elements, or other contexts, may be far more difficult.

6. At this point you should be alert to the elements. Thus, in your life, in the coming pages, and in the course you should be able to identify which elements are occurring ("Here the writer is drawing a conclusion").

7. You should be asking more questions about the elements.

8. You may be confused where before you didn't always even realize there was something to be confused about. (As paradoxical as it sounds, sometimes confusion indicates progress.)

9. Look back at the outcomes listed for Chapter 5 (page 115). They are not over and done with. You should be able to elaborate on them in a somewhat deeper way now because you can fit them in with the elements. You should also be able to give new examples.

Ideas for Writing

(General guidelines for "Ideas for Writing" are on page 116.) The elements of reasoning are the *parts* of thinking, and that gives them an almost unlimited applicability. Ideas for writing about them are also almost unlimited. Writing about them at this stage requires you not to be a perfectionist: your understanding and practical use of them are not as sharp as they will become. With that in mind, you can try writing about any **one of the elements** (for example, assumptions: How do assumptions work in people's lives or in disciplines?); about **inter-relations between pairs** of them (for example, How do the questions you ask shape the conclusions you come to? And how do the conclusions you come to shape the questions you ask?); about **how to transfer them** from one course to another; about **applying them** (or some of them) to life issues you will face (such as your own thinking about marriage or your choice of an area of study to pursue in school); about how developing your skills with them helps develop **critical-thinking character traits** (see pages 351–352); about **problems** you face in taking ownership of them.

Tell Your Story

(The idea behind "Tell Your Story" and some suggestions about responding to it are on page 117.) Think about and discuss your personal history—your story—in relation to the elements of reasoning. For example:

> **purpose**: How have your goals and purposes changed over the course of your life? What influenced you to take on those goals in the first place, and what influenced you to change the ones you have changed? How do you anticipate your goals changing in the future?

> **questions or problems**: Contrast the questions that were most on your mind five years ago with those that are most on your mind now. How have you changed? Or: What are some of the major problems you have faced, ones that may have shaped who you are today?

In a similar way, tell your story with respect to the main **assumptions** you have made in your life, to how you have gotten in touch with the **consequences** of your actions, and so forth. Telling your story in relation to the elements can give you an insight into your life you often cannot get any other way.

CHAPTER 6 Exercises

These beginning exercises will help you become familiar with going around the Circle of Elements.

6.1 Choose some problem or question you have. It can be in the field you're studying, but it may be better to begin with one from your personal life.

Think through each of the elements with respect to the problem or question you have chosen. Go around the circle as Chris did with respect to marrying Sean.

(It is best to begin with a problem that's familiar to you and not too difficult. The purpose is to become familiar with identifying the elements. Also, note any questions you have about how the elements apply.)

6.2 Go around the circle again. This time take a question from the field itself. Again choose one that you feel comfortable with; don't choose one that requires you to stretch too much in your thinking. The goal here is to become comfortable thinking with the elements. (After you are finished, again note any questions that arise in you about how the elements apply. Compare the questions with the ones you identified in Exercise 6.1.) Try to pinpoint areas where the elements are not clear to you.

6.3 Go around the circle again. This time choose a problem in the way you relate to the subject matter you're studying. For example, "Why am I studying anthropology?" "How does this course in communications fit into my life?"

The following exercises deal with individual elements rather than with going around the circle as a whole, but remember that the elements do not operate in isolation. Instead, they fit together to form the logic of the problem or question. (There will be more exercises on the elements when you are ready to apply them more directly to the field or discipline you are studying [Chapter 10] and to put them together with the standards of critical thinking, at the end of Chapter 5.) Each question in Exercises 6.4 through 6.13 is about one element. Each contains a list of topics, situations, excerpts, or questions. Identify that element in each of the items listed. (Your instructor may have you do some of these exercises as critical discussion in groups, rather than as individual written responses. If so, he or she may ask you to write a brief report on the discussion.)

6.4 Purpose.

    a. Identify the purpose of three important regular activities in your life.

    b. What is the purpose of Chapter 5 in your textbook?

    c. What are your instructor's goals for you in this class? Be specific.

    d. Try to identify an activity in your life where you do not entirely know your purpose.

    e. Pick out three activities you engage in regularly where you tend to lose sight of your purpose.

6.5 Question at issue.

    a. Identify the main problem in how you get along with someone you are close to.

    b. What is the question at issue in Chapter 6 of this critical-thinking text?

    c. What are three main problems experts are addressing in the field you are studying? (Though these may not be problems you will actually be studying, they will be problems at the cutting edge of the field.) If you don't know, describe a realistic way of finding out.

    d. Here is part of a table of contents for an art book[4]:

CHAPTER 6. SPACE

Geometric Projections 143

Scientific Perspective 144

Atmospheric Perspective 156

Space in French Impressionism 160

Cezanne's Perspective of Color 162

The Uncanny Space of Cubism 164

On the basis of this very limited amount of information, try to identify three major questions at issue to be addressed in the chapter.

e. Using only the table of contents, apply Exercise 6.5d to a chapter from a subject-matter book in this course.

6.6 Assumptions.

a. Identify assumptions you make about someone who is important in your life.

b. Identify assumptions that person makes about you (check with the person afterward).

c. Identify a theory that is important in the field you are studying. (Write an SEE-I for it.)

d. Try this exercise even if you know very little about economics. Identify two assumptions in this excerpt from an economics textbook:

> The concept of "needs" encourages all-or-nothing thinking. That's why economists prefer the concept of *demand*. Demand is a concept that relates *amounts people want to obtain to the sacrifices they must make to obtain these amounts.*[5]

e. Identify two assumptions from an important paragraph near the beginning of your textbook.

6.7 Implications and consequences.

a. Identify some implications and consequences of the syllabus for your course.

b. What are some implications and consequences of an important decision that is coming up for you?

c. Here are three claims from a psychology text: "Probably the best-known herbal remedy for memory is ginkgo . . . . Americans spend several hundred million dollars on it per year. Yet controlled studies comparing ginkgo with a placebo show that its effects on memory in normal individuals are minimal, even non-existent."[6] Use your best judgment to identify some important implications of that claim.

d. Choose three important sentences from your text. Identify the implications of each.

6.8 Information.

a. Focus on an important decision you need to make: what information do you have about it?

b. For the same decision, what information do you need?

c. Identify the five most important pieces of information from a chapter of your text (or some other reading). Describe how that information fits together.

d. Summarize and describe the subject-matter information you will need to do well in this course.

e. Describe a situation in your life where you made a bad decision because you lacked information that was readily available to you.

f. Describe the research (information gathering) it is appropriate for you to engage in as part of being in this course.

6.9 Concepts.

a. Focus on a relationship you have with someone, a relationship that has a specific name (e.g., sister, mother, friend, business partner, teammate). What is your concept of that relationship? (e.g., What is it to be someone's sister?)

b. Describe your concept of "learning the subject" in the discipline you are studying.

c. Think about the concept *animal*. That seems like a straightforward concept: We all know what an animal is. But consider this:

Until 2008, cockfighting was legal in Louisiana. In cockfighting, two roosters are placed in a ring. They violently peck and gouge one another until one dies. Onlookers cheer. Louisiana also has a long-standing law prohibiting cruelty to animals. Before 2008, the attorney general reconciled these two laws by ruling that cockfighting is permissible because roosters are not animals!

Of course that's ridiculous. Of course the attorney general knew that roosters are animals. What he ruled was that when lawmakers prohibited cruelty to animals, they did not intend for it to apply to roosters. So, roosters are not *legally* animals.

Your state has a law prohibiting cruelty to animals. What are some animals that you are legally allowed to kill with a painful death? So what is the concept of *animal*, legally, in your state?

d. Identify the three main concepts in Chapter 5 of your textbook.

6.10 Conclusions, interpretations.

a. Identify three conclusions you have drawn about the importance of critical thinking in classes.

b. In your book, find an example of an interpretation the author is giving. Describe the information that the interpretation is based on.

c. After some careful reflection, give an example of when you have seriously misinterpreted another person's behavior. What information did you base your interpretation on? How should you have interpreted that information?

d. A psychology experiment was performed to see when people would violate a cultural norm against littering. Robert Cialdini and his colleagues tested the conditions under which drivers would litter a parking lot:

> Specifically, when the experimenters had previously littered the parking lot with fliers, the majority of the drivers simply followed suit—probably thinking, "After all, if no one cares about the cleanliness of the parking lot, why should I?" Interestingly enough, people were much less likely to litter if there was one piece of litter on the ground nearby than if the parking lot was completely free of litter. The reason is that seeing one piece of litter reminds us of litter—and shows us that the vast majority of people are subscribing to that norm. If the parking lot is free of litter, most people probably do not even think about the norm and, therefore, will be more likely to litter mindlessly.[8]

What part of the excerpt is information, and what part of it is interpretation?

6.11 Point of view.

a. Describe the difference between your instructor's point of view on the subject matter of this course and your point of view on it.

b. Describe two prominent points of view within the discipline you are studying.

c. The editors of an anthology in social ethics describe the views of Peter Singer, a famous advocate of animal rights:

> Singer rejects speciesism, which he defines as a prejudice or attitude of bias in favor of the interests of members of one's own species and against those of members of other species. In his view, speciesism is analogous to racism and sexism. Just as we have a moral obligation to give equal consideration to the interests of all human beings, regardless of sex or skin color, so, too, we have a moral obligation to give equal consideration to the interests of animals. Insofar as animals, like humans, have the

capacity to suffer, they have an interest in not suffering. Not to take that interest into account is speciesist and immoral.[9]

> Describe Singer's point of view in your own words (not in the editor's words).

d. In a single paragraph, succinctly describe the point of view of the discipline you are studying.

e. Describe your point of view on the issue of memorization versus critical thinking in your courses.

6.12 Alternatives.

a. Identify some goal you want to achieve in relation to this class. Describe a way you can achieve that goal. Then, describe another way to achieve that goal. Then, describe yet another way.

b. Look back over the responses you've given to any of the questions before this. Pick out two that you are least satisfied with. Describe why. Revise them by writing alternative responses.

c. Focus on an important decision you have to make: Identify two (if possible, three) realistic choices you have?

d. Describe how thinking in terms of alternatives is important within the discipline you are studying. Give clear examples.

6.13 Context.

a. Describe how the field you are studying fits into the context of other closely related fields (e.g., if it is a social science, how is it similar to and different from the other social sciences?).

b. Describe the historical background of the field you are studying.

c. Identify an area or activity that is important to you, maybe the kind of music you like, the kind of sports or leisure activity you engage in, the kind of occupation you are interested in, the kind of books you read. Sketch out as well as you can when that particular area or activity was invented, discovered, or became widespread. Try to get a sense of how ancient or how recent it is.

d. Read the first chapter of your text and describe how it sets forth the context of the field you are studying.

e. Describe a situation where, because of your personal history or your cultural background, you were unable to grasp something important that was going on. Then, describe a situation where your history or cultural background gave you a deeper insight into what was going on.

6.14 Try the outcomes (page 154). Just go through the list of outcomes and see how many of them you understand well with your book and notes closed.

6.15 Look on pages 351–352 for a brief description of some critical-thinking character traits. Describe how *fair-mindedness* is important in thinking things through using the elements of reasoning.

DAILY PRACTICE
At incorporating critical thinking into your life and your learning

Before you start Exercise 6.16, look back at the instructions on pages 122–123.

6.16 **Spend a day on an element. Keep a log.** Pick one of the elements. For example, spend your day looking for assumptions. Write down any of them you can find. Note whether they were assumptions that were clear in the person's mind or ones the person was unaware of. Look for assumptions underlying your own statements and those of other people, in the way software works (or doesn't work), in advertising, in classes, everywhere. Feel free to ask people, "Excuse me, but I'm doing a critical-thinking assignment. I just heard you speaking. Are you making the assumption that _____?"

In your log, write down any questions that come up for you about assumptions. Those may be questions you'll want to ask in class, of your teacher, or of a classmate.

Wait a few days. Then choose another element to spend a day on. Go through all of them, including context and alternatives. By the time you have finished, you should be significantly better at identifying the elements and using them in practice.

6.17 Group work. Answer with an element. Sit in groups of four people, A, B, C, and D. Everyone takes turns asking questions of A. The questions can be anything, but try to ask different kinds. Before actually answering the question, A identifies the element he or she is using. Afterward, switch roles: everyone quizzes B, then C, then D. For example:

Question: What's your name?

A: A piece of information. My name is A.

Question: Where do you live?

A: Another piece of information (it's getting boring). My address is . . .

Question: Why are you taking this class?

A: My major purpose is . . .

Question: What is this stupid exercise for?

A: The question at issue, from your point of view, is "What is this stupid exercise for?"

6.18 In the Discipline: Metacognitive Discussion. Choose one element per class. Discuss how that element is important in the discipline. Do some pre-thinking and pre-writing the night before as homework. Have concrete examples of that element to share.

STANDARDS FOR THINKING

One of the fundamentals of critical thinking is the ability to assess one's own reasoning. To be good at assessment requires that we consistently take apart our thinking and examine the parts with respect to standards of quality. We do this using criteria based on clarity, accuracy, precision, relevance, depth, breadth, logicalness, and significance. Critical thinkers recognize that, whenever they are reasoning, they reason to some purpose (element of reasoning). Implicit goals are built into their thought processes, but their reasoning is improved when they are clear (intellectual standard) about that purpose or goal. Similarly, to reason well, they need to know that, consciously or unconsciously, they are using information (element of reasoning) in thinking, but their reasoning improves when they make sure that the information they are using is accurate (intellectual standard).

Put another way, when we assess our reasoning, we want to know how well we are reasoning. We do not identify the elements of reasoning for the fun of it or just to satisfy some authority. Rather, we assess our reasoning by using intellectual standards because we realize the negative consequences of failing to do so. In assessing our reasoning, then, we recommend these intellectual standards as minimal:

clarity	relevance	logic
accuracy	depth	significance
precision	breadth	fairness

These are not the *only* intellectual standards a person might use. They are simply among the most fundamental. In this respect, the elements of thought are more basic because the eight elements we have identified are *universal*; they are present in all reasoning of all subjects in all cultures for all time. On the one hand, one cannot reason with no information about no question from no point of view

165

with no assumptions. On the other hand, there is a wide variety of intellectual standards from which to choose—such as credibility, predictability, feasibility, and completeness—that we don't use routinely in assessing reasoning.

As critical thinkers, then, we think about our thinking with these kinds of questions in mind: *Am I being clear? Accurate? Precise? Relevant? Am I thinking logically? Am I dealing with a matter of significance? Is my thinking justifiable in context?* Typically, we apply these standards to one or more elements.

7.1 *Think for Yourself*

IDENTIFYING INAPPROPRIATE STANDARDS

Can you identify a class you took in the past, either in high school or in college, in which you think your work was graded, at least in part, by one or more inappropriate standards? If so, what was the class? What was the standard? What was the result? Can you see the importance in education of basing all grades on appropriate intellectual standards? Write out or orally explain your answer.

TAKE A DEEPER LOOK AT UNIVERSAL INTELLECTUAL STANDARDS

Thinking critically requires command of fundamental intellectual standards. Critical thinkers routinely ask questions that apply intellectual standards to thinking. The ultimate goal is for these questions to become so spontaneous in thinking that they form a natural part of our inner voice, guiding us to better and better reasoning. In this section, we focus on the standards and questions that apply across the various facets of your life.

Clarity

Questions that focus on clarity include:

- Could you elaborate on that point?
- Could you express that point in another way?
- Could you give me an illustration?
- Could you give me an example?
- Let me state in my own words what I think you just said. Tell me if I am clear about your meaning.

Clarity is a gateway standard. If a statement is unclear, we cannot determine whether it is accurate or relevant. In fact, we cannot tell anything about it because we do not yet know what it is saying. For example, the question, "What can be done about the education system in America?" is unclear. To address the question adequately, we need a clearer understanding of what the person asking the question is considering the "problem" to be. A clearer question might be, "What can educators do to ensure that students learn the skills and abilities that help them function successfully on the job and in their daily decision making?" This question, because of its increased clarity, provides a better guide to thinking. It lays out the intellectual task in a more definitive way.

7.2   *Think for Yourself*

CONVERTING UNCLEAR THOUGHTS TO CLEAR THOUGHTS

Can you convert an unclear thought to a thought that is clear? Suppose you are engaged in a discussion about welfare, and one person says, "Let's face it—welfare is corrupt!" What does this mean? What could it mean?

It could mean some very different things. It could mean, "The very idea of giving people goods and services they have not personally earned is equivalent to stealing money from those who have earned it" (an ethical claim). It could mean, "The welfare laws have so many loopholes that people are receiving money and services that were not envisioned when the laws were initially formulated" (a legal claim). It could mean, "The people who receive welfare so often lie and cheat to falsify the documents they submit that they should be thrown in jail" (a claim about the ethical character of the recipients).

Now, for practice in making thoughts clear, consider this statement: "She is a good person." This statement is unclear. Because we don't know the context within which this statement is being made, we aren't sure in what way she is "good." Formulate three possible meanings of this statement.

Now consider the statement: "He is a jerk." Again, formulate three possible meanings of this statement.

When you become skilled in differentiating what is clear and what is unclear, you will find that much of the time we are unclear both about what we are thinking and about what we are saying.

Accuracy

Questions focusing on making thinking more accurate include:

- Is that really true?
- How could we check to see whether that is accurate?
- How could we find out whether that is true?

A statement may be clear but not accurate, as in, "Most dogs weigh more than 300 pounds." To be accurate is to represent something in accordance with the way it actually is. People often present or describe things or events in a way that is not in accordance with the way things actually are. People frequently misrepresent or falsely describe things, especially when they have an interest in seeing them in a certain way. Advertisers often do this to keep a buyer from seeing the weaknesses in a product. If an advertisement states, "Our water is 100% pure," when in fact the water contains small parts of chemicals such as chlorine and lead, it is inaccurate. If an advertisement states, "This bread contains 100% whole wheat," when the whole wheat has been bleached and enriched and the bread contains many additives, the advertisement is inaccurate.

Good thinkers listen carefully to statements and, when there is reason for skepticism, question whether what they hear is true and accurate. In the same way, they question the extent to which what they read is correct when asserted as fact. Critical thinking, then, implies a healthy skepticism about public descriptions of what is and is not fact.

At the same time, because we tend to think from a narrow, self-serving perspective, assessing ideas for accuracy can be difficult. We naturally tend to believe that our thoughts are automatically accurate just because they are ours and, therefore, that the thoughts of those who disagree with us are inaccurate. We also fail to question statements others make that conform to what we already believe, while we tend to question statements that conflict with our views. However, as critical thinkers, we force ourselves to accurately assess our own views as well as those of others. We do this even if it means facing deficiencies in our thinking.

7.3, 7.4 *Think for Yourself*

RECOGNIZING INACCURATE STATEMENTS

Can you identify a statement you heard recently that was clear but inaccurate? You will find an abundance of examples in everyday statements that people often make in praise or criticism. People in general have a tendency to make two kinds of inaccurate statements: *false positives* about the people they personally like (these would be untrue positive statements about people they like) and *false negatives* about the people they personally dislike (untrue negative things about people they don't like). Politically motivated statements tend to follow a similar pattern. See whether you can think of an example of an inaccurate statement from your recent experience. Write out or orally explain your answer.

IN SEARCH OF THE FACTS

One of the most important critical thinking skills is the skill of assessing the accuracy of "factual" claims (someone's assertion that such-and-so is a fact). In an ad in the *New York Times* (Nov. 29, 1999, p. A15), a coalition of 60 nonprofit organizations accused the World Trade Organization (a coalition of 134 nation states) of operating in secret, undermining democratic institutions and the environment. The nonprofit coalition argued that the working class and the poor have not significantly benefited as a result of the last 20 years of rapid expansion of global trade. They alleged, among other things, the following facts:

1. "American CEOs are now paid, on average, 419 times more than line workers, and the ratio is increasing."
2. "Median hourly wages for workers are down by 10% in the last 10 years."
3. "The top 20% of the U.S. population owns 84.6% of the country's wealth."
4. "The wealth of the world's 475 billionaires now equals the annual incomes of more than 50% of the world population *combined*."

Using whatever sources you can find (including the website of the Turning Point Project, the nonprofit coalition, at www.turnpoint.org), discuss the probable accuracy of the factual claims. For example, find the website (if there is one) of the World Trade Organization. The group might challenge some of the facts alleged or advance facts of its own that put the charges of the nonprofit coalition into a different perspective.

Precision

Questions focusing on making thinking more precise include:

- Could you give me more details?
- Could you be more specific?

A statement can be both clear and accurate but not precise, as in "Jack is overweight." (We don't know how overweight Jack is—one pound or 500 pounds.) To be precise is to give the details necessary for someone to understand exactly what is meant. Some situations don't call for detail. If you ask, "Is there any milk in the refrigerator?" and I answer, "Yes," both the question and the answer are probably precise enough for the circumstance (although specifying how much milk is there might be relevant). Or imagine that you are ill and go to the doctor. He wouldn't say, "Take 1.4876946 antibiotic pills twice per day." This level of specificity, or precision, would be beyond what is useful in the situation.

In many situations, however, specifics are essential to good thinking. Let's say that your friend is having financial problems and asks you, "What should I do about my situation?" In this case, you want to probe her thinking for specifics. Without the full specifics, you could not help her. You might ask questions such as, "What precisely is the problem? What *exactly* are the variables that bear on the problem? What are some possible solutions to the problem—in detail?"

7.5   *Think for Yourself*

RECOGNIZING IMPRECISE STATEMENTS

Can you think of a recent situation in which you needed more details to figure out something and, because you didn't have the details, you experienced some negative consequences? For example, have you ever been given directions to someone's house, directions that seemed precise enough at the time, but when you tried to find the person's house, you got lost because of lack of details in the directions?

First, identify a situation in which the details and specifics were important (for example, in buying a computer, a car, or a stereo system). Then identify the negative consequences that resulted because you didn't get the details you needed to think well in the situation. Write out or orally explain your answer.

Relevance

Questions focusing on relevance include:

- How is this idea connected to the question?
- How does that bear on the issue?
- How does this idea relate to this other idea?
- How does your question relate to the issue we are dealing with?

A statement can be clear, accurate, and precise but not relevant to the question at issue. For example, students often think the amount of effort they put into a course should contribute to raising their grade in the course. Often, however, effort does not measure the quality of student learning and, therefore, is irrelevant to the grade. Something is relevant when it is directly connected with and bears upon the issue at hand. Something is relevant when it is pertinent or applicable to a problem we are trying to solve. Irrelevant thinking encourages us to consider what we should set aside. Relevant thinking stays on track. Thinking often is irrelevant because people lack discipline in thinking; they don't know how to analyze an issue for what truly bears on it. Therefore, they aren't able to think their way effectively through the problems and issues they face.

7.6   *Think for Yourself*

RECOGNIZING IRRELEVANT STATEMENTS

Can you identify a statement you heard recently that was clear, accurate, and sufficiently precise but irrelevant to the circumstance, problem, or issue? Although we all sometimes stray from a question or task, we need to be sensitive to when failure to stay on task may have a significant negative implication.

Identify, first, circumstances in which people tend to introduce irrelevant considerations into a discussion (for example, in meetings, in response to questions in class, in everyday dialogue when they have a hidden agenda or simply want to take control of the conversation for some reason). Write out or orally explain your answer.

Depth

Questions focusing on depth of thought include:

- How does your answer address the complexities in the question?
- How are you taking into account the problems in the question?
- How are you dealing with the most significant factors in the problem?

We think deeply when we get beneath the surface of an issue or problem, identify the complexities inherent in it, and then deal with those complexities in an intellectually responsible way. Even when we think deeply, even when we deal well with the complexities in a question, we might find the question difficult to address. Still, our thinking will work better for us when we can recognize complicated questions and address each area of complexity in the question.

A statement can be clear, accurate, precise, and relevant, but superficial—lacking in depth. Let's say you are asked what should be done about the problem of drug use in America, and you answer by saying, "Just say no." This slogan, which for several years was supposed to discourage children and teens from using drugs, is clear, accurate, precise, and relevant. Nevertheless, it lacks depth because it treats an extremely complex issue—the pervasive problem of drug use among people in our culture—superficially. It does not address the history, politics, economics, psychology, or other important aspects of addiction.

7.7 *Think for Yourself*

RECOGNIZING SUPERFICIAL APPROACHES

Identify a newspaper article containing a statement that is clear, accurate, precise, and relevant but superficial with respect to a complex issue. For example, a number of laws take a Band-Aid® approach to systemic problems such as drugs and crime.

1. State the problem.
2. State how the article deals with the problem and why the approach taken is superficial.
3. Focus on the complexity of the issue, and state how the problem might be dealt with.

Breadth

Questions focusing on making thinking broader include:

- Do we need to consider another point of view?
- Is there another way to look at this question?
- What would this look like from a conservative standpoint?
- What would this look like from the point of view of ...?

A line of reasoning may be clear, accurate, precise, relevant, and deep but lack breadth. Examples are arguments from either the conservative or the liberal standpoint that get deeply into an issue but show insight into only one side of the question.

When we consider the issue from every relevant viewpoint, we think in a broad way. When multiple points of view are pertinent to the issue, yet we fail to give due consideration to those perspectives, we think myopically, or narrow-mindedly. We do not try to enter alternative, or opposing, viewpoints.

Humans are frequently guilty of narrow-mindedness for many reasons: limited education, innate sociocentrism, natural selfishness, self-deception, and intellectual arrogance. Points of view that significantly disagree with our own often threaten us. It's much easier to ignore perspectives with which we disagree than to consider them when we know at some level that to consider them would mean being forced to reconsider our views.

Let's say, for example, that you and I live together and that I like to play loud music, which annoys you. The question is: *Should I play loud music in a room when you are present?* Both your viewpoint and mine are relevant to the question. When I recognize your viewpoint as relevant and then intellectually empathize with it—when I enter your way of thinking to understand it—I will be forced to see that imposing my loud music on you is unfair and inconsiderate. I will be able to imagine what it would be like to be forced to listen to loud music that I find annoying. However, if I don't force myself to enter your viewpoint, I do not have to change my self-serving behavior. One of the primary mechanisms the mind uses to avoid giving up what it wants is unconsciously to refuse to enter viewpoints that differ from its own.

7.8 *Think for Yourself*

THINKING BROADLY ABOUT AN ISSUE

Consider the question: Is abortion morally justified? Some argue that abortion is not morally justifiable, and others argue that it is. Try to state and elaborate on each of these points of view in detail. Articulate each point of view objectively, regardless of your personal views. Present each point of view in such a way that a person who actually takes that position would assess it as *accurate*. Each line of reasoning should be *clear, accurate, precise, relevant,* and *deep*. Do not take a position on it yourself.

Logic

Questions that focus on making thinking more logical include:

- Does all of this fit together logically?
- Does this really make sense?
- Does that follow from what you said?
- How does that follow from the evidence?
- Before, you implied this, and now you are saying that. I don't see how both can be true.

When we think, we bring together a variety of thoughts in some order. When the combined thoughts are mutually supporting and make sense in combination, the thinking is logical. When the combination is not mutually supporting, is contradictory in some sense, or does not make sense, the combination is not logical. Because humans often maintain conflicting beliefs without being aware that we are doing so, it is common to find inconsistencies in human life and thought.

Let's say we know, by looking at standardized tests of students in schools and the actual work they are able to produce, that students are often deficient in basic academic skills such as reading, writing, speaking, and the core disciplines such as math, science, and history. Despite this evidence, teachers frequently conclude that they don't need to change their instruction to improve student learning (and in fact nothing is fundamentally wrong with the way they teach). Given the evidence, this conclusion seems illogical. The conclusion doesn't seem to follow from the facts.

Let's take another example. Say that you know a person who has had a heart attack, and her doctors have told her she must be careful about what she eats to avoid problems in the future. Yet she concludes that what she eats really doesn't matter. Given the evidence, her conclusion is illogical. It doesn't make sense.

7.9   *Think for Yourself*

RECOGNIZING ILLOGICAL THINKING

Identify a newspaper article that contains an example of illogical thinking—thinking that doesn't make sense to you.

1. State the issue the thinking revolves around.
2. State the thinking you believe is illogical and why you think it is illogical.
3. State some implications of the illogical thinking. What are some consequences likely to follow from the illogical thinking?

Significance

Questions that focus on making thinking more significant include:

- What is the most significant information we need to address this issue?
- How is that fact important in context?
- Which of these questions is the most significant?
- Which of these ideas or concepts is the most important?

When we reason through issues, we want to concentrate on the most important information (relevant to the issue) in our reasoning and take into account the most important ideas or concepts. Too often, we fail in our thinking because we do not recognize that, although many ideas might be relevant to an issue, not all are equally important. In a similar way, we often fail to ask the most important questions and become trapped by thinking only in terms of superficial questions, questions of little weight.

In college, for example, few students focus on important questions such as, *What does it mean to be an educated person? What do I need to do to become educated?* Instead, students tend to ask questions such as, *What do I need to do to get an A in this course? How many pages does this paper have to be? What do I have to do to satisfy this professor?*

7.10 *Think for Yourself*

FOCUSING ON SIGNIFICANCE IN THINKING

Think about your life, about the way you spend your time, in terms of the amount of time you spend on significant versus trivial things. As you do so, write the answers to these questions:

1. What is the most important goal or purpose you should focus on at this point in your life? Why is this purpose important? How much time do you spend focused on it?

2. What are the most trivial or superficial things you spend time focused on (things such as your appearance, impressing your friends, chatting about insignificant things at parties, and the like)?

3. What can you do to reduce the amount of time you spend on the trivial and increase the amount of time you spend on the significant?

Fairness

Questions that focus on ensuring that thinking is fair include:

- Is my thinking justified given the evidence?
- Am I taking into account the weight of the evidence that others might advance in the situation?

- Are these assumptions justified?
- Is my purpose fair given the implications of my behavior?
- Is the manner in which I am addressing the problem fair—or is my vested interest keeping me from considering the problem from alternative viewpoints?
- Am I using concepts justifiably, or am I using them unfairly to manipulate someone (to selfishly get what I want)?

When we think through problems, we want to make sure that our thinking is justified. To be justified is to think fairly in context and in accord with reason. If you are vigilant in using the other intellectual standards covered thus far in the chapter, you will (by implication) satisfy the standard of justifiability. We include fairness separately because of the powerful nature of self-deception in human thinking. For example, we often deceive ourselves into thinking that we are being fair and justified in our thinking when in fact we are refusing to consider significant relevant information that would cause us to change our view (and therefore not pursue our selfish interest). We pursue unjustified purposes to get what we want even if we have to hurt others to get it; we use concepts in an unjustified way to manipulate people; and we often make unjustified assumptions, unsupported by facts, that then lead to faulty inferences.

Let's focus on an example in which unjustified thinking resulted from ignoring relevant facts. Let's say, for instance, that Kristi and Abby lived together. Kristi was cold-natured, and Abby was warm-natured. During the winter, Abby liked to have the windows in the house open while Kristi liked to keep them closed. However, Abby insisted that it was "extremely uncomfortable" with the windows closed. The information she used in her reasoning all centered on her own point of view—that she was hot, that she couldn't function well if she was hot, and that if Kristi was cold, she could wear a sweater. Abby was not justified in her thinking. She refused to enter Kristi's point of view to consider information supporting Kristi's perspective because to do so would mean that *Abby would have to give up something*. She would have to adopt a more reasonable, or fair, point of view.

People who are manipulative often use concepts in ways that are not justified. Let's imagine that John, for example, is interested in borrowing Jay's portable stereo for a trip. John, therefore, begins to hang out regularly with Jay. When they are with others, John introduces Jay as his "friend," and Jay comes to define John as his friend. So when John asks to borrow Jay's stereo, Jay readily agrees (because John is his friend). However, when John fails to return the stereo, and Jay asks for it back, John lies and says he lost it. The fact is that John never intended to return the stereo—and obviously never considered Jay a friend. John just used the term *friend* to get what he wanted. He said he was a *friend* specifically to manipulate Jay. Thus John's use of the term *friend* was not fair in context.

When we reason to conclusions, we want to make sure the assumptions we use to come to those conclusions are justifiable given the facts of the situation. For example, all our prejudices and stereotypes function as assumptions in thinking, and prejudices and stereotypes are unjustifiable by their very nature. We often make broad, sweeping generalizations such as:

- Liberals are soft on crime.
- Elderly people aren't interested in sex.
- Young men are interested only in sex.
- Jocks are cool.
- Blondes are dumb.
- Cheerleaders are airheads.
- Intellectuals are nerds.
- Learning is boring.
- School doesn't have anything to do with life.

The problem with assumptions such as these is that they cause us to make basic—and often serious—mistakes in thinking. Because they aren't justifiable, they cause us to prejudge situations and people and draw faulty inferences—or conclusions—about them. For example, if we believe that all intellectuals are nerds, whenever we meet an intellectual, we will infer that he or she is a nerd (and act unfairly toward the person).

In sum, justifiability, or fairness, is an important standard in thinking. It forces us to see how we are distorting our thinking to achieve our self-serving ends (or to see how others are distorting their thinking to achieve selfish ends).

7.11, 7.12   *Think for Yourself*

ANALYZING ASSUMPTIONS FOR JUSTIFIABILITY (FAIRNESS)

Look back at the assumptions you came up with; for each one, decide whether it is justifiable given the situation. For each assumption that is not justifiable, re-create an assumption that would be justified in context.

APPLYING INTELLECTUAL STANDARDS TO EVERYDAY LIFE DISCUSSIONS

Record a discussion/debate between you and several other people (friends or family) on an important controversial issue (for example, "What is the best solution to the drug problem in this country?"). Then play back the recording two or three remarks at a time. Comment on which of the standards are being met and which are violated at each "step" along the way. Notice how seldom people tend to use intellectual standards in their thinking, how unclear everyday thinking often is, and how people may feel just as confident in their positions even after you point out violations of intellectual standards. What does that tell you about them?

EXHIBIT 7.1 *To evaluate thinking, we must apply intellectual standards to the elements of thought.*

Clarity   Understandable; the meaning can be grasped

Could you elaborate further? Could you give me an example? Could you illustrate what you mean?

Accuracy   Free from errors or distortions; true

How could we check on that? How could we find out if that is true? How could we verify or test that?

Precision   Exact to the necessary level of detail

Could you be more specific? Could you give me more details? Could you be more exact?

Relevance   Relating to the matter at hand

How does that relate to the problem? How does that bear on the question? How does that help us with the issue?

Depth   Containing complexities and multiple interrelationships

What factors make this a difficult problem? What are some of the complexities of this question? What are some of the difficulties we need to deal with?

Breadth   Encompassing multiple viewpoints

Do we need to look at this from another perspective? Do we need to consider another point of view? Do we need to look at this in other ways?

Logic   The parts make sense together; no contradictions

Does all this make sense together? Does your first paragraph fit in with your last? Does what you say follow from the evidence?

Significance   Focusing on the important; not trivial

Is this the most important problem to consider? Is this the central idea to focus on? Which of these facts are most important?

Fairness   Justifiable; not self-serving or one-sided

Is my thinking justifiable in context? Am I taking into account the thinking of others? Is my purpose fair given the situation? Am I using my concepts in keeping with educated usage, or am I distorting them to get what I want?

BRING TOGETHER THE ELEMENTS OF REASONING AND THE INTELLECTUAL STANDARDS

We have considered the elements of reasoning and the importance of being able to take them apart to analyze them so we can recognize flaws in our thinking. We also have introduced the intellectual standards as tools for assessment. Now let us look at how we can use the intellectual standards to assess the elements of reason.

EXHIBIT 7.2 *Critical thinkers routinely apply the intellectual standards to the elements of reasoning.*

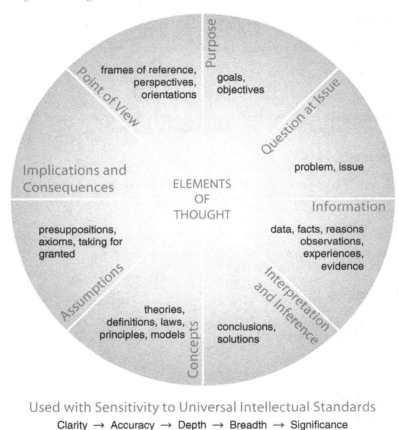

Used with Sensitivity to Universal Intellectual Standards

Clarity → Accuracy → Depth → Breadth → Significance
Precision
Relevance

↓

Fairness

Purpose, Goal, or End in View

Whenever we reason, we reason to some end: to achieve some objective, satisfy some desire, or fulfill some need. One source of problems in human reasoning is traceable to defects at the level of goal, purpose, or end. If the goal is unrealistic, for example, or contradictory to other goals we have, if it is confused or muddled, the reasoning we use to achieve it will suffer.

As a developing critical thinker, get in the habit of explicitly stating the purposes you are trying to accomplish. You should strive to be clear about your purpose in every situation. If you fail to stick to your purpose, you are unlikely to achieve it. Let's say your purpose in being in college is to obtain a degree so you can improve your chances of getting a good job and making a good income. If you keep that purpose clearly in mind and consistently work to achieve it, you are more likely to be successful. But it is easy to become so involved in the social life at college that you lose sight of your purpose and thus fail to achieve it.

As a student interested in developing your mind, you can begin to ask questions that improve your ability to focus on purpose in your classes. For example: *Am I clear about my purpose—in an essay, a research project, an oral report, a discussion? Can I specify my purpose precisely? Is my purpose a significant one? Realistic? Achievable? Justifiable? Do I have contradictory purposes?*

EXHIBIT 7.3 *Criteria for evaluating reasoning.*

When we bring the intellectual standards to bear upon the elements of reasoning, we ask these type of questions in evaluating reasoning:

1. **Purpose:** What is the purpose of the reasoner? Is the purpose clearly stated or clearly implied? Is it justifiable?
2. **Question:** Is the question at issue well-stated? Is it clear and unbiased? Does the expression of the question do justice to the complexity of the matter at issue? Are the question and purpose directly relevant to each other?
3. **Information:** Does the reasoner cite relevant evidence, experiences, and/or information essential to the issue? Is the information accurate? Does the reasoner address the complexities of the issue?
4. **Concepts:** Does the reasoner clarify key concepts when necessary? Are the concepts used justifiably?
5. **Assumptions:** Does the reasoner show a sensitivity to what he or she is taking for granted or assuming (insofar as those assumptions might reasonably be questioned)? Does the reasoner use questionable assumptions without addressing problems that might be inherent in those assumptions?
6. **Inferences:** Does the reasoner develop a line of reasoning explaining well how he or she is arriving at her or his main conclusions?
7. **Point of View:** Does the reasoner show a sensitivity to alternative relevant points of view or lines of reasoning? Does he or she consider and respond to objections framed from other relevant points of view?
8. **Implications:** Does the reasoner show a sensitivity to the implications and consequences of the position he or she is taking?

EXHIBIT 7.4   The Figuring Mind

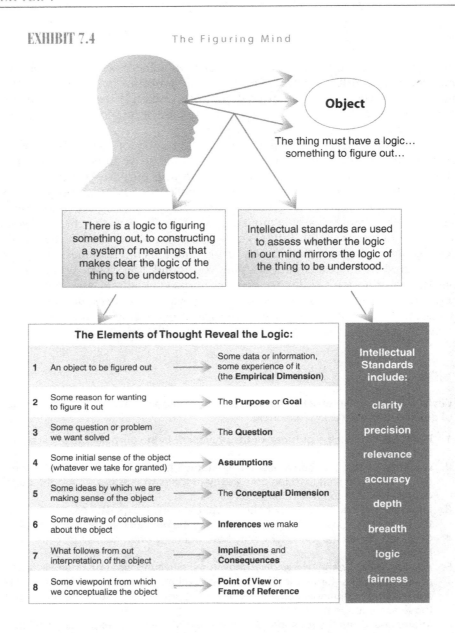

Question at Issue or Problem to Be Solved

Whenever you attempt to reason through something, you are attempting to answer at least one question that emerges from the problem to be solved or issue to resolve. An area of concern in assessing reasoning, therefore, revolves around that very question.

7.13   *Think for Yourself*

BRINGING INTELLECTUAL STANDARDS TO BEAR ON YOUR PURPOSE

Think of an important problem in your life. This can be a problem in a personal relationship, at your place of work, in college, or in another situation. Now state your purpose in the situation *clearly* and *precisely*. What exactly are you trying to accomplish? Is your purpose *fair* or *justifiable*? Is it *realistic*? Explain to a classmate.

An important part of being able to think well is assessing your ability to formulate a problem in a clear and relevant way. It requires determining whether the question you are addressing is important, whether it is answerable, whether you understand the requirements for settling the question, for solving the problem.

As a student interested in developing your mind, you can ask yourself questions that will improve your ability to focus on the important questions in your classes. You can ask: *What is the most fundamental question at issue* (in this lecture, in this chapter, in this discussion)? *What is the question, precisely? Is the question simple or complex? If it is complex, what makes it complex? Am I sticking to the question* (in this discussion, in this paper I am working on)*? Is there more than one important question to be considered here* (in this lecture, etc.)*?*

7.14   *Think for Yourself*

BRINGING INTELLECTUAL STANDARDS TO BEAR ON THE QUESTION AT ISSUE

Go back to the important problem in Think for Yourself 7.13. Now state the problem you are addressing and then the question that emerges from that problem. State your question *clearly and precisely*. What complexities, if any, are inherent in the problem? Is there more than one question you need to address to reason effectively through the problem? Explain to a classmate.

Point of View or Frame of Reference

Whenever we reason, we must do so within some point of view or frame of reference. Any "defect" in that point of view or frame of reference is a possible source of problems in the reasoning.

A point of view may be too narrow, based on false or misleading information, unfair, or contain contradictions. Critical thinkers strive to adopt a point of view that is fair to others, even to opposing points of view. They want their point of view to be broad, flexible, and justifiable and to be stated clearly and adhered to consistently. Good thinkers, then, consider alternative points of view when they reason through an issue.

As a person interested in developing your mind, you begin to ask yourself questions that will improve your ability to focus on point of view in your classes. These questions might be: *From what point of view am I looking at this issue? Am I so locked into my point of view that I am unable to see the issue from other points of view? Must I consider multiple points of view to reason well through the issue at hand? What is the point of view of this author? What is the frame of reference in this discipline? Are different worldviews implicit in these perspectives?*

7.15   *Think for Yourself*

BRINGING INTELLECTUAL STANDARDS TO BEAR UPON POINTS OF VIEW

Continue with the problem in Think for Yourself 7.14. Now state the point or points of view relevant to the issue. State each point of view *clearly and precisely*. Make sure you are considering all relevant points of view (that you are thinking *broadly*), *and that you are representing each point of view accurately* (even if it means sympathetically expressing a view that you do not personally hold).

Information, Data, Experiences

Whenever we reason, there is some "stuff," some phenomena about which we are reasoning. Any "defect," then, in the experiences, data, evidence, or raw material upon which a person's reasoning is based is a possible source of problems.

Reasoners should be assessed on their ability to give evidence that is gathered and reported clearly, fairly, and accurately. Therefore, as a student, you should assess the information you use to come to conclusions, whether you are working on papers for class, reasoning through issues within the subjects you take, or considering a problem in your personal life. Assess whether the information you are using is relevant to the issue and adequate for achieving your purpose, whether you are representing the information accurately or distorting it to fit your own (often self-serving) point of view.

As a student interested in developing your mind, ask yourself questions that will improve your ability to focus on information in your classes. These questions might be: *What is the most important information I need to reason well through this issue? Are there alternative information sources I need to consider? How can I check to see whether the information I am using is accurate? Am I sure that all the information I am using is relevant to the issue?*

7.16   *Think for Yourself*

> ## BRINGING INTELLECTUAL STANDARDS TO BEAR ON THE INFORMATION YOU ARE USING IN REASONING
>
> Continue with the problem you have been working on. Now state the information you are using in your thinking. This could consist of data, facts, or experiences that, in conjunction with your assumptions, lead you to conclusions. It could come from your experience, word of mouth, research, the media, or other sources. State the information clearly. How could you determine whether the information is *accurate and relevant* to the question?

Concepts, Theories, Ideas

All reasoning uses some ideas or concepts and not others. These concepts include the theories, principles, axioms, and rules implicit in our reasoning. Any defect in the concepts or ideas of this reasoning is a possible source of problems in our reasoning.

As an aspiring critical thinker, you begin to focus more deeply on the concepts you use. You assess the extent to which you are clear about those concepts, whether they are relevant to the issue, whether your principles are slanted inappropriately by your point of view. You begin to direct your attention toward how you use concepts, what concepts are most important, how concepts are intertwined in networks.

As a student interested in developing your mind, you begin to ask questions that will improve your ability to focus on the importance of concepts in your classes. These questions may include: *What is the most fundamental concept I need to learn in this class to help me in my life? How does this concept connect with other key concepts in the course? What are the most important theories in this class? Am I clear about the important concepts in the class? What questions do I need to ask to get clear about the concepts the teacher is explaining?*

7.17   *Think for Yourself*

> ## BRINGING INTELLECTUAL STANDARDS TO BEAR UPON THE CONCEPTS YOU USE
>
> Continue with the problem you have been working on. Now state the most important concepts you are using to guide your reasoning. For example, if you are concerned with how you can keep in physical shape while also dedicating enough time to classes, work, family, significant others, and so on, your key concepts might be physical fitness, quality learning, and good relationships. (You usually can find the key concepts you are using in your reasoning by looking at your question and purpose.) Elaborate on each of these concepts so you understand exactly how you are using them. State your concepts *clearly* and *precisely*.

Assumptions

All reasoning must begin somewhere. It must take some things for granted. Any defect in the assumptions or presuppositions with which reasoning begins is a possible source of problems in the reasoning.

Assessing skills of reasoning involves assessing our ability to recognize and articulate assumptions, again according to relevant standards. Our assumptions may be clear or unclear, justifiable or unjustifiable, consistent or contradictory.

As a student interested in developing your mind, you begin to ask questions that will improve your ability to use important assumptions in your classes. These questions could include: *What is taken for granted in this academic discipline* (or in this lecture, or this discussion, or this article, or this experiment)? *Are these assumptions justifiable, or should I question them? What does the author of this textbook assume? Are these assumptions justified, or should they be questioned?*

7.18 *Think for Yourself*

BRINGING INTELLECTUAL STANDARDS TO BEAR UPON YOUR ASSUMPTIONS

Continue with the problem you have been working on. Now state the most important assumptions you are making in your reasoning. What are you taking for granted that might be questioned? Using the previous example of how to keep in physical shape while also dedicating enough time to learning and your key relationships, your main assumptions might be:

1. Intellectual work is/is not more important than relationships.
2. I know enough about fitness to do appropriate exercises.
3. I must spend some time working at a part-time job while in college (rather than getting a student loan).
4. I have enough time to address all of the preceding responsibilities well.

State your assumptions *clearly* and *precisely*. Make sure they are *justifiable* in the context of the issue.

Implications and Consequences

Whenever we reason, implications follow from our reasoning. When we make decisions, consequences result from those decisions. As critical thinkers, we want to understand implications whenever and wherever they occur. We want to be able to trace logical consequences and see what our actions are leading to. We want to anticipate possible problems before they arise.

No matter where we stop tracing implications, there always will be further implications, and the same can be said about further consequences. Any defect in our ability to follow the implications or consequences of our reasoning is a potential source of problems in our thinking. Our ability to reason well, then, is measured in part by our ability to understand and enunciate the implications and consequences of reasoning.

As a student interested in developing your mind, you begin to ask yourself questions that will improve your ability to focus on the important implications in your thinking as a student. These questions could include, for example: *What are the most significant implications of this biological theory, this phenomenon, this economic policy? What are the implications of this political practice? What are the implications of failing to act in this context? If we adopt this course of action, what are the likely consequences? What are the most significant implications of our tendency to solve this social problem in this way rather than in that way? What were the implications* (social, political, economic, cultural) *of the United States' involvement in World War I?*

7.19   *Think for Yourself*

THINKING THROUGH THE IMPLICATIONS OF YOUR REASONING

Continue with the problem you have been working on and state the most important implication of potential decisions you might make. Fill in these blanks: If I decide to do _____, then _____ is likely to follow. If I decide to act differently by doing _____, then _____ is likely to follow.

In this activity, you are emphasizing the *logical* implications and potential consequences of each decision. Make sure you emphasize important implications of each decision. For further practice, what would be the most likely implications of (1) getting married, (2) not staying in college, (3) staying in your hometown all your life, or (4) doing drugs for the fun of it?

Inferences

All reasoning proceeds by steps in which we reason as follows: "Because this is so, that also is so (or is probably so)," or, "Because this, therefore that." The mind perceives a situation or a set of facts and comes to a conclusion based on those facts. When taking this step of the mind, an inference results. Any defect in our ability to make logical inferences presents a possible problem in our reasoning. For example, if you see a person sitting on the street corner wearing tattered clothing, a worn bedroll beside him, and a bottle wrapped in a brown paper bag in his hand, you might infer that he is a bum. This inference is based on the facts you perceive in the situation and what you assume about them. The inference, however, may or may not be logical in this situation.

Critical thinkers want to become adept at making sound inferences. First, you must learn to identify when you or someone else has made an inference. *What key inferences are made in this newspaper article? Upon what are the inferences based? Are they justified? What is the key inference* (or conclusion) *I made in this paper? Was it justified? What is the key inference in this theory, in this way of proceeding, in solving this problem in this way? Is this inference logical? Is this conclusion significant? Is this interpretation justified?* These are the kinds of questions you ask.

As a student interested in developing your mind, you should ask questions that will improve your ability to spot important inferences wherever they occur. Given the facts of this case, is there more than one logical inference (conclusion, interpretation) one could come to? What are some other logical conclusions to consider? From this point on, develop an inference detector, the skill of recognizing the inferences you are making to analyze them.

7.20 *Think for Yourself*

BRINGING INTELLECTUAL STANDARDS TO BEAR ON YOUR INFERENCES

Continue with the problem you have been working on. Now state the inferences, or conclusions, you might come to (from the information you have) in solving your problem. You may have stated these already in Think for Yourself 7.19.

Once you have thought through your potential answers, be clear and precise in stating each one and then state a possible final conclusion. Make sure your inferences make good sense based on the information and concepts you are using.

BRIEF GUIDELINES FOR USING INTELLECTUAL STANDARDS

As we have emphasized, all reasoning involves eight elements, each of which includes a range of possible mistakes. Here we summarize some of the main "checkpoints" the best thinkers use in reasoning. Use these same checkpoints.

1. All reasoning has a *purpose*.
   - Take time to state your purpose *clearly*.
   - Choose *significant* and *realistic* purposes.
   - Distinguish your purpose from related purposes.
   - Make sure your purpose is *fair* in context (that it doesn't involve violating the rights of others).
   - Check periodically to be sure you are still focused on your purpose and haven't wandered from your target.

2. All reasoning is an attempt to figure out something, to settle some *question*, and to solve some problem.
   - Take time to state the question at issue *clearly* and *precisely*.
   - Express the question in several ways to *clarify* its meaning and scope.

- Break the question into sub-questions (when you can).
- Identify the type of question you are dealing with (historical, economic, biological, etc.) and whether the question has one right answer, is a matter of mere opinion, or requires reasoning from more than one point of view.
- Think through the complexities of the question (think through the question *deeply*).

3. All reasoning is based on *assumptions*.
    - *Clearly* identify your assumptions and determine whether they are *justifiable*.
    - Consider how your assumptions are shaping your point of view.

4. All reasoning is done from some *point of view*.
    - *Clearly* identify your point of view.
    - Seek other *relevant* points of view and identify their strengths as well as weaknesses.
    - Strive to be *fairminded* in evaluating all points of view.

5. All reasoning is based on data, *information*, and evidence.
    - Restrict your claims to those supported by the data you have.
    - Search for information that opposes your position as well as information that supports it.
    - Make sure that all information you use is *clear*, *accurate*, and *relevant* to the question at issue.
    - Make sure you have gathered *sufficient* information.
    - Make sure, especially, that you have considered all *significant* information relevant to the issue.

6. All reasoning is expressed through, and shaped by, *concepts* and ideas.
    - *Clearly* identify key concepts.
    - Consider alternative concepts or alternative definitions for concepts.
    - Make sure you are using concepts with care and *precision*.
    - Use concepts *justifiably* (not distorting their established meanings).

7. All reasoning contains *inferences* or interpretations by which we draw conclusions and give meaning to data.
    - Infer only what the evidence implies.
    - Check inferences for their *consistency* with each other.
    - Identify assumptions that lead you to your inferences.
    - Make sure your inferences *logically* follow from the information.

8. All reasoning leads somewhere or has *implications* and consequences.
    - Trace the *logical* implications and consequences that follow from your reasoning.
    - Search for negative as well as positive implications.
    - Consider all possible significant consequences.

7.21   *Think for Yourself*

CHECKPOINTS IN THINKING

For all eight categories outlined, transform each checkpoint into a question or a set of questions; figure out one or more questions that the checkpoint implies. When you have completed your list and you are actively using the questions you formulated, you will have powerful tools for thinking. Under the first category, *All reasoning has a purpose*, for example, the first checkpoint is: *Take time to state your purpose clearly*. Two questions implied by this checkpoint are: *What exactly is my purpose? Am I clear about my purpose?*

EXHIBIT 7.5

PURPOSE		
All reasoning has a purpose.		
Primary standards: (1) clarity, (2) significance, (3) achievability, (4) consistency, (5) justifiability		
Common problems: (1) unclear, (2) trivial, (3) unrealistic, (4) contradictory, (5) unfair		
Principle: To reason well, you must clearly understand your purpose, and your purpose must be fairminded.		

Skilled Reasoners	Unskilled Reasoners	Critical Questions
take the time to state their purpose clearly.	are often unclear about their central purpose.	Have I made the purpose of my reasoning clear? What exactly am I trying to achieve? Have I stated the purpose in several ways to clarify it?
distinguish the purpose from related purposes.	oscillate between different, sometimes contradictory, purposes.	What different purposes do I have in mind? How do I see them as related? Am I going off in somewhat different directions? How can I reconcile these contradictory purposes?
periodically remind themselves of their purpose to determine whether they are straying from it.	lose track of their fundamental object or goal.	In writing this proposal, do I seem to be wandering from my purpose? How do my third and fourth paragraphs relate to my central goal?
adopt realistic purposes and goals.	adopt unrealistic purposes and set unrealistic goals.	Am I trying to accomplish too much in this project?
choose significant purposes and goals.	adopt trivial purposes and goals as if they were significant.	What is the significance of pursuing this particular purpose? Is there a more significant purpose I should be focused on?
choose goals and purposes that are consistent with other goals and purposes they have chosen.	inadvertently negate their own purposes and do not monitor their thinking for inconsistent goals.	Does one part of my proposal seem to undermine what I am trying to accomplish in another part?
regularly adjust their thinking to their purpose.	are unable to do the thinking necessary to achieve their purpose.	What thinking do I need to do to achieve my purpose?
choose purposes that are fairminded, considering the desires and rights of others equally with their own desires and rights.	choose purposes that are self-serving at the expense of others' needs and desires.	Is my purpose self-serving, or is it concerned only with my own desires? Does it take into account the rights and needs of other people?

EXHIBIT 7.6

QUESTION AT ISSUE OR CENTRAL PROBLEM		

*All reasoning is an attempt to figure out something,
to settle some question, or to solve some problem.*

Primary standards: (1) clarity and precision, (2) significance, (3) answerability, (4) relevance

Common problems: (1) unclear and unprecise, (2) insignificant, (3) not answerable, (4) irrelevant

Principle: To settle a question, it must be answerable, and you must be clear about it and understand what is needed to answer it adequately.

Skilled Reasoners	Unskilled Reasoners	Critical Questions
are clear about the question they are trying to settle.	are often unclear about the question they are asking.	Am I clear about the main question at issue? Am I able to state it precisely?
can express a question in a variety of ways.	express questions vaguely and find questions difficult to reformulate for clarity.	Am I able to reformulate my question in several ways to recognize the complexities in the issue or problem?
can break a question into sub-questions.	are unable to separate the questions they are asking.	Have I broken down the main question into sub-questions? What are the sub-questions embedded in the main question?
routinely distinguish questions of different types.	confuse questions of different types and thus often respond inappropriately to the questions.	Am I confused about the type of question I am asking or being asked? For example: Am I confusing a legal question with an ethical one? Am I confusing a question of preference with a question requiring judgment?
distinguish significant from trivial questions.	confuse trivial questions with significant ones.	Am I focusing on trivial questions while other significant questions need to be addressed?
distinguish relevant questions from irrelevant ones.	confuse irrelevant questions with relevant ones.	Are the questions I'm raising in this discussion relevant to the main question at issue?
are sensitive to the assumptions built into the questions they ask.	often ask loaded questions.	Is the way I'm putting the question loaded? Am I taking for granted from the outset something I should be questioning?
distinguish questions they can answer from questions they can't answer.	try to answer questions they are not in a position to answer.	Am I in a position to answer this question? What information would I need to have before I could answer the question?

EXHIBIT 7.7

POINT OF VIEW		

All reasoning is done from some point of view.

Primary standards: (1) flexibility, (2) fairness, (3) clarity, (4) breadth, (5) relevance

Common problems: (1) restricted, (2) biased, (3) unclear, (4) narrow, (5) irrelevant

Principle: To reason well, you must identify those points of view relevant to the issue and enter these viewpoints empathetically and in good faith.

Skilled Reasoners	Unskilled Reasoners	Critical Questions
keep in mind that people have different points of view, especially on controversial issues.	do not credit alternative reasonable viewpoints.	Have I articulated the point of view from which I am approaching this issue? Have I considered opposing points of view regarding this issue?
consistently and accurately articulate other points of view and reason from within those points of view to understand them.	neither value nor practice reasoning within alternative viewpoints; cannot reason with empathy from other points of view.	Let me think aloud within this alternative viewpoint to see whether I can accurately articulate it.
seek other viewpoints, especially when the issue is one they believe in passionately.	can sometimes give other points of view when the issue is not emotionally charged but cannot do so for issues they feel strongly about.	Am I presenting X's point of view in an unfair manner? Am I having difficulty appreciating X's viewpoint because I am emotional about this issue?
confine their monological reasoning to problems that are clearly monological.*	confuse multilogical with monological issues; insist that there is only one frame of reference within which a given multilogical question must be decided.	Is the question here monological or multilogical? How can I tell? Am I reasoning as if only one point of view is relevant to this issue when in reality other viewpoints are relevant?
recognize when they are most likely to be prejudiced for or against a viewpoint.	are unaware of their own prejudices.	Is this prejudiced or reasoned judgment? What is causing me to prejudge in this situation?
approach problems and issues with a richness of vision and an appropriately broad point of view.	reason from within inappropriately narrow or superficial points of view.	Is my approach to this question too narrow? Am I thinking broadly enough to address the issue adequately?

Monological problems are ones for which there are definite correct and incorrect answers and definite procedures for getting those answers. In *multilogical* problems, there are competing schools of thought to be considered. (See the Thinkers Guide to Asking Essential Questions.)

EXHIBIT 7.8

INFORMATION		

All reasoning is based on information: data, evidence, experience, research.

Primary standards: (1) clear, (2) relevant, (3) fairly gathered and reported, (4) accurate, (5) adequate, (6) consistently applied

Common problems: (1) unclear, (2) irrelevant, (3) biased, (4) inaccurate, (5) insufficient, (6) inconsistently applied

Principle: Reasoning can be only as sound as the information it is based on.

Skilled Reasoners	Unskilled Reasoners	Critical Questions
assert a claim only when they have sufficient evidence to support it.	assert claims without considering all relevant information.	Is my assertion supported by evidence? Do I have sufficient evidence to support my position?
can articulate and accurately evaluate the information behind their claims.	don't articulate the information they are using in their reasoning and so do not subject it to rational scrutiny.	Do I have evidence to support my claim that I haven't clearly articulated? Have I evaluated the information I am using for accuracy and relevance?
actively search for information *against* (not just *for*) their own position.	gather information only when it supports their own point of view.	Where is a good place to look for evidence on the opposite side? Have I looked there? Have I honestly considered information that doesn't support my position?
focus on relevant information and disregard what is irrelevant to the question at issue.	do not carefully distinguish between relevant information and irrelevant information.	Are my data relevant to the claim I'm making? Have I failed to consider relevant information?
draw conclusions only to the extent that they are supported by the data and sound reasoning.	make inferences that go beyond what the data support.	Does my claim go beyond the evidence I've cited?
state their evidence clearly and fairly.	distort the information or state it inaccurately.	Is my presentation of the pertinent information clear and coherent? Have I distorted information to support my position?

EXHIBIT 7.9

CONCEPTS AND IDEAS		

All reasoning is expressed through, and shaped by, concepts and ideas.

Primary standards: (1) clarity, (2) relevance, (3) depth, (4) accuracy, (5) justifiability

Common problems: (1) unclear, (2) irrelevant, (3) superficial, (4) inaccurate, (5) justifiable

Principle: Reasoning can be only as clear, relevant, realistic, and deep as the concepts that shape it.

Skilled Reasoners	Unskilled Reasoners	Critical Questions
are aware of the key concepts and ideas they and others use.	are unaware of the key concepts and ideas they and others use.	What is the main idea I am using in my thinking? What are the main concepts others are using?
are able to explain the basic implications of the key words and phrases they use.	cannot accurately explain basic implications of their key words and phrases.	Am I clear about the implications of key concepts? For example: Does the word *cunning* have negative implications that the word *clever* does not?
are able to distinguish special, nonstandard uses of words from standard uses.	are not able to recognize when their use of a word or phrase departs from educated usage.	Where did I get my definition of this central concept? For example: Where did I get my definition of the concept of education, terrorism . . . ? Have I changed the meaning of a concept to fit my own purposes?
are careful to use words in keeping with educated usage.	often use words inappropriately or in ways not justified by the circumstances.	Am I using the concept of *love* appropriately? For example: Do I unknowingly act as if loving a person implies a right to treat him or her discourteously?
think deeply about the concepts they use.	fail to think deeply about the concepts they use.	Am I thinking deeply enough about this concept? For example: The concept of *health care,* as I describe it, does not take into account the patient's rights and privileges. Do I need to consider the idea of health care more deeply?

EXHIBIT 7.10

ASSUMPTIONS		
All reasoning is based on assumptions—beliefs we take for granted.		
Primary standards: (1) clarity, (2) justifiability, (3) consistency Common problems: (1) unclear, (2) unjustified, (3) contradictory Principle: Reasoning can be only as sound as the assumptions it is based on.		
Skilled Reasoners	**Unskilled Reasoners**	**Critical Questions**
are clear about the assumptions they are making.	are often unclear about the assumptions they make.	Are my assumptions clear to me? Do I clearly understand what my assumptions are based upon?
make assumptions that are reasonable and justifiable given the situation and the evidence.	often make unjustified or unreasonable assumptions.	Do I make assumptions about the future based on just one experience from the past? Can I fully justify what I am taking for granted? Are my assumptions justifiable given the evidence I am using to support them?
make assumptions that are consistent with each other.	often make assumptions that are contradictory.	Do the assumptions I made in the first part of my argument contradict the assumptions I am making now?
consistently seek to figure out their assumptions.	ignore their assumptions.	What assumptions am I making in this situation? Are they justifiable? Where did I get these assumptions?
recognize that assumptions lie at the unconscious level of thought and that those assumptions determine the inferences we make.	don't explicitly realize they make assumptions; don't understand the relationship between inferences and assumptions.	What assumptions in my thinking have I never explained? How might these assumptions lead to illogical inferences?

EXHIBIT 7.11

IMPLICATIONS AND CONSEQUENCES		

All reasoning leads somewhere. It has implications and, when acted upon, consequences.

Primary standards: (1) significance, (2) logic, (3) clarity, (4) precision, (5) completeness

Common problems: (1) unimportant, (2) unrealistic, (3) unclear, (4) imprecise, (5) incomplete

Principle: To reason well through an issue, you must think through the implications that follow from your reasoning. You must think through the consequences likely to follow from the decisions you make.

Skilled Reasoners	Unskilled Reasoners	Critical Questions
trace out a number of significant implications and consequences of their reasoning.	trace out few or none of the implications and consequences of holding a position or making a decision.	Have I spelled out all the significant implications of the action I am advocating? If I were to take this course of action, what other consequences might follow that I haven't considered?
articulate the implications and possible consequences.	are unclear and imprecise in articulating possible consequences they articulate.	Have I clearly and precisely delineated the consequences likely to follow from my chosen action?
search for negative as well as positive potential consequences.	trace out only the consequences that come immediately to mind, either positive or negative, but usually not both.	I may have done a good job of spelling out some positive implications of the decision I am about to make, but what are some of the negative implications possible?
anticipate the likelihood of unexpected negative and positive implications.	are surprised when their decisions have unexpected consequences.	If I make this decision, what are some unexpected consequences? What are some variables out of my control that might lead to negative consequences?

195

EXHIBIT 7.12

INFERENCE AND INTERPRETATION		
All reasoning contains inferences from which we draw conclusions and give meaning to data and situations.		
Primary standards: (1) clarity, (2) logic, (3) justifiability, (4) profundity, (5) reasonability, (6) consistency		
Common problems: (1) unclear, (2) illogical, (3) unjustified, (4) superficial, (5) unreasonable, (6) contradictory		
Principle: Reasoning can be only as sound as the inferences it makes (or the conclusions it comes to).		
Skilled Reasoners	**Unskilled Reasoners**	**Critical Questions**
are clear about the inferences they are making and articulate their inferences clearly.	are often unclear about the inferences they are making, do not clearly articulate their inferences.	Am I clear about the inferences I am making? Have I clearly articulated my conclusions?
usually make inferences that follow from the evidence or reasons that are presented.	often make inferences that do not follow from the evidence or reasons presented.	Do my conclusions logically follow from the evidence and reasons presented?
often make inferences that are deep rather than superficial.	often make inferences that are superficial.	Are my conclusions superficial, given the problem?
often make inferences or come to conclusions that are reasonable.	often make inferences or come to conclusions that are unreasonable.	Are my conclusions reasonable?
make inferences or come to conclusions that are consistent with each other.	often make inferences or come to conclusions that are contradictory.	Do the conclusions I came to in the first part of my analysis seem to contradict the conclusions that I came to at the end?
understand the assumptions that lead to inferences.	do not seek to figure out the assumptions that lead to inferences.	Is my inference based on a faulty assumption? How would my inference be changed if I were to base it on a different, more justifiable assumption?

ASK QUESTIONS THAT LEAD TO GOOD THINKING

From what we have emphasized thus far, it should be clear that to emulate the thinking of the best thinkers

- you must become interested in thinking.
- you must become a critic of your own thinking.
- you must be willing to establish new habits of thought.
- you must develop a passion for thinking well.
- you must study the interplay of thoughts, feelings, and desires.
- you must become interested in the role of thinking in your life.
- you must routinely analyze thinking into its elements.
- you must routinely assess thinking for its strengths and weaknesses.
- you must routinely assess your study (and learning) habits.
- you must learn how to think within diverse systems of thought.

In this chapter, we shall explore the role of questions in thinking to make explicit the questions the best thinkers ask.

THE IMPORTANCE OF QUESTIONS IN THINKING

It is not possible to become a good thinker and be a poor questioner. Thinking is not driven by answers but, rather, by questions. If those who laid the foundation for a field—for example, physics or biology—asked no questions, the field would not have been developed in the first place. Every intellectual field is born out of a cluster of questions to which answers are either needed or highly desirable. Furthermore, every field stays alive only to the extent that fresh questions are generated and taken seriously as the driving force in thinking.

To learn a subject is to learn to ask the questions the best thinkers in the field routinely ask.

When a field of study is no longer pursuing answers to questions, it becomes extinct. To think through or rethink anything, one must ask questions that stimulate thought.

On the one hand, questions define tasks, express problems, and delineate issues. Answers, on the other hand, often signal a full stop in thought. Only when an answer generates further questions does thought continue its life as such. This is why you are really thinking and learning only when you have questions. Moreover, the quality of the questions you ask determines the quality of your thinking. When you have no questions, you are not concerned with pursuing any answers.

For example, biologists and biochemists make progress when they ask questions such as: "What are we made of? How do our bodies work? What is life?" They make even more progress when they take their questioning to the subcellular and molecular level. They ask questions about isolated molecules and events on the molecular level: "What are proteins? What are enzymes? What are enzyme reactions? How do molecular events underlie macroscopic phenomena?" (Jevons, 1964). By focusing on these subcellular questions, they can move to important questions such as: "How do vitamins interact with chemistry in the body to produce healthier functioning? How do cancer cells differ from normal cells? What kinds of foods interact with the body's chemistry to lessen the likelihood of the development of cancerous cells?"

A field is alive only to the extent that there are live questions in it.

The best teachers are usually those who understand the relationship between learning and asking questions. As Jevons (1964) says of his students, "Those who asked questions helped me most, but even those who merely looked puzzled helped a little, by stimulating me to find more effective ways of making myself understood."

QUESTIONING YOUR QUESTIONS

When you meet a person for the first time, what questions would you most like to answer about him or her? Another way to put this question is to ask, "What information do you seek about people when you first meet them?" What do these questions (and the information you seek) tell you about your values and concerns? What do they tell you, as well, about the nature of the relationships you tend to form?

Consider the following types of questions based on the elements of reasoning and intellectual standards.

- Questions of *purpose* force us to define our task.
- Questions of *information* force us to look at our sources of information as well as the quality of our information.
- Questions of *interpretation* force us to examine how we are organizing or giving meaning to information and to consider alternative ways of giving meaning.
- Questions of *assumption* force us to examine what we are taking for granted.
- Questions of *implication* force us to follow where our thinking is leading us.
- Questions of *point of view* force us to examine our point of view and to consider other *relevant* points of view.
- Questions of *relevance* force us to differentiate what does and does not bear on a question.
- Questions of *accuracy* force us to evaluate and test for truth and correctness.
- Questions of *precision* force us to give details and be specific.
- Questions of *consistency* force us to examine our thinking for contradictions.
- Questions of *logic* force us to consider how we are putting all our thought together, to make sure that it all adds up and makes sense within a reasonable system of some kind.

8.1 *Think for Yourself*

QUESTIONING THE DEPTH OF YOUR QUESTIONS

Write out your answers to these questions:

Are any of the questions you are focused on in your life *deep* questions?

To what extent are you questioning your *purposes* and goals?

Your *assumptions*? The *implications* of your thought and action?

Do you ever question your *point of view*?

Do you ever wonder whether your point of view is keeping you from seeing things from an opposing perspective? When?

Do you ever question the *consistency* of your thought and behavior?

Do you question the *logicalness of your thinking*?

What did answering these questions, and your reflection on them, tell you about yourself and about your habits of questioning?

DEAD QUESTIONS REFLECT INERT MINDS

Most students ask virtually none of these thought-stimulating types of questions. Most tend to stick to dead questions such as, "Is this going to be on the test?" This sort of question usually implies the desire not to think at all.

We must continually remind ourselves that thinking begins within some content only when questions are generated. No questions (asked) equals no understanding (achieved). Superficial questions equal superficial understanding; unclear questions equal unclear understanding. If you sit in class in silence, your mind probably will be silent as well. When this is the case, you either will ask no questions or your questions will tend to be superficial, ill-formed, and self-serving. You should strive for a state of mind in which, even when you are outwardly quiet, you are inwardly asking questions. You should formulate questions that will lead you to productive learning.

If you want to learn deeply and independently, you should always strive to study so that what you do stimulates your thinking with questions that lead to further questions.

> The best thinkers ask live questions that lead to knowledge and further questions that lead to knowledge and yet further questions.

> Isaac Newton at age 19 drew up a list of questions under 45 headings. His goal was constantly to question the nature of matter, place, time, and motion.

8.2, 8.3 *Think for Yourself*

QUESTIONING AS YOU READ

Read a chapter in one of your textbooks specifically to generate questions. Only when you are asking questions as you read are you reading critically. After reading each section, or every few paragraphs, make a list of all the questions you have about what you are reading. Then try to answer these questions—either by looking in the textbook or by raising them in class.

QUESTIONING YOUR QUESTIONING ABILITY

At this point in your intellectual development, to what extent would you call yourself a skilled or deep questioner? That is, how would you rate the overall quality of the questions you are asking (those that you share with others and those you keep to yourself)? Do you know anyone who you would say is a deep questioner? If so, what makes you think this person questions deeply?

THREE CATEGORIES OF QUESTIONS

Before we go further in our discussion about how to question deeply, we want to introduce a useful way of categorizing questions. This way of classifying questions provides a "jumpstart" in discovering the kind of reasoning a question calls for.

The three categories of questions are:

1. Questions of fact. Questions with one right answer (Factual questions fall into this category.)

- What is the boiling point of lead?
- What is the size of this room?
- What is the differential of this equation?
- How does the hard drive on a computer operate?

2. Questions of preference. Questions with as many answers as there are different human preferences (a category in which mere subjective opinion rules). These questions ask you to express a preference.

- Which would you prefer, a vacation in the mountains or one at the seashore?
- How do you like to wear your hair?

EXHIBIT 8.1 *In approaching a question, it is useful to figure out what type it is. Is it a question with one definitive answer? Is it a question that calls for a subjective choice? Or does the question require you to consider competing answers?*

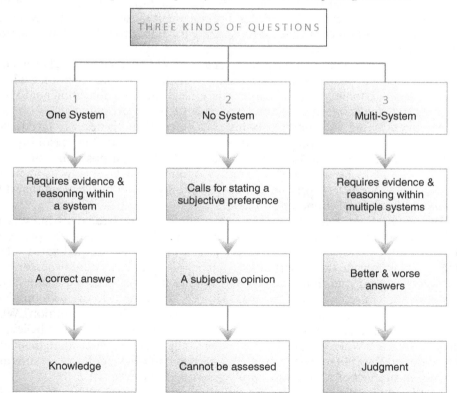

- Do you like to go to the opera?
- What is your favorite type of food?

3. Questions of judgment. Questions requiring reasoning but with more than one defensible answer. These are questions that make sense to debate, questions with better-or-worse answers (well-reasoned or poorly reasoned answers). Here we are seeking the best possible answer given the range of possibilities.

- How can we best address the most basic and significant economic problems of the nation today?
- What can be done to significantly reduce the number of people who become addicted to illegal drugs?
- What is the best thing we can do to save the earth?
- Is abortion morally justifiable?
- Should capital punishment be abolished?

Only the second kind of question (a question of preference) calls for sheer subjective opinion. The third kind is a matter of reasoned judgment. We should rationally evaluate answers to the question by using universal intellectual standards—such as clarity, depth, consistency, and so forth. Some people think of all judgments as either fact or subjective preference. They ask questions that elicit either a factual response or an opinion. Yet, the kind of judgment most important to educated people—and the kind we most want to be good at—falls into the third, now almost totally ignored, category: reasoned judgment.

A judge in a court of law is expected to engage in reasoned judgment. He or she is expected to render a judgment and to base that judgment on sound, relevant evidence and valid legal reasoning. A judge is under the ethical and legal obligation not to base his or her judgments on subjective preferences or on personal opinions.

Judgment based on sound reasoning goes beyond, and is never to be equated with, fact alone or mere opinion alone. Facts are typically used in reasoning, but good reasoning does more than state facts. Furthermore, a position that is well reasoned is not to be described as simply "opinion." Of course, we sometimes call the judge's verdict an "opinion," but we not only expect but *demand* that it be based on relevant and sound reasoning.

When questions that require reasoned judgment are treated as matters of preference, counterfeit critical thinking occurs. In that case, some people come to uncritically assume that everyone's subjective opinion is of equal value. Their capacity to appreciate the importance of intellectual standards diminishes, and we can expect to hear questions such as these: What if I don't like these standards? Why shouldn't I use my own standards? Don't I have a right to my own opinion? What if I'm just an emotional person? What if I like to follow my intuition? What if I think spirituality is more important than reason? What if I don't believe in being "rational"? When people reject questions that call for reasoned judgment and deep thought, they fail to see the difference between offering legitimate reasons and evidence in support of a view and simply asserting the view as true.

Intellectually responsible people, by contrast, recognize questions of judgment for what they are: questions that require the consideration of alternative ways of reasoning. Put another way, intellectually responsible people recognize when a question calls for good reasoning, and they behave in accordance with that responsibility. This means that they realize when a question can be answered in more than one reasonable way. Moreover, they appreciate the responsibility they have to consider alternative ways of looking at the problem, of entering *in good faith* viewpoints that oppose their own before coming to final judgments.

To summarize, we all need to recognize that questions call on us to do one of three things:

1. To express a subjective preference
2. To establish an objective fact (within a well-defined system)
3. To come up with the best of competing answers (generated by competing systems)

We do not fully understand the task we are faced with until we know which of these three is called for in our thinking. Is the question calling for a subjective or personal choice? If so, let's make that choice in terms of our personal preferences. If not, is there a way to come up with one correct answer to this question (a definite system in which to find the answer)? Or, finally, are we dealing with a question that could reasonably be answered differently within different points of view? In other words, is it debatable? If the last, what is the best answer to the question, all things considered?

8.4 *Think for Yourself*

DISTINGUISHING TYPES OF QUESTIONS 1

Make a random list of clear and precise questions. Then decide which questions are factual (with a definite right or wrong answer), which questions are matters of subjective preference, and which questions require reasoning and judgment (within multiple perspectives). To make these determinations, you might think through each question in the following way:

1. Ask, "Are there any facts that a reasonable person would have to consider to answer this question?" (If there are some facts you need to consider, the question is not purely a matter of subjective preference.)

2. If any facts are relevant to the question, would all reasonable persons interpret the fact in the same way? If so, it is a question of fact. If not, the facts presumably can be rationally interpreted differently from competing, reasonable perspectives. It is therefore a question of judgment.

As you study a subject, distinguish among the three types of questions. Look for the questions that have definitive or correct answers. These will be matters settled by definition or fixed, established, and recognized procedures. Identify those questions that are ultimately a matter of personal choice. And, most important, identify those questions that can be legitimately, or at least arguably, approached from more than one point of view. These latter will arise most commonly when there are competing traditions or schools or theories within the discipline. For example, psychology incorporates many competing schools: Freudian, Jungian, Adlerian, rational–emotive, Gestalt, and so on. Many issues in psychology will be reasoned through differently, depending on the reasoner's academic allegiance. These issues will call for considering argumentation from a variety of perspectives and will result in different reasoned judgments.

8.5 *Think for Yourself*

DISTINGUISHING TYPES OF QUESTIONS 2

Identify at least one subject you have studied in school that involves competing traditions or schools of thought. Then identify some questions that would be answered differently, depending on the school of thought used to think through the question. Which of the schools of thought do you best understand or most identify with? How might this school of thought be questioned from the perspective of a competing school of thought?

BECOME A SOCRATIC QUESTIONER

Now that you are beginning to understand how to categorize questions, let us discuss how we can approach questions in general so our questions will lead us to better thinking. As critical thinkers, we want to go beyond questions that are undisciplined, questions that go in multiple directions with neither rhyme nor reason. Therefore, we turn from merely questioning to what might be termed *Socratic questioning*. The word *Socratic* adds systematicity, depth, and a keen interest in assessing the truth or plausibility of things to ordinary questioning.

One of the primary goals of critical thinking is to establish a disciplined, "executive" component of thinking in our thinking, a powerful inner voice of reason, to monitor, assess, and repair—in a more rational direction—our thinking, feelings, and action. Socratic questioning provides that inner voice. Here are some of the fundamentals of Socratic questioning, followed by examples of questions you might ask in Socratic dialogue to probe deeply the thinking of another person.

- Seek to understand—when possible—the ultimate foundations for what is said or believed and follow the implications of those foundations through further questions. (You might ask, for example, "On what do you base your beliefs? Could you explain your reasoning to me in more detail so I can more fully understand your position?")

- Recognize that any thought can exist fully only in a network of connected thoughts. Therefore, treat all assertions as connecting points to further thoughts. Pursue those connections. (You might ask, for example, "If what you say is true, wouldn't X or Y also be so?")

- Treat all thoughts as in need of development. (You might ask: "Could you elaborate on what you are saying so I can understand you better?")

■ Recognize that all questions presuppose prior questions, and all thinking presupposes prior thinking. When raising questions, be open to the questions they presuppose. (You might ask, for example, "To answer this complex question, what other questions do we need to answer?")

8.6   *Think for Yourself*

PRACTICING SOCRATIC QUESTIONING

When you become a Socratic questioner, a systematic questioner, you can question anyone about anything—effectively! Try out your questioning skills by questioning someone you know as systematically and as deeply as you can about something he or she deeply believes. Record the discussion. Follow the suggestions given here. When finished, replay the tape and analyze your Socratic questioning abilities. Did you probe beneath the surface of the other person's thinking? Did you ask for elaboration when needed? Did you pursue connections? Overall, how you would rate yourself as a Socratic questioner?

EXHIBIT 8.2 *Socratic thinking is an integrated, disciplined approach to thinking.*

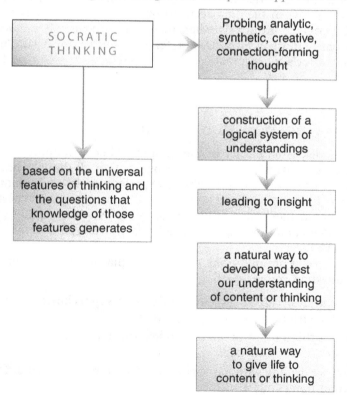

To take your thinking to the level of disciplined questioning, to think or question Socratically, you can go in several directions:

1. You can focus your questions on types of question (fact, preference, or judgment).

2. You can focus your questions on assessment by targeting intellectual standards.

3. You can focus your questions on analysis by targeting the elements of reasoning.

4. You can learn to "unpack" complex questions by developing questions one would have to answer prior to answering the lead question.

5. You can learn to determine the domains of questions inherent in a complex question.

In the following discussion, we will elaborate on these forms of Socratic questioning. Of course, the questions you would ask in a given situation will be determined by the context within which you are thinking. When you become skilled at using these questions, you will see the powerful role they can play in your thinking. With practice, they eventually will become intuitive to you. You will naturally ask questions of clarification when you are unclear and ask questions focused on *information* when the data seem to be inaccurate or otherwise questionable. You will recognize intuitively when people are mistakenly answering questions of judgment with their subjective preference, and so on. Again, intuitive ability comes only after a lot of practice.

Focus Your Thinking on the Type of Question Being Asked

In pursuing questions, Charles Darwin relied on perseverance and continual reflection: "I have never been able to remember for more than a few days a single date or line of poetry."

As discussed earlier in this chapter, when you approach questions systematically, you are able to recognize that all thought has three possible functions: to express a subjective preference, to establish an objective fact (within a well-defined system), or to come up with the best of competing answers (generated by competing systems). Assume that you do not fully understand thinking until you know which type of thinking the question is focused on.

Here are questions you can ask that focus on getting at the type of question you are dealing with:

■ Is the question calling for a subjective or personal choice? If so, let's make that choice in terms of our personal preferences.

■ If not, is this a question that has one correct answer or a definite system in which to find the answer?

■ Or are we dealing with a question that would be answered differently within different points of view?

EXHIBIT 8.3 *Here are five ways to generate questions that lead to disciplined thinking.*

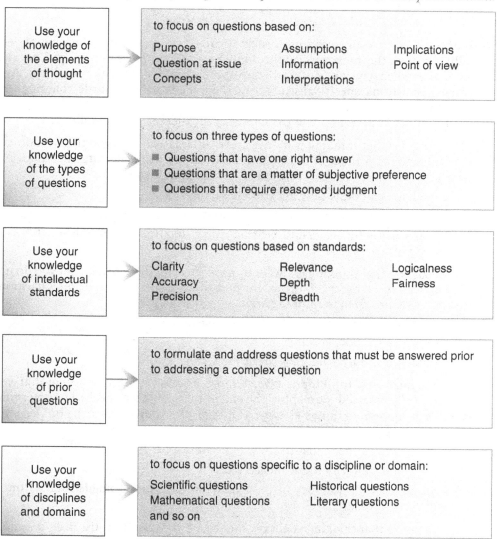

- If so, what is the best answer to the question, all things considered?
- Is this person treating a question of judgment as a question of preference by saying he doesn't have to give reasoning for his answer when the question implies that he does?
- Is this person treating a question of judgment as a question for which there is one right answer?

Focus Your Questions on Universal Intellectual Standards for Thought

When you approach questions systematically, you recognize when people are failing to use the universal intellectual standards in their thinking. You also recognize when you are failing to use these standards in your thinking. And you ask questions, specifically targeting the intellectual standards, that upgrade thinking.

From discussions in previous chapters, the guidelines are as follows.

1. Recognize that thinking is always more or less *clear*. Assume that you do not fully understand a thought except to the extent you can elaborate, illustrate, and exemplify it. Questions that focus on *clarity* in thinking are:

- Could you elaborate on what you are saying?
- Could you give me an example or illustration of your point?
- I hear you saying "X." Am I hearing you correctly, or have I misunderstood you?

2. Recognize that thinking is always more or less *precise*. Assume that you do not fully understand it except to the extent that you can specify it in detail. Questions that focus on *precision* in thinking are:

- Could you give me more details about that?
- Could you be more specific?
- Could you specify your allegations more fully?

3. Recognize that thinking is always more or less *accurate*. Assume that you have not fully assessed it except to the extent that you have checked to determine whether it represents things as they really are. Questions that focus on *accuracy* in thinking are:

- How could we check that to see whether it is true?
- How could we verify these alleged facts?
- Can we trust the accuracy of these data given the questionable source from which they come?

4. Recognize that thinking is always capable of straying from the task, question, problem, or issue under consideration. Assume that you have not fully assessed thinking except to the extent that you have ensured that all considerations used in addressing it are genuinely *relevant* to it. Questions that focus on *relevance* in thinking are:

- I don't see how what you said bears on the question. Could you show me how it is relevant?
- Could you explain what you think the connection is between your question and the question we have focused on?

5. Recognize that thinking can either function at the surface of things or probe beneath that surface to deeper matters and issues. Assume that you have not fully assessed a line of thinking except to the extent that you have determined the *depth* required for the task at hand (and compared that with the depth that actually has been achieved). (To figure out whether a question is deep, we need to determine whether it involves complexities that must be considered.) Questions that focus on *depth* in thinking are:

- Is this question simple or complex? Is it easy or difficult to answer?
- What makes this a complex question?
- How are we dealing with the complexities inherent in the question?

6. Recognize that thinking can be more or less broad-minded (or narrow-minded) and that *breadth* of thinking requires the thinker to think insightfully within *more than one point of view or frame of reference*. Assume that you have not fully assessed a line of thinking except to the extent that you have determined how much *breadth* of thinking is required (and how much has actually been exercised). Questions that focus on *breadth* in thinking are:

- What points of view are relevant to this issue?
- What relevant points of view have I ignored thus far?
- Am I failing to consider this issue from an opposing viewpoint because I don't want to change my view?
- Have I entered the opposing views in good faith or only enough to find flaws in them?
- I have looked at the question from an economic point of view. What is the moral point of view?
- I have considered a liberal position on the issue. What would conservatives say?

8.7 *Think for Yourself*

FOCUSING YOUR QUESTIONS ON INTELLECTUAL STANDARDS

For each of the categories of questions focusing on intellectual standards (see the previous section), try to come up with one situation in which your failure to use intellectual standards had negative consequences. This might be a situation in which you should have asked a question of clarification and didn't or should have asked a question focusing on precision and didn't, and so on. State what happened as a result of each failure. For example, you might recall a time when you asked for directions to someone's house but got lost because you failed to ask questions focused on important details.

Focus Your Questions on the Elements of Thought

Another powerful way to discipline your questions is to focus on the elements or parts of thinking. As you formulate your questions, recall the following guidelines:

1. All thought reflects an agenda or *purpose*. Assume that you do not fully understand someone's thought (including your own) until you understand the agenda behind it. Questions that focus on purpose in thinking include:

- What are you trying to accomplish in saying this?
- What is your central aim in this line of thought?
- What is the purpose of this meeting?
- What is the purpose of this chapter?
- What is the purpose of our relationship?
- What is my purpose for being in college?

2. All thoughts presuppose an *information* base. Assume that you do not fully understand the thought until you understand the background information (facts, data, experiences) that supports or informs it. Questions that focus on information in thinking include:

- On what information are you basing that comment?
- What experience convinced you of this? Could the way you are experiencing the situation be based in distorted views?
- How do we know this information is *accurate*?
- Have we left out any important information that we need to consider?

3. All thought requires making *inferences*, drawing conclusions, creating meaning. Assume that you do not fully understand a thought until you understand the inferences that have shaped it. Questions that focus on inferences in thinking include:

- How did you reach that conclusion?
- Could you explain your reasoning?
- Is there an alternative plausible conclusion?
- Given all the facts, what is the best possible conclusion?

4. All thought involves the application of *concepts*. Assume that you do not fully understand a thought until you understand the concepts that define and shape it. Questions that focus on concepts in thinking include:

- What is the main idea you are using in your reasoning?
- Could you explain that idea?
- Are we using our concepts justifiably?

5. All thought rests upon other thoughts, which are taken for granted or *assumed*. Assume that you do not fully understand a thought until you understand what it takes for granted. Questions that focus on assumptions in thinking include:

- What exactly are you taking for granted here?
- Why are you assuming that?

- Should I question the assumptions I am using about my roommate, my friends, my intimate other, my parents, my instructors, my country?

6. All thought is headed in a direction. It not only rests upon something (assumptions) but also is going somewhere (*implications* and consequences). Assume that you do not fully understand a thought unless you know the implications and consequences that follow from it. Questions that focus on implications in thinking include:

- What are you implying when you say that?
- What is likely to happen if we do this versus that?
- Are you implying that . . .?

7. All thought takes place within a *point of view* or frame of reference. Assume that you do not fully understand a thought until you understand the point of view or frame of reference that places it on an intellectual map. Questions that focus on point of view in thinking include:

- From what point of view are you looking at this?
- Is there another point of view we should consider?
- Which of these possible viewpoints makes the most sense given the situation?

8. All thought is responsive to a *question*. Assume that you do not fully understand the thought until you understand the question that gives rise to it. Questions that focus on questions in thinking include:

- I am not sure exactly what question you are raising. Could you explain it?
- Is this question the best one to focus on at this point, or is there a more pressing question we need to address?
- The question in my mind is this: How do you see the question?
- How is your question related to the question we have been reasoning through?

8.8 *Think for Yourself*

FOCUSING YOUR QUESTIONS ON THE ELEMENTS OF REASONING

From each of the eight categories we just outlined, ask yourself at least one question about your view of marriage (or family). For example, you might begin with the question, "In my view, what is the basic purpose or goal of marriage?" (Answer each question after you ask it.)

Afterward, question a friend about his or her views, using the same questions (you should feel free to ask additional questions as they occur to you). Write out an analysis of your questioning process. Do you notice yourself beginning to think at a deeper level—given the questions you are now asking? Did you focus on all eight elements?

Focus Your Questions on Prior Questions

Whenever we are dealing with complex questions, another tool that is useful in disciplining our thinking is to construct prior questions—questions we need to answer before we can answer a more complex question. Hence, to answer the question, "What is multiculturalism?" we should be able first to settle the question, "What is culture?" To settle that question, we should settle the question, "What are the factors about a person that determine what culture he or she belongs to?" When you learn to formulate and pursue prior questions, you have another important "idea" you can use to develop your ability to learn in any context.

To construct a list of prior questions, simply write down the main question upon which you are going to focus your discussion and then formulate as many questions as you can think of that you would have to answer before you could answer the first. Then determine from this list what question you would have to answer to answer these questions. Continue following the same procedure for every new set of questions on your list.

As you construct your list, keep your attention focused on the first question on the list as well as on the last. If you do this well, you should end up with a list of questions that probe the logic of the first question. As an example of how to construct logically prior questions, consider this list of questions we would need to answer to address the larger question, "What is history?"

- What do historians write about?
- What is "the past"?
- Is it possible to include all of the past in a history book?
- How many of the events during a given time period are left out in a history of that time period?
- Is more left out than is included?
- How does a historian know what to emphasize?
- Do historians make value judgments in deciding what to include and what to leave out?
- Is it possible simply to list facts in a history book, or does all history writing involve interpretations as well as facts?
- Is it possible to decide what to include and exclude and how to interpret facts without adopting a historical point of view?
- How can we begin to judge a historical interpretation?
- How can we begin to judge a historical point of view?

The best questions are those that keep us focused on achieving our most significant goals and purposes.

When you have practiced formulating prior questions to complex questions, you will begin to develop a Socratic questioning tool you can use whenever you need to answer a complicated question. You will notice your mind coming up with questions that are inherent in other questions. You are unpacking questions to answer them better. You should also then begin to recognize when others are failing to consider the complexities in a question.

8.9   *Think for Yourself*

CONSTRUCTING A LIST OF PRIOR QUESTIONS

Formulate a complex question to which you would like to find an answer. Then use the procedure of constructing prior questions until you have a list of at least 10 questions. Afterward, see if you have gained insight into how the first question has to be thought through in light of the prior questions you formulated.

Focus Your Questions on Domains of Thinking

When you are addressing a complex question that covers more than one domain of thought, you can target your prior questions by figuring out the domains of thinking inherent in the question. Does the complex question, for example, include an economic dimension? Does it include a biological, sociological, cultural, political, ethical, psychological, religious, historical, or some other dimension? For each dimension of thinking inherent in the question, you can formulate questions that force you to consider complexities you otherwise may miss. Consider the following question, some of the domains imbedded in the question, and some of the questions imbedded in those domains.

Complex question: What can be done about the number of people who abuse illegal drugs?

Domains inherent in the question, along with some questions we would have to address within each domain before we could answer our complex question, are:

1. Economic
   - What economic forces support drug use?
   - What can be done to minimize the influence of money involved in drug sales?

2. Political
   - What possible solutions to drug abuse are politically unacceptable?
   - Are there any realistic solutions that the power structure would accept?
   - To what extent does the political structure exacerbate the problem?

3. Social/Sociological
   - What social structures and practices support drug abuse?
   - How does gang membership contribute to drug abuse?
   - How does membership within any group contribute to the problem or, conversely, insulate group members from abusing drugs?

4. Psychological
   - How do factors such as stress, individual personality differences, and childhood traumas support drug abuse?
   - What role, if any, does human irrationality play in drug abuse?

EXHIBIT 8.4 *Complex questions have multiple domains.*

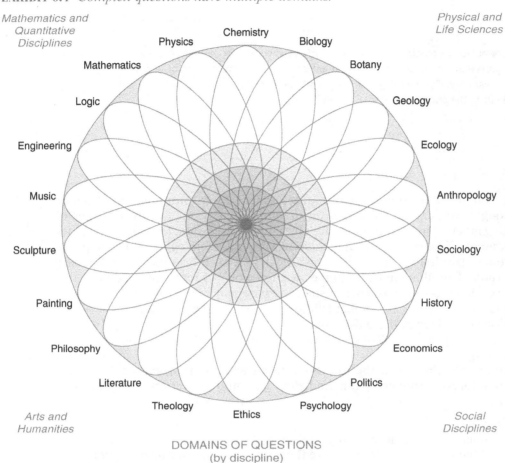

Mathematics and Quantitative Disciplines

Physical and Life Sciences

Arts and Humanities

Social Disciplines

Physics Chemistry Biology
Mathematics Botany
Logic Geology
Engineering Ecology
Music Anthropology
Sculpture Sociology
Painting History
Philosophy Economics
Literature Politics
Theology Ethics Psychology

DOMAINS OF QUESTIONS
(by discipline)

5. Biological
   - How do genetics play a role in drug abuse?
   - What biological changes in the body resulting from drug abuse contribute to the problem?

6. Educational
   - What role are educational institutions now playing to support or diminish the problem?

7. Religious
   - What can religious institutions do to reduce the incidence of drug abuse?
   - What role are they now playing in regard to drug abuse?

8. Cultural
   - What cultural beliefs support the drug-abuse problem?
   - What can we learn from cultures that have a low incidence of drug abuse?

8.10 *Think for Yourself*

FORMULATING QUESTIONS WITHIN DOMAINS OF THINKING

Focus on the question: What can be done to significantly improve the health of the ecosystems on Earth? Using the preceding model, figure out the domains within the question that you would have to think within to address the complexities in the question. Then formulate as many questions as you can within each domain. (The question you are originally addressing determines the domains within which you need to think.)

When we can approach questions to target the domains inherent in them, we are able to ask questions such as:

- What domains of questions are inherent in this complex question?

- Is this person dealing with all the relevant domains within the question?

- Am I leaving out some important domains when reasoning through this issue?

CONCLUSION

Questions play an important role in the minds of the best thinkers. Three important types of questions are questions of fact, questions of preference, and questions of judgment. The best thinkers differentiate these forms of questions because the form of the question determines the kind of thinking the question calls for. The ability to ask questions is not enough in and of itself for the best thinkers. It is necessary to ask important questions relevant to the purposes we are pursuing (including questions that lead us to scrutinize our purposes). Socratic or systematic questioning is a means to disciplined thinking. One method of approaching Socratic questioning is to develop prior questions.

Because there is a sense in which "you think only as well as the questions you ask," you want to force yourself, as a developing thinker, to focus on the role that questions play in your thinking. To what extent are you asking significant questions? To what extent are you able to figure out whether a question is asking for a factual answer, preference, or reasoned judgment? To what extent are you asking questions that follow a disciplined path, leading to rationally defensible answers? To what extent are you able to take apart complex questions, to figure out questions you would have to answer prior to answering those questions? When you are practicing the fundamental questioning steps we have explored in this chapter, you will find yourself progressing as a questioner—and as a thinker.

MASTER THE THINKING, MASTER THE CONTENT

From what we have emphasized thus far, it now should be clear that

- critical thinking requires the development of basic intellectual skills, abilities, and insights.
- becoming a skilled thinker can be compared to becoming skilled in basketball, ballet, or saxophone playing.
- these skills can be used to serve two incompatible ends: self-centeredness or fairmindedness.
- the skills of critical thinking can be learned in a weak sense (skilled but selfish thinking).
- we are focused in this book on the development of critical thinking in a strong sense (skilled, fairminded thinking).
- fairmindedness requires that we develop a network of interrelated traits of mind.
- development as a critical thinker occurs in predictable stages.
- engaging in that development is challenging, requiring planned practice and happening over many years, not weeks or months.
- human egocentrism represents a significant obstacle to fairminded critical thinking.

- to conquer our egocentrism, we must understand, and exercise some control over, the three basic functions of the human mind: thinking, feeling, wanting.

- because we humans spend most of our time thinking about what we personally want or value, we need to question our personal values.

GO BEYOND SUPERFICIAL MEMORIZATION TO DEEP LEARNING

As a student, it is important that you think seriously about what you want to accomplish in each of your classes and in college in general. If you simply want to get by, to do no more than pass your courses, you know the logic of how to do so: You go to class. You find out the minimal requirements of the course. You fulfill those requirements with the least effort possible. You get the grade. You move on to the next semester. After four years and a certain number of course hours, you get a degree. Using this kind of thinking, you think of college merely as a vehicle to get a job. The problem with this "minimalist" strategy is that, in using it, you miss the opportunity to develop skills and insights that you can use for a lifetime. You graduate, but you do not become a lifelong learner.

If, however, you look at college as an opportunity to learn how to learn, to develop your mind, to seek out new ways to look at things, to expand your knowledge, to learn ideas that will help you figure out the problems of your life, you must seek to internalize a set of intellectual skills that will enable you to learn more deeply and more permanently in every one of your courses. With the proper vision of what you are after, you can begin to practice effective thinking in all your classes. And if you strive to develop certain habits of thought and characteristics of mind, such as intellectual humility, perseverance, and fairmindedness, you can transform the way you operate in every challenging context and situation. You will acquire the tools of good thinking and learning. You then will go into each class with powerful questions on the tip of your tongue. You will ask these questions whenever possible. You will ask them while you are silently reading, while engaged in writing, while speaking, while listening.

You will recognize, then, that the content that defines college instruction can be learned only through thinking. You will recognize that when you think poorly while learning, you learn poorly, and that when you think well while learning, you learn well. So, if you are serious about acquiring powerful tools for learning, you must be committed to developing your ability to think well, to reason your way into any body of content, to organize content in your mind, to relate it to your experience, to assess it using appropriate standards.

If, however, you have become subconsciously habituated to rote memorization as your principal tool of learning, if your mode of preparing for an exam is to cram bits and pieces of content into your head, you may get by temporarily, but you will retain little of what you learned. The result, in the long run, will be poor performance, poor learning, and poor habits of thought. You will be of little value to an employer who wants to hire people who can systematically pursue important goals, recognize and analyze significant problems, communicate important meanings, and assess their own performance on the job.

9.1   *Think for Yourself*

THINKING DEEPLY ABOUT WHY YOU ARE IN COLLEGE

What are you trying to accomplish in college? Are you committed to developing your thinking in a deep way? Or are you going to college simply to get a job that requires a degree? Are you going to college just because your friends are going? Are you after the social life that college offers? Or are you not sure what your real motivation is? If you had to complete the following statements, what would you say? My fundamental purpose in going to college is . . . I am committed to. . . . Write out your answer or explain orally.

THE RELATION OF CONTENT TO THINKING

A key insight into content—and into thinking—is that all content represents a distinctive mode of thinking. Math becomes easier as one learns to *think* mathematically. Biology becomes easier as one learns to *think* biologically. History becomes easier as one learns to *think* historically. Parenting

Exhibit 9.1 Thinking is the key to all content.

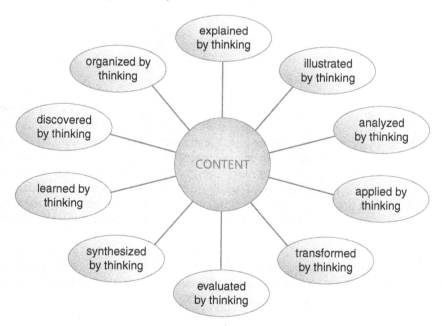

becomes easier as one learns to *think* as a good parent. In Chapter 11, we elaborate on what it means to understand and think through the logic of a course, or indeed of any domain of thinking.

To become motivated to learn what you are studying, you have to understand the connection between content and thinking. If you do, what first appears as dull, dry stuff to memorize can come alive to you. Too many students—and, alas, too many teachers—fail to appreciate this intimate connection. As an opener, consider this: All subjects you study (that is, all content domains) were created by the thinking of humans. They are

generated by thinking, evaluated by thinking,

organized by thinking, restructured by thinking,

analyzed by thinking, maintained by thinking,

synthesized by thinking, transformed by thinking.

expressed by thinking.

They are

learned by thinking,

understood by thinking,

applied by thinking.

If you were to try to take the thinking out of content, you would have nothing, literally nothing, remaining. Learning a way to think is the key to learning any content whatsoever.

UNDERSTAND CONTENT THROUGH THINKING AND THINKING THROUGH CONTENT

The first and most important insight necessary for deep learning is that everything covered in college lectures, and written in college textbooks, is, in the last analysis, nothing more or less than a special way of thinking about a special set of things. To elaborate: Historical content is a special way of thinking about events in the past. Biological content is a special way of thinking about living things. Algebraic content is a special way of thinking about the operations of arithmetic. Physics content is a special way of thinking about mass and energy and their interrelations. Sociological content is a special way of thinking about human behavior in social groups.

There are many ways to begin to grasp the profound truth that all content is nothing more or less than special ways of thinking, ways of figuring out particular things, ways of understanding some set of things through thought. Three ways of beginning to grasp this truth are discussed next.

All content in school is content in a subject; all content in a subject must be thought through. All subjects are areas of study. All areas of study are things we are interested in figuring out. All fields of study have been advanced insofar as we have discovered ways to figure out whatever is being studied. There is no way to figure out something without thinking. There is no way to learn how to figure out something without learning how to think it through. There is no way to learn mathematical content without learning how to figure out correct answers to mathematical questions and problems. There is no way to learn historical content without learning how to figure out correct or reasonable answers to historical questions and problems. There is no way to learn biological content without learning how to figure out answers to biological questions and problems. Any subject or content area can therefore be understood as a mode of figuring out correct or reasonable answers to a certain body of questions. We study chemistry to figure out chemicals (to answer questions about chemicals). We study psychology to figure out human behavior (to answer questions about certain human problems). Subjects can be deeply understood only in this way.

9.2   Think for Yourself

UNDERSTANDING CONTENT AS SOMETHING TO BE THOUGHT THROUGH

Select a subject that is the topic of a class you are now taking or have taken in the past. Make a list of the questions that professionals within the discipline pursue, questions they try to think through to figure out important matters in the field. You may want to look through the first chapter of the textbook for the class, which should provide an overview of the purpose of the discipline, and key questions that thinkers within the discipline traditionally ask. You also might read through the relevant entry in an encyclopedia to identify these key questions. Write out your answer or explain orally.

All Content Is Organized by Concepts

There is no way to learn a body of content without learning the concepts that define and structure it. There is no way to learn a concept without learning how to use it in thinking something through. Hence, to learn the concept of democracy is to learn how to figure out whether some group is functioning democratically or not. To learn the concept of fair play is to learn how to figure out whether participants are being fair in the manner in which they are participating in a game. To learn the concept of a novel is to learn how to distinguish a novel from a play or a short story. To learn the concept of a family is to learn how to distinguish a family from a gang or a club. To learn any body of content, therefore, it is necessary to learn to think accurately and reasonably with the concepts that define the content.

9.3   *Think for Yourself*

IDENTIFYING THE MEANING OF KEY CONCEPTS

Choose a concept, the most basic concept, that is the focus of one of your classes. Write out in your own words your understanding of the concept. Write it out in such a way that you can readily see the significance of the concept in your life.

For example, if you are studying history, you first understand the role that historical thinking plays in our lives. Every human lives within a self-constructed inner history. That history is used every day to make decisions.

For example, if in your understanding of your past, you were always poor in writing or math, you probably would now seek to avoid writing or math classes.

Again, all of your plans for the future are a result of what seems possible and probable to you—given your understanding of your past. Understood in this way, there could be no more important study than that which enables us to improve our historical thinking. Can you see how that would be so? Can you see the study of history in a new light, given this way of understanding the basic concept (humans and historical thinkers)? Now try a key concept of your own choosing. Write out your answer or explain orally.

All Content Is Logically Interdependent

To understand one part of some content requires that we figure out its relation to other parts of that content. For example, we understand what a scientific experiment is only when we understand what a scientific theory is. We understand what a scientific theory is only when we understand what a scientific hypothesis is. We understand what a scientific hypothesis is only when we understand what a scientific prediction is. We understand what a scientific prediction is only when we understand what it is to scientifically test a view. We understand what it is to scientifically test a view only when we understand what a scientific experiment is, and so on. To learn any body of content, therefore, is to figure out (reason or think through) the connections between the parts of that content. No *true* learning of the content is possible without this thinking process.

9.4   *Think for Yourself*

SEEING CONNECTIONS BETWEEN CONCEPTS WITHIN A SUBJECT

Select a subject you are taking currently (or have taken) and draw a diagram showing the links between the most basic concepts within the subject. Then state in your own words how each idea is linked to every other idea. Your thinking will be something like this: To understand "a," you must understand "b," and to understand "b," you must understand "c," and to understand "c," you must understand "d," and so on. Elaborate on each idea as you go so that you can see the connections between them.

Many teachers and students currently approach content not as a mode of thinking, not as a system for thought, or even as a system *of* thought but, rather, as a sequence of stuff to be routinely covered and committed to memory. When content is approached in this lower-order way, there is no basis for intellectual growth, no deep structures of knowledge are formed, and no basis for long-term grasp and control is developed.

By contrast, critical thinking approaches all content explicitly as thinking. It takes thinking apart. It weaves new thinking into old. It assesses thinking. It applies thinking. It is thinking about thinking while thinking to make thinking better: more clear, more accurate, more relevant, more deep, more broad, and more effective.

THINK THROUGH YOUR CLASSES USING YOUR KNOWLEDGE OF THINKING

If learning any content well involves understanding it as a mode of thinking, everything you can discover about thinking offers potential insight into how you should approach college classes. First, let us remind you of eight basic features of all thinking: Whenever we think, we think for a purpose within a point of view based on assumptions leading to implications and consequences. We use concepts and theories to interpret data, facts, and experiences to answer questions, solve problems, and resolve issues. Here are all the elements listed separately:

1. All thinking has a purpose.
2. All thinking raises at least one question.
3. All thinking requires information.
4. All thinking requires concepts.
5. All thinking involves inferences.
6. All thinking involves assumptions.
7. All thinking involves implications.
8. All thinking involves a point of view.

Now let's think about how this knowledge might guide your thinking when thinking through the process of learning college material. As examples:

1. If all thinking entails thinking for a *purpose*, you can always ask yourself, What is the purpose of this assignment? What was the purpose of this character in this story? What is the teacher's purpose in asking me this question? What is my purpose for being in class? What is my purpose for being in college? What are my long-term goals? If you keep central purposes in mind, you will accomplish them more fully.

2. If all thinking requires *information*, you can always ask yourself: What information do I need so I can to reason well through this problem? What information did the researchers use in coming to this conclusion? Upon what information does this historian base her conclusions? What information do I have about how to be successful in college? What information do I have about people who are successful in life? Do I have the information I need to accomplish my most important goals? If you make it a habit to consciously think about the information sources you are using, the quality of your thinking will improve.

3. If all sound thinking is focused on a *question*, you can always ask yourself: What is the key question at issue in this assignment? What is the key question that the researchers focused on? What is the key question at the heart of this story? What is the key problem that I face in becoming successful in college? In life? All good thinkers are good questioners. By learning powerful questions to ask, you will find that you learn more and more and that it becomes progressively easier.

These are just three of the structures of thought that serve as guides for improving thinking. A similar group of questions can be developed for each of the eight structures.

9.5   *Think for Yourself*

FOCUSING ON QUESTIONS IMPLIED BY THE STRUCTURES OF THOUGHT

Choose a subject in a class you are taking. Focus on a different subject than you have in previous Think for Yourself exercises. Complete the following sentences and elaborate on your answer as much as possible.

1. The purpose of this subject is ...
2. The main types of information that professionals in this field of study use are ...
   (This might be research studies in psychology, for example; events from the past in history, for example; information about the universe in astronomy, for example.)
3. Some of the main questions that professionals within this discipline ask are ...

A Caution

No one can do your thinking for you. No one can change you but you. The challenge of becoming the agent of your own growth and development is formidable. We are creatures of habit. We are masters of self-deception. We are highly skilled in self-justification, rationalization, and self-defense. We are not inclined to put burdens on ourselves that others are not requiring of us. Little in academic or social life encourages independent, critical thinking. Although college offers a wonderful opportunity to establish the habits of a lifelong learner, it would be naive to think that all college professors require critical thinking and teach for it.

You may take some history courses in which the professor covers so much historical content in lectures that historical thinking is obscured rather than encouraged. You may take some math courses in which mathematical thinking is sacrificed in favor of memorizing fixed procedures for solving standardized problems. You may take a psychology course in which the multilogical nature of psychological perspectives—that the many competing schools of psychology respond very differently to the same data or problem—is thrown into the background, and the subject is presented as if it were a scientific discipline such as physics or chemistry. You may take a logic course so abstracted from the problems of everyday thinking that you conclude that logic is a waste of time rather than a necessary goal in thinking well.

In short, to some extent, if you are to truly benefit from the content you are studying, you may have to learn at a higher level than the mode of teaching in a class requires of you. To do this, you must develop for yourself the intellectual skills that will enable you to think through the content in a disciplined way, in a way that leads to deep learning, in a way that results in your ability to take the ideas you learn in class, to give them meaning in your thinking, and to use them in your life.

9.6 *Think for Yourself*

CRITIQUING THE QUALITY OF TEACHING

Select a class you are in now or that you have taken in the past, which you think involved high-quality teaching. What precisely does/did the teacher do that led to deep, long-term learning? What can you do as a student to deepen your learning in every class you take? How can you learn as you learned in the best class you took by taking initiative in all your other classes? Or do you think the teacher determines how much you learn and you have little to do with it? Write out your answer or explain orally.

Chapter 10
What Is Critical Thinking within a Field or Discipline?

How can you learn to think critically in a field or discipline? That is, how can you start "learning the discipline" in a deeper, more thoughtful way–not just memorizing information, not just engaging in discussion or debate about it, not just defending your own firmly held beliefs?

One straightforward way you have already begun to try out is to take the elements of reasoning and use them to think through all aspects of the discipline itself. Since the elements are the nuts and bolts of reasoning, to reason within a discipline is to reason out questions within it using those nuts and bolts. When applied to the discipline itself this is called *the logic of the discipline*. But the elements apply equally to all aspects of study in the field: reading in it, writing in it, doing research, analyzing and evaluating positions, theories, arguments, strategies, artworks: all the topics that the discipline addresses.

CRITICAL WRITING

Pre-think what your course will be about. Begin by writing the name of the course (e.g., "Peoples of the World" or "Instructional Management in Special Education"). Write a paragraph or two on what you believe the course will be about: What are the goals of the course? What are the main questions you will address? How will the course fit in with other courses? What implications does it have for your life?

Next, write the name of the discipline that course is in (e.g., *anthropology* in the first case, *special education* or *education* in the second case).

1. Clarify your concept of the discipline by stating it, elaborating on it, exemplifying, and illustrating it (SEE-I).

2. Describe a situation in which you thought through something critically using some of the main concepts in the discipline.

3. Describe a situation in your life (one that actually occurred) in which it would have made sense to think it through critically using the concepts of the discipline, but you didn't.

Definitions and Parts of Critical Thinking: Applied to a Field

So, what *is* critical thinking in a discipline? What is it to think critically in a field such as biology or math, physical education, or nursing, or writing?

One way to approach these questions is by taking the definitions of critical thinking from Chapter 5 and applying them to specific fields. For example, apply Robert Ennis's definition to the field of biology:

Critical thinking in biology is reasonable, reflective biological thinking that is focused on deciding what to believe or do in biology and in the relation between biology and the world at large.

Similarly, we can apply Matthew Lipman's definition to the field of history:

> Critical thinking in history is skillful, responsible thinking that is conducive to good historical judgment, because it is sensitive both to historical contexts and to other contexts which have a relation to history; it relies on historical criteria, and it is self-correcting.

The re-written definitions may be a little cumbersome, but it is worthwhile taking time to ponder what makes thinking in the field you are studying *skillful* or *responsible*. What is involved in being a *reflective* nurse or psychologist? What is it to think in a *reasonable* way in music or political science? What are the main *contexts* a critical-thinking engineer or writer must be sensitive to?

We can also take the three parts of critical thinking discussed in Chapter 5 and apply them to learning a subject. Critical thinking in a field involves asking good questions, reasoning out responses, and believing the results of our reasoning.

Asking the Question

If I am a student thinking critically in a field, I will find myself asking questions in the field: questions about the reading, about what I hear from teachers as well as from other students, about the subject matter, and about my own beliefs and understanding. I won't necessarily ask them out loud, and I will not expect them all to be answered, but with practice, and once I start freeing myself from a passive model of what it is to be a student, I will probably be flooded with questions—far more questions than I can answer.

In fact, that is a good rough-and-ready test of whether you are becoming more of a critical thinker in the field. You will see complexities beneath the surface, ones you never noticed before. You'll notice a lot more places where things are not as clear to you as they seemed before. You may find yourself confused in cases when previously you would not have understood enough even to be confused: before, you would simply have taken notes.

To begin, identify the most central ideas in the course—maybe from the name of the course—and ask yourself, "What are they?" For instance, "What *is* abnormal psychology?" "On the deepest level I can think at, what makes something abnormal?" "What is the purpose of psychology?" In a management course: "What is it to manage an office?" That is a *deep* question, one that you can ask yourself at different points in your life and come up with differing and deeper answers every time. You cannot be an effective office manager unless you re-answer that question when business conditions change, the office changes, or you yourself change.

In a physics course, you can ask, "How does an object get from point A to point B? How does it *do* it? How do forces work? How does energy get transferred?" Don't allow questions like these to be answered simply by definitions the text gives. Definitions are an *aid* to thinking through the question and answer. They are not, by themselves, "the answer."

When Richard Feynman, the Nobel laureate in physics, was a boy, he noticed the ball in his wagon kept rolling even after he stopped the wagon. He asked his father why that happened. His father gave him a profound answer, rooted in a spirit of asking questions: "The general principle is that things which are moving tend to keep on moving . . . . This tendency is called 'inertia,' but nobody knows why it's true."[1] Feynman points out how the answer, inertia, could have been used to stifle the wonder behind the boy's question. But the answer his father gave, promoted further questioning.

It takes practice to improve at critical thinking. That is particularly true of learning to ask questions. If you are like many other students, when you read a paragraph in your text or you listen to a lecture, no questions come up for you at all. As you work on your critical thinking, though, that will change. But guard against the idea that having no questions shows you understand something. For any subject matter that is at all complicated, the opposite is the case: if no questions arise for you, it probably means you do not understand it deeply enough to see the many paths of questioning that arise.

Reasoning It Through

Reasoning in a field can be difficult. Initially, it requires you to recognize both what you know *and* what you need to know but don't. Additionally, it means being able to draw conclusions on the basis of reasons.

Think of the difference between memorizing a list of the causes of World War I and reasoning those causes out. The historians who first formulated the thesis that the war came about as a result of entangling alliances *reasoned* this out as an answer, and so do all the people who rethink this answer for themselves. They re-examine how adequate it is, whether it's deep enough as a cause. They amend it, add to it; some of them end up rejecting the idea that entangling alliances were a major cause of WWI. Jennifer Reed, a history professor, regularly asks her students to work through not just a single set of causes of WWI, but also causes that are geographic, political, economic, social, technological, and personal. She helps students reason out what combination of these causes was necessary and sufficient for the event.[2]

That is an example of reasoning in the field of history. It is entirely different—different in kind—from merely repeating what someone else said about the causes of WWI. In its fullest sense, reasoning in a field involves being able to use the elements (Chapter 6) and standards of critical thinking in the subject matter.

Take a paragraph or two from your text, selected by you or your teacher. The paragraphs may be largely composed of factual material; they may also contain reasoned judgments. But in either case, they are the product of *reasoning*. So picture them as *conclusions*, conclusions that people have drawn from a long process of reasoning. Try to describe the process of reasoning that might have led to these conclusions.

The paragraphs may contain:

■ A set of definitions or classifications → Can you describe the disorganized state of affairs that existed before these definitions and classifications were formulated?

■ Factual matters that are the results of tests or investigations (these may not even be mentioned) → Can you determine the kinds of tests and investigations that led to these results?

■ Biographical or background information → Can you describe the kinds of primary sources that this information is derived from?

Believing the Results

It may seem that, as you become more adept at asking questions in the field and then reasoning through the answers, you will automatically believe the results of your reasoning. But believing the results of your reasoning—or acting on that reasoning—may not follow.

Here is a personal example. I learned in school that heavy objects and light objects fall toward the earth at the same rate. Everyone learns this. It is a scientific law. And, of course, I know that law is true. I learned it many times in school; if you ask me on an exam, I will give the right answer. But despite all that, I strongly suspect that I don't really believe it! That is, in my heart I probably don't believe it: If I had to bet my life on the outcome, without a lot of time to think it over, I'm afraid I might bet that the heavy one would hit the ground first (even in a vacuum).

Here is another example, a far more serious one. One of the hardest things to teach student nurses and other health-care practitioners to do is to wash their hands between patients. It is easy, however, to get student nurses to *say* they will wash their hands. If you ask on a test, "It is important to wash your hands: TRUE or FALSE," they will always get the right answer. They can also correctly explain why hand-washing is necessary. What's difficult is getting them to learn to *do* it.

A few years ago, there was a conference in New Orleans for experts on infectious diseases. These were doctors, not nurses. Some graduate students stationed themselves in the restrooms and counted how many of these doctors washed their hands after using the restrooms. They found that 13 percent of the women and 44 percent of the men

Give some examples of findings in the field you are studying that you don't believe.

These may fall into two distinct categories. The first is where you straightforwardly *disagree* with claims or positions in the field. You may or may not have any of these. If you do, write some of them down.

The second category is much harder to identify. It is where the findings in the field subtly conflict with background stories or accounts you already have in your head. (See pages 255–257.) These background stories may not be fully formulated in your mind; they may not be conscious at all. (My example of heavy versus light objects is an example of this.)

It is especially important to look for this second category as the course progresses. Why is that important? Because if you don't, you won't really be taking the subject matter seriously—and *not* because you disagree, but rather because you have an unexamined story guiding your thoughts. And it may well be a story that you will reject once you have thought about it.

did not. And these were experts in *infectious diseases!*[3] Every one of these experts would tell you that hands are the single main vector for passing infections—but the "knowledge" still didn't work its way into their actions. This strongly suggests they have not completely internalized their thinking about the importance of hand-washing.

Thinking Biologically, Thinking Sociologically, Thinking Philosophically, Thinking Musically . . .

Here is another way to describe what it is to think critically in a field or discipline: The discipline works as a set of lenses through which you can see the world in a more focused way. (Look back at Figure 5.3.) You can picture the discipline's lenses as like the ones inside a microscope or telescope: they let you look more deeply into events or see the distant up close.

Critical thinking in a field is thinking things through *in terms of* the concepts of the field. Critical thinking in biology is *thinking biologically*. Critical thinking in the field of anatomy is *thinking anatomically*. Critical thinking in geography is taking any problem having to do with the spatial ordering of the earth and *thinking it through geographically*. Notice how broad the application of such thinking is: it goes far beyond those problems brought up in the course.

Not all fields have a convenient adverb attached to them, such as "biologically." We can't say someone thinks "nursingly" or "literarily." But we can still use the idea: Critical thinking in nursing is thinking the way an observant, informed, reasonable nurse thinks. Critical thinking in literature is thinking the way a knowledgeable, sensitive, reasonable literary reader thinks.

So what is it to think biologically? Here is an example that gets at it, at least in a negative way. In my critical-thinking course, virtually all students have taken a course in biology, either recently or in the past. So for several years I gave a quiz (not for a grade) in which I asked students to define 10 biological terms. I chose ordinary terms, such as *cell*, and some more specialized terms, such as *mitochondria* or *endoplasmic reticulum*. As you might guess, students' ability to define them differed widely: Some were able to define many of them and some only a few or none. Students did better defining ordinary terms like *cell* than they did defining terms like *mitochondria*. Keep in mind that the course has nothing to do with biology. Several weeks later I gave another quiz and asked students to write a paragraph or two in response to questions like these:

What happens when you cut your finger and get an infection?
How does a person catch sexually transmitted diseases?
What happens when someone gets cancer?
How are babies made?
Why is it harmful to get a suntan?

Students answered these questions in various ways. But in two years of classes, virtually no student's response ever used the word *cell*. And this was the result *whether or not* the student had defined *cell* correctly on the earlier quiz. I conclude from this informal experiment that the term *cell* had not become a significant part of the way these people thought through questions. My judgment is that the students answered these questions in the same way they would have if they had never taken a biology course at all. The concept of cell had not become internalized.

But *cell* is an important concept. It is different from *mitochondria*. For most of us who are not professional biologists, we will probably never confront a problem for which thinking in terms of mitochondria will help us make better choices. But that is decidedly not true of cell: cell is a *powerful* concept. Thinking in terms of cells gives insight into how to answer the ordinary questions we confront daily.

You can think biologically at any level of educational expertise, in high school, in college, as a graduate student in biology, as a professional biologist. At each level, though, you need to incorporate the concept of cell into the way you habitually think through questions. You need to apply that concept not just to questions specifically asked in the course, and not just to those that are labeled "biology questions," but to any question about our life processes where the concept of cell will yield insight and promote better choices.

One of the main goals of a biology course is to help you internalize the most central biological concepts and to learn to think through questions in your life using those concepts. That is what it is to think biologically. Similarly, thinking mathematically is, in a way, seeing the world in terms of quantity. Thinking historically is not the same as knowing a hodgepodge of events and persons from the past. Rather, it revolves around a central question: How are events made meaningful by the past they grow out of?

The Logic of the Field or Discipline

What Is a Field or Discipline?

A common impression is that a field consists essentially of a body of information. It is as if geology were equivalent to all the information we have acquired in geology. But that is an inaccurate and misleading view of a field. True, geologists, professional or amateur, have a good deal of information. But a field is far more than that. Fields are dynamic: they change, grow, evolve. Fields embody a distinctive way, or set of ways, of looking at the world. The perspective of geology is different from the perspective of geography or sociology or psychology.

Practitioners in a field—at whatever level of education—do not simply possess information. Rather, they know how to use that information as well as the concepts that structure it. They are able to apply both of those to new cases. They know how to synthesize the information. They know how to think *about* the field, and they know how to think *within* the field.

The Concept of the *Logic of a Field*

Almost everyone has experienced learning *parts* of a subject, but with no idea at all of how those parts fit together. Though this can happen in any field, it is dramatically true of many people's experience of algebra. You can learn how to solve quadratic equations by factoring, by completing the square, or by applying a theorem for solving radical equations, and not have any idea of how these methods fit together—or even that they *do* fit together.

Similarly, you can learn parts of a subject with no idea of how those parts fit into *the whole.* That also happens with algebra. Very few students finish a course in algebra with an idea of what the whole of algebra is. Many students' experience with a history course is learning lists of events, dates, people, and the relations among them, but with very little idea of what the history of that time and place was *as a whole.*

If you have had that experience, what you were missing was *the logic* of that subject matter. Understanding a whole is not the same as understanding the parts. It is not even the same as understanding all of the parts. Instead, it is understanding parts as they fit together with one another and form a coherent whole: a logic.

Thinking critically in a field is getting hold of the logic of that field. The concept of "the logic of" something is one of the most important concepts in learning to think critically.

Take the U.S. Constitution. You can memorize the entire Constitution (preamble, 7 articles, 26 amendments) and still not know the Constitution in any real sense. Professors of constitutional law probably never memorize it at all. They know the Constitution in quite a different sense. They understand, for example, how to extrapolate from constitutional principles to situations that did not exist at the time the Constitution was written. They understand alternative ways it can be reasonably applied in an era of nuclear secrets, Miranda rights, and responding to terrorist threats. They understand *the logic of* the Constitution. To call it "the" logic does not mean there is only one such logic—there are several in fact. But it means there are coherent ways of thinking through and in terms of the Constitution. It means the Constitution has a distinct set of purposes, which fit together with the assumptions, implications, alternative readings, interpretations, central concepts, key questions at issue, and distinctive points of view embodied in it—all the elements of reasoning, working together. Understanding the Constitution is understanding the logic sufficiently to be able to reason within it.

You can also approach the concept of "the logic of" by considering what you do when you forget something you have learned in a field. Suppose you have memorized something in a course—the dates of the Civil War, for example, or Hobbes' second law of nature, or whether a U- or a V-shaped valley is the result of glaciation. And then you forget it. Because you learned it by memory, you have no recourse but to look it up and then memorize it again. But people who know the logic of a subject won't have to look it up if they happen to forget a detail. Instead, they can *figure it out*. ("Figuring it out" is almost a synonym for "critical thinking.") They can figure it out from the events they know led up to the Civil War and the other events they know followed from it, or from understanding Hobbes' idea of a state of nature and the social contract. They can figure out the shape of a glaciated valley by envisioning how glaciers move, and drawing conclusions.

The subjects taught in school are almost never composed of unrelated individual bits of information. If it seems that way to you, that's only because you have missed the logic of that subject. (There are a few exceptions to this rule; e.g., the keyboard skills used in typing have no logic.[4] But such exceptions are rare. And it is no coincidence that there is no *field* of typing.) In fact, a rough test of whether you grasp the logic of a field is to see how much you feel the need simply to memorize bits of information. The more you feel that need, the less you grasp the logic of the way it all fits together.

What Does the Logic of a Field Consist Of?

Ultimately, we can display the logic of a field by analyzing it in terms of the *elements of reasoning*. A field or discipline embodies a distinctive range of problems and questions. It involves a set of purposes, key assumptions about the world, key concepts and models that people in the field use to gather and categorize information and trace out its implications. It involves a unique and fertile point of view in which people draw conclusions that could not be drawn without the discipline. A good way to describe practitioners is to say they have ownership of the logic of that field.

Here are two abbreviated examples of an analysis of the logic of a discipline. The first is an analysis of earth sciences, and as you read it, notice how the earth-sciences student has a grasp of the field as a whole. She analyzes the field—breaks it down into its essential parts—but she also synthesizes it. This is, of course, not *all* there is to earth sciences. And it is not the only version of a logic of earth sciences. But it assembles fundamental parts of the field for us, displays a vision of the whole, and shows how the parts are interrelated. The second example is a shorter one on the logic of a literature course.

AN ANALYSIS OF THE LOGIC OF EARTH SCIENCES

The main <u>purpose</u> of earth sciences (geology, physical geography) is to explain the composition of the earth, its history, and the physical/geological forces that made it this way. Another goal is to help us locate natural resources so we can use them while also preserving the environment.

The main <u>question at issue</u> in geology is "What is the earth like and how did it come to be this way?" Other important questions: How did the movement of tectonic plates produce the physical features of the earth (mountains, rivers, volcanoes, etc.)? What makes rocks? What is the future of the earth? What can we learn from geology about global warming?

The geological processes on the earth take place within the <u>context</u> of the universe as a whole: the big bang, the birth of our galaxy, the formation of our sun and solar system, including planet earth. Geology as a field fits in the *context* of the natural sciences: physics, chemistry, biology, astronomy.

The <u>information</u> geologists use comes from observations and tests on the composition of rock, air, and water, from precise observation and measurement of natural features, from the fossil record and from stratification.

Geologists make the <u>assumption</u> that we *can* find out about what happened to the earth in the past, that scientific method helps us put natural resources to new uses, and that the earth is best understood by observing data and gathering evidence. A major assumption of earth sciences is that plate tectonics explains the physical features of the earth *[but maybe this is a <u>conclusion</u> based on a huge body of evidence]*.

Some <u>implications and consequences</u> of earth sciences: The geological processes that formed the earth are still going on and will continue into the future. Plate tectonics results in predictions about where various natural resources will be found. Natural resources are limited.

The <u>point of view</u> of geology is a scientific one, based on observation, careful measurement, theory construction, and tests. The geological point of view is characterized by seeing the earth as something to be preserved and nurtured because it is the result of eons-long processes.

The main <u>concepts</u> of earth sciences include plate tectonic theory, convection heat systems, continental drift, subduction; the rock cycle, the hydrologic cycle; geological time.

<u>Conclusions</u>, <u>interpretations</u>: Geology allows us to <u>interpret</u> the land around us as the result of the movement of immense tectonic plates that have shaped the planet. Now when I look at mountains, rivers, or the ground under my feet, I draw <u>conclusions</u> about how they were formed, and that lets me see them in a different way. An important conclusion to draw from studying earth sciences is that the government should consult the geological community about the use of natural resources.

There are <u>alternatives</u> to looking at the earth geologically: some people believe that the earth has always been the way it is now, that it is basically unchanging, or that science and religion are opposed, and we should look at the earth from the point of view of religion only. Some people think the earth was given to humans to use as they see fit.

The value of analyses like these does not consist so much in reading them as in creating them, in thinking them out. Once you have constructed your own analysis, your understanding of details will fit into this logic in a coherent way, and as your understanding deepens, the logic will grow deeper as well.

LOGIC OF A LITERATURE COURSE

- **Purpose:** To think the way a literary reader thinks about his or her life

- **Question at Issue:** How can I think in a deep literary way about stories and about my life in terms of those stories?

(continued)

LOGIC OF A LITERATURE COURSE (*Continued*)

Assumptions:

- That I can learn about life by reading stories deeply

- That I will connect more deeply to stories by seeing them in terms of character, conflict, change

- That a story can be like an old friend—in which I can always find new and worthwhile things

Implications and Consequences:

- That my reading of stories will become deeper during the course

- That I will apply stories to my life in a richer way at the end of the course than at the beginning

- That stories help me understand aspects of my life; that stories also keep aspects of my life hidden from me

Concepts:

- Character
- Plot
- Theme
- Conflict

- The concept of *story* itself → What makes something a story? Just because you write stuff down about things that happened doesn't make it a story.

- Meaningfulness

Information:

- The actual stories we will read in the course

- Sometimes, information about the author, or the context in which the story was written

Conclusions/Interpretations:

- Conclusions about specific stories (e.g., how Holden Caulfield has changed)

- Conclusions I will draw about my life on the basis of the stories: Am I a catcher in the rye too?

- Interpreting items in my life in a different way: the way when you read a book (Shirley Jackson) or watch a movie and you can *see* the world in terms of the story

Point of View:

- The points of view of various characters: What does the story look like from their point of view? (e.g., the kid that Holden Caulfield can't stand)

- Also: developing empathy with alien points of view

Context: I am reading these stories as someone of a certain age, of a certain gender, with a personal history, in a society, in a culture—and all of these shape the stories I read and the way I interpret them.

Alternatives: I have choices—alternatives—about which stories I will let influence me.

Learning the Vocabulary of the Discipline

How can you begin to think in terms of the logic of the discipline you're studying? A good place to start is learning to use the discipline's vocabulary. This is a minimal condition, and it is easy to confuse means and ends. Learning the vocabulary in a field is *a means* to an end. It is an essential means for learning to reason better in the field. But be careful not to think that learning the vocabulary—learning the *names* for concepts in the field—is somehow the *point* of studying in the field. It isn't. Teachers don't stress terminology because it's the purpose of the course. Rather, it's that the purpose cannot be accomplished without the essential terminology. Learning the parts of a flower in a botany course is important, but it is seldom an end in itself. (It is for some people. Some people find value in knowing the precise names of things.) For most people, the vocabulary is important because it increases their ability to think clearly about flowers, to communicate clearly about botany, to gain precision in their observations. These abilities in turn provide insight beyond flowers, insight into how things grow, into fundamental processes of life.

What Is It to Think in a Discipline's Vocabulary?

Of course, thinking in a discipline's vocabulary is not the same as merely memorizing definitions. Haven't you often memorized definitions of terms without really having a handle on what they mean, without being able to use them intelligibly? Disciplines are integrated wholes, and their vocabulary reflects that. Vocabulary in a discipline is like a web: it's interconnected. Thinking of one vocabulary word brings up its connections to other words in the vocabulary. It starts you thinking in terms of logical connections, rather than in terms of fragments. It also brings up the connections between the concepts that lie behind the words. For example, the term *force* in physics should lead you naturally, almost automatically, to think about *mass* and *acceleration*. In an English literature course, the term *stream of consciousness* should bring James Joyce's *Ulysses* to your mind, at least as a background, ready to be applied. In social work, when you think about "enabling behavior," your mind turns naturally to dysfunctionality, control, needs, and a web of other terms.

There is another advantage to learning the vocabulary of the field. Your present vocabulary is saturated with the point of view you grew up with. It has its own connections, and often these run counter to the more accurate, precise, and important connections that have been discovered in the discipline. So, if you think in your present vocabulary of something *in motion*, you are liable to connect to the idea of "something else that puts it in motion" (a force). That's natural, but it is the direct opposite of what we learn from Newton. In Newtonian theory (and in reality), "being in motion" connects to the idea that *nothing* is moving it (no net forces); in reality, things that are moving simply keep moving. (Only when they turn or move faster is there a connection to the idea that a force is moving them.)

The concept of *enabling* in social work is a dramatic example. We often think of helping people who are in a recurring state of need (e.g., helping an alcoholic make it home) as a *good* act, as an act of mercy or unselfishness. Thinking in terms of *enabling*, though, shifts these connections and calls them into question. Now, connections are made to how the one who seems to be helping may be perpetuating a *dysfunctionality* in the person, and how the *enabler* may be *controlling* the situation to meet his or her own *needs*.

To change your way of thinking, you need to change the vocabulary of your thinking.

Fundamental and Powerful Concepts

Here are two basic questions about learning a discipline:

1. If I take a course in a discipline, how can I think critically *within* that discipline?

2. How do I learn to think critically while also amassing the large amount of information—often misleadingly called the content—I may need to learn in the course?

When confronted with these questions, students, and sometimes teachers, often phrase them in terms of a false opposition. They think they have to choose *either* to learn critical thinking *or* to learn content—as if the two were opposed.

They are not at all opposed. Learning content *is* learning to think. If I learn content, but I don't learn to think in terms of that content, then it's not *content* at all. It's just *words*, memorized and soon forgotten words. If I learn that for every action there is an equal and opposite reaction, but I can't explain what that phrase means when given the example of a man pushing against a wall (what is the reaction?), then all I have is a singsong slogan. That is not *content*. Content is not repeating formulas or slogans, nor is it memorizing long lists of information. Rather, I have ownership of a course's content when I *understand* the course concepts, see their implications, relate them to other concepts; when I can raise relevant questions about them, when I can apply them to new situations.

The answer to both questions 1 and 2 has to do with fundamental and powerful concepts.

Understanding Fundamental and Powerful Concepts

What are fundamental and powerful (f&p) concepts? A fundamental and powerful concept is one that can be used to explain or think out a huge body of questions, problems, information, and situations. All fields have f&p concepts, but there are a relatively small number of them in any particular area. They are the most central and useful ideas in the discipline. They are to be contrasted with individual bits of information, or with less general concepts. In the earlier example, "cell" is a far more fundamental and powerful concept than "mitochondria." The idea, then, is that if you can understand the f&p concepts in a deep way, you are in a position to understand a great deal of the rest of the course. You need to learn to think in terms of the fundamental and powerful concepts, to use them to think through any new problem or question that arises.

For example, when I was in college, I liked poetry, particularly the Romantic poets: Keats, Shelley, Wordsworth, and Coleridge. So I took a course in the Romantics. Here is all that I remember from the course: *Michael*, 1800. That is, I remember that Wordsworth's poem *Michael* was written in 1800. That is the sole remnant left from more than 200 names of poems and dates I memorized in that course. This is an example of the opposite of an f&p concept. It is a detail, and it illuminates nothing, not even itself (I don't even remember what *Michael* was about!). What would be an f&p concept in that course? Well, one would clearly be the concept of *romanticism* itself. Romanticism involves a whole way of looking at life: a feeling of deep yearning, a longing for the unknown, the richness of imagination and strong emotions, an intense love of nature, especially for the mystery of nature, for the faraway and the unattainable.

What makes romanticism a fundamental and powerful concept is that once you grasp it deeply, you acquire a concept for understanding and appreciating many Romantic poems. You can then take almost any poem written during that period, understand it as an expression of romanticism, and think it through using the concept of romanticism. That gives you an insight into those poems that you would not have without that concept. Additionally, if you have questions about how those poets lived—about their attitudes toward politics, love, drugs, or religion; or about novels and essays written at the time—you can now think through any of these questions using the concept of romanticism. It is a *powerful* concept.

But the case is far stronger than this: If you can learn to think in terms of f&p concepts—in this case, *romanticism*—then not only are many questions in the course illuminated, but also any number of questions beyond the course, ones that arise long after the course is over. How does romanticism apply to later poets you may read? How does it apply to your own poetry? How about movies? The topics can go on and on. Romanticism is powerful as a concept because it continues to illuminate, far beyond the subject matter of the course. How do you look at *your life* in terms of romanticism? How about the romanticism of science or the law? What are the romantic aspects of your choice of profession, your choices in romantic relationships (the other sense of "romantic"), your self-image? How does the concept of romanticism help you understand yourself and others?

The concept is *fundamental* because it forms the foundation of our understanding of that era and of a great many forms of life that extend beyond that era. It is *powerful* because it is useful in understanding a wide range of questions and problems, issues, and situations.

Although fundamental and powerful concepts are important in *understanding* certain phenomena, they are just as important in fields that emphasize *doing*.

Take the nursing concept *asepsis*. There are many antiseptic procedures, both medical and surgical, some suitable in one situation, some in another, and each one has a subset of steps associated with it. But as a student nurse, you can spend so much time learning these individual procedures that you lose the forest for the trees. It's easy to become engaged in parroting and carrying out rote procedures rather than assessing what to do in a situation by thinking it out. Every nursing teacher has scary stories of nurses unthinkingly carrying out one procedure even though it's obvious the patient is in desperate need of another. So the idea is: Take any situation that arises and think it out with the idea of *asepsis* in mind. How can this situation be made aseptic? With that in mind, you can identify the specific antiseptic procedures called for by a specific situation. If you have to adapt the procedure to an unusual situation, you have a way of doing so—namely, thinking in terms of how to achieve asepsis. It is not a surefire way, of course. But it is a good way, a reasonable way. If, however, all you have done is memorize the specific procedures, you can't determine which part you've forgotten, and you have no insight into why a particular procedure is appropriate for an unusual case. In fact, you may have no real grasp of what a procedure is *for*: it may be just a procedure you follow blindly. When new procedures come along, long after graduation, you have no broader concepts through which to understand them.

To think critically through a course, the f&p concepts need to be learned in a *deep* way. Almost certainly, the teacher of the course I took in Romantic poetry did define romanticism. But it remained just that—a definition. For me, the student, it was one more detail, on a par with "*Michael*, 1800." By contrast, fundamental and powerful concepts should constantly return throughout the course as part of the explanatory context whenever new material is introduced. Given any new material, always raise this question: How is this illuminated by our small stock of f&p concepts? Occasionally, it may be that some new material is not illuminated at all by one of the f&p concepts. That's okay. You should recognize that too. Maybe you should ask about it in class. But what you are aiming for is to make those f&p concepts part of *the way you think*.

All courses have f&p concepts: *Homeostasis* in biology is an example, the concept of *the audience* is one that is central to all writing courses, the concept of *what is justifiable* is at the heart of any ethics course. Most courses and fields have more than one, but not a large number. If you start thinking in terms of 10 or 15 concepts, or more,

IDENTIFYING FUNDAMENTAL AND POWERFUL CONCEPTS

Depending on how far along you are in your course, you may not yet be able to identify the fundamental and powerful concepts. Your teacher may have told you the f&p concepts. If so, do not treat that as just another piece of information. Rather, take those concepts and use them to think out every single important topic or question that arises in the course.

If you are far enough along:

1. Focus on the course as a whole, not on individual parts.

2. Identify three f&p concepts that underlie the whole course. Do this by first identifying *one*. Only then, go on to identify two others that stem from that one. (Use the concept map in Figure 10.1.)

3. Share and discuss the f&p concepts with other students. How do they underlie the field or course as a whole? Are they fundamental enough? The concepts each class member identifies should be similar.

FIGURE 10.1   *A concept map.*

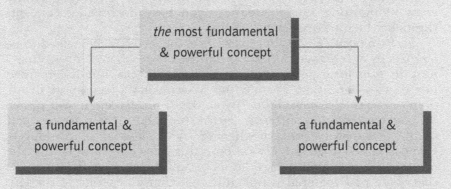

you are already going beyond the fundamental ones to narrower, more specific concepts. Focus instead on a smaller number, trying to get at what is most central:

- To identify the f&p concepts
- To understand how they fit together
- To learn them in a deep way

- To use them in your thinking about every important question or problem that arises in the course
- To use them to begin to think through questions that lie beyond the scope of the course

Using Concept Maps to Display Logical Connections

Concept maps are a useful way of showing the logical connections that exist between concepts (see the example in Figure 10.1). For instance, the field of clinical psychology trains therapists to deal with the psychological disorders of patients. When clinical psychologists work they focus on diagnosing the client, identifying the major causes of the psychological disorder in that client, and carrying out a course of treatment. We can identify five main concepts, then: *clinical psychology*, *psychological disorders*, *diagnosis*, *causes*, and *treatment*. A concept map of these might be drawn as in Figure 10.2.

That's not the only way to map out these concepts, however. You may reason instead that the treatment a clinical psychologist recommends for a patient is not *separate* from the diagnosis and causes, as portrayed in Figure 10.2. Treatment *depends* on the diagnosis the psychologist gives and on the causes of the disorder in that patient. Such reasoning might be depicted as in the map in Figure 10.3. The concept map reflects the system of thinking, the logical connections between concepts.

FIGURE 10.2   *A concept map for psychological disorders.*

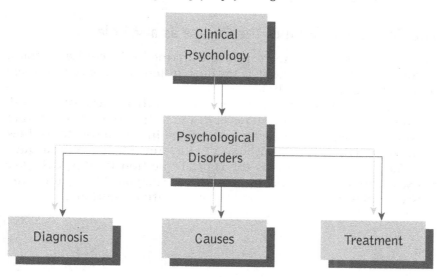

FIGURE 10.3   *An alternative concept map for psychological disorders.*

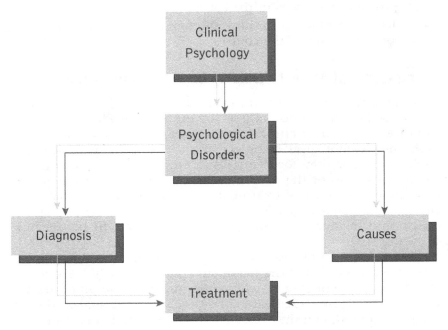

The three concepts, *diagnosis, causes,* and *treatment,* are f&p concepts in clinical psychology. That means that, as you learn to think the way a clinical psychologist thinks, you can reason out virtually any question in the field in terms of how to diagnose it, what its causes are, and how it should best be treated.

The Central Question of the Course as a Whole

Another important way to keep your thinking in the course on track, to grasp the logic of the field, is to think in terms of the central question of the course as a whole.

A course in a field has a central question that it revolves around. It is the unifying question, and everything in the course fits into that question. The way to understand every item in the course, to see how it all fits together, is to understand it in terms of that central question. Take this book. This is the central question it addresses: *How can you learn to think critically in a field or discipline?* Every topic discussed in the book is an aspect of that central question.

the field?" That central question forms the unifying center around which all other topics and questions are organized. Without keeping that central question in mind, the parts of a book (or a course) fall apart into separate and unrelated pieces.

One problem with describing a central question is that it can seem so simple. And it *is* simple—simple in the sense of uncomplicated, not in the sense of easy. Insights that are simple in that sense are often the things most worth saying.

Picture yourself taking a course in educational psychology. You are deluged with educational theories, countertheories, procedures, statistics, case studies, definitions, objectives, and a hundred other items. All of them seem important. This one relates to that one, this other one doesn't. This theorist says X, this other theorist says Y, and a third says Z. In such cases, it sometimes seems almost heroic to see the forest for the trees.

What is the central question? It is, *How does a student learn? And how can I help students learn?*[5] That is what educational psychology is all about. Everything in the course is geared to that one question. You are taking the course in education to get a richer, fuller understanding of how students learn, and how you as teacher can help them learn. To think through any issue critically during the course means to think it through *in terms of* how it contributes to answering that central question. That question provides the structure through which everything else is understood.

There can be more than one central question in a course. It is usually helpful to assume there is only one because it unifies your vision of the course and the field. But you may have to suspend that assumption. For example, the central question in a literature course might be *How can literature enrich and deepen the way I live my life?* That is a profound and far-reaching question. The whole course, every assignment, every poem, drama, or story, and all class discussion, can be seen as addressing that single, central question. But that same course might have another central question. It might focus on the *craft* of writing: *What do writers do to make literature effective?* That is also a central question, one that directs your attention to how writers accomplish what they accomplish: how they use characters, theme, plot, conflict, and literary forms. A third central question might focus on the interaction necessary to make meaning: *How do writer, reader, and society together create meaning in literature?* This too is a question that may underlie the entire course. It directs you to ask, whenever you read *any* piece of literature, in the course or long afterward, *How do we, together, make this work of art?*

Thinking in terms of central questions can change your whole understanding of a course. A good candidate for a fundamental and powerful concept in physical education, for example, is lifelong fitness.

A central question is *How can I promote lifelong fitness?* That is, the suggestion is to think of every activity in a physical education course in relation to how it promotes, or detracts from, lifelong fitness. You can now think through nutrition, sports, and exercise in a different, more global way. Notice how thinking in terms of that central question—and lifelong fitness—can change your perception of potentially damaging sports like football or boxing, at least as part of a physical education program.

Here are some examples of central questions for a few courses:

- **Chemistry:** How are you and the world around you created by chemicals?
- **Composition:** What *is it* to write an effective essay?
- **Economics:** How is society shaped by the decisions people make on the basis of expected costs and benefits?
- **Philosophy:** How can you make sense of your life and of the world around you?

Thinking in terms of the central question may sound easy, but it's actually difficult. The goal is to use the central question in your thinking at every point in the course. Doing so, even some of the time, takes practice and focused attention. It doesn't come naturally. Think about other classes you have taken, and notice how many of them you sat through, from beginning to end, without ever asking yourself the central questions underlying the class, without ever understanding that there even *was* one.

CRITICAL WRITING

Write down, as well as you can at this point in the semester, the central question of the course you are taking. Do this by writing *three* versions of it. With each one, approach it as if it is *the* one and only central question of the course. When you are done—when you have three different questions written down, each attempting to capture the most central question—choose the one that, in your judgment, captures it best. (At a later time, you may well choose a different version.)

A central question is difficult the way a mission statement is difficult. A business, a university, a hospital, or an organization may formulate a mission statement. Many individuals also formulate a personal mission statement. It is a way to keep themselves focused on what is important and allow what's less important to drift away. A person's mission might be "My mission is to respect myself, others, and all things." It is often difficult to formulate a mission statement that captures what you truly think is important, what you think your mission is. By the same token, though, formulating it can be deeply enlightening.

What's even more difficult, however, is keeping the mission in front of you as you go through life: remembering it, keeping it fresh, not letting it become an empty formula, reviewing it as you mature, actually living your life, as much as possible, in accord with it.

The central question of a course operates the same way as a mission statement, and it is difficult in the same way. Like a mission statement, it is a question you can ask yourself over and over. As your education and understanding increase, the depth with which you answer that question will also increase.

- Formulate the central question(s) of the course as a whole.
- Break it down into two or three subsidiary questions. Then figure out how they fit together within the central question.
- Look at every topic in the course and ask, "How does it fit into the central question? How does that topic contribute to answering the central question?"
- Remind yourself of the central question frequently, especially at times when you feel overwhelmed or when you find yourself just going through the motions.
- Reformulate the central question from time to time.
- Push the envelope. Ask, "How is that central question important for my life beyond the classroom?"

SHORT ESSAY

USING FUNDAMENTAL AND POWERFUL CONCEPTS TO THINK THROUGH A CENTRAL QUESTION IN AN INTRODUCTION TO SOCIOLOGY COURSE

Central Question: How do humans behave socially, and why do they behave that way?

If I had to describe how and why humans behave socially in just a few sentences, I would use three fundamental and powerful concepts: social forces, socialization, and norms/sanctions. I would say that "social forces"

(continued)

SHORT ESSAY (*Continued*)

act on people as they grow up and as they go through life. From these social forces, people learn how to behave. They learn which actions and values and things to do are acceptable and which are not. This process is called "socialization"—it is the way people become part of society. Societies have "norms and sanctions." That means a lot of the behavior we think of as individual free choices is brought about by cultural norms that we are taught unconsciously and accept automatically.

A major part of the social forces that influence us comes from the groups we belong to, including the social categories we are in. Some important groups that influence us socially are family, peer groups, our schools, and our religious groups. Social categories are things like a person's race, age, gender, and income level. Each of these groups has norms that tell us, "This is how you're supposed to behave in the group." And each of them has sanctions, meaning, "If you don't behave that way, you will be punished for it." One thing that was hard for me to get is that these norms and sanctions are things we're not aware of. It's not like anybody ever said to me (I'm a male): "Don't wear dresses!" and "If you do, we're going to punish you by laughing at you." It's just something you know as you grow up. You don't even think of people laughing at you as a punishment or "sanction." It's just what people do.

So the way sociology looks at people is very different from the way I looked at people before I began taking this course. I understood the behavior of my friends and family (and even strangers like sports figures and movie stars) on the basis of my personal experience and what I talked about with friends (in sociology, these are called "peer groups"). I also learned a lot from music and movies and TV. I was also brought up with certain values, like in my family they always talk about being a success. You just know things about people—like: you can trust your friends and you can't trust other people as much.

What I didn't think about was how I was "socialized" to take on these values and obey certain norms. I'm not saying that social forces *make* me have certain values, but I can see that they have a strong influence on me (as well as on everybody else). For example, I like football. I play sports sometimes, but what I like most is watching football on TV with my friends. We have a great time!

I always thought that I just liked football. I thought it was my individual choice and nobody else had anything to do with it. My friends and I even act like we are kind of being rebellious and nonconformist in the way we like football. I hate to say it, but we even look down on people who don't like football: I mean, what's wrong with them? But now I realize that there are social patterns to the way we like sports. What my friends and I do is *very much like* what thousands and thousands of other groups (mostly males, like us) do across the country. In fact, when I think about people who don't like sports at all (like maybe they like to dance or bird-watch), I now realize that they probably look down on my football group just the way we look down on them. (My group would be called an "in-group" in my social interactions, and they would be called an "out-group.") I go through some of my own values, and it amazes me how much they are like the values of the groups I belong to. Not all of them, but a lot more than I ever realized.

It's not just sports or movies. We begin to be socialized through our families. Then we continue to be socialized by our peer groups and the way we are categorized into race, gender, and age groups. We don't just learn to like football (if we grew up in England, my friends and I would probably be wild about soccer or cricket!). We are also socialized to take on deep values like being an individual versus following the crowd, or learning to do whatever it takes to succeed in life.

There are other ways someone could try to understand human social behavior—psychologically, economically, politically, maybe even biologically (maybe some of our values are in our genes). So a key to understanding human behavior sociologically is to look for "social forces." If there are a lot of groups that do the same things, have the same values, and follow the same norms, then we should look for the social forces at work making the groups conform.

The Point of View of the Discipline

Disciplines embody a unique way of looking at the world. The point of view (or perspective) of a discipline runs so deep that it can seem as if practitioners of the discipline are seeing a different world from yours, and in a sense they are. Sarah Blaffer Hrdy is a brilliant evolutionary anthropologist, and her description conveys beautifully what it is to think in terms of that field:

> For better or for worse, I see the world through a different lens than most people. My depth of field is millions of years longer, and the subjects in my viewfinder have the curious habit of spontaneously taking on the attributes of other species: chimps, platypuses, australopithecines. This habit of thinking about mothers in broad evolutionary and comparative—as well as cross-cultural and historical—perspectives distinguishes my examination of motherhood from those of the psychoanalysts, psychologists, novelists, poets, and social historians whose work I build on.[6]

This way of thinking is available not just to professional anthropologists like Hrdy but to almost anyone. It can open up clear, accurate, important perspectives for the way we conceptualize our lives. That happens because each discipline has a vision of the world that's embodied in its point of view.

What is involved in "seeing the world from the point of view of the discipline"? Three things (though they are not completely separate):

- Seeing the items in the *domain* of the discipline
- Seeing them in terms of the *concepts* and categories of the discipline
- Seeing the *connections* among those items

The place to begin is by recognizing there is a whole set of objects (or events) that the discipline investigates as its area of expertise. That set is the *domain* of the discipline. The items in that domain are ones that the point of view of the discipline can give you special insight into.

So a good first step toward taking on the perspective of the discipline is at least to identify its domain. Thus the domain of psychology is human behavior (and also the behavior of many nonhuman animals). The domain of chemistry includes chemicals and their interactions. The domain of art history includes artworks (as well as other objects and events that are made meaningful via artworks). The domain of nursing may be hard to describe simply: it includes "nursing situations"—those health-related situations where the field of nursing applies and gives understanding.

But you don't "identify the domain" just by saying the words. Seeing things from the point of view of the discipline involves *seeing* the things in our world *as* items in the domain of the discipline. It is essential not to wall off the domain of the discipline from our ordinary life ("school stuff": see page 257). The domain of psychology covers human behavior. But if I describe it that way I can easily miss its significance. The domain includes *all* human behavior, meaning it includes everything that anyone does or thinks. That's the domain that psychology can give us insight into. To "see" from the point of view of psychology, then, is to notice—consciously notice—those acts of human behavior around me. Similarly, the domain of chemistry includes "chemicals"—but *everything* is made of chemicals. If I describe the domain as "chemicals," I am probably blinding myself to what chemistry is actually talking about: it is talking not about some specialized thing called "chemicals" but about the chemical make-up of *everything*. Thus, to "see" from a chemistry point of view is to look at the world around me—tables, books, chalk, blood, my dog, people—and to see them as assemblages of chemicals. In the same way, it's difficult to imagine an object or event that is *not* shaped and made meaningful by artworks, or any aspect of what we do that is *not* a "health-related situation." And I can "see" them that way.

Thus practitioners in a field don't simply see the same things you do and just call them by different names, as if what you see are some tall weeds by the side of the highway and ecologists merely supply the Latin name for them. That's just a trivial difference. In "seeing" objects and events, disciplines conceptualize them and categorize

> Think back on the visualization of the elements in Chapter 6 (page 141), the one where you were walking down a path, seeing the world in terms of the elements. The world you see as you walk down the path will be strikingly different if you are a geographer, a writer, an economist, an artist, a philosopher. It will be different in the objects or events you focus on (the domain), in the way you categorize them, and in the connections you "see."
>
> Describe the path, as best you can, according to how it would look from the point of view of the discipline of the course you are in.

them in strikingly different ways from the ways we understand them without the discipline. For example, you may be highly aware that you and your fellow waiters at a restaurant are angry at your customers, but once you conceptualize that anger as "cognitive dissonance," suddenly a whole new way of thinking about it (psychology) becomes available to you. This happens because the point of view of the discipline allows us to see not only objects and events differently, but also the *connections* between those objects and events. Thus, when you see weeds, ecologists may see native grasses that are struggling against both crops and invaders from other continents, and managing to survive only because the grasses are located in a small habitat of untended land that humans have inadvertently allowed to revert back to a state close to the great prairies that once covered a huge area of the United States and Canada. You see weeds; ecologists see struggle, balance, succession, history, and loss of genetic diversity.

The same is true of all disciplines. The connections you start to see, as you take on the point of view of a geographer, a writer, an economist, an artist, a philosopher, will furnish a deeper understanding of the world around you. If you let it, this powerful point of view can become part of your standard way of looking at the world.

Impediments to Thinking Critically within a Discipline

The impediments to critical thinking mentioned in Chapter 5 are impediments to thinking critically within a discipline as well. For example, two of the impediments deal with forming a picture of the world based on what we learn from news reports or on what we see in movies, TV, advertising, and other fictionalized accounts. But these sources can also provide us with an uncritical picture of the subject matter in courses we study.

For example, space travel is presented matter-of-factly in fictionalized accounts (often at "warp speed," with stars streaking by, and the "noise" of booster rockets firing). We also see news reports of spacecraft sending incredibly precise data back from Mars or Jupiter. We also hear reputable scientists talk about black holes and the consequent possibility of wormholes through space-time. These are three separate sources of information that really have almost nothing to do with one another: fiction, news bites, scientific reports. But many people put them together uncritically and assume that space travel to other planetary systems is just around the corner. They form an unrealistic picture, one that can easily be an impediment to learning about science. Space travel beyond our tiny system of planets is unlikely ever to happen. Distances are simply too great, our highest speeds are infinitesimally small, and there are physical limits (not just practical limits) to what objects with mass can do. Human space travel beyond the solar system cannot be proved impossible, of course, but it's only a fantasy, probably no more likely than finding out leprechauns actually exist.

You can readily find examples of how the other impediments discussed in Chapter 5 can seriously interfere with your ability to think critically through the subject matter in your courses. Think of the common *fear* of taking math or science and how it interferes with reasoning through questions entirely within people's capacity; or the way we *stereotype* social scientists, nurses, professors, psychiatrists, and students; or the way even within a discipline people identify *egocentrically* with one position or another and go to unreasonable extremes to defend that position; or, *developmentally*, the way a need to feel safe can lead people to major in a subject where they feel in control, even though their real interest is in a different subject entirely.

Background Stories, Background Logic

There are other impediments to critical thinking in a discipline. We enter courses not as blank slates but with *background stories* and accounts already in place. These stories have a logic that shapes how we think within the discipline. We have a story, for example, about chemicals: Chemistry teachers sometimes despair at the persistent background story that if something is made of chemicals, it is therefore bad for you. Chemistry teachers respond to this background story by teaching that this can't be true because everything is made of chemicals. As a student, though, you can hear what your chemistry teacher says, you can write it in your notes, you can give the right answer on exams—and even after all that, once class is over, you can still believe chemicals are bad for you. It is extremely difficult, for example, to understand what it means when biochemists say that *life* is chemistry.

Though these examples are from science, background stories are strong impediments to critical thinking in all fields. You have in you right now, like a default program on your computer, background stories about how business works (including marketing, management, accounting, . . .), what nursing and education are (including all the specializations), how humans interact (psychology, sociology, political science, . . .), what other cultures are like (anthropology, history, . . .), what reality is like (philosophy, science, religious studies, . . .), and how to find answers (librarianship, methods courses, math, . . .). It is not so much that these background stories you have are false. Many of them *are* false, but even if the story has a lot of truth in it, it is probably a very limited truth, and the story will be deeply misleading when it is extended beyond the area where it works.

Even calling them "stories" is misleading because that implies the stories are easily supplanted with new information from your courses. But that doesn't do justice to how deep our background stories run and to how pervasive their influence is. It is hard for the account you learn in your course to get through. Background stories are deep and pervasive in part because they are unexamined and in part because they have *a logic* to them. That is, our background stories are not just stories; rather, they embody a whole way of thinking about things.

Here is another example. Most people have a picture of how evolution is supposed to work according to Darwinism. Yet, that picture is deeply misguided, often straight-out wrong. How many of the following do you think of as part of the theory of evolution?

- Life progresses by evolution.
- There are higher and lower forms of life.
- Evolution has something to do with how individuals adapt to their environment.
- The fittest organisms tend to survive.
- Organisms have a drive (or an instinct) to reproduce.
- Organisms also have a drive (or an instinct) for self-preservation.
- Evolution has something to do with whether an individual survives.
- Humans are more evolutionarily advanced than chimps.
- The better an organism is able to adapt to its environment, the more likely it is to evolve.
- We live today in the age of mammals; there was once an age of dinosaurs.
- Humans evolved from monkeys or apes.
- Humans are more fit to survive than dinosaurs.
- Humans are advancing evolutionarily in their intelligence.

Notice how these statements have a logic to them: we can reason from one idea to another. We can reason *from* progress *to* higher forms of life, *to* advanced ability to adapt, *to* greater survival, *to* humans as the high point of evolution.

But *all* the statements are deeply flawed. A few of them can be made to fit in with evolution, but only by wrenching them from their ordinary meaning. This whole way of reasoning seriously distorts what the theory of evolution is about. Yet, if you are convinced of any of the statements that make up this logic, you probably cannot get hold of how in the world it could be wrong.

Background stories are so difficult to counteract because they are virtually invisible. We don't see them as background stories at all. We see them simply as *the way things are*. As a result, the background stories influence our interpretation of everything we encounter. We don't even *hear* that the account we learn in our courses contradicts our background story.

Simply becoming aware of our background stories is empowering because it means we can now decide what we are going to believe, and, if we choose, we can decide that by reasoning things out.

School Stuff

Another impediment to critical thinking in a discipline can be illustrated by a couple of math problems Kurt Reusser asked fourth graders.[7]

There are 26 sheep and 10 goats on a ship. How old is the captain?

Most children *add* 26 and 10 to find the age of the captain! Not only that, but the better they are at math, the more likely they are to add to find the age of the captain.

Here is a second problem asked of the fourth graders:

A school is going on a field trip, and they need school buses. There are 140 kids in the school, and each school bus holds 30 kids. How many school buses do they need in all?

The children's answer is "Four, remainder 20"!

What is going on with these answers? It is not that the children cannot do the math. It's that, for the children, there is simply no link between math and reality. For them, math is something you learn in school, and it has nothing to do with real captains or real school buses.

Most of us have this category called "school stuff." It is the stuff we hear about in school, and we keep all this stuff in a special receptacle in our minds. We think, "I have to jump through some hoops to become a nurse, and one of them is taking courses in basic science. But there is no need for me to remember that stuff. It's *just science*; it's *not nursing*."

The temptation to isolate course material as merely school stuff is heightened by ingrained study techniques: passive listening, memorizing information rather than organizing and synthesizing it, simply repeating information from the book or a lecture, not formulating questions. If I think of what I learn in my courses primarily as stuff to be put into notes and regurgitated on exams, there is little chance I will learn much. I will leave class with the same unexamined background stories. These are difficult patterns to break, and it's difficult to make the leap of faith that using critical thinking as a study tool will actually result in better school performance.

TELLING YOUR STORY

It is important to take the subject matter as *your own*, to participate in the construction of your own knowledge.

With that in mind, review some of your personal history. Think back on courses you took more than two years ago:

- What is an example of something you learned in a course that still has major importance in your thinking or in your life?

- What is an example of a course you took that had *no* long-term influence on your life?

Now ask yourself, "How can I make this present course I am taking more like the first example? How can I use it to bring *value* to my life?"

Trusting the Discipline

Talking about trusting the discipline, in the context of critical thinking, implies two seemingly contradictory messages: first, that critical thinking encourages you to question the discipline you are studying; but, second, that it's reasonable for you to trust the discipline you are studying. Each message is reasonable, and each can be exaggerated.

Questioning lies at the heart of critical thinking, and a student in a discipline will be questioning many aspects of it: how to analyze the course material, how to apply it to cases, how to compare and contrast different theories, how to organize the main concepts, and how to evaluate positions in the discipline itself. In a political science course, for example, you may be asked to compare and contrast various political systems, to evaluate them, and maybe to reject one or another. In an ethics course, you may be asked to evaluate competing arguments about the morality of abortion or killing animals for food, and maybe come to a well-reasoned decision.

That questioning attitude can leave you with the impression that a goal of critical thinking is to be skeptical about what you learn in a discipline. This is particularly true when the course covers topics you've experienced firsthand—relationships, sports, dieting, family, power structures, art. It's easy to leave the course with your ideas about those topics completely unaffected. Or, having read competing accounts of marriage, you can come to believe that everyone in the field has his or her own theory about the subject. You can conclude that each account of marriage is just one of many, with no better backing than a host of others. Each account can become something to be doubted automatically, certainly no better than your own view of marriage or the one you were brought up with.

The idea that the subject matter is just "school stuff" can increase that skepticism. At the least, it can lead you to the impression that course content is not something to be taken too seriously. You can quickly say, "There are so many different views about political systems or abortion or marriage, that I am no better off than when I entered the course. It's all just a matter of opinion." But that would be a mistake.

To a great degree, the findings in a discipline, the material presented in texts and courses in that field, can be trusted. In fact, compared to other sources of knowledge in our society, the content of the disciplines studied in school can be trusted to a remarkable degree. Disciplines do have built-in sources of distortion, and you need to be aware of these. For example, experts in the discipline are much more trustworthy in their central results than they are in their application of those results to actual situations, especially complex situations. Thus in physics we know the laws that govern physical processes such as the weather, but that doesn't mean physics can tell us what the temperature will be a week from Thursday in Colorado Springs. It can't. (As paradoxical as it sounds, it seems that physics can be used to *prove* we will never be able to predict next week's exact weather on the basis of physics.)

Another source of distortion is that discipline experts are as human as anyone, so they can be guided by egocentricity and developmental factors just the way you and I can. A third source of distortion is actually rooted in a strength of the discipline: disciplines by their nature cannot pay attention to all factors that affect a situation. A discipline pays attention only to those factors that it studies. Thus, if you are studying adolescent development in a psychology class, you are learning to think the way a developmental psychologist thinks. You get insight into adolescents by looking at their patterns of physical, cognitive, social, and personality changes, based primarily on experiments and correlational studies. In thinking the way a psychologist thinks, you concentrate on the psychological factors in adolescent development, and not on the anthropological, legal, economic, medical, and literary factors.

It is important, then, not to accept the discipline without question. As a student, though, it is hard to appreciate how much emphasis is usually placed on critical-thinking standards by teachers in their presentations, by the authors of textbooks, by scholars in the field. Very seldom is a book used in a course "just someone's opinion."

Compare that to editorials or opinions on TV, newspapers, or on-line, or to politicians, lobbyists, advertisers and some other "advocates": Many of them (though not all) are actively trying to influence you to accept their own view of the matter. In contrast, virtually any textbook on controversial issues presents many different viewpoints. Authors of texts work hard to eliminate bias. (A frequent criticism of textbooks is that they *include too many* points of view rather than too few, that they are *bland* rather than biased.) Scholarly work is scrutinized by others in the field who have extensive knowledge and skills (peer review). (One observation is that in science [in contrast to dogmatic areas] no one is praised more than someone who refutes accepted theories.) None of this implies that authors are always successful in eliminating bias or egocentricity. Of course not. But they are far more successful than people who don't even try to root out bias or who present only their own side of an issue.

Trusting a discipline, then, does not mean believing it completely or automatically. It means taking it seriously, treating it as something to be learned from, rather than as something to be doubted automatically or put aside or rejected out of hand. After consideration, you may reject an idea or find it inadequate in one way or another. But to trust a discipline means to "try it on," to think in terms of it and see how it helps you understand the world in a new and richer way.

INTERNALIZING THE FIELD

Consider:

> (1a) Suppose you are selling your car to a man who doesn't know much about cars, and he is willing to pay you much more than you know the car is worth. What should you do?

In many ways, this is just an ordinary everyday question.

Now consider something different. In ethics courses, two major ethical perspectives are usually addressed: rights theory and consequentialist theory. Rights theory directs you to ask, roughly, "Whose rights are being violated by the action? Is this the fair way to act?" Consequentialist theory directs you to ask, roughly, "What are the positive and negative consequences of the action for all concerned?" Thus a teacher, as part of an ethics course, might ask an essay question:

> (1b) Address the following from either a rights perspective or a consequentialist perspective, or both: Suppose you are selling your car to a man who doesn't know much about cars, and he is willing to pay you much more than you know the car is worth. What should you do?

So one way to bring the point home about internalizing the discipline and getting out of the grip of "school stuff" is to see that there is a strong sense in which questions (1a) and (1b) are virtually *the same question*.[8] Part of the point of any course is that we should look at ordinary everyday situations in terms of the central concepts in the discipline. The intent is for this to hold long after the course is over. If it doesn't, the course may have missed you.

It is reasonable to apply a similar degree of trust even in matters that are far more controversial and deeply personal. For many people, for example, understanding the Bible is a deeply personal and intensely significant part of their lives. But, if you want to find out what the Bible is saying, if that is important to you, a reasonable way to go about it is to take a course in biblical studies. The authors you are likely to read in such a course will be biblical scholars, familiar with a wide variety of viewpoints and interpretations—not just with others who agree with them. They have read primary sources carefully. They have come to reasoned conclusions about the dating of manuscripts, and when and by whom those manuscripts were written. Most likely they know the original languages. They are intimately familiar with both the historical periods and the archaeological record. Their writings have been subjected to peer review.

Such extensive research is not found in most other sources you might consult, such as television documentaries, websites, sermons by religious leaders, evangelists on the radio, or the newest *New York Times* best seller.

Of course, the trustworthiness of the field does not imply that scholars are necessarily *right*. They could be wrong for any number of reasons—and you should think critically about their conclusions and their evidence, their interpretations and the context, the assumptions they make and the alternatives they ignore. They *are*, however, the best source you are likely to find. Moreover, if they are later shown to be wrong, it will most likely be by a member of the same community of critically thinking historians and biblical scholars.

The same can be said for just about any topic, no matter how controversial or personal. In fact, the more important a topic is in

---

COMMON SENSE

One of the things disciplines often do is contradict common sense. If that happens, you should feel a need to question the common sense. Disciplines are full of carefully amassed evidence, reasoned argumentation, and critiques by others. Common sense is not subject to any of these, certainly not in any systematic way. It is not common sense that the desk you are sitting at is 99 percent empty space; that being cold and wet has nothing to do with catching cold; that ulcers are caused by bacteria, not stress; that, objectively, there is no such thing as color; that the vast majority of us are capable of acting the way the Nazis did. Though these examples contradict most people's common sense, all, according to the most complete evidence we have, are clearly true.

---

your life, the more important it is to take a course in it, to read a textbook in the area. Here is a brief list of topics that are important to many people, and those people would benefit tremendously by consulting and taking seriously the discipline's findings and viewpoints:

- dieting
- healthy attitudes toward death and dying
- causes of crime in the United States
- global warming
- cloning
- the morality of abortion, the rights

- of animals, sexual morality
- the causes of "terrorism"
- the efficacy of herbal remedies
- the litigious nature of our society
- parapsychology, telekinesis

When You Disagree

There may be inaccuracies in your text or in lectures. That is quite possible. But be wary of concluding too quickly that lectures or texts are inaccurate or biased. If what the book says is contrary to your own experience, carefully consider a number of questions before concluding that the text is off-base. For example:

- Did I understand clearly what was said and what was meant, in context?
- Is my disagreement based merely on common sense? What is the real evidence for the commonsense view?
- Are my beliefs based on sources I have accepted uncritically?
- Is my own experience limited? Is it applicable only in one area?
- Do I have a vested interest in disbelieving what is in the text? Is my ego bound up with accepting one view over another?
- Do I feel some fear I may be unaware of at having my worldview shaken up? Do the findings in the discipline make me angry?

Some Outcomes

The outcomes listed here may be premature at this point. You may need further practice (maybe a lot of further practice) to do them well. But you should be making a beginning.

At the end of this chapter . . .

1. SEE-I: You should be able to state, elaborate, exemplify, and illustrate what is meant by the main concepts in this chapter: "the logic of a discipline," "the importance of vocabulary in a discipline," "fundamental and powerful concepts," "the central question of a course," and "the point of view of a discipline."

2. You should be able to *analyze the logic of the discipline* you are studying in a clear and accurate way (although not necessarily in a way that shows a deep or broad grasp of the discipline).

3. You should be *generating questions* within the discipline using the elements of reasoning. ("What are the implications of calling this artwork baroque?" "What information and assumptions is this theory based on?")

4. You are beginning to *use the vocabulary* of the discipline when you describe problems or situations.

5. You should be able to think through at least some important problems using *fundamental and powerful concepts* in the course. You should be able to carry this through in a way that is reasonably clear and accurate, though again not necessarily with

the depth or breadth that will come as you apply those concepts to an ever-widening range of problems and topics.

6. You can *identify the central question of the course*, at least tentatively. You should be able to describe how virtually every problem or question that arises in the course is an aspect of that central question.

7. You should be able to *describe the point of view of the discipline*: the domain, categories, and connections one sees when looking at the world through that point of view. You should be able to give your own examples of these. But more than that, you should be starting to actually *see* the world with that point of view.

8. You should be able to *state, elaborate*, and *give your own examples* of impediments to thinking critically within the discipline.

9. You should be able to *integrate* the outcomes of this chapter with those from Chapters 5 and 6 (pages 115 and 154). You should now be able to *explain* and *apply* those earlier outcomes to the discipline in a broader, deeper way.

Ideas for Writing

(General guidelines for "Ideas for Writing" are on page 116.)

1. What role do *questions* play in the discipline you are studying? How about *reasoning*? How about the challenge of *believing the results*?

2. Think about the distinction between seeing the discipline you are studying as a system of thinking versus seeing it as a body of information. What would you say are the key differences between the two? How might that affect someone taking a course in the discipline?

3. On pages 351–352, there is a brief description of some intellectual character traits of a critical thinker. As well as you can at this point in your learning, describe what it would be like for someone to be *intellectually engaged* in the field you are studying? (For example, suppose you are in a writing course. What would it be like for someone to be *committed* to being a writer?)

4. There are any number of questions you can write about in relation to the discipline you are studying: What impact does the discipline have on the world? What impact should it have? What would be the implications and consequences if people in general took the findings or expertise of the discipline seriously? How do people often fail to take account of it in our political, social, legal, or educational institutions? How are the discipline's fundamental and powerful concepts, and the central questions it addresses, essential in the world outside school? How would young people benefit from thinking through the point of view of the discipline (at their level)? Generate some of your own ideas to write about in relation to the discipline you are studying.

Tell Your Story

(The idea behind "Tell Your Story" and some suggestions about doing it are on page 117.)

I. What is your attitude toward the discipline you are studying? How has your attitude toward it changed over the years, maybe even before you ever took a course in it? What are some factors that might help you personally to become more open to it?

2. Have you ever thought about what it would be like for you to have a degree in the field you are focusing on in this course? Or, even more, picture what it would be like to be a professional in this field. What would stand in the way for you?

3. Do you have a category like "school stuff" in your mind? If so, how strong is it? To what extent does it prevent you from taking the discipline seriously?

4. Consider the central question of the course you are taking, and reflect on background stories you carry with you as "answers" to it. Because we are so unaware of our background stories, spelling them out is usually very difficult, but you may have some real insights here. To write on this question, you probably have to let go of some of the restraints you usually impose on your thinking. So, if it's a course in political science, how do

you think politics or government really works? If it's a course in nursing, what's your picture of how to treat people who are sick?) Adapt the question to the domain of the subject matter you are studying. Then reflect on how you acquired your background story.

5. Think of the fundamental and powerful concepts in your course or discipline. What was your idea of them before you ever entered this course? Even if the words in the concepts are unfamiliar to you, the concepts themselves may well have operated in your thinking all along, without your being aware of it. How have these f&p concepts had an impact on your life?

CHAPTER 10 Exercises

The exercises contain examples from a wide variety of disciplines. Few of these examples will be in the subject you are studying. But what the exercises ask you to do is directly relevant to the field you are studying. The exercises were chosen because they bring home important points about critical thinking in any field.

If possible, after answering the question as it stands, see if you can adapt it to the discipline you are studying.

10.1 Analyze the logic of a discipline-based course you are taking by "going around the circle" with respect to it. If you wish, you can use the "Logic of a Literature Course" (pages 237–239) as a model.

10.2 Here are two paragraphs from a composition text:

> Whenever you write, your goal is to communicate effectively with the people who are going to read what you write. These readers are considered your audience. Sometimes your audience might include specific people such as your classmates, your instructor, your friends, your family, or your boss. At other times, you might be writing for the general public that reads your local newspaper.
>
> As you write, ask yourself: Who is going to read this? How much do they already know about my topic? What are their attitudes about my topic? The answers to these questions can help you identify your audience. . . . Once you have analyzed your audience, you will be better able to decide on the content, vocabulary, and tone that are most suitable for your paper.[9]

   a. Use the elements of reasoning to describe how the authors reason from point to point in the two paragraphs.

   b. Do the same kind of analysis with different paragraphs from the readings in your course.

10.3 Critical thinking involves asking good questions: Write down five questions you have about the discipline you are studying. They should be good questions, ones where learning the answer is important to you. If you have trouble thinking of such questions, what conclusions do you draw?

10.4 With your book closed, write an SEE-I for the main concepts in this chapter: "the logic of a discipline," "the importance of vocabulary in a discipline," "fundamental and powerful concepts," "the central question of a course," and "the point of view of a discipline."

10.5 Critical thinking is authentic. Consider math problems. Students often prefer certain math problems because all they have to do is the computations or the calculator work. They hate word problems. That's natural. Computations have a much safer feel to them because you have a good idea of how to proceed. The problem does not look so open-ended. Critical thinking, however, applies to real-life problems with a quantitative aspect. Think them through mathematically, and only then do the computation or calculator work.

   a. Having any realistic understanding of math shows that buying lottery tickets makes no sense at all. People in math often call lotteries "the stupidity tax." Why, mathematically, do you think that is?

   b. Think of credit card debt: What exactly are you *buying* with the interest you pay?
   → What are some areas of your life where you need to think mathematically?

10.6 Logic of a field. What is the difference between thinking ethically and thinking legally? Give some examples to illustrate the difference.

10.7 Vocabulary of the discipline. As the course goes along, keep a log of terms you can define but still don't really understand. Keep a log of vocabulary words in the field that you can apply directly to your life as you live it now.

10.8 Look in the Table of Contents of a textbook in a class you are taking, and draw a concept map of the main themes of the book. Alternatively, make a concept map of the fundamental and powerful concepts for this course.

10.9 **Group work.** In groups of four, critically discuss the central question of the course. Try to come to a consensus on what it is, how it unifies the course as a whole, how it fits in with the central questions of other related fields. Then write down the central question of three other courses you are currently taking (or ones you have taken as recently as possible).

Compare the central questions to the one you identified for this course. How are they similar? What are the striking differences? How do they fit with one another?

10.10 Look back at the box on "Internalizing the Field" (pages 260–261), and adapt it to the field you are studying in this course. Take three or four questions as they might be asked from the point of view of the field you are studying. (For example, in a sociology course: "From the point of view of a structural-functional analysis of the family, what main roles do families play in human society?")

Next, ask the same question, but leave off the whole first half. Try to phrase it in ordinary non-academic language: "How do families work?"

How do the two versions of the question seem different to you? From the point of view of the field, to what extent are the questions the same or different?

10.11 **Critical writing for self-assessment.** Construct your own pre-test and post-test on critical thinking in a subject matter. Choose an important question in the course. It may not be the central question, but it should be very important. Maybe you can write it by adapting the title of a chapter or group of chapters in the text. Here are some examples:

Life sciences: How does the body work?

Education: How do children learn?

Geology: How do landforms come about?

Business: How does one manage a business?

Composition: How does someone write a good argumentative essay?

Write out an answer to this near the beginning of the course. You will be thinking it out as you compose your response. When your answer is written, put it away somewhere, and don't refer back to it. Give it time to sink into the background.

Near the end of the course (and without looking at your first answer), write out an answer to the same question.

Then compare the two, but not just with respect to the information each contains (this will obviously increase substantially by the time the semester is over). Compare them with respect to:

- How you have organized the information
- How well you have grasped the logic of the answer
- How well you are able to see the parts working together as a whole (synthesis).

You should also notice a marked improvement in the accuracy, importance, precision, and depth of your response.

10.12 As a study skill, memorizing does not work very well. What can you do instead? (Consider the effectiveness of your study habits for your coursework. Suppose you were going to a doctor for a serious medical condition. Would you want your doctor to have studied in medical school the way you study for your classes? Why or why not? How would you want your doctor to have studied?)

10.13 As an illustration, draw a concept map of critical thinking as you understand it so far.

10.14 Here is a concept map based on a new management paradigm in a management textbook.[10]

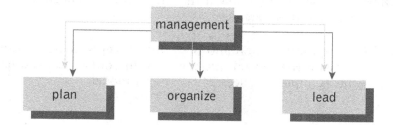

By thinking of the logic of this paradigm, can you see what is missing as a fundamental and powerful concept?

10.15 Impediments. Take each of the impediments listed in Chapter 5 (pages 94–103) and give an original example of how each might be an impediment to thinking critically in the discipline you are studying in this class. Be specific.

10.16 Why would you (or someone else) think that humans are more fit than dinosaurs? Evaluate the reasoning.

10.17 Group work. Focus on the background story you have for this course. (This is difficult work.)

Individually, take five of the most important concepts in the field. (A good place to get them is from the headings in the table of contents in the text.) Before you read anything about them in the book, write down your main ideas about them: how you understand them, how they work. For example, suppose it is a course in sociology and one of the chapters is entitled "Cultural Diversity." Explain what cultural diversity is, how it works, how it comes about, what effects it has, how you feel about it—whatever seems important to you. (Notice that this is an ill-defined question. You'll have to adapt it to your field.)

Now, discuss your responses in groups of four. Your aim in this is not to argue your points with others. It is to formulate a clear understanding of the background story that is operating in you.

Next, read the book and compare your story with the account in the book. Discuss this with the same group of four people. But your goal is not to find out if you were right or wrong. It is still to get a conscious grasp of your background story or logic, and to compare it to the logic of the discipline you are studying.

10.18 "We don't really know if the sun will rise tomorrow." Evaluate this statement.

10.19 Using fundamental and powerful concepts, write a short essay on the central question of your course. You can use the example on pages 249–251 as a model.

10.20 SEE-I. Look back over the contents of Chapter 10:

- Find a clarifying *statement* (or definition) in the chapter.
- Find an *elaboration* of an idea in it.
- Find an example; then find a contrasting example.
- Find an illustration.

10.21 Read the brief description of critical-thinking character traits on pages 351–352. Describe how intellectual empathy and intellectual humility enter into the learning of the discipline you are studying.

DAILY PRACTICE
At incorporating critical thinking into your life and your learning.

Before you start on Exercises 10.22 through 10.24, look back at the instructions on pages 122–123. Again, the key is to do the exercises as often as possible, daily if you can, in small repeated intervals, rather than doing them in a single big burst of effort.

10.22 Engage with the fundamental and powerful concepts. After you or your teacher have identified these in your course, spend a day in your life as usual, but as you do, start applying the fundamental and powerful concepts in a conscious, self-aware way. You don't have to be advanced as a thinker to feel the power of this. The exercise is to look for situations that can be understood better (or differently) by applying the fundamental and powerful concepts. Thus, if the concept is *romanticism*, I would spend intensive, focused time looking at almost everything—ordinary events, people, things, interactions—through the lens of romanticism. How can I use that concept to understand my quest for an education, my preference for driving versus public transportation (or vice versa), the people I choose (and do not choose) for friends, movies I like, books, anything?

10.23 **Engage with the central question of the discipline.** After you (or your teacher) have identified the central question in your course, spend a short period of time each day, for several days, asking yourself that question and applying it to what you encounter as you live your life. For example, suppose the question is, "What do writers do to make literature effective?" You could spend your day creatively applying this question in any number of ways: "How would a writer describe this situation effectively?" "How *have* writers I've read described this kind of situation effectively?"

Engage in this ongoing activity with the central question of your course.

10.24 **Spend a day observing through the point of view of the discipline.** At the beginning, you don't necessarily have to *explain* anything. Just *notice*, observe. (Observe not just visually, but with your other senses as well—and especially with your mind.)

Go through your daily life as usual, only notice—and write down—all the items you encounter that are in the domain of the discipline you are studying. Try also to observe in terms of connections—at least wonder about the connections between the objects and events you observe and other concepts in the field.

For example, suppose you are studying physics. You see leaves moving on a tree, and notice that you are seeing forces at work, energy being transformed. You see your hands writing in your journal, and you notice that you are seeing push–pull forces of muscles; you are seeing a lever at work as you get up from your chair, and so on.

Another example: Suppose you are studying the Impressionists in an art history course. You see colors and shapes dissolving as you look out the window, and that boundaries aren't nearly as exact as you thought they were; you see that shadows are blue or purple as Monet saw them, not really black at all; you see the effects of snow and how it turns things blue rather than white; you let your eyes unfocus and allow yourself to see black foreground and bright background switch places as Manet did.

In your journal, write down as many examples as you can (at least 12 to 15) of things or connections that you see differently when you are viewing them from the point of view of the discipline. Describe the differences briefly.

DISCOVER HOW THE BEST THINKERS LEARN

A man may hear a thousand lectures, and read a thousand volumes, and be at the end of the process very much where he was, as regards knowledge. Something more than merely admitting it in a negative way into the mind is necessary, if it is to remain there. It must not be passively received, but actually and actively entered into, embraced, mastered. The mind must go half-way to meet what comes to it from without.

John Henry Newman, *The Idea of a University* (1853)

The best thinkers are skilled learners. They take charge of their learning. They, in essence, design it—plan it out. You plan learning by becoming clear as to what your goals are, what questions you have to—or want to—answer, what information you need to get, what concepts you need to learn, what point of view or perspective you need to adopt. Skilled learners figure out the logic of what they are trying to understand. Skilled learners have strategies for studying well—and continue to develop strategies as they become more skilled at thinking. As you read through this chapter, you should begin to explicitly choose and practice a range of strategies that take you out of the mainstream of most students—who have in effect no powerful learning strategies.

We will begin with 18 ideas or strategies expressed simply. Most of these strategies will be explained and exemplified throughout the chapter. The strategies of close reading and substantive writing (two of the most important tools for learning) will be covered in a separate chapter.

273

Exhibit 11.1 Critical thinkers have confidence in their ability to figure out the logic of anything they choose.

The spirit of
critical thinking

18 IDEAS FOR IMPROVING YOUR STUDIES

Idea # 1: Make sure you thoroughly understand the requirements of each class—how it will be taught and what will be expected of you. Ask questions about the grading policies and for advice on how best to prepare for class.

Idea # 2: Become an active learner. Begin to work ideas into your thinking by actively reading, writing, speaking, and listening.

Idea # 3: Think of each subject you study as a form of thinking. (If you are in a history class, your goal should be to think historically; in a chemistry class to think chemically; etc.)

Idea # 4: Become a questioner. Engage yourself in lectures and discussions by asking questions. If you don't ask questions, you probably won't discover what you do and do not know.

Idea # 5: Look for interconnections. The content in every class is a *system* of interconnected ideas, never a random list of things to memorize. Don't memorize like a parrot. Study like a detective, always relating new learning to previous learning.

Idea # 6: Think of your instructor as your coach. Think of yourself as a team member trying to practice the thinking exemplified by your instructor. For example, in an algebra class, think of yourself as going out for the algebra team and your teacher as demonstrating how to prepare for the games (thinking within the discipline).

Idea # 7: Understand the textbook as the thinking of the author. Your job is to think the thinking of the author. For example, role play the author frequently. Explain the main points of the text to another student as if you were the author.

Idea # 8: Consider class time as a time in which you *practice* thinking (within the subject) using the fundamental concepts and principles of the course. Don't sit back passively, waiting for knowledge to fall into your head like rain into a rain barrel. It won't.

Idea # 9: Relate content whenever possible to issues and problems and practical situations in your life. If you can't connect it to your life, you don't understand it at a deep enough level to use it in your thinking.

Idea # 10: Figure out what study and learning skills you need to develop. Practice those skills whenever possible. Remember that recognizing and correcting your weaknesses is a strength.

Idea # 11: Frequently ask yourself: Can I explain this to someone well enough for them to accurately understand it? (If not, you haven't learned it.)

Idea # 12: Seek the key concept of the course during the first couple of class meetings. For example, in a biology course, try explaining what biology is in your own words. Then relate that definition to each segment of what you learn afterward. Fundamental ideas are the basis for all other ideas.

Idea # 13: Routinely ask questions to fill in the missing pieces in your learning. Ask yourself: "Can I elaborate on this? Can I give an example?" If you cannot give examples of what you are learning you are not connecting what you are learning to your life.

Idea # 14: Test yourself before each class by trying to summarize, orally or in writing, the main points of the previous class meeting. If you cannot summarize the main points, you haven't learned them.

Idea # 15: Learn to test your thinking using intellectual standards: "Am I being clear? accurate? precise? relevant? logical? Am I looking for what is most significant?"

Idea # 16: Use writing as a tool for learning by writing summaries in your own words of important points from the textbook or other reading material. Formulate your own test questions. Then write out answers to your questions.

Idea # 17: Frequently evaluate your listening. Are you actively listening for main points? Can you summarize what your instructor is saying in your own words? Can you elaborate what is meant by key terms?

Idea # 18: Frequently evaluate the depth of your reading. Are you reading the textbook actively? Are you asking questions as you read? Can you distinguish what you understand from what you don't understand?

11.1 *Think for Yourself*

WHERE DO YOU STAND?

To what extent have you "designed" any part of your learning (in high school or college)? Have you ever developed any strategies for learning? Can you name one? Did it work (if you can think of one)? If you can't think of any strategies you use to learn, why not? On a scale of 1 to 10, how skilled would you say you are as a learner?

THE LOGIC OF A TYPICAL COLLEGE CLASS

Because you are learning through the medium of college classes, it is helpful to understand the logic of college classes. To understand the logic of college classes, consider college in the light of its history and traditions.

College today is a product of college yesterday. Traditions alive in college instruction go back hundreds of years. For example, the most common way for professors to try to get students to learn a body of knowledge is to state that body of knowledge to them in a sequence of lectures and then to ask students, largely on their own, to internalize that knowledge outside of class. In this design, quizzes and examinations are usually interspersed among the lectures as means of assessing the extent to which the students have learned what the lectures covered.

Often a quiz is not given for six weeks or more. When this traditional teaching approach is used, students often revert to two strategies, neither of which is conducive to deep learning:

1. Taking random, but disconnected, notes during the lecture (focusing on points that might be on the test)

2. Intensive cramming one or two nights before the quiz or test (striving to store a large amount of information in short-term memory)

Under these conditions, many students go from the passive to the desperate learner, from being largely inactive as a learner to being frantic as a learner. On the other hand, students who are naturally "good" at memorization generally get higher grades in lecture-based classes than students who struggle to memorize content. Consequently, these students erroneously connect high grades with skilled learning. In other words, because memorization leads to high grades, they conclude that when they memorize content, they are learning at a deep level. In this model, students formulate a concept of learning that is superficial and transitory.

11.2   Think for Yourself

ARE YOU A PASSIVE LEARNER?

To what extent would you say that you match the traditional college student learning pattern above (largely passive, periodically frantic)? To what extent do you think this pattern is effective for deep learning? Why have you fallen into this pattern (if you have)? Or why haven't you fallen into this pattern (if you have not)?

Becoming a Skilled Thinker

The ideal of college can be expressed in a number of ways. However, no matter how it is expressed, certain basic skills and dispositions must be included in the definition for it to accurately characterize the educated person. The educated person, for example, must be:

1. proficient in close reading and substantive writing;

2. able to acquire and effectively use significant information, reason well, communicate effectively, solve problems, and exercise sound personal and professional judgment;

3. proficient in formulating and assessing goals and purposes, questions and problems, information and data, conclusions and interpretations, concepts and theoretical constructs, assumptions and presuppositions, implications and consequences, and points of view and perspectives;

4. able to think clearly, accurately, precisely, relevantly, deeply, broadly, and logically;

5. intellectually perseverant, intellectually responsible, intellectually disciplined, intellectually humble, intellectually empathic, and intellectually productive;

6. reasonable, ethical, and effective in reasoning through complex problems, both globally and in one's personal life;

7. a lifelong learner with the capacity to deal effectively with a world of accelerating change, intensifying complexity, and increasing interdependence.

It should be clear to you that these characteristics and skills will not emerge simply as the result of regularly taking notes in lecture and cramming for quizzes and exams. If you value the ends expressed in the above ideals, if you want to develop as an educated person, you will have to establish personal imperatives that set you apart from your fellow students. You will have to develop habits that few of your peers are developing. You must rise above peer group expectation (and possibly peer group scorn) and learn for reasons of your own and at a deeper level.

You must recognize that to acquire knowledge, you must construct it in your mind. You must translate it from the thoughts of someone else into your thoughts. To think it into your mind, you must be able to state it, elaborate upon it, exemplify it, and illustrate it. You must become proficient in taking ownership of ideas. Ideas may come from lectures, from textbooks, or from other sources. But do not be deceived by your ability to restate ideas in the same words that the instructor or text originally expressed them. A parrot, a tape recorder, or a rote memorizer is not a knower. Until you can express an idea in your own words and exemplify it from your own experience, it is not yours; you do not *know* it.

11.3   *Think for Yourself*

DO YOU OWN THE IDEAL?

Which of the goals stated above do you most identify with? Which the least? Why? Note that goals 3, 4, and 5 presuppose some knowledge of critical thinking. Consider one of these goals—for example, learning to be more proficient in using "concepts and theoretical constructs." How could you begin to incorporate this goal more thoroughly into your strategies for learning?

The Design of a Typical College Class and the Typical College Student

Although all college students take college classes, few master the logic of any academic discipline they study. Few students understand how college classes get designed or what challenges they themselves face in the learning process. Here are some important background facts:

1. Every field of study is subject to continual and (in most cases) enormous expansion.
2. Textbooks, which are the basis for most college classes, are getting larger and larger, and lectures are, in turn, tending to cover more and more content.
3. Most students do not know how to organize content as a system of meanings, to bring content into their thinking as a connected, interrelated system.
4. Most students use periodic cramming to pass their exams.
5. Most students read, write, and listen at a superficial level.
6. Most students lack intellectual standards by which to assess their own thinking and learning.

11.4   *Think for Yourself*

RATING YOURSELF AGAIN

How would you rate yourself on items 3, 4, 5, and 6 above? Comment on each separately. Then comment on what you consider the implications of your answers to be. For example, for number 5, if you read at a superficial level, what is a consequence of your limited reading ability?

The facts presented above have a number of important implications:

1. Most college exams are constructed so that the majority of students can pass them—that is, the majority of students can memorize well enough to pass them. (If a significant number of students were to fail the exams, the instructor would get low evaluations from the students.)

2. Grade inflation is rampant.

3. Most students probably could not pass the final exams for courses six months after the courses end.

4. Most students do not learn to think in the broader context of the course (e.g., they take history courses but do not learn to think historically; they take science courses but do not learn to think scientifically).

An important implication of these facts is that college generates a great deal of self-deception: Instructors who certify students as understanding subjects they do not truly understand; students who forget most of what they temporarily cram into their heads; accrediting teams and accrediting departments that show no real evidence that students are learning what they claim they are learning.

Skilled thinkers want to do more than survive in college. They want their college education to help them become effective lifelong learners and thinkers.

11.5 *Think for Yourself*

THE PROBLEM OF SELF-DECEPTION

To develop as a critical thinker, you must be willing to face the fact that humans engage in a great deal of self-deception. Self-deception in college is part of the broader problem of self-deception in human life. Do you see any ways in which you have deceived yourself in terms of your learning? In your personal relationships? Do you see any ways in which teachers you have had in the past deceived themselves? Do you see any ways in which your friends are deceiving themselves?

For each class you take, it is important for you to understand how that course is designed. This includes figuring out the logic of the course through an analysis of the course syllabus, the textbook, and how the instructor has introduced the course. Every course in which you enroll has some essential things to look for. First, what are the official requirements of the class? What is the assigned reading, writing, and planned testing or assessment? When will papers, if any, be due? When will quizzes and tests occur? These are some obvious things to look for.

However you study, you want to meet the formal requirements at a high level. But there is something more important than merely getting passing grades. It is learning to think within the disciplines you study, internalizing core concepts, and gaining the most basic insights underlying the disciplines. It is important to make the mode of thinking in the discipline a permanent part of your thinking. To aim at these high goals, you might routinely ask and pursue three interconnected key questions:

1. What is the central underlying concept of the course or subject?
2. What form(s) of thinking is (are) essential to this course or subject?
3. How can I begin to think within the logic of the subject?

Let us consider these in order.

FIGURE OUT THE UNDERLYING CONCEPT OF YOUR COURSES

If you look at the sequence of items a course covers as if they were random bits and pieces of information, the course will seem to lack any underlying unity. But virtually all courses have some inherent unity that, when understood, ties all the learning of the course together like a tapestry. This unity typically is found in foundational concepts that define the subject and its goals.

For example, if you understand that the important "facts" of history are the product of historical thinking, and recognize the basic patterns that underlie such thinking, you have a way of looking at everything covered in the textbook and lectures—namely, as products of historical thought. You then read the textbook and listen to the lectures in a special way, seeking to find components of historical thought. You recognize that, to understand any written history, you must understand

1. the historian's goals or purposes.
2. the questions or problems that are the primary focus of the historian.
3. the historian's specific selection of historical events he or she considers relevant to his or her questions.
4. the historian's interpretations of the events and the significance of those events.
5. the theoretical concepts the historian is using to interpret the events.
6. the underlying assumptions that help define the historian's perspective.
7. the implications of studying the historical events from a given perspective.
8. the historical point of view that shapes the historical reasoning throughout.

If, in addition, we recognize that everyone thinks historically every day of his or her life, we study history differently. For example, each and every day of our lives, we use in our thinking a story that entails our personal history. That story, or the way we view our past, determines the decisions we make today and the plans we make for the future. Our own personal history, then, reflects our historical assumptions, concepts, and point of view. It leads us to ask certain questions with certain purposes in mind. It leads us to make particular inferences, based on historical information, that then lead to implications.

When you see history in this richly interconnected way, you look for the historical goals and questions that are defining the construction of any and all historical accounts. You notice what events are included and look for what is left out of the historical account. You look at key historical conclusions historians come to, the key assumptions made, the underlying historical points of view. Yet, most history classes have little impact on the historical thinking of students. Therefore, most students lack the organizing idea behind the discipline of history. They lack insight into the logic of historical thinking. As a result, their own historical thinking remains unmodified by their "study" of history. They never internalize deep and important historical concepts that, if internalized, would enable them to think critically about the past and to apply historical concepts in everyday life.

Consider another subject—economics. If we understand the concept of scarcity as the underlying concept in economics, we study economics in a special way. We realize that all other concepts that economists use are related to this central idea behind economics: that it is not possible for any one of us to have everything we want (the fact of scarcity) and, as a result, all of us have to give up some things to get other things. What people are willing to give up to get something else forms the basis for their economic decision making. Power enters economics when some people control what is scarce and highly desired and can thereby "force" people who want what is scarce to make significant sacrifices to obtain such scarcities. This "power" is an important concept in economics.

Here is the skeleton for some other organizing ideas:

- *Mathematics* as the development of a language for quantification
- *Algebra* as arithmetic with unknowns
- *Sociology* as the study of how the life of humans is shaped by the groups in which they are members
- *Physics* as the study of mass and energy and the interrelations between the two
- *Philosophy* as the study of ultimate questions and their reasoned answers
- *Biochemistry* as the study of the chemistry of life at the molecular level

11.6   *Think for Yourself*

GETTING THE KEY IDEA

For practice, attempt to formulate the basic idea behind history, economics, or any other discipline. Explain that idea to a friend. Encourage him or her to ask you questions. See whether you can explain the significance of understanding the underlying idea behind a subject as an important first step in understanding the subject—and that every concept within the subject must be integrated into this key organizing idea. (We recommend that you use textbooks and/or encyclopedias in formulating core concepts.)

FIGURE OUT THE FORM OF THINKING
ESSENTIAL TO COURSES OR SUBJECTS

The organizing concept behind a course is often the organizing concept behind a subject or discipline. If you understand this core concept, you should be able to formulate the eight central structures that define any form of thought:

1. What are the *goals* or objectives of the course or discipline?
2. What *questions* or problems will be central?
3. What *concepts* will be fundamental?
4. What *information* will I use in reasoning well within the subject?
5. What *point of view* or frame of reference do I need to learn to reason within?
6. What *assumptions* define the course or discipline?
7. What kinds of *conclusions* will I need to learn how to reason to?
8. What are the pay-offs (*implications*) of reasoning well within this discipline?

If we are correct in what we said about all subjects being forms of thought, each of your classes offers an invitation to think within one or more of those forms. Your ability to reason well within any subject will directly depend upon your ability to understand the *thinking* that defines the subject, to think the kind of thinking that professionals in the discipline think.

Consider the following thinking on the part of a student taking a course in history:

> To do well in this course, I must begin to think historically. I must read the textbook not as a bunch of disconnected stuff to remember but, instead, as the thinking of the historian. I must begin to think like a historian myself. I must begin to be clear about historical purposes. (What are historians trying to accomplish?) I must begin to ask historical questions (and recognize the historical questions being asked in the lectures and textbook). I must begin to sift through historical information, drawing some historical conclusions. I must begin to question where historical information comes from.
>
> I must notice the historical interpretations that historians form to give meaning to historical information. I must question those interpretations (at least sufficiently to understand them). I must begin to question the implications of various historical interpretations and begin to see how historians reason to their conclusions. I must begin to look at the world as historians do, to develop a historical viewpoint. I will read each chapter in the textbook, looking explicitly for the elements of thought in that chapter. I will actively ask historical questions in class from a critical-thinking perspective. I will begin to pay attention to my own historical thinking in my everyday life. In short, I will try to make historical thinking a more explicit and prominent part of my thinking.

Students who approach history classes as historical thinking begin to understand the historical dimension of other subjects as well. For example, they begin to recognize that every subject itself has a history and that the present state of the subject is a product of its historical evolution. What's more, historically thinking students notice the overlap between history as a study of the relatively recent past of humans (in the past 30,000 years) and the much longer history of humans (canvassed in anthropology). They are able to place these past 30,000 years (which seem like such a long time when we first think about it) into the larger historical perspective of anthropology, which begins its study of the human past some 1.5 million or more years ago when our ancestors were small, hairy, apelike creatures who used tools such as digging sticks and clubs, walked upright, carried their tools, and lived on plant food.

Further, they see this longer history as breaking down into stages: from hunting and gathering civilizations to agricultural civilizations to industrial civilizations to post-industrial civilizations. And that's not all. They then are able to place this historical perspective into a still larger historical view by shifting from anthropological thinking to geographical thinking. They realize that human history is itself a small part of a much older history, that of mammals, and that the age of mammals was preceded by an age of reptiles, and that age by the age of coal plants, and that age by the age of fish, and that by the age of mollusks. They then can take the next step and grasp that geological history, even though reaching back thousands of millions of years, is comparatively short when compared to that of the solar system, and that of the solar system is comparatively short when compared to the galaxy, and that of the galaxy is comparatively short when compared to the history of the universe itself.

The capacity to think historically in larger and larger time spans continues to develop as the study of all subjects is transformed by a developing sense of the drama of time itself. Historical thinkers then are able to shift from history to prehistory, from prehistory to anthropological history, from anthropological history to geological history, and from geological history to astronomical history. In this ever-expanding perspective, the history of human knowledge is pitifully short: a millisecond geologically, a milli-millisecond astronomically. Only a second ago, astronomically speaking, did a species emerge—*Homo sapiens*, which drives itself and creates the conditions to which it itself must adapt, in new and unpredictable ways. Only a millisecond ago did a species emerge that has the capacity, but not the propensity, to think critically.

11.7   Think for Yourself

DEVELOPING YOUR THINKING

Examine in detail the extract quoting a student thinking about history (see page 282). Write out some thinking of your own about any subject you are studying. Construct parallel sentences if you wish, but try to begin to see how each of the parts fits and contributes to an organized way of understanding a body of content and learning within any system of thought.

Then read and explain to a classmate or a friend what you wrote. Encourage him or her to ask you questions whenever what you say is not clear. Only when you can accurately articulate the logic of a course in your own words and elaborate on that logic can you begin to use it in your thinking. Once you finish, you can begin to think about how your thinking within this discipline can help you gain insights into other disciplines as well.

THINK WITHIN THE LOGIC OF THE SUBJECT

Once you have some sense of what you are aiming at as a whole, when you can articulate the key organizing idea within a subject, begin to plan your learning in parts, in light of the order or sequence in which content is being presented in the class and in the textbook. Then go to class armed with questions generated by reading your class notes and the textbook. You also might read encyclopedia entries for help with the basic logic of a subject. Some possible start-up questions are:

What is the main *goal* of studying this subject?

What are people in this field trying to accomplish?

What kinds of *questions* do they ask? What kinds of problems do they try to solve?

What sorts of *information* or data do they gather?

How do they go about gathering information in ways that are distinctive to this field?

What is the most basic idea, *concept*, or theory in this field?

How should studying this field affect my *view* of the world?

How are the products of this field used in everyday life?

These questions can be contextualized for any given class day, chapter in the textbook, and dimension of study. For example, on any given day, you might ask one or more of the following questions:

What is our main *goal* today?

What are we trying to accomplish?

What kinds of *questions* are we asking? What kinds of problems are we trying to solve?

What sort of *information* or data do we need?

How can we get that information?

What is the most basic idea, *concept*, or theory that we need to understand to solve the problem we are most immediately posing?

How should we look at this problem? What *point of view* should we adopt?

How does this problem relate to everyday life?

11.8   *Think for Yourself*

ASKING GOOD QUESTIONS

Using these questions as a stimulus for your thinking, write out, for any class you are taking, a series of questions that enable you to think your way into the subject of the course. Compare your questions with the questions of another student.

THE LOGIC OF BIOCHEMISTRY

Let us now explicate the logic of one discipline by analyzing some key passages from the kind of text you might find in a book on the subject. Consider the following quote:

[In biochemistry] … attention is directed to the problems of finding out how molecular events underlie macroscopic phenomena, with special reference to the modes of action of vitamins, drugs, and genetic factors. One kind of job that biochemists undertake is, of course, to isolate compounds from living things and determine their structures. In this they share the preoccupation of other kinds of biologists with spatial form.

Biochemistry includes a sort of submicroscopic anatomy that elucidates structure on the minute scale of molecules. The classical anatomists cut up bodies to describe the parts of which they are made insofar as they are visible to the naked eye. Microscopy revealed a whole new world of structure and organization smaller than this, and … cells became the focus of interest. With the advance of chemistry, it gradually became possible to tackle biological architecture even on the molecular scale.

The grand strategy remains the same—a better understanding of living things in terms of their constituent parts. The tactics, however, … depend on the order of size of the parts being examined. For gross anatomy, the scalpel is appropriate; for cellular structure, the microscope; for parts as small as molecules, the relevant techniques are those we call chemical.… Seen in this light, biochemistry is the logical extrapolation of dissection. The idea is epitomized in the expression "molecular biology."…

Merely to determine structure, however, is far from the summit of the ambitions of biochemists. They are interested not only in what the constituents of living things are like, but also in what they do—in the way that chemical processes underlie the more obvious vital manifestations. The continuous change that is one of the most striking characteristics of life rests on unceasing chemical activity inside living organisms. Biochemistry thus continues another classical tradition of biology in linking form with function. Like anatomy divorced from physiology, static divorced from dynamic biochemistry … fails to … increase man's power over nature. Life, after all, is a matter of keeping events going, not only of maintaining structures; and biochemists seek to elucidate events as well as structures by isolation.

By and large, then, while the techniques of biochemistry are chemical, its problems are the basic ones of biology. Chemistry is its means, biology its end. It is the extreme extension of that approach to the phenomena of life that seeks to explain them in terms of the sub-units of which living organisms are composed. Of this kind of biological analysis, it represents the ultimate state—ultimate because pushing the analysis a stage further, from the molecular level down to the atomic, leaves no characteristically biological kind of organization, the atoms being the same in the inorganic realm.… Biochemistry concentrates on the farthest removal from immediate biological reality; insofar as it concerns itself with molecules, it remains remote from intact organisms. Data on the molecular level have to be related to observations made on more highly organized, less disrupted systems. (Jevons, 1964)

Biochemical Goals

It is clear from this passage that the goals of biochemistry are to determine the biochemical foundations of life and, through those means, to develop a rational chemotherapy. It aims to be a fundamental kind of biology, to use chemistry and events on the molecular scale, typified by proteins and single enzyme reactions, and then "moves on to their collaboration and organization above the molecular level in subcellular particles."

Biochemical Questions

The chemical concepts address the phenomena of life. From isolated molecules and questions, biochemistry is concerned with these questions: What are we made of? How do our bodies work? What is life? More particularly: How do molecular events underlie macroscopic phenomena of life? What compounds underlie living things? What is their structure? And what do they do?

How do vitamins work in the body? How do drugs work? How do genetic factors influence both? What molecular parts of living organisms are the special concern of biochemistry? (What are proteins, carbohydrates, and fats? What do they do? What are nucleic acids? What do they do?) How do enzymes catalyze virtually every reaction in living organisms? What is the role of enzymes in biological thought? How can we understand the biochemical unity of living matter? What is the similarity of yeast and muscle? What do proteins do inside living organisms? How can we correlate observations made at different levels of organization? How can we design drugs and create a rational chemotherapy? How can we produce drugs that target undesirable events in living creatures?

Biochemical Information

From the questions above, we can begin to see the kinds of information that biochemists seek: information about proteins and enzymes as the kind of chemical units out of which life is constructed, about the process of catalysis as the means by which key chemical reactions essential to the construction of life take place, information about artificial lifelike reactions (such as the study of a single enzyme reaction in a test tube), information about the variety of enzymes in living cells, about the molecular structures within cells, about multi-enzyme systems and how they operate, and so on.

Biochemical Judgments

From the biochemical information above, biochemists clearly seek to make judgments about the important properties of enzymes, their protein nature, the agents that make things happen in living organisms, metabolism, the complex process of maintenance and growth of which life basically consists.

Biochemical Concepts

From the biochemical judgments above, we have to understand a number of essential concepts to understand the logic of biochemistry: the concept of levels of organization of life processes (at the molecular level, at the subcellular particle level, at the cellular level, at the organ level, and at the level of the total organism);

the concept of life structures and life processes; the concept of the dynamics of life; the concept of proteins, enzymes, catalysis, and metabolism as reducible to a consecutive series of enzyme-catalyzed reactions; the concept of the unity of life processes amid a diversity of life forms; and so on.

Biochemical Assumptions

From the biochemical concepts above, some key assumptions behind biochemical thinking are that life has biochemical foundations; that these foundations are found at the molecular level; that the techniques of chemistry are most fitting for the study of life at the molecular level; that it is possible to use chemical concepts to explain life; that it is possible to analyze and discover the structure and dynamics of isolated molecules and events on the molecular scale; that proteins and enzymes are key agents in fundamental life processes; that enzyme reactions are crucial to understanding life; and that it is possible, ultimately, to develop a rational chemotherapy that can be used in medicine and everyday life planning to kill unwanted life processes while strengthening or maintaining desirable ones.

Biochemical Implications

The present logic of biochemistry has specific and general implications. The specific implications have to do with the kind of questioning, the kind of information-gathering and information-interpreting processes that biochemists are using today. (For example, the state of the field implies the importance of focusing questions and analysis on the concepts above, of seeking key answers at the molecular level, involving proteins, enzymes, and catalyzed chemical reactions.) The general implications are that, if modern biochemical theory is on the right track, we will be increasingly able to enhance human and other forms of life and diminish disease and other undesirable states (by application of chemotherapy).

Biochemical Point of View

The biochemical viewpoint is directed at the molecular level of life and sees that level as providing for the most fundamental disclosures about the nature, function, and foundations of life. It sees the essential techniques to be chemical. It sees the essential problems to be biological. It sees life processes at the molecular level to be highly unified and consistent. It sees life processes at the whole-animal level to be highly diversified. It sees the processes at the molecular level to be the key, along with genetics, to the explanation of diversity at the macroscopic level.

Clearly, as soon as we understand the basic logic of biochemistry and situate ourselves somewhere in a course in biochemistry, the questions we bring to class will be contextualizations of this logic for the following generic types:

What is our main goal today?

What are we trying to accomplish?

What kinds of questions are we asking? What kinds of problems are we trying to solve?

What sort of information or data do we need?

How can we get that information?

What is the most basic idea, concept, or theory that we need to understand to solve the problem we are posing most immediately?

How should we look at this problem?

How does this problem relate to everyday life?

On one day, the class may be focusing on a particular concept such as catalysis, on another day big molecules, on another day subcellular particles, on another co-enzymes, on another energy transactions, on another DNA. Understanding the overall logic of biochemistry will enable you to make sense of where you are, why it is significant, and how to relate it to what came before and what will come after.

THE LOGIC OF FOUR ADDITIONAL DISCIPLINES

Now consider the logic of biology that would likely be implicit in a standard biology textbook. This is followed by three additional logics: that of ecology, aerospace engineering, and electrical engineering.

The Logic of Biology

Biological Goals

Biology is the scientific study of all life forms. Its basic goal is to understand how life forms work, including the fundamental processes and ingredients of all life forms (i.e., 10,000,000 species in fragile ecosystems).

Biological Questions

The questions biology is concerned with are: What is life? How do living systems work? What are the structural and functional components of life forms? What are the similarities and differences among life forms at different levels (molecule, organelle, cell, tissue, organ, organism, population, ecological community, biosphere)? How can we understand the biological unity of living matter?

Biological Information

The kinds of information biologists seek are: information about the basic units out of which life is constructed, the processes by which living systems sustain themselves, the variety of living systems, and their structural and functional components.

Biological Judgments

Biologists seek to make judgments about the complex processes of maintenance and growth of which life basically consists.

Biological Concepts

A number of essential concepts are basic to understanding the logic of biology: the concept of levels of organization of life processes (at the molecular level, at the subcellular particle level, at the cellular level, at the organ level, and at the level of the total organism), the concept of life structures and life processes, the concept of the dynamics of life, the concept of the unity of life processes amid a diversity of life forms, etc.

Biological Assumptions

Some of the key assumptions behind biological thinking are: that there are foundations to life; that these foundations can be identified, studied, described, and explained; that it is possible to use biological concepts to explain life; that it is possible to analyze and discover the structure and dynamics of living systems and their components; that all forms of life reproduce, grow, and respond to changes in the environment; that there is an intricate and often fragile relationship between all living things; that all life forms, no matter how diverse, have common characteristics: 1) they are made up of cells, enclosed by a membrane that maintains internal conditions different from their surroundings, 2) they contain DNA or RNA as the material that carries their master plan, and 3) they carry out a process, called metabolism, which involves the conversion of different forms of energy by means of which they sustain themselves.

Biological Implications

There are specific and general implications of the present logic of biology. The specific implications have to do with the kind of questioning, the kind of information-gathering and information-interpreting processes being used by biologists today. For example, the state of the field implies the importance of focusing questions and analysis on the concepts above, of seeking key answers at all levels of life systems. The general implications are that we have the knowledge, if not always the will, to understand, maintain, and protect forms of life.

Biological Point of View

The biological viewpoint is focused on all levels and forms of life. It sees all life forms as consisting in structures and understood through describable functions. It sees life processes at the molecular level to be highly unified and consistent. It sees life process at the whole-animal level to be highly diversified.

The Logic of Ecology

Purposes of Ecologists

Ecologists seek to understand plants and animals as they exist in nature, with emphasis on their interrelationships, interdependence, and interactions with the environment. They work to understand all the influences that combine to produce and modify an animal or given plant and, thus, to account for its existence and peculiarities within its habitat.

Questions Ecologists Ask

How do plants and animals interact? How do animals interact with each other? How do plants and animals depend on one another? How do the varying ecosystems function within themselves? How do they interact with other ecosystems? How are plants and animals affected by environmental influences? How do animals and plants grow, develop, die, and replace themselves? How do plants and animals create balances between each other? What happens when plants and animals become unbalanced?

Information Ecologists Use

The primary information used by ecologists is gained through observing plants and animals themselves, their interactions, and how they live within their environments. Ecologists note how animals and plants are born, how they reproduce, how they die, how they evolve, and how they are affected by environmental changes. They also use information from other disciplines, including chemistry, meteorology, and geology.

Judgments Ecologists Make

Ecologists make judgments about how ecosystems naturally function, about how animals and plants within them function, about why they function as they do. They make judgments about how ecosystems become out of balance and what can be done to bring them back into balance. They make judgments about how natural communities should be grouped and classified.

Concepts that Guide Ecologists' Thinking

One of the most fundamental concepts in ecology is ecosystem. Ecosystem is defined as a group of living things, dependent on one another and living in a particular habitat. Ecologists study how differing ecosystems function. Another key concept in ecology is ecological succession, the natural pattern of change occurring within every ecosystem when natural processes are undisturbed. This pattern includes the birth, development, death, and then replacement of natural communities. Ecologists have grouped communities into larger units called biomes. These are regions throughout the world classified according to physical features, including temperature, rainfall, and type of vegetation. Another fundamental concept in ecology is balance of nature, the natural process of birth, reproduction, eating and being eaten, which keeps animal and plant communities fairly stable. Other key concepts include imbalances, energy, nutrients, population growth, diversity, habitat, competition, predation, parasitism, adaptation, coevolution, succession and climax communities, and conservation.

Key Assumptions Ecologists Make

Ecologists assume that patterns exist within animal and plant communities; that these communities should be studied and classified; that animals and plants often depend on one another and modify one another; and that balances must be maintained within ecosystems.

Implications of Ecology

The study of ecology leads to numerous implications for life on earth. By studying balance of nature, for example, we can see when nature is out of balance, as in the current population explosion. We can see how pesticides, designed to kill pests on farm crops, also lead to the harm of mammals and birds, either directly or indirectly through food webs. We can also learn how over-farming causes erosion and depletion of soil nutrients.

The Point of View of Ecologists

Ecologists look at plants and animals and see them functioning in relationship with one another within their habitats and needing to be in balance for the earth to be healthy and sustainable.

The Logic of Aerospace Engineering

Purpose

Aerospace engineering develops aerial and space-based systems for defense, scientific, commercial, civil, and recreational markets and missions. General mission needs within those markets include transportation, earth and space sensing, and communications. Typically, the products are vehicles such as rockets, airplanes, missiles, satellites, and spacecraft, although the products may also include the ground support equipment or imbedded hardware or software.

Key Questions

What are the detailed design features of the system that best satisfy the stated mission or market requirement? How will we design, build, test, and support aerospace vehicles?

Point of View

The conceptual mission profile typically provides the organizing framework for all design requirements and design decisions. The attempt is to define value principally from the perspective of the organizational leader who is sending the vehicle on some mission flight (and paying for the flight). Other perspectives may also be relevant: pilots, maintainers, manufacturing, and logisticians, as well as technologists (structural engineers, aerodynamicists, controls engineers, propulsion engineers, and relevant others). Politicians will likely be influential in large aerospace programs. Public opinion, concerned with ethical or environmental issues, are often relevant and, if so, must be considered.

Key Concepts

These include all those concepts associated with classical physics, with some particular emphases: Newtonian and orbital mechanics, conservation of mass, momentum and energy, low- and high-speed aerodynamics, material properties and lightweight structures, and propulsion technologies.

Key Assumptions

Assumptions are in part shared by all scientists and engineers. One assumption is that the universe is controlled by pervasive laws that can be expressed in mathematical terms and formulas. Additionally, aerospace engineers assume that an aerospace solution will invariably entail the integration of multiple technological disciplines and the resolution of competing design tensions, including aerodynamics, astrodynamics, stability and control, propulsion, structures, and avionics. Furthermore, the aerospace system will be a system of systems, which must also fit and interface with a larger system. (For instance, air cargo airplanes must fit and communicate with the air traffic control structures; missiles must fit with existing launch rails; satellites must fit on independently developed launch vehicles.)

Data or Information

Aerospace engineers employ experimental and computational data, legacy designs, regulatory requirements, market studies, or mission needs statements.

Inferences, Generalizations, or Hypotheses

The conclusion of most aerospace engineering activity is a product ready for delivery to a customer.

Implications

Aerospace engineering products and services have wide-ranging implications linked with global, national, and local economics; ethics; defense; security; environmental effects such as noise and pollution; and infrastructure such as airports, any of which may impact the quality of life in communities and regions.

The Logic of Electrical Engineering

Purpose

Electrical engineering develops electrical and electronic systems for public, commercial, and consumer markets. It is tremendously broad, spanning many domains, including recreational electronics, residential lighting, space communications, and electrical utilities.

Key Questions

What are the detailed design features of the system that best satisfy the stated mission or market requirements? How will we conceive, design, implement, and operate electrical and electronic products and systems?

Point of View

The point of view is commonly that of the design and manufacturing team. Other relevant points of view include the customer, stockholders, marketing, maintainers, and operators.

Key Concepts

These concepts include electromagnetism (Maxwell's equations), electrochemical properties of materials, discrete and analog mathematics, resistance, current, charge, voltage, fields and waves, and so on.

Key Assumptions

Assumptions are in part shared by all scientists and engineers. One assumption is that the universe is controlled by pervasive laws that can be expressed in mathematical terms and formulas and that those principles can be used to model electrical systems. Electrical engineers assume that some important market needs can be best met through electrical and electronic products. Additionally, electrical engineers frequently assume that their work must be integrated with other engineering disciplines (such as mechanical, chemical, and so forth) in the design and implementation of a product.

Data or Information

Electrical engineers employ experimental and computational data, legacy designs, regulatory requirements, market studies, or mission needs statements.

Inferences, Generalizations, or Hypotheses

The conclusion of most electrical engineering activity is a product ready for delivery to a customer.

Implications

Electrical engineering products and services have wide-ranging implications that span global, national, and local economics; public infrastructure; health care; and communications, with potential for positive and negative quality-of-life impacts on communities and regions.

MAKE THE DESIGN OF THE COURSE
WORK FOR YOU

At the beginning of any course you take, ask yourself: How am I going to learn so as to make the design of the class work for me? What am I going to do to get actively involved? How am I going to develop essential insights, understandings, knowledge, and abilities? How am I going to learn to reason my way to the answers to questions in the field?

Early in the course, seek an explanation of the most fundamental concept of the course. As you proceed through the course, you should seek to integrate all features of the course into a comprehensive understanding to see the course, and the subject, as a comprehensive whole.

Exhibit 11.2 The logic of science.

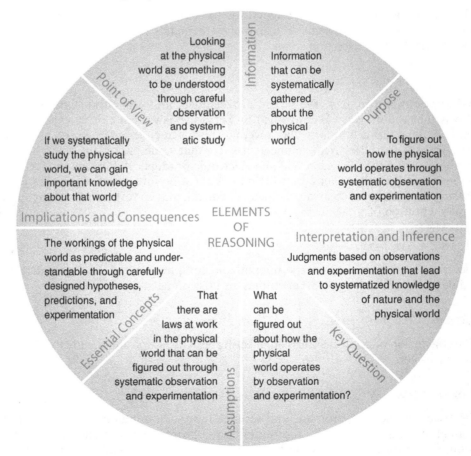

11.9 Think for Yourself

WRITING OUT THE LOGIC OF A COURSE

Using the examples of biochemistry, biology, ecology, aerospace engineering, and electrical engineering, as well as the more abbreviated logic of American history on pages 296–297, write out the logic of a course you are now taking or have taken in the past. Use textbooks, encyclopedias, and other resources as references. You might also refer to Exhibits 11.2–11.7, which give the basic logic of several subjects.

Exhibit 11.3 The logic of history.

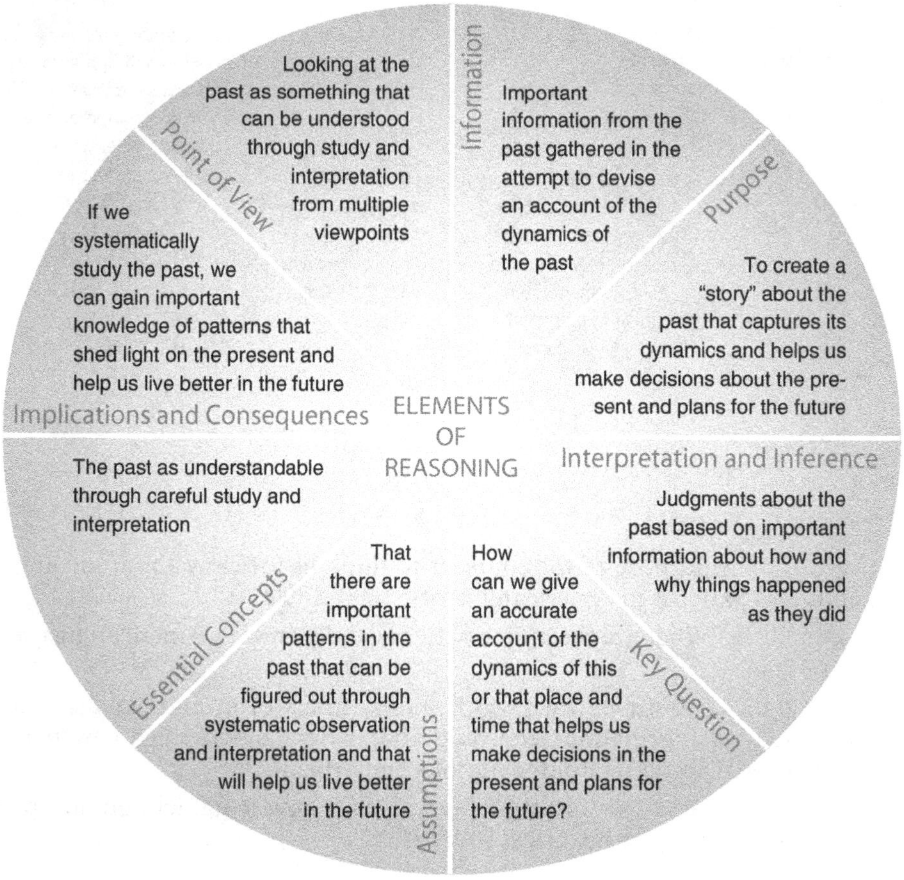

ELEMENTS OF REASONING

Point of View
Looking at the past as something that can be understood through study and interpretation from multiple viewpoints

Information
Important information from the past gathered in the attempt to devise an account of the dynamics of the past

Purpose
To create a "story" about the past that captures its dynamics and helps us make decisions about the present and plans for the future

Implications and Consequences
If we systematically study the past, we can gain important knowledge of patterns that shed light on the present and help us live better in the future

Interpretation and Inference
Judgments about the past based on important information about how and why things happened as they did

Essential Concepts
The past as understandable through careful study and interpretation

Assumptions
That there are important patterns in the past that can be figured out through systematic observation and interpretation and that will help us live better in the future

Key Question
How can we give an accurate account of the dynamics of this or that place and time that helps us make decisions in the present and plans for the future?

Exhibit 11.4 The logic of business.

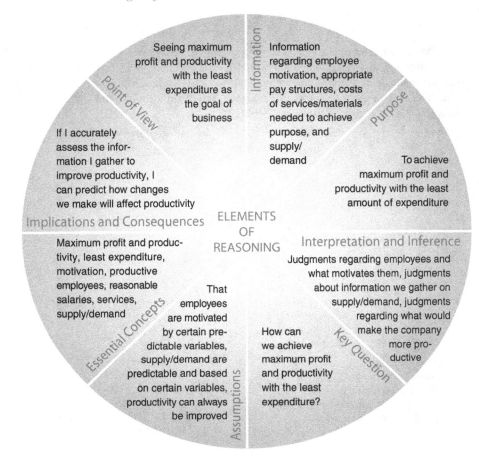

Sample Course: American History, 1600–1800

1. **Purpose.** The purpose of the course is to think historically about the major trends and patterns in American history, 1600–1800.

2. **Key question.** What are the major patterns and trends in American history, 1600–1800?

3. **Information.** The students will work with a variety of primary and secondary sources of information: records, diaries, letters, biographies, newspapers, and historical accounts from textbooks and articles.

4. **Skills of interpretation.** The students will learn how to gather and interpret data from a variety of historical sources.

5. **Essential concepts.** The students will need to learn how to use basic historical, economic, political, and religious concepts, as well as those from social life and values.

6. **Assumptions.** The fundamental assumption behind this course is that it is possible for entry-level students to gain insight into the patterns and events in American life, 1600–1800, that shed light on contemporary problems.

7. **Implications.** Students who reason well about events in 17th- and 18th-century American life should be able to see connections with events in the 20th century.

8. **Point of view.** Students will learn how to reason as both a conservative and a liberal historian, integrating economic, political, and social analyses.

Exhibit 11.5 The logic of abnormal psychology.

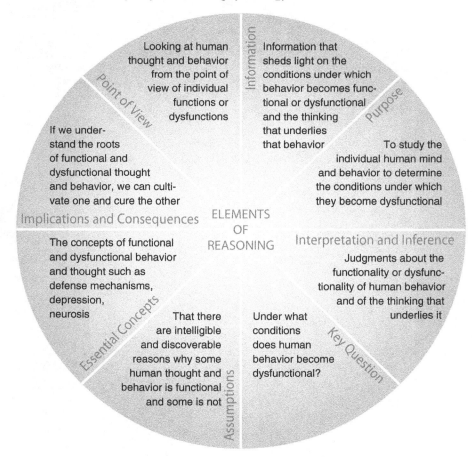

Exhibit 11.6 The logic of philosophy.

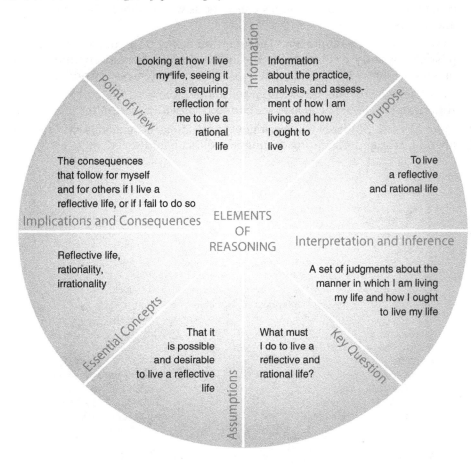

Exhibit 11.7 The logic of sociology.

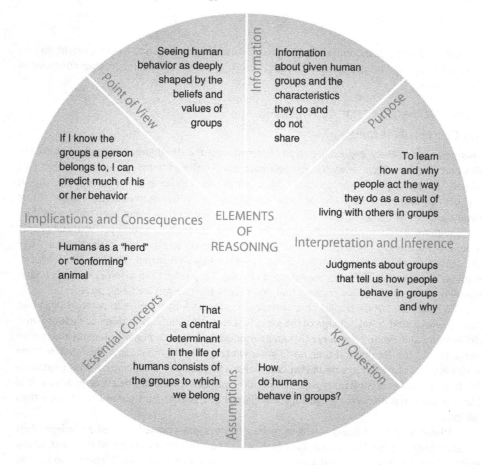

Point of View

Seeing human behavior as deeply shaped by the beliefs and values of groups

Information

Information about given human groups and the characteristics they do and do not share

Purpose

To learn how and why people act the way they do as a result of living with others in groups

Implications and Consequences

If I know the groups a person belongs to, I can predict much of his or her behavior

Humans as a "herd" or "conforming" animal

ELEMENTS OF REASONING

Interpretation and Inference

Judgments about groups that tell us how people behave in groups and why

Essential Concepts

That a central determinant in the life of humans consists of the groups to which we belong

Assumptions

Key Question

How do humans behave in groups?

11.10   Think for Yourself

EVALUATING THE LOGIC OF A COURSE

E xamine the course description below for a Critical Thinking course. To what extent do you think it is based on the concept of critical thinking in this book? Support your conclusions with reasons.

CLASS SYLLABUS: CRITICAL THINKING

Key Concept of the Course

This course is entirely and exclusively concerned with the development of potential capacities that all of you have, even though you have not developed them—capacities in that part of your mind known as your "intellect." Most people don't develop their intellect. They use it ineffectively and often mainly to rationalize or justify their infantile or egocentric drives. Most people are not in charge of their ideas and thinking. Most of their ideas have come into their mind without their having thought about them. They unconsciously pick up what the people around them think. They unconsciously pick up what is on television or in the movies. They unconsciously absorb ideas from the family in which they were reared. They are the products, through and through, of forces they did not choose. They reflect those forces without understanding them. They are like puppets that don't know their strings are being pulled.

To become a critical thinker is to reverse that process—by learning to practice skills that enable one to start to take charge of the ideas that run one's life. It is to think consciously and deliberately and skillfully in ways that transform oneself. It is to begin to remake one's own mind. It is to run for the first time one's inner workings and to understand the "system" one is running. It is to develop a mind that is analogous to the body of a person who is physically fit. It is like an excellent dancer who can perform any dance that can be choreographed. It is like a puppet that discovers the strings and figures out how to gain control of the way they are pulled.

Whenever you are doing a task in or for the class, ask yourself: Would an independent observer watching me closely conclude that I am engaged in taking charge of my mind, of my ideas, of my thinking, or would such a person conclude that I am merely going through the motions of formally doing an assignment, trying to get by with some formula or procedure memorized by rote?

General Plan

The class will focus on practice, not on lecture. It will emphasize using your own mind to figure things out, not memorizing what is in a textbook. On a typical class day, you will be in small groups practicing "disciplined" thinking. You will be regularly responsible for assessing your own work, using criteria and standards discussed in class. If at any time in the semester you feel unsure about your grade, you should request an assessment from the professor. For every class day, you will have a written assignment that involves disciplined thinking. Out of class, you will enter disciplined reflections in a journal, using a special format.

READING, WRITING, SPEAKING, LISTENING, AND THINKING

Let us turn now to reading, writing, speaking, and listening. Clearly, these activities are important to your success as a student. If you are a skilled *reader,* you are able to master a subject from a textbook alone, without benefit of lectures or class discussion. Many excellent readers have become educated through reading alone.

Or consider *writing.* The art of writing well forces us to make explicit the ideas we understand and how we understand those ideas in relation to each other. Often, we have the illusion that we understand an idea until we try to place our understanding into written words. Suddenly we see problems. We discover that we cannot state what we understand clearly, or we have trouble elaborating, or we find it difficult to give apt examples or illustrations. Writing to learn is a powerful tool in learning deeply and well. Those who cannot write out what they are learning are often poor learners.

Speaking is another powerful tool in learning. If we can explain to another person what we are learning, we typically take our learning to a deeper level. This is why we have the saying, "In teaching, you will learn." Entering into an oral dialogue with other learners is a powerful tool in learning—if the speaking in that dialogue is skilled. Of course, poorly discussed ideas may lead to "activated ignorance," the illusion that we understand when we do not. In this case, speaking solidifies misunderstanding rather than furthering understanding. For this reason, you want to make sure that you acquire oral skills so you can express yourself well, ask appropriate questions, and assess your learning.

Listening well is probably the least understood of the four modalities of communication we are considering. Much student listening is unskilled—passive, associational, unquestioned, superficial. Poor listening leads to incomplete internalization and even to blatant misunderstanding.

Reading, writing, speaking, and listening are all modes of *thinking.* Your primary goals as a student should be to learn how to think like a good reader (while reading), like a good writer (while writing), like an effective speaker (while speaking), and like an insightful listener (while listening). Happily, these four different modes of thinking are interrelated, so that learning to take charge of one is significantly related to learning to take charge of the other three. This is true precisely because each is a form of thinking, and all forms of thinking share generic characteristics—as we have emphasized throughout this book.

Irrespective of whether you are reading, writing, speaking, or listening, you want your thinking to be clear, precise, accurate, relevant, responsive to complexity, as broad as the issue requires, and focused on the appropriate point(s) of view. Good readers, writers, speakers, listeners, and thinkers recognize that they each have agendas, deal with questions and problems, use information, make inferences and draw conclusions, make assumptions, and reason within a point of view. And they consider the implications and consequences of their reasoning.

Consider writing as an example. All intellectual deficiencies in writing can be explained as deficiencies in the elements of thinking reflected. These deficiencies are, typically, in violations of the standards for thinking. Consider:

- When you write sentences that can be interpreted in many different ways and you do not make clear which meaning you intend, you demonstrate that you are writing, and presumably thinking, in a vague way.
- When you do not give concrete examples and illustrations to make your point clear, you demonstrate that you do not know how to clarify your thought or, for some reason, have chosen not to.
- When you do not make clear—with appropriate transitional words and critical vocabulary—the logical relations between the sentences you write, you make evident that you are not thinking in terms of the logic of your thought, that you do not fully understand the structure of your own reasoning.
- When you do not analyze key concepts and lay bare their logic, you make evident that you are weak at conceptual analysis.
- When you do not make clear the question or issue you are dealing with or you drift, for no apparent reason, from one issue to another, you reveal that you lack the intellectual discipline and focus to appreciate what each issue you raise requires of you. You demonstrate that you lack a sense of relevance.
- When you make sweeping judgments about a philosophical position that you have not sufficiently analyzed empathetically, you demonstrate intellectual arrogance.

Take reading as another example. All intellectual deficiencies in reading can be explained as deficiencies in the elements of thinking reflected, typically, in violations of the standards for thinking. Consider:

- When you are unable to identify the *agenda* of a text, there is a problem in your reading (or in the text).
- When you are unable to identify the *key questions* of a text, there is a problem in your reading (or in the text).
- When you are unable to identify the *key information* in a text, there is a problem in your reading (or in the text).
- When you are unable to identify the *key concepts* in a text, there is a problem in your reading (or in the text).
- When you are unable to identify the *key assumptions* in a text, there is a problem in your reading (or in the text).
- When you are unable to identify the *key implications* in a text, there is a problem in your reading (or in the text).
- When you are unable to identify the *key point of view* in a text, there is a problem in your reading (or in the text).

Speaking and listening can be analyzed in a similar way. Let us now apply these principles to the reading of an article or essay.

FIGURE OUT THE LOGIC
OF AN ARTICLE OR ESSAY

O ne important skill for understanding an essay or article is the analysis of the parts of the author's reasoning. Once you have done this, you can evaluate the author's reasoning by using intellectual standards.

11.11   Think for Yourself

ANALYZING THE LOGIC OF AN ARTICLE

T ake an article that you have been assigned to read for class, completing the logic of it using the template below. When you become practiced in using this approach, you will have a powerful intellectual tool for understanding the reasoning of any author.

THE LOGIC OF "*<NAME OF THE ARTICLE>*"

1. The main *purpose* of this article is _____. *(Here you are trying to state as accurately as possible the author's purpose for writing the article. What was the author trying to accomplish?)*

2. The key *question* that the author is addressing is _____. *(Your goal is to figure out the key question that was in the author's mind when he or she wrote the article. What was the key question the article addressed?)*

3. The most important *information* in this article is _____. *(You want to identify the key information the author used, or presupposed, in the article to support his or her main arguments. Here you are looking for facts, experiences, data the author is using to support his or her conclusions.)*

4. The main *inferences/conclusions* in this article are _____. *(You want to identify the most important conclusions the author comes to and presents in the article.)*

5. The key *concept(s)* we need to understand in this article is (are) _____. By this concept, the author means _____. *(To identify the concept, ask yourself: What are the most important ideas that you would have to understand to understand the author's line of reasoning? Then elaborate briefly on what the author means by these concepts.)*

6. The main *assumption(s)* underlying the author's thinking is (are) _____. *(Ask yourself: What is the author taking for granted that might be questioned? The assumptions are generalizations that the author does not think he or she has to defend in the context of writing the article, and they are usually unstated. This is where the author's thinking logically begins.)*

7. a. If we take this line of reasoning seriously, the *implications* are _____. *(What consequences are likely to follow if people take the author's line of reasoning seriously? Here you are to follow the logical implications of the author's position. You should include implications that the author states, if you believe them to be logical, but you should do your best thinking to determine what you think the implications are.)*

   b. If we fail to take this line of reasoning seriously, the *implications* are _____. *(What consequences are likely to follow if people ignore or reject the author's reasoning?)*

8. The main *point(s) of view* presented in this article is (are) _____. *(The main question you are trying to answer here is: What is the author looking at, and how is he or she seeing it? For example, in this book, we are looking at education and seeing it as involving the development of intellectual skills. We also are looking at learning as the responsibility of students.)*

FIGURE OUT THE LOGIC OF A TEXTBOOK

Just as you can understand an essay or article by analyzing the parts of the author's reasoning, so can you figure out the logic of a textbook by focusing on the parts of the author's reasoning within it. To understand the parts of the textbook author's reasoning, use the template in Think for Yourself 11.12, below.

11.12 Think for Yourself

FIGURING OUT THE LOGIC OF A TEXTBOOK

Using the template below, figure out the logic of a textbook from a current class you are taking or any textbook you choose. Be as detailed as is necessary for someone new to the field of study you are focused on to understand the logic of the textbook.

1. The main *purpose* of this textbook is _____. *(Here you are trying to determine the author's purpose for writing the textbook. What was the author trying to accomplish?)*

2. The key *question(s)* that the author is addressing in the textbook is (are) _____. *(You are trying to figure out the key question(s) in the author's mind when he or she wrote the textbook. What is the key question the textbook answers? Here, you might identify the broadest question the textbook answers, along with the most important sub-questions it focuses on.)*

3. The most important kinds of *information* in this textbook are _____. *(You want to identify the types of information the author uses in the textbook to support his or her main arguments [e.g., research results, observations, examples, experience].)*

4. The main *inferences/conclusions* in this textbook are _____. *(You want to identify the most important conclusions the author comes to and presents in the textbook. Focus on this question: What are the most important conclusions the author presents, conclusions that, if you understand them, shed important light on key beliefs in the field?)*

5. The key *concept(s)* in this textbook is (are) _____. By these concepts, the author means _____. *(To identify these concepts, ask yourself: What are the most important ideas that you would have to understand to understand the textbook? Then precisely elaborate on what the author means by these basic concepts. Begin with the most fundamental concept presented, such as science, biology, or psychology. These usually can be found in the first chapter. Then identify the other significant concepts that are deeply tied into the most fundamental concept.)*

6. The main *assumption(s)* underlying the author's thinking is (are) _____. (*Ask yourself: What is the author taking for granted that might be questioned? Assumptions are sometimes generalizations that the author does not think he or she has to defend in the context of writing the textbook. The assumptions are sometimes stated in the first chapter as the key assumptions underlying the subject area.*)

7. a. If people take the textbook seriously, the *implications* are _____. (*What consequences are likely to follow if readers take the textbook seriously? Here you are to follow the logical implications of the information and ideas in the textbook. You should include implications that the author argues for, if you believe them to be well founded, but you should do your best thinking to determine what you think the implications are.*)

   b. If people fail to take the textbook seriously, the *implications* are _____. (*What consequences are likely to follow if the author's thinking is ignored in a situation when it is relevant?*)

8. The main *point(s) of view* presented in this textbook is (are) _____. (*The main question you are trying to answer here is: What is the author looking at, and how is he or she seeing it? For example, the author might be looking at science and seeing it as "our main tool in helping us to better understand the physical world and how it operates."*)

CRITERIA FOR EVALUATING AN AUTHOR'S REASONING

Now that you have worked through the logic of an article, a textbook, or both, you are ready to assess the author's reasoning by focusing on how well the author uses each of the elements of reasoning within the article or book. Choose the logic of either the article or the textbook. For the one you choose, go through each of the elements, or parts, of the author's reasoning and evaluate them using the intellectual standards outlined here:

1. Focusing on the author's *purpose:* Is the purpose well stated? Is it clear and justifiable?

2. Focusing on the key *question* that the written piece answers: Is the question at issue well stated (or clearly implied)? Is it clear and unbiased? Does the expression of the question do justice to the complexity of the matter at issue? Are the question and purpose directly relevant to each other?

3. Focusing on the most important *information* the author presents: Does the writer cite relevant evidence, experiences, and information essential to the issue? Is the information accurate and directly relevant to the question at issue? Does the writer address the complexities of the issue?

4. Focusing on the most fundamental *concepts* at the heart of the author's reasoning: Does the writer clarify key concepts when necessary? Are the concepts used justifiably?

5. Focusing on the author's *assumptions:* Does the writer show a sensitivity to what he or she is taking for granted or assuming (insofar as those assumptions might reasonably be questioned)? Or does the writer use questionable assumptions without addressing problems that might be inherent in those assumptions?

6. Focusing on the most important *inferences* or conclusions in the written piece: Do the inferences and conclusions the author makes follow clearly from the information relevant to the issue, or does the author jump to unjustifiable conclusions? Does the author consider alternative conclusions where the issue is complex? Does the author use a sound line of reasoning to come to logical conclusions, or can you identify flaws in the reasoning somewhere?

7. Focusing on the author's *point of view:* Does the author show a sensitivity to alternative relevant points of view or lines of reasoning? Does he or she consider and respond to objections framed from other relevant points of view?

8. Focusing on *implications:* Does the writer show a sensitivity to the implications and consequences of the position he or she is taking?

A TEST TO REPEAT IN EVERY CLASS AND SUBJECT

We have shown how every academic field has its own logic or system of meanings. To learn the field is to learn to think within the system. This is true whether one is talking of poems or essays, paintings or choreographed dances, histories or anthropological reports, experiments or scientific theories, philosophies or psychologies, specific events or general theories. Whether we are designing a new screwdriver or working out a perspective on religion, we must create a system of meanings that makes sense to us. To learn the system underlying a discipline is to create it in our mind. This requires that our thinking be permanently re-shaped and modified. As you study a subject, periodically ask yourself:

Can I explain the underlying system of ideas that defines this subject? (This is like writing the encyclopedia entry for it.)

Can I explain its most basic ideas to someone who doesn't understand it (answering their questions about it)?

Could I write a glossary of its most basic vocabulary (minimizing technical terms in my explanations of meaning)?

Have I written out the basic logic of the subject? (Its key goal is ... etc.)

Can I compare and contrast the logic of the subject I am learning with that of other subjects I have learned?

To what extent can I relate this subject to significant problems in the world?

To what extent has thinking in this field helped me become more intellectually humble, persevering, autonomous ...?

HOW TO DETECT MEDIA BIAS AND PROPAGANDA IN NATIONAL AND WORLD NEWS

The logic behind bias and propaganda in the news media is simple, and it is the same the world over. Each society and culture has a unique worldview, which colors what they see and how they see it. News media in the cultures of the world reflect the worldview of the culture they write for, but the truth of what is happening in the world is much more complicated than what appears to be true in any culture. To be a critical reader of the news media in any society, one must come to terms with this truth and read accordingly. Critical thinking is a complex set of skills that reverses what is natural and instinctive in human thought.

As we pointed out previously, the uncritical mind is unconsciously driven to identify truth in accordance with the following tacit maxims:

"It's true if I believe it."

"It's true if we believe it."

"It's true if we want to believe it."

"It's true if it serves our vested interest to believe it."

The critical mind consciously seeks the truth in accordance with the following instinct-correcting maxims:

"I believe it, but it may not be true."

"We believe it, but we may be wrong."

"We want to believe it, but we may be prejudiced by our desire."

"It serves our vested interest to believe it, but our vested interest has nothing to do with the truth."

Mainstream news coverage in a society operates with the following maxims:

This is how it appears to us from our point of view; therefore, this is the way it is.

These are the facts that support our way of looking at this; therefore, these are the most important facts.

These countries are friendly to us; therefore, these countries deserve praise.

These countries are unfriendly to us; therefore, these countries deserve criticism.

These are the stories most interesting or sensational to our readers; therefore, these are the most important stories in the news.

Critical readers of the news reverse each of these maxims. This chapter explains how to do this and thereby reduce the influence of bias and propaganda on the mind.

DEMOCRACY AND THE NEWS MEDIA

Nothing could be more irrational than to give the people power and to withhold from them information, without which power is abused. A people who mean to be their own governors must arm themselves with the power which knowledge gives. A popular government without popular information or the means of acquiring it is but a prologue to a farce or a tragedy, or perhaps both.

—James Madison

Democracy can be an effective form of government only to the extent that the public (that rules it in theory) is well-informed about national and international events and can think independently and critically about those events. If the vast majority of citizens do not recognize bias in their nation's news; if they cannot detect ideology, slant, and spin; if they cannot recognize propaganda when exposed to it, they cannot reasonably determine what media messages have to be supplemented, counterbalanced, or thrown out entirely.

On the one hand, worldwide news sources are increasingly sophisticated in media logic (the art of "persuading" and manipulating large masses of people). This enables them to create an aura of objectivity and "truthfulness" in the news stories they construct. On the other hand, only a small minority of citizens are skilled in recognizing bias and propaganda in the news disseminated in their country. Only a relatively few are able to detect one-sided portrayals of events or seek out alternative sources of information and opinion to compare to those of the mainstream news media. At present, the overwhelming majority of people in the world, untrained in critical thinking, are at the mercy of the news media in their own country. Their view of the world, which countries they identify as friends and which as enemies, is determined largely by those media (and the traditional beliefs and conventions of their society).

This slanted information is not a "plot" or a "conspiracy." It is simply a matter of educational background and economic reality. Journalists and news editors are themselves members of a culture (German, French, Mexican, Chinese, Korean, Japanese, Indonesian, Russian, Algerian, Nigerian, North American, etc.). They share a view of the world with their target audience. They share a nationalized sense of history and allegiance, often a religion, and a general belief system. An Arab editor sees the world differently than an Israeli editor. A Pakistani editor sees the world differently than an Indian editor. A Chinese editor sees the world differently than an American editor. The same is true of news reporters and other journalists.

What's more, news people work under severe time restrictions (in constructing their stories) and limitations of space (in laying out or presenting their stories). It is hardly surprising that profound differences are reflected in news coverage from nation to nation and from culture to culture.

In any case, only those who understand the conditions under which world media operate have a chance of controlling the influence of their national media upon them. Our goal in this chapter is to help our readers lay a foundation for transforming the influence of the media on their lives. It is in all of our interests to critically assess, rather than mindlessly accept, news media pronouncements. We hope we can aid readers to become more independent, insightful, and critical in responding to the content of news media messages and stories.

12.1   Think for Yourself

CONTRASTING WORLDVIEWS

Are you familiar with any worldview that contrasts with the worldview of your culture? If so, discuss with another student the similarities and differences between the beliefs of your culture and those of a different culture. If not, see whether you can locate a characterization of one worldview that contrasts with the worldview of your home culture.

For example, if you see the world from the perspective of a North American "Christian" culture, accumulate some information about the perspective of a Middle Eastern "Muslim" culture. Find a news source on the Internet that provides coverage of world events from that alternative cultural perspective. Discuss the differences you find in the same events being covered in these contrasting ways. See whether you can notice your prejudice in favor of your home culture.

MYTHS THAT OBSCURE THE LOGIC
OF THE NEWS MEDIA

The media foster a set of myths regarding how they function. Believing these myths impedes the ability to view the news from a critical perspective. The myths include the following:

- that most news stories are produced through independent investigative journalism
- that news writers simply report facts in their stories and do not come to conclusions about them
- that fact and opinion are clearly separated in constructing the news
- that there is an objective reality (the actual "news") that is simply "reported" or described by the news media of the world (our news media writers reporting on this objectively; the media of foreign enemies systematically slanting and distorting it)
- that what is unusual (novel, odd, bizarre) is news; what is usual is not.

12.2   Think for Yourself

FINDING THE ROOT CAUSES OF MYTHS ABOUT THE MEDIA

Discuss with another student what you think are the root causes of one or more of the above myths. Ask why people would believe these myths.

"OBJECTIVITY" IN THE NEWS MEDIA

The logic of constructing news stories is parallel to the logic of writing history. In both cases, for events covered there is *both* a massive background of facts *and* a highly restricted amount of space to devote to those facts. The result in both cases is the same: 99.99999% of the "facts" are never mentioned at all (seeExhibit 12.1).

Most people, having given up on getting a set of unadorned facts, align themselves with whichever spin outlet seems comfortable.

Wall Street Journal
(May 7, 2004)

If objectivity or fairness in the construction of news stories is thought of as equivalent to presenting all the facts and only the facts ("All the news that's fit to print"), objectivity or fairness is an illusion. No human knows more than a small percentage of the facts, and it is not possible to present all the facts (even if one did know them). It isn't even possible to present all the *important* facts, for many criteria compete for determining what is "important." We therefore must always ask: What has been left out of this article? What would I think if different facts had been highlighted here? What if this article had been written by those who hold a point of view opposite to the one embedded in the story as told?

Exhibit 12.1 What happens in the world on any given day.

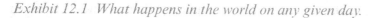
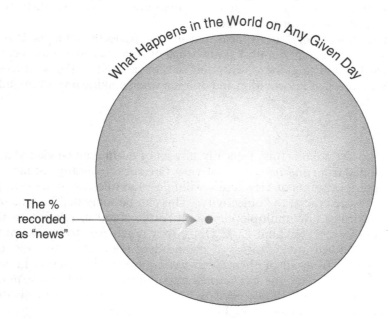

The %
recorded
as "news"

For example, people commonly consider facts to be important to the extent that the facts have significant implications for them personally: Is any given event going to affect what I want? How much is it going to cost me? How is it going to influence my income, my living conditions, my leisure, my convenience? How some given event is going to affect others, especially others far away and out of sight, is quite another matter. There is therefore a wide divergence among the news media of the world as to what is presented as "significant" in the world.

The media focus on what their readers personally care about. Thus, even if their readers are irrational in some belief (e.g., they harbor some irrational hate), the media nevertheless will treat that hatred as rational. Hence, when slavery was commonly accepted in the United States, the media presented slavery as "natural." When the country became divided on the issue, the media followed suit (each paper presenting as right what its readers believed to be right).

Consider how news media treat what is "shocking" or "exciting" or "disgusting" or "delightful" to a social group. For example, a woman sunbathing on a beach with bare breasts is commonplace on the French Riviera (and therefore is not condemned and her behavior is not treated as "news"), but the same woman would be arrested and punished for sunbathing in a similar way at a beach in Lebanon (and therefore would be condemned and her behavior treated as "news"). Or again, during the Olympic Games, each country's news media focus their attention on those events in which their nation's athletes are expected to do well. And when one of their athletes wins a gold medal in an event, this event is presented to the home audience as if it were much more important than the events in which they won no medals. National audiences often are "thrilled" by their "victories" and uninterested in victories of others.

Human "objectivity" is an ideal that no one perfectly achieves. It requires a great deal of intellectual humility (knowledge of our extensive ignorance) and begins by freely admitting one's own point of view as well as the need to consider competing sources of information and opinion when making important judgments.

Points of View

Newspapers tend to signal the importance of an article or image by the prominence of its placement.

New York Times International (May 11, 2004)

The key point is this: Typically, any set of events can be viewed and interpreted from *multiple* points of view. Openness to a range of insights from multiple points of view and a willingness to question one's own point of view are crucial to "objectivity." This can be suggested in a diagram that illustrates how multiple viewpoints often stand in relation to the same set of events (Exhibit 12.2). Objectivity is achieved to the extent that one has studied a wide range of perspectives relevant to an issue, obtained insights from all of them, seen weaknesses and partiality in each, and integrated what one has learned into a more comprehensive, many-sided whole. Each perspective should serve to "correct" exaggerations or distortions in the others and to add facts not highlighted in the others.

We gain in "objectivity" (in conceptualizing both history and the news) to the extent that we can put stories and narratives into a rich historical context and comment on them from multiple points of view. For example, to understand the

Exhibit 12.2 Six points of view focused on the same set of events.

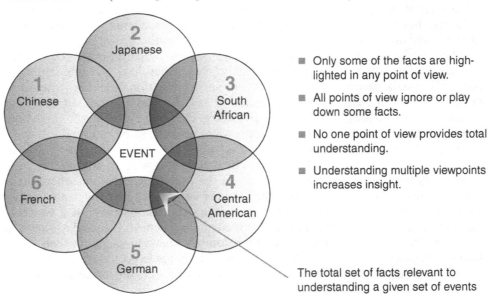

- Only some of the facts are highlighted in any point of view.
- All points of view ignore or play down some facts.
- No one point of view provides total understanding.
- Understanding multiple viewpoints increases insight.

The total set of facts relevant to understanding a given set of events war between Great Britain and its colonies in North America (1776–1783), one must look at the events from at least three points of view: that of the British government, that of the Colonial leaders, and that of the indigenous peoples.

To achieve objectivity, we need to:

1. identify the point of view from which a given news story or historical account is constructed,

2. identify the audience it is written for,

3. recognize what points of view it is negating or ignoring,

4. distinguish the raw facts behind the story from the interpretation and spin being put on those facts.

When we do this, we are not as easily manipulated. We are able to exercise greater independence of judgment. We get a greater sense of what elements of the story or account are most credible and which are the least credible. Of course, it is hard to do any of these if we have not also discovered multiple sources for information and a way to determine when those sources are most credible.

12.3 *Think for Yourself*

IDENTIFYING THE INTERESTS OF READERS

Analyze the front section of a newspaper to identify the viewpoint of the paper's primary audience. See whether you can figure out what the readers of that paper—the people willing to buy—think is important. How would you characterize the readers' primary point of view? How do they see the world? What do they want to read about? What would they rather not read about?

Forms of Objectivity

"Objectivity" may appear in three ways. Two are genuine. One is a façade, a counterfeit of objectivity. These forms of objectivity are discussed next.

The Objectivity of Intellectual Humility

The first form of objectivity is based on the possibility of developing intellectual humility, knowledge of our ignorance. Thus, a critical consumer of the news knows the difference between hearing a story and verifying the truth of that story. A critical consumer of the news knows that what is presented as fact in the news may not be fact. It may be propaganda, misinformation, distortion, or half-truth. Knowing this, critical consumers of the news "bracket" what they hear, read, and see in the news. Recognizing that they don't themselves know the facts, they "suspend" belief. They take in information in a tentative fashion. ("This may or may not be true.") For example, "objective" jurors will not come to a conclusion of guilt or innocence after hearing only one side of a case.

Unfortunately, intellectual humility is a rare quality in human life. The majority of people in the world have been exposed to a limited range of views and have been most influenced by the viewpoint that is dominant in their own culture. As a result, they take themselves to be in possession of the *Truth*. This confidence is actually proof of their lack of objectivity. They do not know what intellectual humility is, and they do not take steps to achieve it.

The Objectivity of Fairminded, Multidimensional Thinking

A second form of objectivity goes beyond the first. Fairminded, multidimensional thinking is based on intellectual humility and on having done substantial intellectual work in reasoning within multiple conflicting points of view in addressing questions, problems, and issues of significance. It is connected to positive insight into the complexity and many-sidedness of most important world issues and large-scale conflicts. Those who have achieved this state can insightfully role-play multiple perspectives on a multitude of issues. They can identify and weigh relative strengths and weaknesses within those perspectives. They are comfortable playing the role of dissenter, although they don't dissent for the sake of dissent. They reject party lines, sociocentric mindsets, and intellectual conformity. They are intellectually independent, intellectually perseverant, and have intellectual integrity.

Sophistic Objectivity

The third form of objectivity is "sophistic." This intellectual state results from studying a range of views with the overriding motivation to defend a predetermined choice. This mindset is common in intellectuals who make their income (and achieve their prestige) as apologists for powerful interests. The temptation to become an apologist for a well-established point of view or economic interest is enormous because money, position, and prestige are involved. Lawyers and politicians, as well as public relations experts, are typically ready to play such a role.

Most national news commentators routinely play such a role. They present positions consistent with a picture of the world shared by most of their readers or viewers. Their audience views them as objective only to the extent that what they present reflects mainstream views.

> How many photos of naked Iraqis does one want to see?
>
> Col Allan, editor in chief, *New York Post* (May 10, 2004)

> What is on the front page is more difficult to avoid than what is inside.
>
> *New York Times International* (May 11, 2004)

12.4   Think for Yourself

INTERNALIZE THE FORMS OF OBJECTIVITY

Explain to another student (in your own words) the three forms of objectivity described. Have your partner try to explain them to you. For each one, state your understanding, elaborate, and give an example from your own experience.

THE PERCEPTION OF BIAS
IN THE MAINSTREAM

Quite naturally, but uncritically, people think of those who agree with them as objective and those who disagree with them as biased. Thus, if news commentators present mainstream views with a liberal spin, they are viewed as "objective" only by the liberals in the audience. If mainstream views are given a conservative spin, they are viewed as "objective" only by the conservatives in their audience. The media therefore present liberal or conservative slants on the news in accordance with their audience's views.

Propaganda and News Story Writing

Webster's New World Dictionary defines *propaganda* as "any systematic, widespread dissemination or promotion of particular ideas, doctrines, practices, etc., to further one's own cause or to damage an opposing one." Given this definition, there is no clear-cut dividing line between news story writing with a given cultural audience in mind, on the one hand, and constructing propaganda on the other hand. Both systematically play down or seek to minimize the worth of opposing perspectives or points of view. The logical similarity is striking. Even historical writing can take on the character of propaganda when it is written to "glorify" or "demonize" certain groups of people by suppressing or ignoring information that does not support its preconceptions and favored ideology.

> . . . [B]ecause of the nudity and humiliation on display in the Iraq photographs, many newspapers have chosen to put articles about them on the front page, but the images inside.
>
> *New York Times International*
> (May 11, 2004)

Because the word *propaganda* carries with it a negative connotation (suggesting deception or distortion), few news writers would admit that the word applies to their stories. Yet, if one receives most of one's news from a single cultural or national source, the likely impact on the mind will be that of distortion and deception. Most people, as a result, are trapped in one worldview (because they have received a steady diet of stories and accounts articulated from that perspective and have not seriously considered any alternatives).

This does not mean, of course, that a given worldview is unvaried. Not everyone who shares a viewpoint agrees on every issue. Not every German agrees with every other German. Still, a significant difference exists between those who see the world from a German perspective and those who see it from, say, a Japanese or a Mexican perspective. What's more, although essentially every point of view carries some insight, it doesn't follow that each has *equal* insight.

It is usually much easier for people to recognize the truth of these tendencies when they are thinking about the news coverage in other nations or cultures—especially when those other nations and cultures differ greatly from their own. For example, Israelis easily recognize bias and propaganda in Arab coverage although they see little in their own coverage, and vice versa.

When President George W. Bush of the United States gave a speech identifying Iran, Iraq, and North Korea as an "axis of evil," his speech was received favorably by the majority of Americans. It was taken as a follow-up of the President's promise to "rid the world of evil." A wave of patriotic fervor was sweeping the nation. The national news media had engendered a communal sense of rage. For the overwhelming majority of Americans, the American government stands for high ideals (liberty, justice, democracy, free enterprise, human rights). The President defending the country against its enemies with the might of its armed forces is an image that inspires patriotic emotions.

The speech, however, was not received in the same way abroad. Bush was roundly condemned by the news media in Iran, Iraq, and North Korea and was viewed as arrogant and out of touch with the complexities of reality by "allies" of the United States. Here are some of the ways the French and German media conceptualized the speech to their national audiences (*New York Times,* January 31, 2002, p. A12):

- "In France, the afternoon daily *Le Monde* ran a front-page cartoon of Mr. Bush in battle fatigues and a headline saying, 'Mr. Bush points out his latest enemies'."
- "A television editorialist on LCI, France's 24-hour news station, said the speech belonged to 'a sheriff convinced of his right to regulate the planet and impose punishment as he sees fit'."
- "In Germany, an editorial in the daily *Suddeutsche Zeitung* offered Chancellor Gerhard Schroder sympathy as he heads for Washington tonight. 'Poor Gerhard Schroder,' the editorial says. 'It can't be easy being the first grumpy European to appear at the throne of the freshly anointed American Caesar'."

Here is a sense of the news media coverage in Iran and North Korea, taken from the same source:

- "Bush intends to divert public opinion from the Middle East issue and to prepare the domestic grounds for continuing his support of Israel in its brutal oppression of the Palestinian nation." (Iran state radio report)
- "North Korea's official media scoffed at Mr. Bush for identifying the nation as among the world's most dangerous. It said his 'loudmouthed threat' was intended to justify an American military presence in South Korea."

In virtually every case, it is easier to persuade people that foreign press coverage is biased than to persuade those same people of their own national press bias. Every nation's press coverage of the "news" appears to the mass public of that culture as expressing self-evident truth—because the news is routinely presented within the worldview of the mass public that consumes that news.

When trapped in a culture-bound view of the world, one thinks within a web of self-serving assumptions, thinking that it is others (our national or cultural enemies and opponents) who use propaganda and manipulation while we, being honest and just, always give the other side its due. Others use propaganda and manipulation.

We freely express the truth. This mindset is not the product of a conspiracy or intrigue. It is the natural and predictable outcome of national news media attempting to make a profit by presenting events in the world to a home audience.

12.5   Think for Yourself

INTERNALIZE THE CONCEPT OF PROPAGANDA

Explain to another student (in your own words) the concept of propaganda described above. Have your partner try to explain it to you. State your understanding, elaborate, and give an example. Do you have a different concept of propaganda? Explain.

Protecting the Home Audience from Guilt Feelings

The events for which news coverage is most taboo in mainstream media news are deeds that indict the home culture or society of ethical wrongdoing. Consider, for example, the extent of civilian suffering following the dropping of atom bombs on the cities of Hiroshima and Nagasaki by the United States military. Although some debate has taken place in the United States media on these acts, to our knowledge the U.S. mainstream media have presented little documentation of the enormous suffering caused by those events.

One might compare, for example, documentation of the suffering of civilians in German extermination camps (which has been, and continues to be, extensive) with that of the Japanese populations of Hiroshima and Nagasaki when subjected to massive atomic radiation. Searching the 50 years since the event, we found only one article in one American newspaper, the Santa Rosa *Press Democrat* (in Northern California) documenting in detail the suffering of the civilian population. The article was a guest editorial by David R. Ford, who worked in 1965 for a CBS television affiliate in Honolulu and now lives in the Santa Rosa, California, area. Here are excerpts (without the horrific details) from his editorial:

> We are certainly not going to let images with nudity or gore or violence go on the air.
>
> John Banner,
> executive producer of
> ABC's *World News Tonight*

> In 1965 ... I spent a vacation in Hiroshima, Japan. My purpose: To interview the sick and dying 20 years after the atomic bomb was exploded over that city on Aug. 6, 1944 ... I began the visit in the women's ward.

What follows in the article are detailed images of suffering that American readers would find extremely painful to imagine their government as inflicting (200,000 civilians died in Hiroshima alone on that day). The American reporter said to a Japanese victim,

> "But we dropped millions of pamphlets warning citizens to evacuate the cities." He looked into my eyes. "No paper was ever dropped. No warning was ever given."

12.6   *Think for Yourself*

IDENTIFYING UNETHICAL GOVERNMENT ACTIONS

Identify a news story, either from the mainstream news or from an alternative news source, that focuses on one or more ethical wrongdoings sanctioned by your government or culture, actions that people within the country would like to avoid knowing or thinking about. Write a summary of the story and identify the reason(s) people would like to avoid thinking about the issue. How is the "wrongdoing" treated? Is it highlighted, or is it hidden?

FOSTERING SOCIOCENTRIC THINKING

The key insight is this: The major media and press in *all countries of the world* present events to the world in terms that presuppose or imply the "correctness" of the ideology (or ideologies) dominant in the country. Our hope is not in changing the news media. News reporters and editors operate within a system of economic imperatives and constraints that dominate their work. Their audience is captive to an acculturated conception of the world.

Rather, as aspiring critical consumers of the mass media, we must learn to recognize that mainstream news is inevitably based on a sociocentric view of the world. We must learn how to recognize national and cultural bias. There is no reason to suppose that the ideology dominant in our culture is more accurate or insightful than that of any other culture. Presuming that one's own culture is exceptionally truthful in presenting its picture of the world is evidence not of insight but instead of ethnocentrism. Sociocentrism is a fundamental characteristic of all countries and cultures. The news media function as unwitting agents of social conventions and taboos.

Many examples of sociocentric thinking can be found in the mass media. The media are an inherent part of the culture within which they function. And, again, those in the media must "sell" their stories. Their papers, news broadcasts, and magazines must be economically successful to remain in business.

> Pressure to increase the profits of media companies has not been an isolated phenomenon. Throughout the American economy, there is unprecedented pressure to maximize profits, putting shareholder value ahead of all other considerations. The corporations that own the news media are subject to all the business trends and economic demands that have reshaped American business in the 1980s and 1990s, affecting nearly every part of society. (Downie and Kaiser, p. 25)

Because much of the thinking within any given culture is sociocentric in nature to begin with, the news media have little choice but to package what they produce within a sociocentric framework. The vehicles of large-scale social communication within a society inevitably serve that society and advance its self-image. Biased coverage is the rule, not the exception.

The mainstream news media around the world are thus biased toward their country's "allies" and prejudiced against their "enemies." They therefore present events occurring in the countries of their allies in as favorable a light as possible,

Exhibit 12.3 A mutually reinforcing relationship fostering sociocentric thinking.

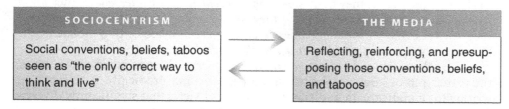

highlighting their "positive" deeds while downplaying their negative ones. When generating news stories about their "enemies," the opposite treatment inevitably follows. Generating positive stories about the admirable characteristics of one's enemies is unacceptable. At the same time, negative stories about enemies are always popular, routinely generated and highlighted. The ability of a news consumer to identify these biased stories in action and mentally "rewrite" them with an opposing bias is a crucial critical thinking skill. With this skill, one sees slanted constructs everywhere in the news. And when one sees through the bias, its persuasive effect on the mind disappears.

12.7   Think for Yourself

IDENTIFYING SOCIOCENTRIC THINKING IN THE NEWS

Locate one news story exemplifying the fact that reporters, as a rule, uncritically accept the social conventions and taboos of their culture.

For example, on the front page of the typical American newspaper, it is common to see, from time to time, a picture of the President of the United States shaking hands with another leader, or arriving somewhere on an airplane, or walking on the front lawn of the White House with his dog, smiling and appearing happy—in other words, looking "presidential." Somehow, this makes people within the culture feel confident in their president. It is a form of "authority worship." The convention that this picture exemplifies is the cultural norm of idolizing persons in positions of power.

See if you can find a story wherein the reporter feeds into social conventions or taboos— for example, a story of a woman being taken to jail for appearing topless in public or a story of someone going to prison for growing and selling marijuana. These types of stories would be candidates because they represent cultural conventions.

SLANTING STORIES TO FAVOR PRIVILEGED VIEWS

Every journalist knows intuitively which terms to use when characterizing the favored and unfavored players on the world stage (as pictured within a cultural perspective). We *plan* ... they *plot*. We are *clever* ... they are *sneaky*. We form *strategies* ... they *conspire*. We have *convictions* ... they are *fanatics*. We are *proud* ... they are *arrogant*. We *stand tall* ... they *brag* and *bluster*. We build weapons to *defend* ourselves ... they build weapons to *threaten* us. We *intervene* ... they *invade* ... We have *religious convictions* ... they are *fanatics*. We are *freedom-fighters* ... they are *terrorists*. We violate treaties when they are *obsolete* ... they violate treaties because they are *irresponsible, untrustworthy, unethical*.

Journalists routinely select words that reinforce the prevailing views among the readership or audience for whom they are writing. Ironically, if newspersons writing for a mainstream audience were to adopt views that significantly diverged from those dominant in their society and presented the news in accordance with those views, they would be considered "biased" and "irresponsible." If you think in accordance with mainstream views, you are a "responsible" thinker; if not, you are "irresponsible."

The exception occurs, of course, if significant numbers of people in the culture hold conflicting views, as in the conflict between liberal and conservative perspectives (expressed differently in most cultures). In this case, both points of view are presented in both favorable and unfavorable terms (depending upon whether the source is dominated by conservatives or liberals). Nevertheless, if one's views do not fall into either the mainstream liberal or conservative purview, one is dismissed as a "radical." Radicals are irresponsible by definition (because they do not agree with one of the two traditional views).

The following newspaper excerpts exemplify how the news media across the world do not report the news objectively but instead cater to the views of their readers.

*"The War Americans Don't See"**

Source: *Press Democrat*, April 4, 2003, editorial by Rami G. Khouri, executive editor of the *Daily Star*, a Beirut newspaper

> The Arab press—like Arab public opinion as a whole—predominantly opposes the British and American attack on Iraq, and does not hesitate to say so in its front page headlines, articles and photographs. Yet the press is neither monolithic nor uniformly anti-American.... Samples ... from front pages this week in the Arabic language (and in Algeria's case, French-language) press demonstrate the United States and the Arab world do see a different war unfolding. But the front pages of leading newspapers in and around the Arab world include both American and Iraqi perspectives and feature dramatic photographs that show United States forces as both aggressors and humanitarians.
>
> One recent front page photo showed an Iraqi civilian pouring tea for an American soldier. More common, though, are images of dead and maimed Iraqi children, parents wailing over the coffins of relatives killed by American bombings, extensive damage of Iraqi civilian buildings and Iraqi civilians being humiliated by American and British troops. Sometimes, an image that would get an innocuous description in an American newspaper is given a more sinister interpretation in the Arab press.

*Reprinted with permission by the author.

Coverage tends to mirror ideology. The quality regional press like *Asharq al Awsat* and *Al Hayat,* edited in London and printed throughout the Middle East, are the most balanced. More ideological papers with narrow readerships reflect the sentiments of their financial backers and tend to cater to the nationalistic, political and emotional views of their audiences. The tone of opinion columns and editorials is heavily anti-American. Only occasionally do Arab writers like Ghassan Tueni in Beirut's *AN Nahar* call for the end of Saddam Hussein and his regime (and that is coupled with a rejection of American occupation).

Commentary.   This editorial supports the thesis that the press in every country presents events in the world as confirming what their audience (and the backers of their newspaper) already believe. This thesis is borne out at a national level and a regional level as well. Hence, the *Press Democrat* (published in a liberal area of California) carries this editorial, which argues that the Arab press is not entirely biased against the United States. Its title emphasizes the need for Americans to broaden their sources of information ("The War Americans Don't See"). In contrast, the *New York Times*, in reporting on the Arab press, strongly suggests that it is biased against the United States and Israel, whereas the U.S. press, we are tacitly led to believe, is objective, balanced, and fair. See the next excerpt.

"Arab Media Portray War as Killing Field"

Source: *New York Times*, April 4, 2003

This article refers to a picture of a boy glaring from the debris of a bombed building while a woman wearing a veil screamed while standing over the prone body of a relative. The picture was blended from two separate pictures into one image on the website of *Al Watan*, a popular Saudi newspaper. The meaning intended for readers—that the war in Iraq should be seen as a never ending vicious onslaught by America and its allies on innocent Arabs. According to the article, the Israeli flag was superimposed on the American flag. Ghastly stories of powerless people stream into TVs and newspapers and into the lives of Arabs all over the world. The message to Arab people is that American troops are heartless murderers, and that their only hope for self-respect is to resist this onslaught. The article suggests that Arab newspapers are increasingly running headlines that frankly accuse soldiers of deliberately murdering innocent people.

Commentary.   This article implies that there is no truth in the Arab media's coverage of civilian casualties in the Iraq war. The *New York Times* readership is basically conservative, overwhelmingly supporting both the Israeli government and the U.S.-led invasion of Iraq. The readership is therefore primed to reject any coverage of the war that negatively portrays U.S. forces, the U.S. government, or the Israeli government. Because the article heavily criticizes the Arab media's coverage of the Iraq war, the story is not "buried"; rather, it is given a prime place in the paper (front page).

12.8   Think for Yourself

IDENTIFYING BIAS AGAINST OTHER COUNTRIES

Identify a news story that favors your country's viewpoint and therefore is biased against the viewpoint of another country. Use the format above to write a summary of the story (with quotes). Then comment on how the story is slanted to support your country's viewpoint.

How to Obtain Useful Information from Propaganda and Standard News Stories

Obtaining useful information, even from propaganda and one-sided news stories, is possible, but only if one learns to read, hear, or view the stories critically. This means that we must analyze the stories with a clear awareness of the point of view they embody, recognizing the attempt to influence our thinking and beliefs. We must analyze them as we analyze one side of a multi-sided argument. One-sided presentations are not the truth pure and simple, although they contain at least part of the truth, the part that supports the side in question. What's more, in standard news stories, something of the opposing point of view is often mentioned (though, usually, in fine print, deemphasized in the last few paragraphs of the story, or couched in terms or quote marks, suggesting that the reader should dismiss it).

Critical readers recognize one-sidedness and seek out viewpoints that are dismissed or ignored. They also note which stories are highlighted (e.g., on the front page) and which are buried in the background (e.g., on page 24). Some key questions we should ask when analyzing and interpreting news stories are:

- Who is the intended audience?
- What point of view is being privileged?
- What point(s) of view is (are) being dismissed or played down?
- How can I gain access to the point of view being negated (from those who most intelligently understand it)?
- Which stories are featured on the front page? Why?
- What information is "buried" in the article? Why?

12.9, 12.10   Think for Yourself

INTERNALIZING IDEAS

Based on your understanding of the logic of the media, discuss with another student why some stories are highlighted (put on the front page) and others are played down (placed in a small article in an obscure section of the paper).

ANALYZING NEWS STORY PLACEMENT

Read through the front section of a newspaper. Your local paper might do, but try to use a fairly large newspaper containing national and international news. Find examples of relatively unimportant but highlighted (on the front page, for instance) articles and examples of important but buried stories.

Steps in Becoming a Critical Consumer of the "News"

1. Understand the basic agenda of "news story construction." Always keep in mind that the ultimate purpose of mainstream "news story fabrication" is to sell "stories" for a profit to specific audiences (each with certain beliefs, values, and prejudices). It is not to educate. It is not to be fair to all sides (all sides are rarely represented in the target audience). To sell news stories to an audience, one must construct those stories carefully in such a way as to engage intended readers and reinforce or validate their beliefs, values, prejudices, and worldview. Journalists typically come from those who share the beliefs, values, prejudices, and worldview of the intended audience. The "slanting" of the story then is achieved "naturally."

Constructing news stories for an audience requires that one determine:

a. what the audience would consider a "story" (what they would, and would not, be interested in),

b. what about a story would be considered most relevant and what about it would be considered least relevant to the audience (therefore, what to play up and what to downplay),

c. how to construct "leads" or "headlines" for a story (to create an initial definition for the reader),

d. how much space or time to give a particular story,

e. how to relate the story to other stories and to the audience's picture of themselves and their world, and

f. how to tell the story so it sounds "professional" (objective and unbiased to the readers, a mere accounting of bare facts).

2. Use one's knowledge of the logic of news story construction, first, to deconstruct stories in the news and then to reconstruct them imaginatively with alternative biases and slants. One becomes a critical consumer of the news media, first, by understanding the agenda of the news media, the criteria the news media use in constructing the news (deciding what a "story" is, what stories to cover, how to cover them to get the highest ratings or sell the most newspapers or magazines). Skilled consumers of the news learn how to identify and assess national, social, and political emphases and agendas. They learn how to read between the lines and how to imaginatively recast *stories-as-told* into alternative *stories-as-they-might-have-been-told* from other points of view.

3. **Learn how to redefine issues, access alternative sources (both within and outside the mainstream), put events into a historical perspective, and notice and assess assumptions and implications.** Systematic questioning and assessment are crucial to the critical processing of media messages.

4. **Learn how to identify low-credibility stories by noticing vested interests or passion associated with content.** Stories are least credible when the interests of the producer or receiver of a story are involved or when the passions of a mass audience are involved (mass fear, anger, hatred, patriotism, etc.). When a nation is at war, for example, stories about the war told by the nation's press (including all explanations of it) are suspect because all nations produce mass propaganda during war to build support for it. Another such case would be stories about persons involved in taboo sexual acts (approved in other societies) because the reader's disgust would command telling the story in such a way as to justify that disgust as a reasonable response ("Nudists Arrested," "Sexual Predator Condemned"). Stories that arouse mass passions typically are highly one-sided in nature and thus should have low credibility to those who think critically.

12.11   *Think for Yourself*

IDENTIFYING AND ANALYZING BIASED NEWS STORIES

Locate a news story (in a newspaper) that appears biased or is told from a slanted view. Identify:

1. The bias(es) inherent in the story.
2. The viewpoints that are ignored or distorted.

Then state how the story would have to be constructed if it were to fairly represent all relevant viewpoints.

Media Awareness of Media Bias

To what extent are the news media aware of bias and propaganda in their own constructions? This question does not have a definitive answer. All journalists are aware that they are writing for an audience. It does not follow, however, that they have thought through the implications of this. Certainly, some journalists are much more aware than others.

In the United States, Israel is a favored "ally," so mistreatment or abuse of the Palestinians by the Israelis is usually covered under the idea of "justified reprisal." Because Fidel Castro of Cuba is viewed within the United States as an enemy, mainstream news writers routinely present Castro and Cuba in a negative light, ignoring or explaining away any achievements of the Cuban government (such as universal medical coverage and a low infant mortality rate). If and when persons in the news media recognize patterns of news coverage such as these, they must be careful in writing about them—lest they themselves be labeled "irresponsible" and "biased."

Sensitivity to Advertisers

Every group within a culture is not equally important to the news media. National media are biased in favor of national culture, religion, dominant beliefs, and social values. But within any complex culture, some groups play a more powerful role than others within media logic. For example, much news media profit comes from advertisers. These advertisers are not pleased if they, or the interests they represent, are cast in a bad light by the media they finance. News media, therefore, avoid generating stories that negatively feature major advertisers.

Put another way, because news media outlets can select from among a large mass of potential stories and cannot, in any case, carry more than a small percentage of what is available, they naturally, all other things being equal, choose to avoid or play down stories that are irritating to their advertisers. There are, of course, exceptions to this pattern. A lot depends on the "splash" the story would make or whether it is already "out."

Sensitivity to Government

National news media are sensitive to the power of government. For one, national governments typically license and regulate news media by law. For another, much national news is given to news media through high governmental officials and agencies. For these reasons, news media personnel hesitate to criticize the national government in certain fundamental ways.

For example, if the national government names some other group or nation as an enemy, the national news media generally present the "enemy" as unfavorably as they can. If the government attacks another nation militarily, the national news media line up like cheerleaders at a sporting event. The news media are typically apologists for the policies and acts of the national government.

An exception occurs when elements in the national news media are linked to a political party not presently in power. Their protection then comes from the power and interests represented by the opposition party. Then they are beholden to the views and beliefs of their political supporters. In the United States, certain news outlets are sometimes more influenced by the Democrat or Republican parties, but both parties unite around the same basic worldview and beliefs of the broader society. Both identify the same countries as friends or enemies; both are responsive to major economic forces and concentrations of wealth and power.

The basic logic is the same. The media are presenting the news within a point of view. The point of view represents interests affecting media profitability and is deeply entrenched in social ideology. The news media focus on profit, although that focus is obscured and kept in the background.

The national television networks have trimmed their reporting staffs and closed foreign reporting bureaus to cut their owners' costs. They have tried to attract viewers by diluting their expensive newscasts with lifestyle, celebrity, and entertainment features, and by filling their low-budget, high-profit, prime-time "newsmagazines" with sensational sex, crime, and court stories. (Downie and Kaiser, 2002, p. 10)

12.12   Think for Yourself

IDENTIFYING NEWS STORIES THAT PANDER TO THE GOVERNMENT

Identify a news story in which one or both of the following are true:

1. An action of your government is shown in a positive light when it should be shown in an objective, or even negative, light given the circumstances.
2. Negative actions of your government are downplayed when they should be highlighted (due to their implications).

Sensitivity to Powerful Interests

News media sources try to maximize their profit while minimizing costs. Investigative journalism is more expensive than prepackaged stories (news from press releases, news conferences, and speeches). Realizing that their position of power within the culture is threatened if they fail to maintain a favorable public image, powerful economic interests continually invest in marketing their image to the public. There is therefore a symbiotic relationship between powerful media sources (which need news stories) and powerful economic interests (which generate and disseminate news stories in their interest). This is true in virtually all nations.

Powerful industries such as manufacturing, communications, agriculture, weapons producers, airlines, the criminal justice industry (prisons, police, lawyers, social workers, prison contractors), construction, banking, auto, insurance, public relations and advertising, broadcasting, and entertainment—all are involved in shaping the daily news in their interest. Governmental agencies and persons in positions of power in the executive, legislative, judicial, military, and intelligence communities are all involved in shaping the daily news in their interest. Religious groups, professional groups, unions, and other groups organize around vested interests and invest heavily in shaping the daily news in their interest.

From the Great Depression in the 1930s through World War II and the beginning of the Cold War in the 1950s, reporters seemed to reflect establishment views more often than they exposed the failings and foibles of the powerful. They seldom challenged government news management or the press agentry of private business and the entertainment industry. (Downie and Kaiser, p. 19)

Because most people's fundamental source of information about the world comes through the mass media, favorable news media coverage is a significant variable in achieving a favorable public image.

12.13   Think for Yourself

IDENTIFYING STORIES THAT FAVOR BUSINESS INTERESTS

Identify a news story in which business interests are favored over the interests of the people (or the environment) and, yet, the media fail to highlight this fact in the story.

Sensitivity to Competitors

News media provide the news in light of the news that other media outlets focus on. When some of the major outlets treat a story as "big," the others typically pick it up so as not to be viewed as deficient in coverage. Major media move as one "herd," following the leaders slavishly. National and international coverage differ very little from one newspaper to another within any given country.

12.14   Think for Yourself

ANALYZING NEWSPAPERS FOR SIMILARITIES AND DIFFERENCES

For any given day, purchase three mainstream newspapers. Then analyze them to see how they differ and how they are similar (focusing on the front section). Consider these questions:

1. To what extent do the three papers cover the same national news?

2. To what extent do they cover the same international news?

3. To what extent do they cover the same stories in the same or a similar way (in terms of placement and slant of the stories)?

4. After completing your analysis, what do you conclude about how mainstream newspapers cover the news in your country?

The Bias toward Novelty and Sensationalism

The "news" typically is constructed with a systematic bias in favor of reporting what is novel, bizarre, sensational, or odd. What happens every day—no matter how intrinsically important—is often sacrificed. But great social problems typically are embedded in day-to-day events that are repeated thousands of times. The individual events underlying these problems are often not dramatic or "odd" (but pathetically common).

On the one hand, if a large bank systematically overcharges millions of customers a small amount of money, it succeeds in stealing millions of dollars. But such a practice probably will not be considered news. If, on the other hand, a solitary bank robber makes off with $10,000, that will make the news. If millions of children are bullied in schools every day and suffer lifelong damage from that experience, that probably will not be considered news. But if a child has sex with another child at school, that will be considered news. If millions of children go to bed hungry every night all over the globe, that is not news. But if one school serves caviar during the school lunch, that is news. If women and children are sold every day in an international slave trade, that is not news. But if a solitary teacher has a sexual relationship with a student, that is news.

12.15   *Think for Yourself*

IDENTIFYING SENSATIONALISM IN THE NEWS

Identify a news story in which some behavior is sensationalized. You are looking for a story that is blown out of proportion in terms of importance (while other important stories are ignored).

Critical Consumers of the News

Manipulating critical consumers of the news is difficult because:

- They study alternative perspectives and worldviews, learning how to interpret events from multiple viewpoints.
- They seek understanding and insight through multiple sources of thought and information, not simply through those of the mass media.
- They learn how to identify the viewpoints embedded in news stories.
- They mentally rewrite (reconstruct) news stories through awareness of how stories would be told from multiple perspectives.
- They analyze news constructs in the same way they analyze other representations of reality (as some blend of fact and interpretation).
- They assess news stories for their clarity, accuracy, relevance, depth, breadth, and significance.
- They notice contradictions and inconsistencies in the news (often in the same story).
- They notice the agenda and interests served by a story.
- They notice the facts covered and the facts ignored.
- They notice what is represented as fact (that is in dispute).
- They notice questionable assumptions implicit in stories.
- They notice what is implied (but not openly stated).

- They notice what implications are ignored and what implications are emphasized.

- They notice which points of view are systematically put into a favorable light and which in an unfavorable light.

- They mentally correct stories reflecting bias toward the unusual, the dramatic, and the sensational by putting them into perspective or discounting them.

- They question the social conventions and taboos being used to define issues and problems.

> The media world we inhabit is without exception a world of "spin."
>
> *Wall Street Journal*
> (May 7, 2004)

12.16   Think for Yourself

REWRITE A NEWS STORY

Using a daily newspaper, choose a story you think you can rewrite from another viewpoint. Rewrite the story. Explain the changes you have made and why you have made them.

Questions for the News Media

Is It Possible for the News Media to Reform?

To provide their publics with nonbiased writing, journalists around the world would have to, first, enter empathically into worldviews to which they are not currently sympathetic. They would have to imagine writing for audiences that hold views antithetical to the ones they hold. They would have to develop insights into their own sociocentrism. They would have to do the things that we have suggested are done by critical consumers of the news.

The most significant problem is that, were they to do so, their articles would be perceived by their public as "biased" and "slanted," as propaganda. These reporters would be seen as irresponsible, as allowing their personal point of view to bias their journalistic writings. Imagine Israeli journalists writing articles that present the Palestinian point of view sympathetically. Imagine Pakistani journalists writing articles that present the Indian point of view sympathetically.

The most basic point is this: Journalists do not determine the nature and demands of their job. They do not determine what their readers want or think or hate or fear. The nature and demands of their job are determined by the broader nature of the society itself and the beliefs, values, and worldviews of its members. It is human nature to see the world, in the first instance, in egocentric and sociocentric terms. Most people are not interested in having their minds broadened. They want their current beliefs and values extolled and confirmed. Like football fans, they want the home team to win and, when it wins, to triumph gloriously. If it loses, they want to be told that the game wasn't important, or that the other side cheated, or that the officials were biased against them.

As long as the overwhelming mass of people in the broader society are drawn to news articles that reinforce and do not question their fundamental views or passions, the economic imperatives will remain the same. The logic is parallel to that of reforming a nation's eating habits. As long as the mass of people want high-fat, processed foods, the market will sell high-fat and processed foods to them. And as long as the mass of people want simplistic news articles that reinforce egocentric and sociocentric thinking, articles that present the world in sweeping terms of good and evil (with the reader's views and passions treated as good and those of the reader's conceived enemies as evil), the news media will generate such articles for them. The profit and ratings of news sources with their fingers on the pulse of their readers and viewers will continue to soar.

12.17 Think for Yourself

CAN THE MEDIA REFORM?

Explain in your own words the reasoning used in concluding that the news media will never reform. Discuss the implications of this reasoning. Do you agree?

Is the Emergence of a "Critical Society" Possible?

In a concluding chapter of his classic book, *Folkways*, published in 1906, William Graham Sumner raised the possibility of the development of "critical" societies, by which he meant societies that adopt critical thinking as an essential part of their way of life. Sumner recognized that critical thinking "is our only guarantee against delusion, deception, superstition, and misapprehension of ourselves and our earthly circumstances." He recognized education as "good just so far as it produces a well-developed critical faculty." He says:

> The critical habit of thought, if usual in a society, will pervade all its mores, because it is a way of taking up the problems of life. People educated in it cannot be stampeded.... [They] are slow to believe. They can hold things as possible or probable in all degrees, without certainty and without pain. They can wait for evidence and weigh evidence, uninfluenced by the emphasis or confidence with which assertions are made on one side or the other. They can resist appeals to their dearest prejudices and all kinds of cajolery. Education in the critical faculty is the only education of which it can be truly said that it makes good citizens.

No country or culture in the world routinely fosters education as Sumner conceived it. As things now stand, such education is the rare exception in any society. The detection of bias and propaganda in the news media is possible only for those who are willing to be diligent in pursuing news from multiple sources representing multiple alternative cultural and national standpoints. It is possible only for those who—in their reading and thinking and judging—are willing to swim against the tide.

12.18 Think for Yourself

IMAGING A CRITICAL SOCIETY AND ITS IMPLICATIONS

What are some of the ways your life would probably have been different had you been raised in a critical society? What are some of the realities we face, given that people in the world are largely irrational?

FINDING ALTERNATIVE SOURCES OF INFORMATION

To find sources of information supporting the dominant views within a culture is not difficult. The problem for most of us is finding well-thought-through views that question the mainstream news. Thus, in the former Soviet Union, for example, it was hard to gain access to views that critiqued the Soviet line. It is always a minority of thinkers motivated to look beyond the dominant views who dig beneath the surface and bring forward what is unpleasant or painful to the majority. Critiques of a society within a society are typically hard to come by.

The main point is that every society in the world today has mainstream and dissenting views. And it is important to recognize that we are not saying that dissenting views are correct and mainstream views are incorrect. Insights can be gained from all major conflicting worldviews. What is most important is to locate both mainstream and dissenting views (expressed in their most articulate and insightful forms). The ideal, for any given important issue, is access to a full range of views, as expressed by their most skilled and insightful defenders.

In doing this, one faces two problems:

1. to locate a full range of views and
2. to locate well-informed spokespersons for each major position in the spectrum.

Let us look at the United States. American mainstream views can be found in any of a large number of major American newspapers (the *New York Times*, the *Washington Post*, the *Baltimore Sun*, the *Boston Globe*, the *Chicago Tribune*, the *Cleveland Plain Dealer*, the *Los Angeles Times*, the *Minneapolis Star Tribune*, the *Philadelphia Inquirer*, the *Sacramento Bee*, the *San Francisco Chronicle*, and so on). Similar lists of mainstream newspapers could be produced for other countries in the world. Of course, there would be some overlap in viewpoints between mainstream newspapers from various nations and cultures, depending on the extent to which they share religious views, economic interests, and political traditions.

Locating dissenting views within nations and cultures is more difficult, depending on the extent to which dissenters are forced to go "underground." The best general source for the views of important dissenters is through the scholarly magazines and presses of the world. In some cases, a person can locate publications dealing with issues in greater depth than the mainstream news.

In the United States, for example, *The Nation* is one such publication. Founded in 1865, it has, from its beginnings, provided an outlet for intellectually dissenting points of view. Its contributors include Nelson Algren; Hannah Arendt; W. H. Auden; James Baldwin; Willa Cather; Emily Dickinson; John Dos Passos; W. E. B. DuBois; Albert Einstein; Lawrence Ferlinghetti; Robert Frost; Carlos Fuentes; Emma Goldman; Langston Hughes; Henry James; Martin Luther King, Jr.; D. H. Lawrence; Robert Lowell; Thomas Mann; H. L. Mencken; Arthur Miller; Pablo Neruda; Octavio Paz; Sylvia Plath; Ezra Pound; Bertrand Russell; Jean Paul Sartre; Upton Sinclair; Wallace Stevens; I. F. Stone; Gore Vidal; Kurt Vonnegut; Alice Walker; and William Butler Yeats. Clearly, this is a valuable source for non-mainstream points of view. In addition to providing a weekly magazine on controversial political and cultural issues, *The Nation* also has established a digital archive covering 6,500 issues. (See www .archive.thenation.com.)

All sources of news and commentary should be read critically, carefully analyzed and assessed, and used as vehicles for intellectual independence, as sources for *part* of the truth, not as vehicles of *The Truth*. The ideal is freedom from any one point of view or perspective.

BECOMING AN INDEPENDENT THINKER

To detect bias and propaganda in the news media requires a commitment to thinking for oneself. The process of becoming an independent thinker is furthered significantly by reading the writings of famous dissenters, thinkers who in their day questioned the mainstream view. Each of the persons below critiqued the mainstream views of his or her day. Each thought outside the cultural box.

Thomas Paine, *Common Sense,* 1776

William Lloyd Garrison, *The Journal of the Times* and *The Liberator,* 1831

Wendell Phillips, *Speeches, Lectures, and Letters,* 1863

Margaret Fuller, *Memoirs* (2 vols.), 1852

Henry David Thoreau, *Essay on Civil Disobedience,* 1849

Emma Goldman, *My Disillusionment with Russia,* 1923

Henry George, *Social Problems,* 1883

Thorstein Veblen, *The Vested Interests and the Common Man,* 1919

John Peter Altgeld, *Our Penal Machinery and Its Victims,* 1884

Lincoln Steffens, *The Struggle for Self-Government,* 1906

William Graham Sumner, *Folkways,* 1906

Gustavus Myers, *History of the Great American Fortunes* (2 vols.), 1907

Jose Ortega y Gasset, *The Revolt of the Masses,* 1932

William J. Lederer, *A Nation of Sheep,* 1961

H. L. Mencken, *Prejudices* (6 vols.), 1977

Eric Hoffer, *The True Believer,* 1951

Matthew Josephson, *The Robber Barons,* 1962

Bertrand Russell, *Unpopular Essays,* 1952

C. Wright Mills, *The Power Elite,* 1959

Howard Zinn, *A People's History of the United States,* 1995

Ralph Nader, *The Ralph Nader Reader,* 2000

Edward S. Herman, Noam Chomsky, *Manufacturing Consent,* 2002

12.19, 12.20   *Think for Yourself*

FAMILIARITY WITH DISSENTING VIEWS

How many, if any, of these dissenting authors are you familiar with? Have you read a book by any of them? If not, why? Do you begin to see the extent to which you have been socially conditioned to think within a mainstream point of view?

READ VIEWS OF DISSENTING THINKERS

Get a book or article by any of the authors in the preceding list and read some part of the book or article. You will have to read enough to get an idea of this author's views. Then write a short summary of her or his views. Why do you think we have placed this author's name on our list of independent thinkers?

Buried, Ignored, or Underreported Stories

Of the millions of events that take place in the world on any given day, only a tiny percentage of them (a couple of hundred) are made into "news" stories (for a given culture). The stories selected typically confirm the dominant cultural viewpoint of the society. Stories that disconfirm the dominant cultural viewpoint are ignored, underreported, or buried (given little coverage and attention). Stories that are buried in the reporting of one culture, however, may be front-page news in the reporting of another.

This phenomenon is intensified when there is conflict between cultures. In this case, when the same event is covered, it is conceptualized very differently. For example, in wartime, each side tells the story of the conflict to its home audience in self-serving terms. Hence, although both sides commit atrocities, the media on each side highlight only the atrocities of the enemy while suppressing, denying, or minimizing their own atrocities. Each side conceptualizes itself as representing the forces of good (decency, justice, and so on) and its enemies as representing the forces of evil. The predictability of this self-serving function of mass media is highlighted in research into the mutual "image of the enemy":

> Enemy-images mirror each other—that is, each side attributes the same virtues to itself and the same vices to the enemy. "We" are trustworthy, peace-loving, honorable, and humanitarian; "they" are treacherous, warlike, and cruel. In surveys of Americans conducted in 1942, the first five adjectives chosen to characterize both Germans and Japanese (enemies) included *warlike,* and *cruel,* none of which appeared among the first five describing the Russians (allies); in 1966, all three had disappeared from American characterizations of the Germans and Japanese (allies), but now the Russians (no longer allies, although more rivals than enemies) were warlike and treacherous....
>
> The enemy-image acts like a distorting lens, which overemphasizes information that confirms it and filters out information that is incompatible with it. Thus the mass media play up incidents of an enemy's treachery or cruelty and ignore examples of humanitarian or honorable behavior. (Jerome Frank, *Chemtech,* August 1982, p. 467)*

In the pages that follow, we provide examples of stories that were buried, ignored, or underreported in the U.S. mass media. The buried stories were given low priority and minimal coverage in the major media. The ignored stories were found in dissenting alternative, non-mass media publications. In each case of an ignored story, pay special attention to how the story would disconfirm the dominant U.S. image of itself and/or of its role in the world were it to be highlighted in the mass media. If buried or ignored stories actually were emphasized in the mass media, they would damage the public image of the United States as committed to freedom, justice, human rights, preservation of the earth's resources, international law, and democracy.

Keep in mind that the media in all countries project a favorable self-image of their own culture by selecting what is and is not covered, what is given a positive spin and what is given a negative spin. Our examples focus on what has been underreported or suppressed in the mass media in the United States because we expect that the majority of our readers will be U.S. citizens. Our analysis could be paralleled in a similar study of the mass media's treatment of news *within any given country or culture.* Of course, the extent to which news is distorted within any country varies among countries and can be determined only through in-depth analysis, story by story.

1. Do respected countries in the world consider the U.S. a danger to world peace?
"Arrogance May Come Back to Haunt U.S.," editorial by Nicholas Kristof (Source: *New York Times*, Feb. 3, 2003.)

> The European edition of *Time* magazine has been conducting a poll on its website: "Which country poses the greatest danger to world peace in 2003?" With 318,000

---

*Reprinted in part from Frank, Jerome, *Chemtech,* August 1982, p 467. Published 1982 American Chemical Society.

votes cast so far, the responses are: North Korea, 7 percent; Iraq, 8 percent; the United States, 84 percent.

Comment: We did not find this fact reported in the U.S. mass media except as a passing comment in an editorial. The notion that the United States might be the country that poses the greatest danger to world peace is, of course, deeply incompatible with the U.S. self-image.

2. Is the United States responsible for the deaths of more than half a million civilians in Iraq?   **"The Betrayal of Basra,"** by Chuck Sudetic (Source: *Mother Jones*, Nov/Dec. 2001. *Mother Jones* is a dissenting, non–mass media source for news and commentary.)

> For ten years the United States has been the staunchest advocate of maintaining a tight blockade on Iraq's access to foreign goods and its oil revenues. These restrictions have failed to loosen Saddam's grip on power. They have failed to force him to give up what is left of Iraq's chemical, biological, and nuclear weapons programs. What the sanctions have done, however, is kill....
>
> According to an estimate by Amatzia Baram, an Iraq analyst at the University of Haifa in Israel, between 1991 and 1997 half a million Iraqis died of malnutrition, preventable disease, lack of medicine, and other factors attributable to the sanctions; most were elderly people or children. The United Nations Children's Fund puts the death toll during the same period at more than 1 million of Iraq's 23 million people.

According to this article, the Iraqi people

> have come to see Saddam's worst enemy, the United States, as their enemy as well.... Washington abandoned [its] revolt against Saddam in 1991. Now [the] bitterness is tangible. And it will be ripe for exploitation by anti-American demagogues and terrorists for years after Saddam is gone.

The article quotes an Iraqi now living in the U.S.: "These people are not going to forget what has happened to them. In their eyes it is genocide. And people do not forget genocide."

3. Does the United States have a responsibility to live in accordance with the international treaties it signs?   **"Bush Seeks Exemption for Pesticide"** (Source: *Press Democrat*, Feb. 9, 2003; mass media news source.)

According to this news source, in 1987, along with 182 other countries, the U.S. signed the Montreal Protocol, a treaty calling for the elimination of chemicals that harm the ozone layer. But according to the article, U.S. farmers say there are no good alternatives to the use of methyl bromide, "a clear, odorless gas that is injected into the soil every 18 months to kill worms, insects, rodents, and diseases.... The chemical was to be banned by 2005 in developed nations."

The article states that the Bush administration therefore directed the EPA to seek an exemption for 16 uses of the chemical. The article quotes David Doniger, policy director of the climate center of the Natural Resources Defense Council: "We knew there were going to be some hard cases that needed extra time. But we never anticipated that the agribusiness industry would abuse the process and the Bush administration would kowtow to the growers and chemical companies this bad. It is thumbing its nose at the international treaty."

According to this article, "bromide from methyl bromide is roughly 60 times more destructive to ozone on an atom-per-atom basis than the chlorine from CFCs" (chemicals once widely used in aerosols).

Comment: This article was buried toward the back of a local news section.

4. Does the U.S. army operate a school that trains military officers in torture and murder techniques?   **"New Army Plan for Torturers' School"** (Source: *CounterPunch*, Feb. 1–15, 2000; *CounterPunch* is a dissenting, non–mass media source of news and commentary.)

According to *CounterPunch,* the School of the Americas, located in Fort Benning, Georgia, and run by the U.S. Army, is an institution "that has turned out 60,000 graduates, including many of the most vicious killers and torturers in the Latin American military. . . . Year after year the U.S. Army has seethed at the growing campaign aimed at the School of the Americas. . . . The annual protest rallies and civil disobedience outside Fort Benning have swelled in numbers, with 15,000 demonstrating last fall and 900 committing civil disobedience."

The article goes on to say that because of these demonstrations, the Army recognizes the need to change its image. Thus the Secretary of the Army has drafted legislation that would replace the School of the Americas with the United States Military Institute for Hemispheric Security Cooperation. According to the article, "same place, new name." The article contends that the function of the new school will mirror that of the old one, "which is, as it has always been, the preparation of fresh cadres of military officers able and willing to carry out the proper custodial functions required of them by the American Empire."

5. Is it humane for mentally ill inmates in U.S. prisons to be subjected to long-term solitary confinement?   **"The SuperMax Solution,"** editorial by Regan Good (Source: *The Nation*, March 3, 2003; *The Nation* is a dissenting, non–mass media source for news and commentary.)

According to this editorial, mentally ill inmates are increasingly confined to long-term solitary cells—known as supermax confinement. "Confined to their cells, alone, twenty-three hours a day, inmates eat, sleep, defecate, urinate, read and write (if they are able), watch TV or listen to the radio (if they are allowed) in the same 8-by-12 cell, often for years on end. The monotony, sensory deprivation, and mandated idleness . . . is especially torturous for inmates who have a serious mental illness." The article states that inmates must "earn" their way out of such confinement by correcting their behavior. But as Jean Maclean Snyder, an attorney representing mentally ill prisoners at Tamms prison, points out, many mental ill inmates can't "behave" in solitary confinement, by definition. "There is nothing to be good at, there is no behavior allowed." This article points out that, at any given moment, "there are about 25,000 people in long-term solitary confinement in the United States."

Comment: On a related point, in 1998, the *New York Times* (Oct. 5) reported that Amnesty International was citing the United States for violating fundamental human rights within its own country, criticizing the U.S. criminal justice system for widespread cruelty and degrading practices. According to the *Times*, Pierre Sane, Secretary General of AI, said, "We felt it was ironic that the most powerful country in the world uses international human rights laws to criticize others but does not apply the same standards at home."

6. To what extent has America been involved in crimes against humanity?   **"War Criminals, Real and Imagined,"** by Gregory Elich (Source: *CovertAction Quarterly*, Winter 2001; *CovertAction Quarterly* is a dissenting news source. The following sections are summaries of information contained in this article, which cites 33 supporting references.)

Indonesia: In 1965, a CIA-backed military coup toppled President Sukarno of Indonesia and brought to power General Suharto. Following the coup, between 500,000 and 1 million civilians were killed by the Suharto government. These civilians were trade unionists, peasants, ethnic Chinese, and members of the Indonesian Communist Party. During this time, the U.S. gave Suharto a list of thousands of communists within Indonesia it wanted killed and supplied him with covert military weapons. Once Suharto became acting president, the U.S. began to send economic aid to the country, and U.S. and Western European advisors helped chart economic policy. U.S. aid rose to $200 million by 1969, after Indonesia passed an investment law favorable to foreign companies. "In the years to come, New Order Indonesia would continue to imprison, torture, and execute several hundred thousand people."

Iran: In 1983, the CIA gave the Khomeini government a lengthy list of communists in the Tudeh Party, targeting these people as a threat, and hoping they would be arrested and executed. Eventually the entire party was eliminated by the Khomeini government, with deaths totaling 10,000 people. The Tudeh party leadership was tortured and forced to make false televised confessions. In 1989, again backed by the U.S. government, a special committee in Iran sentenced and executed 5,000 people from various political parties. Those executed were considered "leftists," and therefore a potential problem in a post-Khomeini government.

Cambodia: In 1975, the CIA-backed Khmer Rouge overthrew the government of Cambodia. Virtually the entire country was turned into a forced labor camp to implement a primitive agrarian economy. During the next four years, 2 million Cambodians died from starvation, disease, and executions. Several hundred thousand were tortured and murdered. When the Khmer Rouge invaded Vietnam, an uprising of Cambodian people and Vietnam troops drove the Khmer Rouge from power. The U.S. backed the Khmer Rouge in launching guerrilla war against the new Cambodian socialist government. Through U.S. efforts, Vietnamese troops that were in Cambodia in support of the fledgling socialist government were driven out. Prince Norodom Sihanouk and Son Sann were forced into power, with U.S. insistence that Khmer Rouge play a major role in the new government. But since the people of Cambodia revolted against this idea, and the possibility of an international tribunal was becoming imminent, the Khmer Rouge offered to turn over its leader, Pol Pot, to the U.S. government. The U.S. refused to take Pol Pot. Yet the U.S. managed to control the U.N. trials against the Khmer Rouge so that the role of the CIA in supporting the egregious actions of the Khmer Rouge were never uncovered.

7. Did the Bush administration threaten Mexico to get its U.N. vote for war on Iraq? **"Let Them Hate as Long as They Fear,"** editorial by Paul Krugman, a columnist for the *New York Times* (Source: *Press Democrat,* March 10, 2003; first published in the *New York Times*.)

According to this editorial, the Bush administration has threatened Mexico in order to get its vote on the U.N. Security Council for an American war on Iraq. *New York Times* columnist Paul Krugman states, "Last week *The Economist* quoted an American diplomat, who warned that if Mexico didn't vote for a U.S. resolution, it could 'stir up feelings' against Mexicans in the United States. He compared the situation to that of Japanese Americans who were interred after 1941, and wondered whether Mexico 'wants to stir the fires of jingoism during the war....' Then came President Bush's Monday interview with Copley News Service. He alluded to the possibility of reprisals if Mexico didn't vote America's way...." According to Krugman's column, Bush said that if Mexico and other countries oppose the U.S., "There will be a certain sense of discipline." Krugman goes on to say, "These remarks went virtually unreported by the ever-protective U.S. media, but they created a political firestorm in Mexico. The White House has been frantically backpedaling, claiming that when Bush talked of 'discipline,' he wasn't making a threat. But in the context of the rest of the interview, it's clear that he was."

8. Did the U.S. government know that Iraq had destroyed its chemical weapons and lie rather than admit its knowledge?   **"The Big Lie?"** by Russ Baker* (Source: *The Nation,* April 7, 2003)

In its March 3 issue, *Newsweek* disclosed that the Bush Administration had deliberately suppressed information exculpating Iraq—information from the same reliable source previously cited by the Administration as confirming that Iraq had developed weapons of mass destruction since the 1991 Gulf War. As damning as this disclosure was, *Newsweek* chose to underplay it.... Here's the background: In the summer of 1995 Saddam's then son-in-law, Lieut. Gen. Hussein Kamel, former minister of

*Used with permission of Russ Baker (www.russbaker.com), an award-winning investigative journalist and essayist. Russ Baker is the editor of WhoWhatWhy.com and author of *Family of Secrets: The Bush Dynasty, America's Invisible Government,* and *The Hidden History of the Last Fifty Years.*

Iraq's military industry and the person in charge of its nuclear/chemical/biological programs, defected and provided what was deemed scrupulously accurate, detailed accounts of those weapons. Kamel's information has been cited as central evidence and a key reason for attacking Iraq.

In his February 5 presentation to the U.N. Security Council, Secretary of State Colin Powell said: "It took years for Iraq to finally admit that it had produced four tons of the deadly nerve agent VX.... This admission only came out after inspectors collected documentation as a result of the defection of Hussein Kamel, Saddam Hussein's late son-in-law." But *Newsweek*'s John Barry revealed that the Administration had excised a central component of Kamel's testimony—that he had personal knowledge that Iraq had "destroyed all its chemical and biological weapons stocks and the missiles to deliver them." ... According to the story, U.N. inspectors had reasons to hush up this revelation, as they were trying to bluff Saddam into revealing more. But what is Powell's excuse for using only half of Kamel's claim? And why did *Newsweek* and the rest of the American media make so little of this major story? *Newsweek* chose to run a short, 500-word item in its "periscope" section rather than put the story on the cover or make it the focal point of a longer article showing that the Bush Administration is rushing to war for no reason at all.... Perhaps it's not surprising that other media failed to pick up on the Kamel story: The big papers and magazines hate to acknowledge they've been scooped by competitors.... The Hussein Kamel revelation is probably the biggest Iraq story to get punted, but it isn't the only significant example.... It's worth noting that British revelations that the National Security Agency spied on diplomats representing U.N. Security Council members during the Iraq deliberations got a small mention in the *Washington Post* and prompted no questions at Bush's press conference.... Cumulatively, Barry's item on Kamel, the revelation that Colin Powell was citing a graduate student's thesis as British "intelligence" and a new revelation that more British "evidence" of Iraqi nuclear arms development cited by the Administration was (according to weapons inspectors themselves) fabricated suggest that a monstrous Big Lie is in process—an effort to construct falsified evidence and to trick this country and the world.

Every citizen in the world needs access to news sources and commentary that question the self-image maintained by the home culture through its own mass media. No culture lives up to the image it projects of itself. How inconsistent the "self-serving" image is with "reality" is a matter for the critically well-informed public to judge. In the case of the United States, the stories above represent a small sampling of stories buried in the mass media coverage or largely unread in the dissenting minority media. Their portrayal of the U.S. is incompatible with the highly positive self-image in the preponderance of coverage in the mass media.

For most U.S. consumers of the news, the self-image of the United States as defender of human rights, individual freedom, democratic values, and social justice is unquestionably justified. What we need to remember, however, is that most consumers of the news media do not know how to bring forward "buried" information. They do not know how to read the news critically. Most have never seriously questioned their country's image. Therefore, they see no reason to seek out dissenting stories or to question highly nationalistic self-portraits. They cannot, therefore, exercise that higher patriotism that comes only through recognition of the vital need for constructive criticism—the patriotism that helps a country become more of what it has promised to be.

12.21   *Think for Yourself*

IDENTIFYING IGNORED AND IMPORTANT STORIES

Identify a buried, underreported, or ignored story in the mainstream media news. You can look for this story either in a mainstream or an alternative newspaper. Then write a summary of the story, with relevant quotes, as we have done for the preceding examples. Add your own commentary. The more skilled you are at finding such stories, the better you will be able to analyze the news critically.

Using the Internet

The Internet can be used to locate both mainstream and dissenting views from virtually any country in the world. Below are three sources we located for non-mainstream viewpoints. As always, we do not offer sources as *The Truth* but, rather, as aids in obtaining alternatives to the content of mainstream media news.

1. **Amnesty International.** In some cases, particularly in countries where those with dissenting views are put in prison or killed, dissenting views must be sought from expatriates rather than from resident citizens. Amnesty International (www. amnesty.org) is a good source for discovering persons whose views are being forcibly suppressed. The organization publishes a quarterly news magazine focused on exposing the violations of human rights by nations all over the globe (*Amnesty Now*). (Visit www.aiusa.org.)

2. **Statewatch.** Another example of the sort of important resource one can locate on the Internet is Statewatch. It serves as a watchdog organization and database whose goal is the monitoring of state and civil liberties in the European Union. To get a sense of its thoroughness, Statewatch has compiled 25,500 entries in its database since 1991, containing news features, sources, and reports. It publishes *Statewatch* six times a year in addition to pamphlets and reports. (Visit www.statewatch.org.)

3. Mother Jones. *Mother Jones* is a nonprofit news organization that specializes in investigative, political, and social justice reporting. They have two main "platforms": a bimonthly national magazine (circulation 240,000), and a website featuring new, original reporting 24–7. Mother Jones offers "smart, fearless journalism" that keeps people informed. Mother Jones believes that being—"informed" is "pretty

much indispensable to a democracy that actually works." Their work is not funded by or beholden to corporations, which allows them a free hand in investigative journalism.

Another strategy is to search the Internet under descriptors such as "Japanese perspectives," "Asian perspectives," "Chinese perspectives," "African perspectives," "Central American perspectives," "South American perspectives," "Islamic perspectives," and so on. This should help you locate a range of cultural and political standpoints.

Additional Alternative News Sources

Below are some non-mainstream scholarly sources of news and background for the news. We assume that you will read these sources with the same criticality we are recommending for mainstream views. Once again, we do not offer these sources as *The Truth* but, instead, as helpful non-mainstream viewpoints providing alternatives to the content of mainstream media news.

Harpers, www.harpers.org

The Progressive, www.progressive.org

CounterPunch, www.counterpunch.org

Common Dreams, www.commondreams.org

Indy Media Center, www.indymedia.org

The Nation, www.thenation.com/

Free Speech T.V., www.freespeech.org/

In These Times, www.inthesetimes.com/

Z Magazine, www.zmag.org/

AlterNet, www.alternet.org/

The Multinational Monitor, www.essential.org/monitor/

Dollars and Sense, www.dollarsandsense.org/

The Guardian, www.guardian.co.uk/

The Village Voice, www.villagevoice.com/

Project Censored, www.projectcensored.org/

12.22   Think for Yourself

CHECKING OUR ALTERNATIVE SOURCES OF THE NEWS

Visit any of the news sources in the above list. Identify two or three significant news stories that represent the stories in a way that differs from the mainstream view.

CONCLUSION

Learning to detect media bias and propaganda in the national and world news takes time to develop. Yet, this is an art essential to intellectual responsibility, integrity, and freedom. This chapter presents a starting place for the development of intellectual analysis and assessment applied to news stories. As we develop in this art, we experience a progressive shedding of layers of social indoctrination and ethnocentricity.

In the end, each of us must decide for ourselves what to believe and how to act. We can do this critically or uncritically, rationally or irrationally, egocentrically or fairmindedly. We can either tacitly accept our social conditioning and its accompanying ideology, or we can make a deliberative, conscious choice to grow beyond that conditioning. The choice is ours. No one can legitimately make that choice for us. If we choose to go beyond our social conditioning and think for ourselves, we can become free persons and conscientious citizens.

DEVELOP AS AN ETHICAL REASONER

One of the most significant obstacles to fairmindedness is the human tendency to reason in a self-serving or self-deluded manner. This tendency is increased by the extent to which people are confused about the nature of ethical concepts and principles. To understand ethical reasoning, the following foundations are essential:

1. Ethical principles are not a matter of subjective preference.
2. All reasonable people are obligated to respect clear-cut ethical concepts and principles.
3. To reason well through ethical issues, we must know how to apply ethical concepts and principles reasonably to those issues.
4. Ethical concepts and principles should be distinguished from the norms and taboos of society and peer group, religious teachings, political ideologies, and the law.
5. The most significant barriers to sound ethical reasoning are the egocentrism and sociocentrism of human beings.

First we will seek to clarify the problem posed by ethics in human life: what ethics is, its basis, what it is commonly confused with, its pitfalls, and how it is to be understood. Following that discussion, we emphasize three essential components in sound ethical reasoning: (1) the principles upon which ethics is grounded, (2) the counterfeits to avoid, and (3) the pathology of the human mind.

WHY PEOPLE ARE CONFUSED ABOUT ETHICS

The ultimate basis for ethics is clear: Human behavior has consequences for the welfare of others. We are capable of acting toward others in such a way as to increase or decrease the quality of their lives. We are capable of helping or harming others. What's more, we are capable of understanding—at least in many cases—when we are helping and when we are harming others. This is so because we have the *raw (though usually undeveloped) capacity* to put ourselves imaginatively in the place of others and recognize how we would feel if someone were to act toward us in the manner in which we are acting toward them.

Even young children have some idea of what it is to help or harm others. Children make inferences and judgments on the basis of that ethical awareness, and they develop an outlook on life that has ethical significance for good or ill. But children tend to have a much clearer awareness of the harm done to them than they have of the harm they do to others:

"That's not fair! He got more than me!"

"She won't let me have any of the toys!"

"He hit me and I didn't do anything to him. He's mean!"

"She promised me. Now she won't give me my doll back!"

"Cheater! Cheater!"

"It's my turn now. You had your turn. That's not fair."

Through example and encouragement, we can cultivate fairmindedness in children. Children can learn to respect the rights of others and not simply focus on their own desires. The main problem is not so much the difficulty of deciding what is helpful and what is harmful but, instead, our natural propensity to be egocentric. Few humans think at a deep level about the consequences to others of their selfish pursuit of money, power, prestige, and possessions. The result is that although most people, independent of their society, ethnicity, and religion, give at least lip service to a common core of general ethical principles—that it is ethically wrong to cheat, deceive, exploit, abuse, harm, or steal from others, that we have an ethical responsibility to respect the rights of others, including their freedom and well-being, to help those most in need of help, to seek the common good and not merely our own self-interest and egocentric pleasures, and to strive to make this world more just and humane—few act consistently upon these principles.

The United Nations' Declaration of Human Rights, which all countries have ratified, articulates universal ethical principles. And a core of ideas defines the domain of ethicality and ethics, for reasonable people, in a broad and global way. Many fail to act in accordance with ethical principles, however. At an abstract level, there is little disagreement. Most people would argue that it is not ethically justifiable to cheat, deceive, exploit, abuse, and harm others merely because one wants to or simply because one has the raw power to do so. At the level of action, though, mere verbal agreement on general principles does not produce a world that honors human rights. There are too many ways by which humans can rationalize their rapacious desires and feel self-justified in taking advantage of those who are weaker or less able to protect themselves. Too many forces in human life—social groups, religions, political ideologies—generate norms of right and wrong that ignore or distort ethical principles. What's more, humans are too skilled in the art of self-deception for mere verbal agreement on abstract ethical principles to translate into the reality of an ethically just world.

Further complicating the picture, the ethical thing to do is not always self-evident—even to those who are not significantly self-deceived. In complex situations, people of seeming good will often disagree as to the application of this or that ethical principle to this or that concrete case. One and the same act often receives ethical praise from some and condemnation from others.

We can put this dimension of the problem another way: However strongly motivated to do what is ethically right, people can do so only if they *know* what is ethically justified, and they cannot know this if they systematically confuse their sense of what is ethically right with their vested interests, personal desires, political ideology, or social mores or if they lack the capacity to reason with skill and discipline in the ethical domain.

Because of complexities such as these, skilled ethical reasoning presupposes the art of self-critique and ethical self-examination. We must learn to check our thinking for egocentrism, sociocentrism, and self-deception. This, in turn, requires development of the intellectual dispositions described earlier in the book, including intellectual humility, intellectual integrity, and fairmindedness.

Sound ethical reasoning often requires a thinker to recognize and get beyond the pitfalls of ethical judgment: ethical intolerance, self-deception, and uncritical conformity. Sound ethical reasoning often requires us to recognize when our reasoning is a reflection of our social indoctrination. Sound ethical reasoning often requires us to enter empathically into points of view other than our own, gather facts from alternative perspectives, question our assumptions, and consider alternative ways to put the question at issue.

Few adults, however, acquire the skills or insights to recognize the complexities inherent in many everyday ethical issues. Few people identify their own ethical contradictions or clearly distinguish their vested interests and egocentric desires from what is genuinely ethical. Few have thought about the counterfeits of ethical sentiment and judgment or have thought through a coherent ethical perspective in light of the complexities and pitfalls of ethical reasoning. As a result, everyday ethical judgments are often an unconscious mixture of genuine and counterfeit ethics, of ethical insight on the one hand and prejudice and hypocrisy on the other—each in a web of beliefs that seem to the believer to be self-evidently true.

Inadvertently, we pass on to our children and students our own ethical blindness, ethical distortions, and closed-mindedness. As a result, many who trumpet most loudly for ethics to be taught in the schools merely want students to adopt their own beliefs and perspectives, however flawed those beliefs and perspectives might be. They take themselves to have *The Truth* in their pockets. They take their perspective to be exemplary of all ethical truths. What these same people fear most is someone else's ethical perspective taught as the truth: conservatives afraid of liberals being in charge, liberals fearful of conservatives, theists of nontheists, nontheists of theists, and so on.

All of these fears are justified. People—except in the most rare and exceptional cases—have a strong tendency to confuse what they *believe* with the truth. "It's true because I believe it" is, as we have already emphasized, a deep subconscious mindset in most of us. Our beliefs simply *feel* like *The Truth*. They *appear to the mind* as the truth. In the "normal" human mind, it is always the others who do evil, are deceived, self-interested, closed-minded—never us. Thus, instead of cultivating genuine ethical principles in students, teachers often unknowingly indoctrinate them, systematically rewarding students for expressing the beliefs and perspectives the teachers themselves hold. To this extent, they *indoctrinate* rather than educate students.

13.1   Think for Yourself

DISTINGUISHING BETWEEN INDOCTRINATION AND EDUCATION

As a person interested in developing your thinking, you must clearly distinguish between indoctrination and education. These two concepts are often confused. Using a good dictionary as your reference, complete the following statements (you may want to look up these words in more than one dictionary for a comprehensive understanding of these terms).

1. According to the dictionary, the meaning of the word *indoctrination* that contrasts with the meaning of *education* is . . .
2. According to the dictionary, the most fundamental meaning of the word *education* that contrasts with the meaning of *indoctrination* is . . .
3. The main difference between education and indoctrination, therefore, is . . .

Once you feel reasonably clear about the essential differences between these terms, think about your previous schooling and figure out the extent to which you think you have been indoctrinated (in contrast to having been educated). Complete these statements:

1. As a student, I believe I have been mainly (educated or indoctrinated). My reasons for concluding this are . . .
2. For example . . .

THE FUNDAMENTALS OF ETHICAL REASONING

To become skilled in any domain of reasoning, we must understand the principles that define that domain. To be skilled in mathematical reasoning, we must understand fundamental mathematical principles. To be skilled in scientific reasoning, we must understand fundamental scientific principles (principles of physics, of chemistry, of astronomy, and so on). In like manner, to be skilled in ethical reasoning, we must understand fundamental ethical principles.

Good-heartedness is not enough. We must be well grounded in fundamental ethical concepts and principles. Principles are at the heart of ethical reasoning.

People thinking through an ethical issue must be able to identify the ethical principles relevant to the specific ethical situation. They also must muster the intellectual skills required to apply those principles fairly to the relevant case or situation. Ethical principles alone, however, do not settle ethical questions. For example, ethical principles sometimes can be applied differently in cases that are ethically complex.

Consider, for instance, the question: Should the United States maintain relations with countries that violate human rights? The most important ethical concepts relevant to this question are justice and integrity, yet matters of practicality and effectiveness clearly must be considered as well. Justice and integrity would seem to require cutting off relations with any country that violates fundamental human rights. But is isolating and confronting these countries the most effective way to achieve these high ethical ends? What's more, history reminds us that nearly all countries violate human rights in one form or another—the United States not excluded. To what extent do we have the right to demand that others live up to standards that we ourselves often fail to meet? These are the kinds of challenging ethical issues often ignored by the naïve and the good-hearted on the one hand and the self-deceived and cynical on the other.

Because ethical reasoning is often complex, we must learn strategies to deal with these complexities. The three intellectual tasks we believe to be the most important to ethical reasoning are:

1. Mastering the most basic ethical concepts and the principles inherent in ethical issues.

2. Learning to distinguish between ethics and other domains of thinking with which ethics is commonly confused.

3. Learning to identify when native human egocentrism and sociocentrism are impeding one's ethical judgments (probably the most challenging task of the three).

If any of these three foundations is missing in a person's ethical reasoning, that reasoning will likely be flawed. Let's consider these abilities in turn.

Ethical Concepts and Principles

For every ethical question, we must identify some ethical concept or set of concepts directly relevant to the question. We cannot reason well with regard to ethical issues if we do not clearly understand the force of ethical terms and distinctions. Some of the most basic ethical concepts include honesty, integrity, justice, equality, and respect. In many cases, application of the principles implied by these concepts is simple. In some cases, it is difficult.

Consider some simple cases. Lying about, misrepresenting, or distorting the facts to gain a material advantage over others is clearly a violation of the basic principle inherent in the concept of honesty. Expecting others to live up to standards that we ourselves routinely violate is clearly a violation of the basic principle inherent in the concept of integrity. Treating others as if they were worth less than we take ourselves to be worth is a violation of the principles inherent in the concepts of integrity, justice, and equality.

Every day, human life is filled with clear-cut violations of basic ethical principles. No one would deny that it is ethically repugnant for a person to microwave cats for the fun of it. Nor is it ethically acceptable to kill people to get their money or to torture people because we think they are guilty and ought to confess.

Nevertheless, in addition to the clear-cut cases are also complicated cases, requiring us to enter into an ethical dialogue, considering counterarguments from different points of view. Consider, for example, the question: Is euthanasia ever ethically justifiable? Certainly, there are any number of instances when euthanasia is not justified. To consider the question of whether it is ever justified, however, we must consider the various conditions under which euthanasia seems plausible. For example, what about cases involving people who are suffering unrelenting pain from terminal diseases? Within this group are some who plead with us to end their suffering by helping them end their lives (because, although in torment, they cannot end their lives without the assistance of another person).

Given, then, that a person so circumstanced is experiencing intense terminal suffering, one significant ethical concept relevant to this question is the concept of cruelty. *Webster's New World Dictionary* defines *cruelty* as "causing, or of a kind to cause, pain, distress, etc. . . . ; *cruel* implies indifference to the suffering of others or a disposition to inflict it on others." Cruelty, in this case, means "of a kind to cause" unnecessary pain. It means allowing an innocent person to experience unnecessary pain and suffering when we have the power to alleviate it—without sacrificing something of equal value.

Once cruelty is identified as a relevant concept, one ethical injunction becomes clear: Strive to act so as to reduce or end the unnecessary pain and suffering of innocent persons and creatures. With this ethical principle in mind, we can seek to determine in what sense, in any given situation, refusing to assist a suffering person should be considered cruel and in what sense it shouldn't.

Another ethical concept that may be relevant to this issue is: Life is good in itself. The principle that emerges from this concept is: Life should be respected. Some would argue that, given this principle, life should not be terminated by humans under any circumstances.

As a reasoner, you should come to your own conclusions. At the same time, you must be prepared to state your reasoning in detail, explaining what ethical concepts and issues seem to you to be relevant and why. You must be prepared to demonstrate that you have given serious consideration to alternative perspectives on the issue, that you are not ignoring other reasonable ways to think through the question at issue. You must be ready to present what you take to be the most relevant and important facts in the case. You must be prepared to do what any good thinker would do in attempting to support reasoning on any issue in any domain of thought. The fact that an issue is ethical does not mean that you can abandon your commitment to disciplined, rational thought.

Or consider: Under what conditions, if any, is animal experimentation justifiable? Again, one relevant ethical concept is cruelty, for anyone informed about animal experimentation knows that sometimes animals are subjected to extreme pain, anxiety, and suffering in the name of scientific inquiry. People for the Ethical Treatment of Animals (PETA), a proactive animal rights organization, focuses on the negative implications of animal experimentation. PETA, on its website, makes claims such as the following:

■ Every year, millions of animals suffer and die in painful tests to determine the "safety" of cosmetics and household products. Substances ranging from eye shadow and soap to furniture polish and oven cleaner are tested on rabbits, rats, guinea pigs, dogs, and other animals, even though test results do not help prevent or treat human illness or injury. In these tests, a liquid, flake, granule, or powdered substance is dropped into the eyes of a group of albino rabbits. The animals often are immobilized in stocks from which only their heads protrude. They usually receive no anesthesia during the tests. Reactions to the substances include swollen eyes. The rabbits' eyelids are held open with clips. Many animals break their necks as they struggle to escape.

■ Chimpanzees are popular subjects for AIDS research, although their immune system does not succumb to the virus. Chimpanzees also are used in painful cancer, hepatitis, and psychological tests, as well as for research into artificial insemination and birth control methods, blood diseases, organ transplants, and experimental surgery. Their use in military experiments is suspected, but such information is kept secret and is hard to verify. Chimpanzees are highly active and socially oriented. When kept isolated in laboratories with no regular physical contact with either humans or chimps, they quickly become psychotic. Because adult chimpanzees are strong and often unmanageable, and because infected chimpanzees cannot be placed in zoos or existing sanctuaries, many chimpanzees are killed before the age of 10.

■ More than 205,000 new drugs are marketed worldwide every year, most after undergoing the most archaic and unreliable testing methods still in use: animal studies. Many physicians and researchers publicly speak out against these outdated studies. They point out that unreliable animal tests allow dangerous drugs to be marketed to the public and also may prevent potentially useful drugs from being made available. Penicillin would not be in use today if it had been tested on guinea pigs—common laboratory subjects—because penicillin kills guinea pigs. Likewise, aspirin kills cats, while morphine, a depressant to humans, is a stimulant to cats, goats, and horses. Human reactions to drugs cannot be predicted by tests on animals because different species (and even individuals within the same species) react differently to drugs.

The Physician's Committee for Responsible Medicine reports that sophisticated non-animal research methods are more accurate, less expensive, and less time-consuming than traditional animal-based research methods.

Some argue that, in experiments in which animal suffering cannot be avoided, the suffering is ethically justified because in the long run the knowledge gained from this experimentation reduces the pain and suffering that humans would otherwise endure. These proponents of experimentation argue that minimizing human pain and suffering is a superior ethical end to that of minimizing animal pain and suffering.

When reasoning through complex ethical questions, then, skilled ethical reasoners identify the ethical concepts and facts relevant to those questions and apply those concepts to the facts in a well-reasoned manner. In coming to conclusions, they consider as many plausible ways as they can of looking at the issue. As a result of such intellectual work, they develop the capacity to distinguish when ethical questions are clear-cut and when they are not. Even when ethical issues are not clear-cut, it may be important to exercise our best ethical judgment.

The Universal Nature of Ethical Principles

For every ethical issue, there are ethical concepts and principles to be identified and used in thinking through the issue. Included in the principles implied by these concepts are the rights articulated in the Universal Declaration of Human Rights. This set of rights, established on December 10, 1948, by the General Assembly of the United Nations, holds that the

> recognition of inherent dignity and of the equal and inalienable rights of all members of the human family is the foundation of freedom, justice, and peace in the world.... Disregard and contempt for human rights have resulted in barbarous acts which have outraged the conscience of mankind, and the advent of a world in which human beings shall enjoy freedom of speech and belief and freedom from fear and want has been proclaimed as the highest aspiration of the common people.

The Universal Declaration of Humans Rights was conceived as "a common standard of achievement for all peoples and all nations." It is a good example of an explicit statement of important ethical principles.

Here are a few of the principles laid out in the 30 articles of the declaration:

- All humans are born free and equal in dignity and rights.
- Everyone has the right to life, liberty, and security of person.
- No one shall be held in slavery or servitude.
- No one shall be subjected to torture or to cruel, inhuman, or degrading treatment or punishment.
- Everyone has the right to a standard of living adequate for the health and well-being of himself/herself and of his/her family.
- Everyone has the right to education.
- Everyone has the right to freedom of peaceful assembly and association.

- Everyone is entitled to all the rights and freedoms set forth in this Declaration, without distinction of any kinds, such as race, color, sex, language, religion, political or other opinion, national or social origin, property, birth, or status.

- All are equal before the law and are entitled without any discrimination to equal protection of the law.

13.2   Think for Yourself

RECOGNIZING VIOLATIONS OF HUMAN RIGHTS BASED ON UNIVERSAL ETHICAL PRINCIPLES

One ability essential to sound ethical reasoning is the ability to identify ethical principles relevant to the ethical issue at hand. In this activity we would like you to identify two articles in the newspaper or examples from books in which you believe someone's rights have been violated. This might include the violation of animal rights or human rights. Assume for this exercise that the factual claims in this reading are accurate. Complete the following statements:

1. The main substance of this article is...
2. The reason this article suggests to me at least one violation of human rights is...
3. The universal ethical principle(s) violated is/are...

Although the principles outlined in the Universal Declaration of Human Rights are universally accepted in theory, even democratic countries do not necessarily live in accordance with them. For example, the *New York Times* ("Amnesty Finds 'Widespread Pattern' of U.S. Rights Violations," Oct. 5, 1998, p. A11) reported that Amnesty International was citing the United States for violating fundamental human rights. The Amnesty International report stated that "police forces and criminal and legal systems have a persistent and widespread pattern of human rights violations."

In the report, Amnesty International protested a U.S. failure "to deliver the fundamental promise of rights for all." The report states, "Across the country thousands of people are subjected to sustained and deliberate brutality at the hands of police officers. Cruel, degrading, and sometimes life-threatening methods of constraint continue to be a feature of the U.S. criminal justice system."

Pierre Sane, Secretary General of Amnesty International for 6 years, said, "We felt it was ironic that the most powerful country in the world uses international human rights laws to criticize others but does not apply the same standards at home."

Every country agrees in theory to the importance of fundamental human rights. In practice, though, they often fail to uphold those rights.

13.3   *Think for Yourself*

IDENTIFYING VIOLATIONS OF HUMAN RIGHTS
BASED ON UNIVERSAL ETHICAL PRINCIPLES

Identify a newspaper article that either directly or indirectly implies at least one governmental violation of human rights. Complete the following statements:

1. The main substance of this article is ...

2. The reason this article suggests to me at least one governmental violation of human rights is ...

3. The universal ethical principle(s) violated is/are ...

Distinguishing Ethics from Other Domains of Thinking

In addition to understanding how to identify ethical concepts and principles relevant to ethical issues, skilled ethical reasoners must be able to distinguish between ethics and other domains of thinking such as social conventions, religion, and the law. Too often, ethics is confused with these other modes of thinking. Commonly, for example, social values and taboos are treated as if they define ethical principles.

Thus, religious ideologies, social "rules," and laws often are mistakenly taken to be inherently ethical in nature. If we are to accept this amalgamation of domains, by implication every practice within any religious system is necessarily ethical, every social rule is ethically obligatory, and every law is ethically justified. We could not judge, then, any religious practices—such as torturing unbelievers—as unethical.

In the same way, if ethics and social conventions were one and the same, every social practice within any culture would necessarily be ethical—including social conventions in Nazi Germany. We could not, then, ethically condemn any social traditions, norms, mores, and taboos—however ethically bankrupt we think them to be. What's more, if ethics and the law were inextricable, by implication every law within any legal system would be ethical by definition—including laws that blatantly violate human rights.

It is essential, then, to learn to routinely differentiate ethics and other modes of thinking that are commonly confused with ethics. This will enable us to criticize commonly accepted, yet unethical, social conventions, religious practices, political ideas, and laws. No one lacking in this ability can truly live a life of integrity.

Ethics and Religion

Theological reasoning answers metaphysical questions such as:

> What is the origin of all things? Is there a God? Is there more than one God? If there is a God, what is his/her nature? Are there ordained divine laws expressed by

God to guide our life and behavior? If so, what are these laws? How are they communicated to us? What must we do to live in keeping with the will of the divine?

Religious Beliefs Are Culturally Variant

Religious variability derives from the fact that theological beliefs are intrinsically subject to debate. There is an unlimited number of alternative ways for people to conceive and account for the nature of the "spiritual." The *Encyclopedia Americana*, for example, lists more than 300 religious belief systems. These traditional ways of believing adopted by social groups or cultures often take on the force of habit and custom. They are then handed down from one generation to another. To the individuals in any given group, their particular beliefs seem to them to be the *only* way, or the only *reasonable* way, to conceive of the "divine." They cannot see that their religious beliefs are just one set among many possible religious belief systems. Consider some examples of theological beliefs confused with ethical principles.

- Members of majority religious groups often force their beliefs on minorities.
- Members of religious groups often act as if their theological views are self-evidently true, scorning those who hold other views.
- Members of religious groups often fail to recognize that "sin" is a theological concept, not an ethical one. ("Sin" is theologically defined.)
- Divergent religions define sin in different ways (but often expect their views to be enforced on all others as if a matter of universal ethics).

Religious beliefs, when dominant in a human group, tend to shape many, if not all, aspects of a person's life—with rules, requirements, taboos, and rituals. Most of these regulations are ethically neither right nor wrong but simply represent social preferences and culturally subjective choices.

It is every person's human right to choose his or her own religious orientation, including, if one wishes, that of agnosticism or atheism. That is why there is a provision (Article 18) in the United Nations Declaration of Human Rights concerning the right to change one's religious beliefs:

> Everyone has the right to freedom of thought, conscience, and religion; this right includes freedom to change his religion or belief ...

Beliefs about divinity and spirituality are notoriously divergent and therefore are not compulsory. There is no definitive way to prove any one set of religious beliefs to the exclusion of all others. For that reason, religious freedom is a human right. One can objectively prove that murder and assault are harmful to persons, but not that a lack of belief in God is.

That ethical judgment must trump religious belief is shown by the undeniable fact that many persons have been tortured and/or murdered by people motivated by religious zeal or conviction. Indeed, religious persecution is commonplace in human history. Humans need recourse to ethics in defending themselves against religious intolerance and persecution.

Consider this example: If a religious group were to believe that the firstborn male of every family must be sacrificed, all parents in that group would consider themselves ethically obligated to kill their firstborn male. Their religious beliefs would lead them to unethical behavior and lessen their capacity to appreciate the cruel nature of their acts.

Furthermore, a society must be deemed unethical if it accepts among its religious practices any form of slavery, torture, sexism, racism, persecution, murder, assault, fraud, deceit, or intimidation. Remember, atrocities have often been committed during religious warfare. Even to this day, religious persecution and religiously motivated atrocities are commonplace. No religious belief as such can justify violations of basic human rights.

In short, theological beliefs cannot override ethical principles. We must turn to ethical principles to protect ourselves from intolerant and oppressive religious practices.

13.4   *Think for Yourself*

DISTINGUISHING BETWEEN ETHICS AND RELIGION

Focus on one commonly held religious belief system to identify possible confusion between theological beliefs and ethical principles. See whether you can identify any practices within the religion that might be critiqued as unethical. See also if you can identify any practices the religion considers unethical that one might argue are actually ethical. Select any religion about which you are sufficiently knowledgeable to find possible problems of the sort we are considering. As an example, remember the case of those religious believers who think that a woman who commits adultery should be stoned to death.

Ethics and Social Conventions

Let us return to the relationship of ethics and social conventions. For more than a hundred years in the United States, most people considered slavery to be justified and desirable. It was part of social custom. There can be no question that, all along, this practice was unethical. Moreover, throughout history, many groups of people, including people of various nationalities and skin colors, as well as females, children, and individuals with disabilities, have been victims of discrimination as the result of social convention treated as ethical obligation. Yet, all social practices that violate ethical principles deserve to be rejected by ethically sensitive, reasonable persons no matter how many people support those practices.

Unless we learn to soundly critique the social mores and taboos that have been imposed upon us from birth, we will accept those traditions as "right." All of us are deeply socially conditioned. Therefore, we do not naturally develop the ability to critique social norms and taboos effectively.

Schools and colleges often become apologists for conventional thought; faculty members often inadvertently foster the confusion between convention and ethics because they themselves have internalized the conventions of society. Education, properly so called, should foster the intellectual skills that enable students to distinguish between cultural mores and ethical precepts, between social commandments and ethical truths. In each case, when conflicts with ethical principles are present, the ethical principles should rule.

Socially or Culturally Variant Practices

Cultural diversity derives from the fact that there are an unlimited number of alternative ways for social groups to satisfy their needs and fulfill their desires. Those traditional ways of living within a social group or culture take on the force of habit and custom. They are handed down from one generation to another. To the individuals in a given group, they seem to be the *only* way, or the only *reasonable* way, to do things, and these social customs sometimes have ethical implications. Social habits and customs answer questions such as these:

- How should marriage take place? Who should be allowed to marry, under what conditions, and with what ritual or ceremony? Once a couple marries, what role should the male play? What role should the female play? Are multiple marriage partners possible? Is divorce possible? Under what conditions?

- Who should care for the children? What should they teach the children about proper and improper ways to act? When children do not act as they are expected to act, how should they be treated?

- When should children be accepted as adults? When should they be considered old enough to be married? Who should they be allowed to marry?

- When children develop sensual and sexual desires, how should they be allowed to act? With whom, if anyone, should they be allowed to engage in sexual exploration and discovery? What sexual acts are considered acceptable and wholesome? What sexual acts are considered perverted or sinful?

- How should men and women dress? To what degree should their body be exposed in public? How is nudity treated? How are those who violate these codes treated?

- How should food be obtained and how should it be prepared? Who is responsible for obtaining food? Who for preparing it? How should it be served? How eaten?

- How is the society "stratified" (into levels of power)? How is the society controlled? What belief system is used to justify the distribution of scarce goods and services and the way rituals and practices are carried out?

- If the society develops enemies or is threatened from without, how will it deal with those threats? How will it defend itself? How does the society engage in war, or does it?

- What sorts of games, sports, or amusements will be practiced in the society? Who is allowed to engage in them?
- What religions are taught or allowable within the society? Who is allowed to participate in the religious rituals or to interpret divine or spiritual teachings to the group?
- How are grievances settled in the society? Who decides who is right and who wrong? How are violators treated?

Schools traditionally function as apologists for conventional thought; those who teach often inadvertently foster confusion between convention and ethics because they themselves have internalized the conventions of society. Education, properly so called, should foster the intellectual skills that enable students to distinguish between cultural mores and ethical precepts, between social commandments and ethical truths. In each case, when social beliefs and taboos conflict with ethical principles, ethical principles should prevail. Consider the following examples of societies confusing ethics with social conventions.

- Many societies have created taboos against showing various parts of the body and have severely punished those who violated them.
- Many societies have created taboos against giving women the same rights as men.
- Many societies have socially legitimized religious persecution.
- Many societies have socially stigmatized interracial marriages.

These practices seem (wrongly) to be ethically obligatory to those socialized into accepting them.

Ethics and Sexual Taboos

Social taboos are often matters of strong emotions. People are often disgusted when others violate a taboo. Their disgust signals to them that the behavior is unethical. They forget that what is socially repugnant to us may not violate any ethical principle but, instead, may merely differ from social convention. Social doctrines regarding human sexuality are often classic examples of conventions expressed as if they were ethical truths. Social groups often establish strong sanctions for unconventional behavior involving the human body. Some social groups inflict unjust punishments on women who do no more than appear in public without being completely veiled, an act considered in some cultures as indecent and sexually provocative. Sexual behaviors should be considered unethical only when they result in unequivocal harm or damage.

Our overall goal—which we hope this chapter will inspire readers to pursue—is to become so proficient in ethical reasoning and so skilled in distinguishing matters of ethical principle from matters of social taboo, legal fact, and theological belief that you will rarely confuse these domains in your experience and, rather, render to each of them their due consideration and weight in specific cases as they might arise in your life.

13.5   Think for Yourself

DISTINGUISHING BETWEEN ETHICS AND SOCIAL CONVENTION

Prior to and during the civil rights movement in the United States, many whites believed that blacks were intellectually inferior to them. This belief gave rise to laws that denied basic human rights to blacks. It would be hard to find a clearer case of socially accepted conventions leading to socially defended unethical practices.

Identify one newspaper article that embodies the confusion between social conventions and ethical principles. Look for an article in which a commonly held social belief results in the denial of some person's or group's basic human right(s).

1. The substance of this article is . . .
2. The reason this article implies at least one violation of human rights is . . .
3. The universal ethical principle(s) violated was . . .

Ethics and Political Ideology

A political ideology provides an analysis of the present distribution of wealth and power and devises strategies in keeping with that analysis. It provides either a "justification" of the present structure of power or a "critique." It seeks either to protect and maintain the way things are or to change them. It seeks to change things in small ways or in big ways. It compares the present to the past and both to a future it projects.

Conservative ideologies "justify" the status quo or seek a return to a previous "ideal" time. Liberal ideologies critique the status quo and seek to justify "new" forms of political arrangements designed to rectify present problems. Reactionary ideologies plead for a "radical" return to the past; revolutionary ideologies plead for a "radical" overturning of the fundamental ("corrupt") structures. Conservative ideologies consider the highest values to be private property, family, God, and country. Liberal ideologies consider the highest values to be liberty, equality, and social justice.

Ideological analyses have highly significant ethical implications. Put into action, they often have profound effects on the well-being of people. What is more, the ideologies officially espoused by politicians are often widely different from the personal ends they pursue. Virtually all political ideologies speak in the name of the "people." Yet most of them, in fact, are committed to powerful, vested interest groups who fund their election campaigns. The same people often end up ruling, independent of the "official" ideology. Thus, in the post-Soviet power structure, many of those who were formerly powerful in the Communist party are now among the most prominent and acquisitive neo-capitalists.

The bottom line is that politicians rarely act for ethical reasons. Struggling against each other for power and control, political movements and interests often sacrifice ethical ideals for practical advantage. They often rationalize unethical acts as unavoidable necessities (for example, "forced on them" by their opponents). And they systematically use propaganda to further vested interest agendas.

Ethics and the Law

As students interested in developing your ethical reasoning abilities, you should be able to differentiate ethics and the law. What is illegal may or may not be a matter of ethics. What is ethically obligatory may be illegal. What is unethical may be legal. There is no essential connection between ethics and the law.

Laws often emerge out of social conventions and taboos. And, because we cannot assume that social conventions are ethical, we cannot assume that human laws are ethical. What is more, most laws are ultimately made by politicians, who routinely confuse social values with ethical principles. As we have said, their primary motivation is, except in special cases, power, vested interest, or expediency. For example, from 1900 through 1930, American politicians, in response to an electorate dominated by fundamentalist religious believers, passed laws that made it illegal for anyone, including doctors, to disseminate any information about birth control. The consequence was predictable: hundreds of thousands of poor and working-class women suffered severe injuries or death from the effects of illegal drugs and unsanitary abortions. To "criminalize" behavior that goes against social conventions is one of the time-honored ways for politicians to get reelected. Consider the following examples of people confusing ethics with the law.

- Many sexual practices (such as homosexuality) have been unjustly punished with life imprisonment or death (under the laws of one society or another).
- Many societies have enforced unjust laws based on racist views.
- Many societies have enforced laws that discriminated against women.
- Many societies have enforced laws that discriminated against children.
- Many societies have made torture and/or slavery legal.
- Many societies have enforced laws arbitrarily punishing people for using some drugs but not others.

Acts That Are Unethical In and Of Themselves

For any action to be unethical, it must inherently deny another person or creature some inalienable right. The following classes of acts are unethical in and of themselves. Any person or group that violates them can properly be criticized from an ethical standpoint:

- SLAVERY: Owning people, whether individually or in groups
- GENOCIDE: Systematically killing with the intent to eliminate a whole nation or ethnic group
- TORTURE: Inflicting severe pain to force information, get revenge, or serve some other irrational end

- SEXISM: Treating people unequally (and harmfully) by virtue of their gender
- RACISM: Treating people unequally (and harmfully) by virtue of their race or ethnicity
- MURDER: The premeditated killing of people for revenge or pleasure or to gain advantage for oneself
- ASSAULT: Attacking an innocent person with intent to cause grievous bodily harm
- RAPE: Forcing an unwilling person to have sexual intercourse
- FRAUD: Intentional deception that causes someone to give up property or some right

WE MUST LEARN TO DISTINGUISH AMONG QUESTIONS OF ETHICS, SOCIAL CONVENTIONS, RELIGION, AND THE LAW

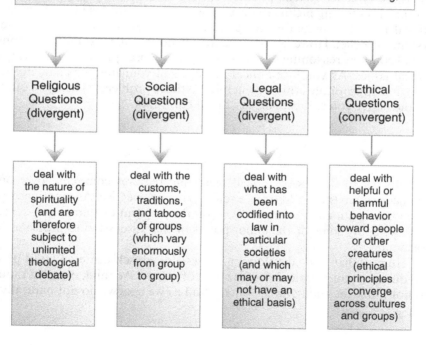

If we are ever to reach a point in human development where skilled ethical reasoning is the norm, each of us must cultivate in ourselves the ability to determine whether any belief system, practice, rule, or law is ethical. To be skilled at ethical reasoning means to develop a conscience not subservient to fluctuating social conventions, theological systems, or unethical laws. Consistently sound reasoning in any domain of thought presupposes practice in reasoning through cases and issues in that domain. As we face problems in our lives, we must distinguish the ethical from the non-ethical and the pseudo-ethical and apply appropriate ethical principles to those problems that are genuinely ethical problems. The more often we do so, the better we become at ethical reasoning.

Religious Questions (divergent)	Social Questions (divergent)	Legal Questions (divergent)	Ethical Questions (convergent)
deal with the nature of spirituality (and are therefore subject to unlimited theological debate)	deal with the customs, traditions, and taboos of groups (which vary enormously from group to group)	deal with what has been codified into law in particular societies (and which may or may not have an ethical basis)	deal with helpful or harmful behavior toward people or other creatures (ethical principles converge across cultures and groups)

- ▪ DECEIT: Representing something as true which one knows to be false to gain a selfish end harmful to another
- ▪ INTIMIDATION: Forcing a person to act against his interest or to deter from acting in his interest by threats or violence
- ▪ Putting persons in jail without telling them the charges against them or providing them with a reasonable opportunity to defend themselves
- ▪ Putting persons in jail, or otherwise punishing them, solely for their political or religious views

13.6   Think for Yourself

DISTINGUISHING ETHICS AND SEXUAL CONVENTIONS

Make a list of sexual practices in your culture considered acceptable in the society, and make a list of those considered taboo. For each one, decide whether the sexual custom, rule, or taboo is either ethical, unethical, or ethically neutral. Remember that for the behavior to be unethical, it must harm or have the great potential to harm someone, objectively speaking.

It is important for you to develop your ability to determine for yourself whether any belief system, practice, rule, or law is inherently ethical. To be skilled at ethical reasoning means to develop a conscience that is not subservient to unethical laws; to fluctuating social conventions; or to controversial, theological systems of belief. However, consistently sound ethical reasoning, like consistently sound complex reasoning of every type, presupposes practice in thinking through ethical issues. As you face ethical problems in your life, the challenge will be in applying appropriate ethical principles to those problems. The more often you do so, the better you will become at ethical reasoning.

Understanding Our Native Selfishness

In addition to the above, ethical reasoning requires command over our native tendency to see the world from a self-serving perspective. As mentioned previously, human irrational tendencies focus on the problem of human self-centeredness. Here we apply some of the major points of that discussion to problems in ethical reasoning.

Humans naturally develop a narrow-minded, self-centered point of view. We feel our own pain; we don't feel the pain of others. We think our own thoughts; we do not think the thoughts of others. And as we age, we do not naturally develop the ability to empathize with others, to consider points of view that conflict with our own. For this reason, we often are unable to reason from a genuinely ethical perspective. Empathy with the thinking of others, then, is not natural to humans. Nevertheless, it is possible to learn to think through ethical issues critically. With the proper practice, we can acquire the skill of considering situations from opposing ethical perspectives.

As we have argued in previous chapters, the human tendency to judge the world from a narrow, self-serving perspective is powerful. Humans typically are masterful at self-deception and rationalization. We often maintain beliefs that fly in the face of the evidence before our eyes and engage in acts that blatantly violate ethical principles. What's more, we feel perfectly justified in doing so.

At the root of every unethical act lies some form and degree of self-delusion. And at the root of every self-delusion lies some flaw in thinking. For instance, Hitler confidently believed he was doing the right thing in carrying out egregious acts against the Jews. His actions were a product of the erroneous beliefs that Jews were inferior to the Aryan race and that they were the cause of Germany's problems. In ridding Germany of the Jews, he believed himself to be doing what was in the best interest of his Germany. He therefore considered his actions to be completely justified. His unethical reasoning resulted in untold human harm and suffering for millions of people.

To become skilled at ethical reasoning, we must understand that it means doing what is right even in the face of powerful selfish desires. To live an ethical life is to develop command over our native egocentric tendencies. It is not enough to espouse the importance of living an ethical life. It is not enough to be able to do the right thing when we ourselves have nothing to lose. We must be willing to fulfill our ethical obligations at the expense of our selfish desires. Thus, having insight into our irrational drives is essential to living an ethical life.

13.9   Think for Yourself

IDENTIFYING YOUR UNETHICAL BEHAVIOR

Each of us engages in unethical behavior, but few of us recognize that we do. To become highly skilled at ethical reasoning, we must become everyday observers of our own thoughts and actions. Over the next week, closely observe your behavior to catch yourself doing something unethical (such as being selfish or hurting someone unjustifiably).

Complete the following statements for five "unethical" acts:

1. The situation in which I behaved unethically was as follows . . .
2. The unethical action I engaged in was . . .
3. The reason(s) this act was unethical is . . .
4. The basic right(s) I violated is . . .
5. To avoid behaving unethically in future such situations, I should . . .

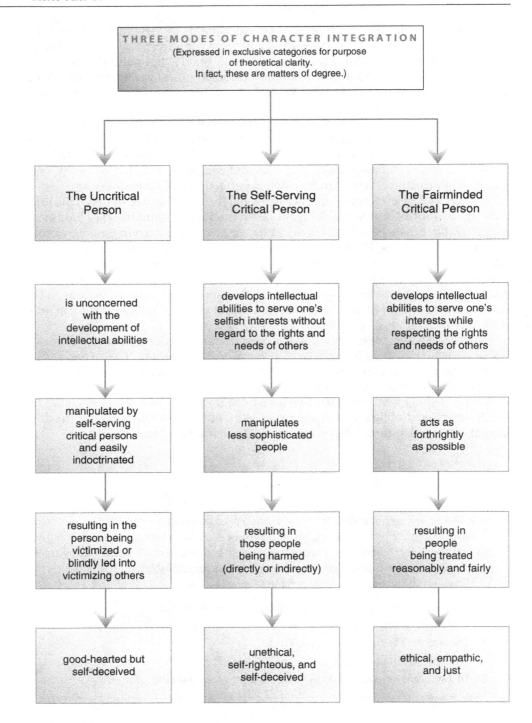

THREE MODES OF CHARACTER INTEGRATION
(Expressed in exclusive categories for purpose
of theoretical clarity.
In fact, these are matters of degree.)

The Uncritical Person

is unconcerned with the development of intellectual abilities

manipulated by self-serving critical persons and easily indoctrinated

resulting in the person being victimized or blindly led into victimizing others

good-hearted but self-deceived

The Self-Serving Critical Person

develops intellectual abilities to serve one's selfish interests without regard to the rights and needs of others

manipulates less sophisticated people

resulting in those people being harmed (directly or indirectly)

unethical, self-righteous, and self-deceived

The Fairminded Critical Person

develops intellectual abilities to serve one's interests while respecting the rights and needs of others

acts as forthrightly as possible

resulting in people being treated reasonably and fairly

ethical, empathic, and just

CONCLUSION

To develop as an ethical reasoner, then, we must deeply internalize the fundamental roots of ethics. This means learning to identify and express ethical concepts and principles accurately. It means learning how to apply these principles to relevant ethical situations and to differentiate ethics from other modes of thinking that are traditionally confused with ethics.

Finally, it means taking command, with intellectual humility, of one's native egocentrism. Without such an organized, well-integrated, critically based approach to ethics, some counterfeit of ethics, but not ethics itself, is the likely result. To date, all across the world, ethics has routinely been confused with other domains of thinking. The use of ethics and its misuse have been nearly one and the same.

Chapter 14

Putting It All Together: Answering Critical-Thinking Questions

It would be natural at this point if you felt a large number of fragments swirling around in your head. First, there are the 8+ elements. Then, there are the standards, seven of them discussed in some detail. There are fundamental and powerful concepts, the central question, and the point of view of the discipline. There are also a number of impediments to critical thinking, and they may overlap significantly with ways you normally think things through. At this point, you probably have a mixed grasp of the elements, the standards, and critical thinking as a whole.

You are probably good at identifying some of the elements when you read a chapter or think through a problem on your own, and you are not nearly as good at identifying some of the other elements. You may be strong on identifying an author's purpose or the information an author is providing, but you may not be clear about the exact difference between conclusions and implications, and you may have trouble telling an assumption from a concept.

364

The same is probably true of your grasp of the standards. You may find that you are regularly giving examples to make your thinking clearer. Yet it may be difficult to tell when you have reasoned through a question sufficiently.

These all improve with practice and instruction—checking back with the book frequently, doing the exercises, or receiving feedback from your teacher. You may still be concerned that you don't see clearly how this all fits together. You may wonder, "Where am I in the process? How do I get an overview?" "I need some kind of a map, so I know which way to go, which critical-thinking move to make, and why." "I understand how to go around the circle and how to do a Standards Check, but how can I turn my critical thinking into an actual paper?" If you feel that way, it's based on a sound instinct. Part of understanding anything, critical thinking included, is seeing *the whole* and *the parts* in perspective: seeing how it all fits together. The purpose of this chapter is to give a sense of the whole, to provide a map.

The Core Process of Critical Thinking in a Discipline

So, what do critical thinkers do?

Core Process (QEDS)

- They address a question or problem (**Q**).
- They think it through using the elements of reasoning (**E**).
- When appropriate, they reason out all aspects of the issue through the lens of the discipline (**D**).
- As they do this, they monitor their reasoning using the critical-thinking standards (**S**).

That's the core process of critical thinking, the heart of it. Critical thinkers who have never taken a course in critical thinking engage in this core process. They may not consider all the elements or consciously name them as they think; they may not consciously realize that they are thinking in terms of a discipline they have internalized; and they may not be explicitly aware that they are using the standards, but if you

FIGURE 14.1   *The core process of critical thinking in a discipline.*

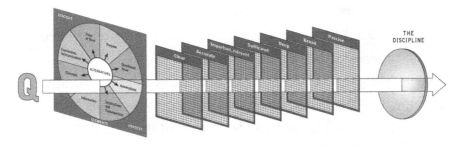

examine their reasoning, you will see that they are thinking about their purpose or their assumptions; they are using discipline-based concepts when it makes sense to do so; they are checking to be sure they are being accurate and that they have focused on the important parts of the problem.

Figure 14.1 offers a rough map of the core process **QEDS**, an annotated version. Now you should be in a better position to know what it's a map of and what the parts are. Figure 14.1 is just a rough map, of course. Thinking is not as linear as this implies: when you think through something critically, you don't necessarily start with the question (Q), *then* go to the elements, *then* to the discipline, and *then* to the standards. You can think it out in that order if you wish, but the role of the standards is more of a persistent monitoring of your thinking. As you think through the question using the elements, you are striving to be clear, to stick to the important parts of the problem, to be accurate, to consider the problem sufficiently. You also use the standards at the end, to check on your reasoning and revise it to make it better. You ask yourself: "Okay, I tried to be accurate in what I was saying. Did I succeed? Do I need more evidence?" or: "I worked at being clear as I wrote my paper. But do I need to elaborate on what I said to make it clearer? Do I need another example, or maybe a contrasting example?"

If the question you are trying to address is one that's in a discipline, then you have to think it through using the fundamental and powerful concepts, relating it to the central question, and looking at it from the point of view of that discipline. Ask yourself, "How do people in this discipline address such questions? How do they go about answering such questions?" If it's a question in anthropology, you need to engage in thinking anthropologically. If it's a question in engineering, you have to think it through the way an engineer would. (See Chapter 10, pages 232–233.)

Even if it's a question outside the discipline, about your personal life, or about some decision you have to make, it is reasonable to think it out from the point of view of disciplines that are relevant to that question. A fundamental thesis of this book is that thinking things through in terms of disciplines gives people insight. So, if you have a decision to make about diet, exercise, or smoking, it will help to ask, "How can I think this out biologically? nutritionally? medically?" You may also gain insight by asking, "How can I think it out psychologically? (How does my psychological way of thinking influence the decisions I make about dieting, exercise, smoking?) How can I think it out historically? (How does my society's history with regard to dieting, exercise, and smoking affect me and guide my choices?)" Literature, math, sociology: each of these, and many others, can not only help you understand the issues in a deep way, they can also help you make better decisions.

Doing More Than the Core Process

Thinking in Terms of Critical-Thinking Processes

The core process, then, involves questions, elements, discipline-based thinking, and standards. For some questions, however, you may have to add to the core. A helpful way to conceptualize this for yourself is to think in terms of critical-thinking processes such as analysis, synthesis, evaluation, and a number of others.

You have already engaged in many of them. *Analysis* is a critical-thinking process of breaking something down into its component parts. You engaged in the process of analysis every time you broke something down into the elements of reasoning. At its root, analysis is going around the circle of elements. If you have gone around the circle with respect to a chapter in your text, you have analyzed the chapter in terms of its purpose, its main question at issue, its main assumptions, and so on.

You haven't merely broken the chapter down into its component parts, however. You have also gained an understanding of how those parts fit together as a coherent whole. In this book, we have been describing this whole as the logic of the question: after going around the circle, you have a good grasp of the logic of the chapter. This "bringing together into a whole" is often called the process of *synthesis*. So, in going around the circle, seeing each of the elements and grasping the logic of the question or topic, you have already been engaged in the critical-thinking processes of analyzing and synthesizing.

Depending on what is called for in the question, however, you still may have to do more than engage in the core process. You may have to engage in other processes besides analysis and synthesis. You may have to *compare and contrast* two different positions on euthanasia, for example. You may have to *evaluate* what a particular author says. You may need to *apply* a theory in the discipline to a new case. You may have to do some actual *decision-making* about a course of action. You may have to engage in some *action*—writing a paper, performing the part of Mercutio, or designing an experiment. Notice that *action*—doing something—is classified here as a critical-thinking process. As with any of the other processes, you want your actions to be infused with your best thinking. Even more broadly, you can rethink your life in an ongoing way using critical thinking. That is living in such a way that you are in touch with the elements (for instance, your goals and assumptions) and with the standards (for instance, paying attention to what is important and deep for you). Thus, according to this book, *living mindfully* is a critical-thinking process.

Each of these critical-thinking processes is built from the elements and standards. We can add these critical-thinking processes to the core process, as shown in Figure 14.2.

Doing Less Than the Core Process

FIGURE 14.2 *Critical-thinking processes.*

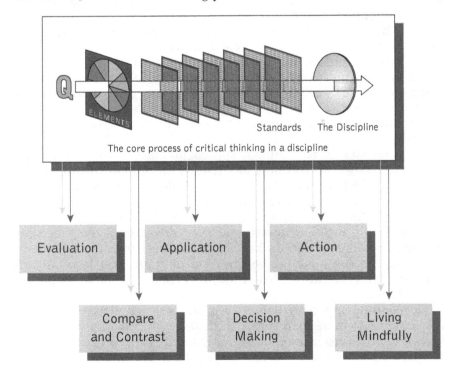

The core process is the centerpiece of critical thinking. Many times you have to do more than this core process just to address the various complexities of an issue. You may have to add the lenses of the disciplines themselves, and you may have to add other critical-thinking processes.

On the other hand, you often have to do less than the core process. You may take an author's position on animal rights and simply identify a crucial assumption behind it. Sometimes, that will be all that's necessary. The act of simply identifying a single element can be a deep insight in your critical thinking. Moreover, getting into the habit of identifying that single element can be a vital step in the development of your ability to think well. It can be valuable to you all by itself, without even addressing the other elements.

Consider *consequences*. By simply focusing on anticipating the *consequences* of your decisions, you can make a crucial transformation in your life, especially if you do it in a regular way. To a certain degree, this benefit can be independent of how you handle the other elements. Of course, your thinking may be deeper if you also pay attention to the other elements. Nevertheless, the act of focusing on consequences all by itself can change your thinking and actions in a dramatic way.

That is true for the standards as well. Consider accuracy. In a classical Greek play, one character, Antigone, sees divine law and the ties of family as having more validity than the claims of human law; the opposing character, Creon, sees human law as taking precedence over religious injunctions and family ties. A crucial step in addressing the play mindfully is to do more than reporting on what the two characters see as valid. The crucial step is for *you* to evaluate that validity yourself. Reflecting on the accuracy or inaccuracy of each of those principles can open up many profound truths.

For any given problem, the elements and standards are not all equally important. The decisions about which of them to focus on, whether to go all the way around the circle, or whether to engage in one or more of the other critical-thinking processes—all of these are themselves critical-thinking decisions.

How Do *You* Fit into the Picture? Becoming a Critical Thinker

Critical thinking isn't done in a vacuum. It is always done by some particular person, someone who brings his or her own repertoire of skills and traits of mind, feelings, wants and needs, strengths and weaknesses. All of these influence how you do your critical thinking. Critical thinking can affect who you are and what you are able to accomplish. Similarly, who you are and what you are able to do affects the quality and direction of your critical thinking.

One trait that distinctly helps you become more of a critical thinker is if you *enjoy* it. Many people find that they do. If you enjoy thinking critically and figuring things out, or if you feel a sense of satisfaction or strength in being able to reason through issues well, it can have a major effect on the quality of your thinking and the quality of your life. But even if you don't enjoy it (or don't enjoy it *yet*), there are skills and traits you can work on to develop as a critical thinker. Some of these you may already possess, maybe to a considerable degree. With some, you may be really weak. Even accomplished critical thinkers have deficiencies in some of their skills and traits (that's part of being human), and even ones you are strong in may temporarily desert you in some circumstances. As your strengths increase, you may find that even if at first you didn't enjoy the process of thinking critically, you do now.

The traits listed below are *transformative*. As you become highly skilled at listening, for example, and as you practice your listening skills often, it starts a transformation in you: *you* start to become a good listener. It starts to become part of who you are.

So as you go through the list below, think of them not so much as skills but as character traits, habits, dispositions, attitudes, aspects of your personality.

A well-developed critical thinker is:

- A good listener
- Someone who speaks thoughtfully
- Someone who searches for explanations (who gets at the "why" of things)
- An observant person
- Someone who seeks out reliable information when making important decisions
- Someone who is centered: proactive rather than reactive
- Someone open to new ideas: not stubborn, not closed minded
- A truth-seeker
- A critical reader, a critical writer (someone who is reliably clear, accurate, and relevant in both areas)
- Someone who seeks to understand other people:
  - → their reasons and motivations
  - → their emotions
  - → their points of view
- A self-aware person: aware of
  - → strengths and weaknesses
  - → abilities and disabilities
  - → his or her own tendencies toward egocentrism

Critical-Thinking Character Traits[1]

Critical-thinking traits are parts of a person's character. Many of the traits are difficult to acquire to a full degree, or to act on in a consistent way. But we can improve in all of them. With commitment and practice, we develop them in ourselves over time. To a very real extent, you cannot think critically, in the discipline or in your life, unless you develop the traits in yourself. Critical thinkers:

- Have **confidence in reason**. They believe in trying to figure things out. They rely on thinking their way through questions and issues, to the best of their ability, rather than relying on the other influences that shape their thinking without their knowing it.

- Have **intellectual humility**. They recognize and own up to what they don't know, in all its fullness. As difficult as it is to admit sometimes, they realize that they make mistakes and are often less than perfect in their reasoning. They can accept criticism, and learn from it.

- Are **intellectually courageous**. They face up to challenges to their settled beliefs and habitual ways of thinking. They are willing to change their point of view—even a deeply held one—when that is the reasonable thing to do.

- Are **intellectually empathetic**. They willingly commit themselves to thinking through the logic of any point of view, without regard to whether they agree with it or not. They do that not just "in their heads": they are willing to *feel the force* of the logic inherent in that other point of view.

- Have **intellectual integrity**. They hold themselves to the same high intellectual standards they hold others to. They are "truth-seekers": in thinking through an issue, they are committed to giving the most reasonable account they can, even if the price of that is high.

- Are **fair-minded**. They do their best to be balanced and impartial when trying to understand, analyze, evaluate or apply any belief or point of view, no matter how different from their own.

- Are **intellectually engaged**. They are involved, on a deep and satisfying level, in wanting to understand things and think them through. They feel a strong desire to immerse themselves in an intellectual topic. They *like* thinking critically.

- Have **intellectual perseverance**. They are willing to stick with important intellectual tasks for as long as it takes to reach a reasonable conclusion.

■ Are **intellectually autonomous**. They think for themselves. They are committed to it. They habitually use the best reasoning they are capable of, including elements, standards, and the discipline, with awareness of the bigger picture.

For me, the best way to think of the traits is as something I'm on my way toward. I'm stronger in some, weaker in others, but I can work on them. Though they are often challenging for me, whenever I take even small steps toward exercising them, I start to feel like a fuller person.

Thinking Through Important Critical-Thinking Questions

Even with an overview, a series of maps, and a sketch of how you might fit in the picture, you may still be wondering what to do to think your way through a critical-thinking question in the discipline. How do you go about it? How do you start? How do you carry it through? How do you tell whether you have done it well? How do you improve? This section takes you through the basics of answering a critical-thinking question. It will also provide a more detailed exploration of putting it all together. Below, in outline form, is the core process of critical thinking. It is an overview of putting it all together, thinking through an important critical-thinking question.

THE CORE PROCESS:

QEDS
Look at the <u>q</u>uestion.
Think it through using the <u>e</u>lements.   } KEEP THE
Think it through in terms of the <u>d</u>iscipline.   } <u>S</u>TANDARDS
                                                       <u>I</u>N MIND

How to Start: Begin by Stepping Back

The most common ways to start thinking through a critical-thinking question are often not very effective. One typical way to start is just to start. I simply begin answering the question, relying on my mind to have sorted things out—or rather, hoping that my mind has sorted things out. Another common way to start is to look for information. I have to write a four-page paper about poverty in the United States. It has to have three references. So I scroll down the list of entries from my Internet search. I find three that look okay. I take a chunk of information from each and put it in my paper. I make sure it equals four pages.

A third common way to begin is not to have the slightest idea how to begin. I wait until time pressure drives me to answer the question at the last minute. By that time the situation is desperate, so I'll be satisfied with just having something to turn in—anything. I can't afford the luxury of spending time trying to think things out.

There are more fruitful ways to think through a question and try to answer it. These ways begin with a central critical-thinking move: reflection. Take a metacognitive step, a step back. The question is in front of you. The natural impulse is to answer it, but don't do that yet. Instead, take a step back from the question, detach yourself from it. Don't ask yourself, "What is the answer?" Instead, ask yourself, "What is the question asking? What does it call for? What would I have to do in order to answer it?" If you get the flavor of these stepping-back questions, you'll find that by thinking critically, you can construct a strategy for answering them.

> Read the box on pages 347–357. Then pick out some questions from your text. Choose some from later in the book, ones that come after chapters you have not read yet. Outline briefly what you need to do in order to answer those questions.
>
> Try the same thing with two or three questions from other courses you are taking.
>
> Later, at the end of this chapter, try the same activity again. Assess how much your abilities have improved.

THINKING CRITICALLY ABOUT QUESTIONS

Here are a few questions from textbooks in different fields, and how I might step back from them to see what I need to do to think through them critically. (These are not the only ways to approach these questions, of course, but they are good ways to start.) Notice that each of the responses focuses on *how* to answer the question critically, not on actually answering it.

1. Here is a question from a geography text. The text gives a half-page labeled "Critical Thinking: Tombouctoo." There are two paragraphs telling about the city of Tombouctoo (Timbuktu), which was a fabulously

(continued)

THINKING CRITICALLY ABOUT QUESTIONS (Continued)

rich, important urban market city on an ancient caravan route across the Sahara. Then the trade routes changed and Tombouctoo was bypassed; it's now a poor, mostly deserted city that plays no important role in today's world. The book then asks:

> Compare Tombouctoo's location with that of Trabzon on the Black Sea in modern-day Turkey. Among which great empires was Trabzon once a major contact and trading point? How important is it today? Do you know of any other once-great cities that have declined as trade routes bypassed them?[2]

What do I need to do to answer the question critically?

a. Well, since the question calls for a comparison (a critical-thinking process), I will need to read about Trabzon. Even before reading, though, I can assume that Trabzon too was an urban trading center in a place where trade routes focused, and that it too was later bypassed. So, I will not simply be gathering information about Trabzon. I am thinking geographically: I am seeing that *"place"* (in this case, a city's position on a trade route) determines a great deal about that city—its prosperity, its origin, maybe its decline when bypassed. *Place* is a central concept in geography. So I am thinking in terms of a *system*, a *logic*. Figure 14.3 is a concept map of that system.

FIGURE 14.3 *A concept map of our critical thinking about Tombouctoo.*

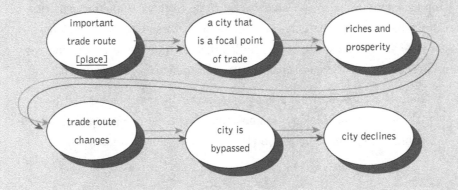

b. As I step back from the question, I also start thinking about another one of the elements, *purpose*: Are most cities located in a certain place for the purpose of cornering trade on some trade route? Is that how cities are founded?

c. The book then asks me to apply this geographical thinking to other once-great cities. For this, I can use my concept map. I begin at the beginning with once-important trade routes. Do I have any examples of that, either in my background knowledge or from other courses? (Some trade routes come to mind: there is the Oregon Trail; there is Route 66; there was the trade between Europe and America before the American Revolution.) I will then expect to find → cities that were a focal point of trade, that → achieved riches and prosperity, but → when trade routes changed, I should expect to find → cities that were bypassed and → then seriously declined. That is following the logic.

(There are implications of the critical thinking so far. I am surprised to find that a city's prosperity does not depend as heavily as I thought on the intelligence and individual business decisions of its inhabitants; those decisions, no matter how smart, may be overridden by the city's place on a bypassed trade route. It is even possible that I might later make a personal decision about where to live based partly on this geographical insight.)

2. Here is a question from a composition textbook. The question asks simply:

What is your definition of obscenity?[3]

Then you are directed to read a paragraph that quotes various Supreme Court justices saying that they can recognize obscenity even without an adequate definition. The paragraph also contains the current Supreme Court criteria for obscenity: "a work must be 'patently

(*continued*)

THINKING CRITICALLY ABOUT QUESTIONS (*Continued*)

offensive' and lack artistic, literary, political, or scientific value to be declared legally obscene." What many people would do at this point is just give their offhand opinion of obscenity. But as I step back from the question, I remind myself that I need to be clear and accurate, and take account of a wide range of possible obscenity cases. A good way to begin might be to write out a thoughtful SEE-I for the concept of *obscenity*. But I also know there are two major sides to this issue. On one side, I need to feel the pull of free speech and the need for free expression. There is a logic, a system, to that way of thinking. But I also feel the pull of those who are offended by obscenity, those who feel children and others can be harmed by it. There is a logic to that way of thinking also. Regardless of which side I am on, I need to write out the logic of both points of view. Doing so will make my written response much deeper and richer.

3. Here is a "Review Question" in a history text:

How did slavery shape Southern society?[4]

This question shows the difference between "learning history" passively versus thinking critically in history. I can answer the question by reading the relevant part of the chapter and writing down the six main ways the book says that slavery shaped Southern society. That's one way. A more meager way is to read the single paragraph of the chapter's "Conclusion." It gives a one-sentence answer to the question. Either way, it looks like a question requiring only recall on my part. If I happen to know some details from lectures or on my own, fine, but that's not expected. I will just find the place in the book where the topic is talked about, so that I can "review" it.

There is not much opportunity here to think the way a historian does. Historians seldom simply repeat an account given by others. Instead, they re-think that account—they look for implications; they give interpretations; they try to make their understanding deeper, more comprehensive. The field of history is a lot more exciting and creative than simply regurgitating information.

I could do some historical thinking about the question:

- What in the American experience is illuminated by thinking about it in terms of the impact of slavery?
- How does this relate to slavery and questions of race in earlier chapters?
- How does the legacy of slavery still have an impact in the present?
- How can I gather evidence about these questions? What primary sources could I use?

4. Another "Review Question" from a different history text:

Discuss the 1928 election as a mirror of the divisions in American society.[5]

Since it asks me to "discuss," it looks like it might call for critical thinking. Really, though, it's merely asking me to repeat a "discussion" already given in the book. It is just a pseudo–critical-thinking question. If I'm going to think critically about the divisions in American society, I'll have to do it on my own.

Q: Looking at the Question

Systems Thinking

A major help in seeing how to answer a critical-thinking question comes when you think in terms of how many "systems" you need to use in order to answer it. Take a simple ethical dilemma as an example. You are a parent, and you wonder whether to tell your young child that there is no Santa Claus. You feel the pull of two systems. One system centers on the importance of honesty; the other centers on the importance of preserving the magic of childhood. This is not a battle simply between one principle and another. Rather, each principle is part of a system; each has a logic that you can think in terms of. What is your concept of honesty? Why is it important? What are its limits? The same questions apply to the importance of preserving the magic of childhood. To answer this question critically, then, you have to think it through using *both* systems.

Thinking through any complex issue requires that you feel the pull of the different systems involved in the question. Then, it requires you to weigh the importance of each and give each system an adequate voice. Maybe you can come to a definite conclusion about the issue, maybe not. But the heart of addressing it is thinking it through in terms of different systems.

Think of the question on page 355 about defining obscenity. To think through this issue critically, you must think in terms of at least two different systems, one centering on free speech and the other centering on people's desire to be protected from what is offensive to them. If you write an essay on obscenity and think it through using only one of these systems, it will be seriously flawed as a piece of critical thinking. You treated a complex question as if it required only one system to think it through. That would automatically diminish the quality of your response.

The word "system" is a good one because it is so flexible. Consider how it applies to a range of examples:

Question: In what major ways did Leonardo embody the spirit of the Renaissance?

Systems to think in terms of: System #1: how Leonardo thought, wrote, lived, and painted—the system that unifies these. I need to grasp the logic of this. I can't just begin writing or just collect information. Next I have to think of system #2, the Renaissance: its values, its tendencies, how it differed from other periods. It is clear that this is a *system* because I could use this Renaissance way of thinking to address topics we have never considered in class. With a solid grasp of that system, I could try to describe how a Renaissance person would think about almost anything—clothes, money, business, travel. Specifically, I could see how much of this system, the spirit of the Renaissance, fits in with the system I saw in Leonardo.

If this is a piece of writing I have to do about Leonardo and the Renaissance, or a presentation in class, thinking it out in terms of multiple *systems* provides a logical outline of how to go about my task effectively and practically. I'll have to do *research*—but I realize by now that research is not just gathering information. It is gathering information as it is linked together by a system or logic. In this case, it is both those systems described previously, plus a third—the way they fit together.

Question: How can I improve my test scores in my political science class?

Systems to think in terms of: You need to think this out in terms of the type of test the teacher gives in this course and the study strategy that fits that type of test. The way tests and strategies fit together is system #1. Thus, if the test is one that emphasizes sheer recall of individual facts, a good strategy might be to use the SEE-I process for important terms, to memorize them using flash cards, or (most effectively) to understand them in terms of the fundamental and powerful concepts of the discipline and the central question of the course. On the other hand, if the test requires overall understanding and reasoning in the discipline, memorizing won't work at all. A good strategy would be to engage in critical reading of the text and critical listening during class discussion, and to spend study time outlining in terms of fundamental and powerful concepts and the central question.

System #2 centers on *you*, what your study strengths and weaknesses are, the amount of time you're willing to invest in improving your test scores in this class, what is feasible to do in the amount of time you have.

Question: What is the atomic mass of hydrogen?

System to use? → You calculate it, using the formula.

Alternative system to use → you look it up on the periodic table.

Question: An exercise from a composition text: "Identify and correct any comma splices in the following paragraph."

System to use? → You look up "comma splice" in the index and apply the rule to the paragraph. Or, you have already internalized the rule: you check the system "in your head."

Question: How much water per day does a person need, on average, to stay healthy.

System to use? → You find the answer from a reliable source.

Almost any issue that is really important, in your life or in the discipline, will require you to think in terms of more than one system. On the other hand, some questions (for example, the last three above) require only a single system to answer them. (Many factual-type questions fall into this category.) Sometimes such questions are decribed as not requiring critical thinking. But that's misleading. It is true that they seldom require *deep* or *broad* critical thinking, but they do require us to be clear, accurate, relevant, precise and sufficient in our answers. Moreover, even if there is only "one system" to consult, we sometimes have a "wrong system" already in place in our minds. With commas, for example, a seriously misleading "system" that people often use is thinking that a comma represents a pause, and so whenever I would pause in a sentence, I should use a comma.

Even in a question as simple as the one about how much water per day a person needs, the source I consult has to be a *reputable* one, and that requires me to make a critical-thinking judgment. People sometimes answer such questions by simply using a Google search, clicking on a link, and reporting the result. Though there is nothing wrong with using Google, it is a tool, and it has to be used thoughtfully. Even for looking up a "fact," the links listed on the Google search page can be unreliable for any number of reasons (bias, poor research, vested financial interests, rumor-mongering, pushing an agenda, and so forth). For example, suppose I'm given the question: "How much water per day does a person need, on average to stay healthy?" So I do a Google search using the key-words "water per day health." In the first link listed, a reader asks how much water per day a person needs. Google then directs me to the next site which says, "The experts have always said, on aver-age, that eight eight-ounce glasses per day will suffice. However, that might not be enough." If I settle for this answer, though, I'll be far from being accurate. The story about needing eight glasses of water per day turns out to be a myth: other more reputable web-sites (for example, the Mayo Clinic or *Scientific American*) say that there is no scientific basis for the claim and that (except in special circumstances) most of the water we need daily comes in the food we eat.[6]

> An effective "research path" for answering one-system questions is often to look them up in a reliable source. What are some of the main research paths (including reliable sources, if that is relevant) you would take to answer one-system questions in the discipline you are studying?

Thinking in terms of systems, using reasoned judgment to weigh the pull of one system against another, is the heart of answering important questions in disciplines. In each family of disciplines, we are required to do something simi-lar: to think in terms of the various systems that are central to that discipline, how those systems interact, modify one another, and sometimes conflict. We also must think in terms of the systems in the world that the discipline investigates.

E: Thinking It Through Using the Elements

So, you start off with a question to answer. You interpret it. You iden-tify the system or systems that you need to use to answer it. You apply these to the question. What do you need to do now?

You have to use the elements of reasoning; go around the circle (page 127).

Some Questions Need to Be Thought Through Fully; Some Don't

Suppose the question you are considering is important to you. Maybe it's a paper, a major assignment, a presentation in class, or your preparation for an essay exam. Maybe it's something that is important to you personally or professionally—a decision about how to budget your time between work, school, family, and recreation; or how to deal with a client, patient, student, or customer who does not fit the usual profile and requires special help.

You need to go around the whole circle.

Why? Because any one of the elements could turn out to be crucial for this problem. And, besides, this is an *important* question to you. You need to give it the time and attention it deserves in your thinking. With practice, thinking in terms of the elements can become as comfortable and natural as looking where you're going when you drive. Even if you spend only a minute or so on each element, make it a focused minute, with your attention riveted on that element as it applies to the question.

After going around the circle, step back once again. Do some synthesis and re-assemble the logic of the question and your answer to it as a whole.

On the other hand, maybe the question you're addressing is not such an important one; maybe it doesn't need to be treated as fully. Maybe, as you read it, one, two, or three of the elements jump out as the ones you should focus on. You don't always have to go around the full circle.

Here is an example (several others are given in the exercises). A political science text contains a short essay on the issue of gay and lesbian rights. It then asks:

> What is Your Opinion? Should churches and other religious institutions take positions on political issues and candidates?[7]

A critical-thinking response: the element *point of view* stands out from the question. To think this through, you have to give full weight both to those who favor such a thesis and to those who are against it. You have to give the strongest reasons on each side and state them fair-mindedly.

A second element is *implications and consequences*. What, in your most reasonable judgment, will result if churches and religious institutions *do* back political issues and candidates?

A third element stands out: *information*. You can give a thoughtful, balanced answer to this question or just shoot from the hip. You may have an impression about this question, but this is a political science course, not a place to trade unsupported opinions. You need to find information that is as accurate and up to date as possible.

S: Using the Standards

The standards are present in every single act of critical thinking. (If no critical-thinking standards are used, it's not critical thinking at all.) To think in terms of the standards you can:

- Use the standards check (pages 334–335)
- Evaluate around the circle (pages 331–332).

  You use the standards both:

- *While* you are answering a question.
- *Afterward*, when you are checking your work, and revising it to make it better.

Like the elements, the standards are something you need to internalize. That comes as you practice using them, especially as you consciously and explicitly practice using them. You will be better at some standards than others, and that can change from one topic to another.

Internalizing and incorporating even one standard into your way of thinking can substantially improve your thinking everywhere. Take *depth*. Looking for underlying complexities or underlying explanations can make your understanding of almost everything around you deeper. For example, often when people reason, they have a goal, and then they think out the means for achieving the goal. That's critical thinking, but it is probably not *deep* critical thinking. If I think about it more deeply, I'll ask myself what complexities will arise as a carry out those means, what problems will arise. I'll also ask myself, "What are some of the problems that will come about if I *do* achieve that goal?"

D: Thinking It Through in Terms of the Discipline

When you think critically about a question through the lens of a discipline, you use the whole QEDS core process (page 345). The elements and standards are essential in addressing any question. When we add the discipline, we can focus on four key approaches. Each of them is different, but all of them overlap to a considerable degree:

- systems
- fundamental and powerful concepts in the discipline
- the central question of the discipline
- the point of view of the discipline.

Systems

When you identify the discipline-based systems involved in the question, it gives you a key insight into how to go about answering it. It is a great benefit to think in terms of such systems. It means that you don't start off from zero, and you don't start off from unexamined background stories that may be misleading. Focusing on discipline-based systems gives you a framework for addressing a question in a way that is knowledgeable, centered, and often impressive.

In a straightforward way, thinking a question through in terms of the discipline means learning to think in terms of the main systems that are used in that discipline. Part of thinking in systems is knowing the preferred way that type of question is addressed in that discipline. There is a variety of systems, but here are some examples, together with some of the disciplines they might apply to:

- Use well-established theories and laws (natural sciences)
- Use respected points of view within the discipline (literary criticism, art theories)
- Use case studies and expert practice (business, health sciences)
- Use studies, experiments and their findings (social sciences)
- Use highly regarded opposing points of view (philosophy, political science).

All of these clearly involve thinking things through in terms of systems in the discipline.

Fundamental and Powerful Concepts, Central Question, Point of View of the Discipline

Recall that fundamental and powerful concepts are those basic concepts that lie at the heart of a discipline or course (see pages 241–244). (As a reminder, examples might be: homeostasis in biology, Romanticism in literature, supply and demand in economics.) The central question of the course is usually closely related: it is the most central question that the course is addressing (see pages 246–249). This book speaks of the central question as if there were only one, and that is the ideal case. There may in fact be several closely related central questions, but there cannot be many. (A biology example might be, "How do living things work?" Or, breaking that down only a little further, "How does the body work?" "How did organisms come to be the way they are [the origin of species]?" "How are life-forms in a community interdependent?") The point of view of a discipline is that distinctive way practitioners in the field look at things: it includes the domain (the objects or events the discipline focuses on), the way the items in that domain are categorized or classified (these form a system of concepts), and the connections someone in the discipline "sees." It is a major goal of the course that you incorporate those fundamental and powerful concepts, central questions, and point of view into your thinking patterns.

FIGURE 14.4 *Concept map for thinking about the influence of place.*

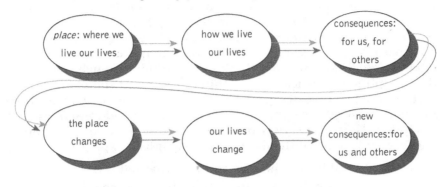

In an earlier example, we worked through a geography question about Tombouctoo and cities on trade routes. We worked it through using the system illustrated in Figure 14.3 on page 354. But we can think it through more deeply as shown in Figure 14.4.

Probably the most fundamental and powerful concept in geography is *place* or *the influence of place*. So, as you think the answer out in terms of this specific system, you are asking yourself, "How does the influence of place determine the fate of cities?"

You have already been addressing this question, but in a much more specific way, when you reasoned out how changing trade routes affect the prosperity of cities. But thinking it out explicitly in terms of *place* is much more conscious—and much more fundamental and powerful. Now, your answer to this question will relate to all the other topics you have learned to think out in terms of *place*. Instead of this being merely one specific system (amid hundreds of other specific systems), all the geographical systems you use are unified by the fundamental and powerful concept of *place*. Not only is the fate of cities influenced by their place on a trade route, but our lives in countless dimensions are also heavily influenced by *where* we live them.

The same is true for the central question. As you think through specific systems, or research some specific information, you relate it to the central question in the course. The central question and the fundamental and powerful concepts are usually closely linked. The central question in a geography course might be: How does the geography of *where* something happens influence *what* happens?

This is thinking geographically. It is thinking the way a geographer thinks. It allows us to see the world from the point of view of the discipline. Geographers can visit Tombouctoo or Washington, D.C., or Los Angeles, or the city or town you live in, and they'll see

Fundamental and powerful concepts sometimes sound unimportant when you write them down. "Place" may seem that way. Part of what makes concepts fundamental and powerful is that they are deep. So you have to make a conscious effort to see them as deep. "Place" can seem unimportant, but it can be incredibly deep: Without being a geographer, it's hard to comprehend just how fundamental and powerful it is, how much of people's lives—how they live, what they do for a living, whom they marry, when they die—is determined by *place.*

it in very different categories from those a non-geographer will see. As I write this paragraph, I am in a coffee shop in New Orleans. I see people (who look different from one another), old buildings (with balconies and high ceilings), streets (paved with shells rather than gravel), flat land; I smell gumbo in the air, feel the humidity (even in late September), and hear sounds of Cajun music. Looking with the eyes of a geographer, though, I see all of those plus a lot more: subtropical weather patterns, the ecosystems and topography of the alluvial lands of the Mississippi delta, cultural diffusion, the ongoing migration of populations. I automatically understand a great deal more about what I see.

When I wrote the lines above this, back in 2004, I did not anticipate Hurricane Katrina coming to destroy much of New Orleans and the Gulf Coast. Geographers did. By thinking in terms of *place,* they—virtually unanimously—knew a hurricane was coming, a devastating one, if not in that year then in another, but soon.

Why Use Fundamental and Powerful Concepts, Central Questions, and Point of View?

So why do this? Why add to your work in a course by thinking things through using fundamental and powerful concepts?

It's a misleading question. Though it is more work in the short run, it's not *much* more work. It just looks like more on paper, and because you're not used to it. It is really a shift in *emphasis.* Sometimes answering the question in terms of fundamental and powerful concepts comes in just a flash of realization, an Aha! After you get used to this way of thinking, it will make *all* the questions in the discipline much more answerable. In fact, it will cut down on the work you have to do. What *is* work is memorizing and retaining a hundred different pieces of information or thinking through a hundred unrelated specific systems. And then you're left with that sinking feeling as those memorized bits and pieces disappear without a trace—and it is as if you did it all for nothing, or just for a number on a transcript somewhere. Many of those pieces, though—maybe all of them—can be thought through far more efficiently (and even retained!) when you use fundamental and powerful concepts and central questions.

Critical Writing: Using the Core Process To Write a Paper

The heart of critical writing—as of critical anything—is reasoning through a question using both the elements and standards. What follows is a set of steps that can help turn your critical thinking into a piece of critical writing. These are general steps: they have to be adapted to fit the question, problem or topic you are writing on. Your teacher may have guidelines that will be more applicable than the general steps here.

Often when people write a paper, they just pick their main points "out of the air." Sometimes they don't even start with a thesis statement, but even if they do, their main points may still simply be ones that happen to come to mind. Critical writing is significantly different from that. It grows from the logic of a topic (pages 146–148), from analyzing the topic by going around the circle, so you see the interrelated parts of it and how they fit together in a coherent whole. In critical writing, then, both the thesis statement of your paper and all your main points come directly out of the logic of the topic. The *topic* of your paper is the question at issue you are addressing, and your paper is the way you answer that question. The content of your paper is therefore really the same as your analysis (or at least the most important parts of it), but written out and developed in paragraphs. The *thesis statement* is the important parts of your analysis crystalized into a single sentence. Thus everything grows from the logic, from going around the circle. As a result, the parts of your paper form a well-integrated whole.

There are six steps—three on pre-writing, two on the actual writing, and one on revision—so the process may look daunting at first glance. But you are already familiar with most of it. You are already used to writing an analysis by going around the circle, to doing a Standards Check, and to using SEE-I. What remains is to pick out the *main points* of your analysis, crystallize them into a *thesis statement*, and let the *logical outline* of your paper flow from them. You then have to *support the weak points* in your reasoning, and write the paper itself using SEE-I to develop your points. Of course, no set of steps will guarantee that the product you come up with will automatically be a finished piece of critical writing. There is a lot more to writing than can be listed. The steps described here may help substantially.

The whole process of critical writing can be compressed into three short sentences: **Reasoned analysis** of a topic generates the **structure** of the paper. The structure exposes the **weak points** and generates **writing the paper** itself using SEE-I. **Reflection and revision** lets you **complete** the paper as a piece of critical writing.

Step One: Reasoned Analysis.

Writing a paper begins with **going around the circle** of elements, analyzing and laying out the logic of the topic you are addressing: its purpose or goals, the main question at issue, the main information your paper will be presenting on the topic, the main assumptions you are making in the paper, and so forth. The analysis will include any research you have done that you plan to incorporate into your paper. It will also include the *multiple systems* (pages 357–360) you use to reason your way through the topic or question.

This is a pre-writing step. It will result in something like Chris's analysis of the logic of getting married (pages 149–153) or the analysis of the logic of earth sciences (pages 236–237) or perhaps like an analysis you have done by going around the circle (page 127). The result will be a bulleted list of well-thought-out responses to each of the 8+ elements and a sense of the logic of the topic as a whole. This is a solid foundation for writing.

You need to make a reasonable choice about how full your analysis needs to be. You may decide to include *more*—or *less*—than the core process. *More:* You can incorporate the discipline or other processes into your reasoning in a rich way. As you go around the circle, then, your analysis might well include fundamental and powerful concepts, the central question, the point of view of the discipline, and other insights from your course; it can involve evaluation, comparison and contrast, and so forth. *Less:* Or you may decide to focus on just a few of the elements, those you judge to be most crucial: there may be time pressure, for example (as in writing a timed essay exam), or you may have deeply ingrained paper-writing habits that are hard to break. There is a choice here you have to make.

You finish Step One by doing a **Standards Check** (pages 334–335). This is a reflection and revision step. The more important your piece of writing is for you, the more beneficial it is to confront the questions in the Standards Check in a conscientious and open way. If your writing project requires research, you have to check on whether the information you report is accurate, whether the sources you have used are reliable, and whether you have exercised intellectual integrity (page 351) by giving credit to your sources. And as you write the paper itself, you'll still be using the standards: checking for clarity, accuracy, relevance, and so forth. You'll be asking yourself if you should go deeper (exploring more of the complexities) or broader (looking at other points of view).

Going around the circle and then doing a Standards Check gives you a **reasoned analysis**, the foundation for critical writing.

Step Two: Structure. The structure of your paper involves figuring out **the main points** you will be making, formulating a **thesis statement** in relation to them, and then constructing a **logical outline** of your paper. Again, everything flows from going around the circle.

Using your reasoned analysis of the topic from Step 1, you figure out the **main points** of your paper by focusing on those parts of the analysis that are most important for making your case in the paper you are writing. The most important points may be just a few of the elements, or they may include all or most of them. From these main points will emerge both your thesis statement and the logical outline of your paper.

You can then formulate the **thesis statement** of your paper directly from the main points. It is a sentence that crystallizes and unifies them, taken all together. It is a statement of the way you will be addressing the topic overall. The thesis statement will also be a touchstone to help you keep in mind how your main points fit together to make your paper a coherent whole. (There is an intimate connection between the main points of your paper and your thesis statement. Many writers formulate their thesis statement *first*, and then derive their main points from it; also, they often go back and forth between the two, adjusting each to get them to fit together well. The key thing is that both main points and thesis statement come from a reasoned analysis.)

The **logical outline** of your paper also comes directly from the main points, written in outline form. (Thus four main points will give the body of your paper four main sections.) In fact, if you write out the main points as sentences, they will often be usable directly as topic sentences in the body of the paper itself.

Step Three: Weakpoints. If your paper says something substantive, there will almost certainly be weak points. The challenge is to **identify** them, to notice where the weaknesses lie, and then to **support** them with back-up.

Identifying weakpoints. Picture someone who strongly disagrees with what you are saying or at least is very skeptical. Ask yourself: Which of your main points would the person be most likely to take issue with? Those are weak points. Alternatively, the weakest points in your outline—the ones someone would object to—may be parts you have *not* stated. Maybe the objection would focus on unstated assumptions you are making or on a consequence you haven't noticed. If that happens, you need to state the weak point explicitly in your outline so you can support it. In critical writing, you don't hide the weak points of your paper. Rather, you put them out in front, you support them, and you let readers evaluate them for themselves.

Weak points are often difficult to see because as you write your paper you may become more and more attached to what you are saying. It can almost blind you to the objections someone else may raise. Here again the standards help. You can ask, from the point of view of someone who disagrees, "Is this relevant? Is the case being made sufficient? Is it accurate?"

→ A good rule of thumb is to take it as a *requirement* that you identify at least one important weakpoint in your outline.

Supporting the weak points. The weak points in your paper are ones that need to be supported—with reasons, with argument, with elaboration, with more information. You then need to incorporate that support into your outline.

Pause and reflect. At this point, you should have a fairly complete outline (although it can still be revised). You have the main points written out and organized. The weakest of your points are supported. You have a sense of the whole. You are clear about the purpose of your paper and the question at issue you are addressing.

Now is a good time for reflection, for contemplating the writing you are about to do, the logical structure it will rest on. This is a good time for making revisions to your thought process.

Step Four: Writing the Paper.

The **introduction** can be just a paragraph or it can be a longer section. In it, you lay out for the reader the question at issue you'll be addressing in the paper, how you plan to answer it (your thesis statement), and your goals or purpose in writing the paper. You may also decide to summarize the main points you will be presenting in the body of the paper and the point of view you will be using to answer the question at issue.

Write **the body of the paper**. With the clear, logical outline you have constructed, writing the paper should be considerably more satisfying than if you just started writing from scratch, saying the first things that come into your mind and hoping it will work out.

A good way to write the body of your paper is to use SEE-I throughout (pages 108–111). Start off with just your first main point. *State* it clearly in a sentence or two. Then *elaborate* on it, explaining it more fully, in more detail. This may take several paragraphs. (You'll want to keep the audience in mind as you do, realizing that you will have to explain a lot more to the reader than you think you have to. After all, you've *done* the analysis; you've organized it coherently; you've seen how the parts fit together—*of course* it seems clear to you. But you have to put yourself in the place of someone who has not thought about this issue very much before. You have to elaborate enough so the reader understands you clearly.) Continuing the SEE-I, you next give a good *example*, maybe more than one, of that first main point. Maybe you can give a *contrasting example* so the reader can pinpoint what you are saying. Then, when appropriate, you give a good *illustration*. Again, the goal is to help the reader see exactly what you are saying, exactly what you mean.

Do this in turn for each of your main points, including the supporting ones. Your paper will grow organically. All the points you are making will be important ones. The sentences you write will not be filler. Rather, each of them will be directly relevant to the individual point you are making and to the overall development of your paper.

FIGURE 14.5 *Critical writing.*

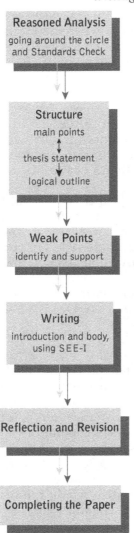

Step Five: Re-read, Reflect, and Revise.   You have written almost the whole paper now. Although it's OK to write the concluding section right away, this is a good time to reflect again and to revise what you have written. Read over the paper. Check for clear topic sentences, for breaks in the logical flow from one main point to the next, for weakpoints that need further back-up. Check for grammar and spelling too. It is often beneficial to take a break now, if you can, maybe to wait a day or two to get a fresh look at the paper you've written. It often helps if do this before writing the concluding section. You need to guard against the feeling of finality, of being done with it. Your paper is still a work in progress.

This is also a good time to work with someone else. Have others read your paper. Get feedback. Ask them to make a mark every time they have to go back and read a sentence a second time. That is a good indication that you need to re-write that part.

Step Six: Completing the Paper. Write **the concluding section**. Again, this can be a single paragraph or it can be longer. In this section, you may want to recapitulate the question at issue you were addressing, your thesis statement, and your main purpose in writing the paper. You may also want to sum up how you have answered the question. Readers should feel they have been brought full circle now. They should have a clear sense of the logic of your paper.

The Work of Critical Thinking

Whether it is in writing or reading, in analysis or evaluation, in the discipline as well as in your life outside school, critical thinking creates value. It takes effort, especially before you get used to it. But it has clear practical benefits that far exceed the effort. It will produce better answers, better grades, in more courses, in more professions, with ultimately less work, than any alternative. More than that, it gives insight that can make your life richer, by bringing the elements, the standards, and the disciplines into learning to think things through.

Some Outcomes

As you finish this book . . .

1. You should be able to *state, elaborate, give examples* and *illustrations* (SEE-I) of the core process of critical thinking and how it applies in the discipline.

2. You should be able to *describe the path* you would take to think through a question, any question, and give examples of it as well.

3. Based on the way you've learned to think critically in this discipline, you should be able to *apply* the same processes to other courses you are taking. Taking this course, in this discipline should make many other courses and disciplines clearer for you. You should be able to give examples of this.

4. You should be able to *identify, describe,* and *give examples* of some of your main strengths and some of your main weaknesses as a critical thinker.

5. You should be able, at least in a preliminary way, to *identify*, *elaborate on*, and *give examples* and *illustrations* of some of the main critical-thinking character traits. You should also be able to *give examples* of when you or others have exemplified (or not exemplified) the trait.

6. You should be able to *identify* and *explain* the systems you would use to respond critically to questions.

7. You should be able to *engage in critical writing*: able to write a paper on a topic by going around the circle of elements, using the standards, constructing a logical outline, supporting weak-points, and using SEE-I for development.

8. You should feel a growing mastery of the outcomes in earlier chapters. You should be able to take any outcome from any chapter in this book and:

   ■ State, elaborate, exemplify and illustrate it
   ■ Relate it to critical thinking in the discipline you are studying
   ■ Describe how it fits into critical thinking as a whole.

As with some of the outcomes in the other chapters in this book, your accomplishments may not be as secure as the outcomes listed above might lead you to believe. Critical thinking takes time, practice, and commitment.

Ideas for Writing

(General guidelines for "Ideas for Writing" are on page 116.)

1. What are some standard activities that, in your best judgment, would work out better for all concerned if the people who engaged in them exercised more critical thinking? Explain.

2. Make the previous question more specific. What are some standard human activities that, in your judgment, would work out better for all concerned → if people reflected on their purpose more? → if people reflected more deeply on their assumptions? [continue, focusing on other elements]; → if people paid more attention to being clear? → to being accurate? [continue, focusing on other standards]; → if people reflected on what we can learn from biology, → from sociology [continue, focusing on the discipline in this course and on other disciplines you are studying]. Explain.

3. Explain the core process of critical thinking as if to someone who has never taken a class either in it or in the discipline you are studying. What are the overall benefits (within the course, in other courses, in life outside of school) of thinking critically from the point of view of the discipline? In your judgment are there significant disadvantages as well? Explain.

4. Look over the critical-thinking character traits again. To what extent can a person slowly build strengths in one or more of these traits in his or her life? What are some ways a person might go about doing that?

5. Think of writers. Many people are intellectually engaged in writing. They find it fulfilling; they take pride in doing it well; they develop themselves and their beliefs in their writing. Or think of Jane Goodall, going out to observe chimps in the wild. Or think of people who are deeply drawn to being in health-care, or science, or literature. Again, the name for that is intellectual engagement. What would it be like if you were intellectually engaged in a discipline (maybe the discipline in this course)? How would it affect the questions you ask, the answers you accept, the implications you search for . . . ?

6. Create your own ideas for writing in relation to this book, this discipline, this course.

Tell Your Story

(The idea behind "Tell Your Story" and some suggestions about doing it are on page 117.)

1. Look back at the "Tell Your Story" questions from Chapter 5. Your personal history has changed a little since then, in that you have read this book and reflected on critical thinking across the curriculum. Respond to some of those questions again, focusing on any changes that may have taken place in you since then. If possible, it is better to revisit them near the end of the semester. (Remember, that any changes will probably seem subtle or slight. Change takes time and practice.)

2. Choose one of the critical-thinking character traits to reflect on (for example, *intellectual courage*), and write it in the blank:
Who in your life has shown significant _____?
Describe your experiences with that person. Give examples.

   By contrast, who in your life has *seemed* to value_____, but in reality did not value it much? Describe your experiences here as well.

3. Have you ever found yourself taking a course "just for a grade?" Or giving answers that you think the teacher expects of you, without even wondering whether it made sense to you? By contrast, have you taken courses in areas you are intensely interested in? Or given answers that, after carefully thinking them through, seemed to you to be right? How were these experiences different for you? Do you see one as more positive than the other?

4. What is something in your life that *you* are intellectually engaged in? It will be a topic that you are intensely interested in, one you want to learn about, often not just for any practical good it will do you, but for its own sake. What disciplines or areas in school could you become intellectually engaged in? What about them appeals to you?

CHAPTER 14 Exercises

The exercises to Chapter 14 are geared to addressing questions in your specific discipline or disciplines. Those questions will be everywhere: asked in the text, asked by your instructor, by fellow students, by you. Some will be unasked but implicit in the readings and the class experience. You need to practice analyzing and answering these by using QEDS within the discipline, and you need to receive feedback from classmates and from instructors.

   14.1 Go around the circle in the discipline; do a Standards Check.

   a. Go around the circle with respect to the discipline as a whole. Make this a pre-test: keep your answer, but don't look at it during the semester. Repeat this analysis near the end of the course as a post-test; do a Standards Check; compare the two; assess how your understanding of the discipline has changed and deepened.

b. Go around the circle with respect to an important sub-discipline in your field (e.g., if your discipline is psychology, → analyze experimental psych, or social psych, etc.; business → marketing, accounting, etc.). Do a Standards Check.

c. Go around the circle with respect to the family of disciplines yours belongs to (e.g., social sciences, natural sciences, arts, humanities, business). Do a Standards Check.

d. Go around the circle with respect to this book on thinking critically. Do a Standards Check.

14.2 Here is an excerpt from a text on nutrition:

> In your lifetime, you are going to read thousands of newspaper and website headlines, as well as watch and listen to countless television and radio reports. Your critical thinking skill in evaluating the sources and information being presented will be your best friend when it comes to deciding which blurbs to believe. This skill may also save you considerable money by helping you avoid nutrition gimmicks. When it comes to assessing nutrition information in the media, it's worth your time and effort to find out where it came from and why (or if) you should care.[8]

For Exercises 14.3 through 14.7: Briefly describe the system or systems you would use to think it through to a reasonable answer. If it requires only one system to answer it, identify some questions you could ask to infuse it with more critical thinking.

14.3 A question from a biology text:

> If all organisms had not descended from a common ancestor, and did not possess many common genes and mechanisms of development, would we be able to perform valid medical research [for humans] using mice and in some cases, Drosophila? Why or why not?[9]

[Drosophila, I find out from the text, are fruit flies.]

14.4 A book on the history of the arts:

> SUMMARY. After reading this chapter you should be able to: Identify and explain the political and religious conditions that led to the Reformation, including the theological and dogmatic contentions of Erasmus, Luther, Zwingli, Calvin, and Montaigne.[10]

14.5   A question on a legal case from a business law text:

> Intoxication. Betty Galloway, an alcoholic, signed a settlement agreement upon her divorce from her husband, Henry Galloway. Henry, in Betty's absence in court, stated that she had lucid intervals from her alcoholism, had been sober for two months, and was lucid when she signed the settlement agreement on September 22, 1978. Betty only moved to vacate the settlement agreement on September 27, 1978, after she had retained present legal counsel. On January 23, 1979, Betty was declared incompetent to handle her person and affairs, and a guardian and conservator was appointed. Betty, through her guardian, sued to have the settlement agreement voided. Who wins? [*Galloway v. Galloway*, 281 N.W.2d 804 (N.D. 1979)][11]

14.6   One of 20 "Review Questions" in a chapter of a geology textbook:

> What is the cataclysmic event called in which an exploding star produces all of the elements heavier than iron?[12]

14.7   Someone asks you to give your reaction to the question of abortion.

14.8   Analyze the following passage in terms of the elements and standards. It is a paragraph from the Constitution of the Islamic Republic of Iran:

> The family unit is the foundation of society and the main institution for the growth and advancement of mankind . . . . It is the principal duty of the Islamic government to regard women as the unifying factor of the family unit and its position. They are a factor in bringing the family out of the service of propagating consumerism and exploitation and renewing the vital and valuable duty of motherhood in raising educated human beings . . . . As a result motherhood is accepted as a most profound responsibility in the Muslim viewpoint and will, therefore, be accorded the highest value and generosity.[13]

14.9   My geology text lists 28 "important terms" and 14 main points of "summary" for Chapter 2 alone. Chapter 2 is on minerals. Chapter 3 (on igneous rocks) lists 35 additional "important terms" and 15 main points of "summary." That's in 46 pages of the book, and there are over 600 pages all together. At this rate, by the end of the book I'll have to know almost 800 important terms and around 400 main points of summary. What can I do?

14.10   What elements would you focus on to answer the following question from a literature text? It follows a story by Ernest Hemingway, "The Short Happy Life of Francis Macomber," and it asks a question about the three main characters.

> What do Wilson, Francis, and Margot each think it means to be a real man? What would you guess Hemingway thinks?[14]

14.11   Why do many people (including you, maybe) spend so much money on their weddings? What is the best way to lose weight? Why is Chicago so much more prosperous than Buffalo, New York? Why are the Rockies so much higher than the Appalachians? Why do young people, on average, drive faster than older people? Why do people like watching sports so much?

14.12   Look again at the questions in Exercise 14.11. Notice that you may not know enough about the relevant disciplines to identify the systems you would use to answer them critically. Write out some ordinary, everyday questions that might be illuminated by the discipline in *this* course. What systems would you use to think it through?

14.13   **Writing thesis statements.** Look at any written examples of your course work in which you have analyzed something by going around the circle. For each one, do the following: pick out the main points from it as if you were going to write a paper. Then write out a thesis statement for the projected paper. Do this by crystalizing the main points into a single sentence.

14.14   **Critical writing.** In Exercise 14.1a, you gave an analysis of the discipline you are studying by going around the circle with respect to it. Now write a paper about the logic of that discipline: from your analysis, construct a logical outline, choose your main points, write out a thesis statement, support the weakest points, write the introduction, write the body of the paper using SEE-I, and (after a time to reflect and revise) write the concluding section.

14.15   Write a paper about getting married from your point of view. Use Chris's analysis of marriage (pages 149–1535) as a model from which to construct your own. The analysis you give is the foundation of your paper. From it select the most important points (try to choose only three or four) and try to choose three or four and crystalize them into a well-written thesis statement. Pick out the weakest points—the ones that are most in need of support. Picture someone who disagrees with your analysis—maybe one of your friends or even someone you used to be involved with romantically. If possible, incorporate the discipline you are studying into your analysis and outline.

Alternatively, write a paper about getting married from Chris's point of view.

14.16 In your course, find an issue, a problem, or a critical-thinking question important enough to merit going around the full circle. Then, do the analysis and synthesis by going around the circle. Do a Standards Check.

14.17 Look carefully at some critical-thinking questions in your subject textbook. Identify the elements of reasoning that stand out and must be addressed in answering the questions.

14.18 Take some important paragraphs from readings in your course. Analyze them in terms of the elements and standards (as in Exercise 14.8).

14.19 SEE-I runs all the way through this book. That's because it is so widely usable. For example, suppose you are a student learning about X: without SEE-I, all you have is the *impression* that you understand X; with SEE-I, on the other hand, you have (a) a *test* of whether you actually do understand it; (b) a record of what you did understand; and (c) a study guide for the future.

Look back at three or four questions in this book, or some "Ideas for Writing," or questions from "Tell Your Story." Envision how much richer and clearer your response would be if you had included an SEE-I.

14.20 **Group work. Answer with critical thinking.** Sit in groups of four.

A asks a question in the discipline or related to it. The group gets two minutes for thinking.
B describes the systems that need to be thought through to answer the question.
C explains which elements need to be addressed to answer it.
D (having taken some notes) does a Standards Check on B's and C's responses.
Switch roles.

14.21   **Group work.** Discuss critically:

- How does Figure 14.1 work? How does it describe critical thinking?
- How much work will it take to engage in critical thinking in this course? To what extent will it save work?
- Will it transfer to other courses? to day-to-day life?

14.22   Look back at the outcomes for each of the chapters. Look only at the "Outcomes" section—don't look back at other parts of the text. See how many of the outcomes you can accomplish now. When you are finished, evaluate how clearly, accurately, and relevantly you did them.

DAILY PRACTICE
At incorporating critical thinking into your life and your learning

Look back at the instructions on pages 122–123. Remember that a major difficulty of engaging with critical thinking is bringing yourself to actually do it. The skills, though vitally important, are not enough.

14.23   **Engage with critical thinking.** Spend a period of time each day practicing your critical thinking as a whole. Listen. Observe. Read. Write. As you do, notice the elements. Notice the standards—their presence or absence. Apply the fundamental and powerful concepts. Question things using the central question. Observe and connect using the point of view of the discipline. Put it all together.

14.24   **Engage with the character traits of being a critical thinker.** Look on page 351–352 for a list of some character traits associated with being a critical thinker. Although these have not been explained in detail, spend some time each day exercising a trait, as you understand it. On one day, you might practice intellectual humility: admitting when you don't know things; explicitly taking back views you have when you realize you don't have the evidence to back them up; recognizing areas that matter to you where you don't really know very much; confronting the large number of beliefs that have simply been passed on to you (by peers, by entertainment, by popular culture) that you haven't really examined. The next day, do the same for another one of the traits on the list.

14.25   **Engage with critical writing.** You should have a host of questions now, about the discipline and about your life. Hold one of them in front of your mind and describe how you would go about writing a paper on it. Think of the elements it would involve most importantly and how you would turn it into a logical outline. Get a sense of the whole. Construct a thesis statement. Then, identify the weakest points and describe how you would support them. Think about how you would use SEE-I to develop your paper.

You don't have to do this all at once, and you don't have to actually write the paper. You can take notes, but the important thing is just to think it out, step by step. Try this with different questions.

Notes

Chapter 5

1. "A Taxonomy of Critical Thinking Skills and Dispositions," in *Teaching Thinking Skills: Theory and Practice*, ed. Joan Boykoff Baron and Robert J. Sternberg (New York: Freeman, 1987), 9–26. I especially like Ennis's definition, not only because it is the classic one (I believe his first formulation of it came in 1964), but because Bob told me, years later, that it was because of my arguments at the Second International Conference on Critical Thinking at Sonoma State (back in 1982) that he added the "or do" to the end of his definition. I hold deeply that critical thinking needs to be infused in our doings (anything from recycling waste to riding my bike) as much as in our believings.

2. Matthew Lipman, *Thinking in Education* (Cambridge: Cambridge University Press, 1995).

3. The answer is that they stay in prison until they die. Actually, in Louisiana a person can be sentenced to life in prison for many crimes, including drug offenses and armed robbery. For these people too, "life" means life.

4. Michael Scriven, *Reasoning* (Point Reyes, CA: Edgepress, 1976), 26.

5. Frederick H. Martini, *Fundamentals of Anatomy & Physiology*, 7th ed. (San Francisco: Pearson, 2006), 23.

6. Teresa Audeskirk, Gerald Audeskirk, and Bruce E. Byers, *Biology: Life on Earth*, 8th ed. (Upper Saddle River, NJ: Pearson, 2008), 202.

7. Penelope J. E. Davies, et al., *Janson's Basic History of Western Art*, 8th ed. (Upper Saddle River, NJ: Pearson, 2009), 17.

8. Brian M. Fagan, *People of the Earth: An Introduction to World Prehistory*, 13th ed. (Boston: Prentice Hall, 2010), 87.

9. Rachel Herz, *The Scent of Desire: Discovering Our Enigmatic Sense of Smell* (New York: William Morrow, 2007), 51.

Chapter 6

1. Adapted from Richard Paul © The Foundation for Critical Thinking, www.criticalthinking.org; cct@criticalthinking.org. Reprinted with permission.

2. Richard T. Wright, *Environmental Science: Toward a Sustainable Future*, 10th ed. (Upper Saddle River, NJ: Pearson, 2008), 644.

3. *Courage to Change* (New York: Al-Anon, 1992), 115.

4. John Adkins Richardson, *Art: The Way It Is* (Englewood Cliffs, NJ: Prentice Hall, 1973), 6.

5. Paul Heyne, *The Economic Way of Thinking*, 7th ed. (New York: Macmillan, 1994), 22.

6. Scott O. Lilienfeld, et al., *Psychology: A Framework for Everyday Thinking* (Boston: Pearson, 2010), 201.

7. No. The passage implies only that ginkgo does not work for normal people. It leaves open the question of whether it works for non-normal people.

8. Elliot Aronson, *The Social Animal* (New York: Worth, 2008), 30.

9. Thomas A. Mappes and Jane S. Zembaty, *Social Ethics: Morality and Social Policy* (Boston: McGraw-Hill, 2007), 482.

Chapter 10

1. Richard Feynman, *What Do You Care What Other People Think?* (New York: Norton, 1988), 16.

2. Jennifer Reed, conversation with author.

3. *Tampa Tribune*, September 17, 1996.

4. Actually they do have a bit of a logic: the keyboard was originally designed to slow down your typing. That's why the keys are in an "illogical" arrangement that makes you use your weakest fingers to strike the most frequent letters.

5. This question comes from Anisa Al-Khatab, conversation with author.

6. Sarah Blaffer Hrdy, *Mother Nature: A History of Mothers, Infants, and Natural Selection*, (New York: Pantheon, 1999), xi.

7. Adapted from Kurt Reusser, "Problem Solving Beyond the Logic of Things," cited in A. H. Schoenfeld, "On Mathematics and Sense Making: An Informal Attack on the Unfortunate Divorce of Formal and Informal Mathematics," in J. Voss, D. Perkins, and J. Segal (eds.), *Informal Reasoning and Education* (Hillsdale, NJ: Erlbaum, 1990), 311–343.

8. They are not exactly the same question. (I have, for example, omitted virtue ethics). The point is that to answer the ordinary everyday question we have to explicitly consider the two ethical theories.

9. Lynn Quitman Troyka and Jerold Nudelman, *Steps in Composition*, 7th ed. (Upper Saddle River, NJ: Prentice Hall, 1999), 31.

10. Stephen P. Robbins, *Managing Today*, 2nd ed. (Upper Saddle River, NJ: Prentice Hall, 2000), xiii.

Chapter 14

1. A fuller description of the traits of mind can be found in Paul and Elder, *Critical Thinking*, (2006), 2–19.

2. Edward F. Bergman and Tom L. McKnight, *Introduction to Geography* (Upper Saddle River, NJ: Prentice Hall, 1993), 148.

3. Troyka and Nudelman, 128, 161.

4. Jennifer D. Keene, Saul Cornell, and Edward T. O'Donnell, *Visions of America: A History of the United States*, vol. 1 (Boston: Prentice Hall, 2010), 280.

5. John Mack Faragher et al., *Out of Many: A History of the American People*, vol. 2, brief 2nd ed. (Upper Saddle River, NJ: Prentice Hall, 1999), 444.

6. The first site is http://www.answers.google.com/answers. This site then directs us to "The Importance of Water and Human Health" (n.d.), http://www.freedrinkingwater.com/water-education/water-get-enough.htm. Contrast: Mayo Clinic Staff, "Water: How Much Should You Drink Every Day?" (17 April, 2010), http://www.mayoclinic.com/health/water/NU00283, or Karen Bellenir, "Fact or Fiction? You Must Drink 8 Glasses of Water Daily" (4 June 2009), http://www.scientificamerican.com/article.cfm?id=eight-glasses-water-per-day. Sources accessed 7 March 2010.

7. Neal Tannahill, *American Government: Policy and Politics*, 10th ed. (Boston: Longman, 2010), 87.

8. Joan Salge Blake, Kathy D. Munoz, and Stella Volpe, *Nutrition: From Science to You*, (San Francisco: Benjamin Cummings, 2010), 17.

9. David Krogh, *Biology: A Guide to the Natural World*, 2nd ed. (Upper Saddle River, NJ: Prentice Hall, 2000), 325.

10. Dennis J.Sporre, *The Creative Impulse: An Introduction to the Arts*, 5th ed. (Upper Saddle River, NJ: Prentice Hall, 2000), 383.

11. Henry R. Cheeseman, *Contemporary Business Law*, 3rd ed. (Upper Saddle River, NJ: Prentice Hall, 2000), 242.

12. Edward J. Tarbuck and Frederick K. Lutgens, *Earth: An Introduction to Physical Geology*, 9th ed. (Upper Saddle River, NJ: Pearson, 2008), 624.

13. Quoted in Margaret L. King, *Western Civilization: A Social and Cultural History*, vol. 2 (Upper Saddle River, NJ: Prentice Hall, 2000), 928.

14. Pamela J. Annas and Robert C. Rosen, *Literature and Society* (Upper Saddle River, NJ: Prentice Hall, 2000), 279.

INDEX